MIGRANTS & CITY-MAKING

MIGRANTS & CITY-MAKING

Dispossession, Displacement, and Urban Regeneration

Ayşe Çağlar and Nina Glick Schiller

Duke University Press • Durham and London • 2018

Printed in the United States of America on acid-free paper ∞
Typeset in Minion and Trade Gothic type by BW&A Books, Inc.

Library of Congress Cataloging-in-Publication Data
Names: Çaglar, Ayse, author. | Schiller, Nina Glick, author.
Title: Migrants and city-making : multiscalar perspectives
on dispossession / Ayse Çaglar and Nina Glick Schiller.
Description: Durham : Duke University Press, 2018. |
Includes bibliographical references and index.
Identifiers: LCCN 2018004045 (print) |
LCCN 2018008084 (ebook) |
ISBN 9780822372011 (ebook) |
ISBN 9780822370444 (hardcover : alk. paper) |
ISBN 9780822370567 (pbk. : alk. paper)
Subjects: LCSH : Emigration and immigration—Social
aspects. | Immigrants—Turkey—Mardin. | Immigrants—
New Hampshire—Manchester. | Immigrants—Germany—
Halle an der Saale. | City planning—Turkey—Mardin. |
City planning—New Hampshire—Manchester. | City
planning—Germany—Halle an der Saale.
Classification: LCC JV6225 (ebook) |
LCC JV6225 .S564 2018 (print) | DDC 305.9/06912091732—dc23
LC record available at https://lccn.loc.gov/2018004045

Cover art: Multimedia Center, Halle Saale. Photo: Alexander
Schieberle, www.alexschieberle.de

To our mothers and fathers,
Sitare and Adnan Şimşek and
Evelyn and Morris Barnett, who
understood the importance of
having daughters who wrote books.

With great appreciation of the
two mothers who so courageously
and patiently waited for this one.

In memoriam, Evelyn Barnett,
1919–2017.

CONTENTS

LIST OF ILLUSTRATIONS

ACKNOWLEDGMENTS

We would like to acknowledge the support of the following institutions that made this book possible through financial assistance, research offices, and facilities: the Max Planck Institute for Social Anthropology; the Center for the Humanities, University of New Hampshire; the University of Vienna; Central European University, the Max Planck Institute for the Study of Religious and Ethnic Diversity; the University of Manchester; and Malmö University.

We also are grateful for the personal support of Günther Schlee, Bettina Mann, Viktoria Giehler-Zeng, Viola Stanisch, Manuela Pusch, Bert Feintuck, Dudley Dudley, Steven Vertovec, Peter van der Veer, Katif Araz, and Yehuda Elkana. Special thanks to Hubert Weterwami, Helene Simerwayi, and their children, who have been an ongoing inspiration for this book.

This book would not have been possible without the support of our partners and children: Arif Çağlar and Leyla and Sinan Çağlar; Steve Reyna and Rachel Schiller, Devan Aptekar, Naomi Schiller, Noah Biklen, Zander Reyna and Kate Reyna Lalier, Brenda and Damon Reyna, and Bradon Reyna. Our special thanks to Sinan for his continuing support and patience as he grew up in the company of this book.

In addition, we had the assistance of the following research colleagues: Dr. Thad Guldbrandsen, Dr. Seda Yüksel, Dr. Evangelos Karagiannis, and Dr. Minh Nguen. We were assisted in fieldwork and our interviews by a range of outstanding and insightful researchers, including Geraldine Boggs, Peter Buchannan, Faten al Hassun, Molly Messinger, Ronn Mueller, Markus Rau, Martin Sieber, Emila Smallridge, Julia Wenger, and Julia Wenzel. Invaluable technical support was provided by Daniele Karasz, Katrin Kremmel, Alexandra Sindrestean, Karen Alexander (copyediting), Robert Schultze (photography), Dr. Oğuz Tanındı and Jutta Turner (cartography).

We were graciously received by city and political officials in Halle/Saale, Manchester, New Hampshire, and Mardin, and we wish to thank them for their generous assistance. This research was made possible only by multiple residents of each city who welcomed us with sociability, kindness, and wisdom.

Funding was provided by a MacArthur Foundation Human Security grant; by a University of New Hampshire Excellence grant and Faculty Development grants; by the Center for the Humanities, including the James H. Hayes and Claire Short Hayes Chair in the Humanities; by a Central European University research grant; by the University of Vienna, Max Planck Institute for the study of Religious and Ethnic Diversity (Minerva Fellowship); and by the Max Planck Institute for Social Anthropology.

Multiscalar City-Making and Emplacement

PROCESSES, CONCEPTS, AND METHODS

The world is very different from the year 2000, when we began our long-term research into relationships between migrants and three seemingly disparate cities.[1] Mardin, Turkey, lies on the Turkish-Syrian Border; Manchester, New Hampshire, is in the northeastern United States; and Halle/Saale, Saxony-Anhalt, is part of formerly socialist eastern Germany. Today, the significance of war and crises of capital accumulation and political power are more evident around the world, including in these three cities, although crisis and social and economic transformations have gained visibility in each of the cities in different ways. As the world changed and our research project developed in response to these changes, we came to better understand the multiscalar relationships and the multiple actors, including each city's migrants, that were reconstituting each locality.

By the time we had finished this book, the province of Mardin had become a war zone, with several districts and villages bombed and blockaded by the Turkish army.[2] The devastation of the city-region is a violent reminder of how changing conjectural conditions in a particular place can—within less than a year—transform a center of global urban regeneration into a space of wreckage and devaluation. In the spring of 2015, posh hotels, tourist destinations, and "quaint" Syriac Christian village and religious sites, which were showcased as historic places of multireligious dialogue and openness, were attracting a seemingly ceaseless flow of tourists and international delegations. A short time later, these places stood empty. They not only mocked recent hopes of regional renewal but also embodied future possibilities for new cycles of urban regeneration and capital accumulation. However, at present, the dreams of Mardin's leaders to regenerate their city by globally marketing its vibrant, multireligious past lie in ruins as people flee for their lives.

By 2016 in Manchester, New Hampshire, city leaders had curbed their enthusiasm for large-scale regeneration plans and defunded one of the city's major public redevelopment agencies. However, the local economy was experiencing the stimulus of a renewed arms industry to supply the wars in the Middle East, including the fighting in Syria close to the Turkish-Syrian border. In Halle, the general failure of redevelopment plans to attract private capital, despite vast public expenditure, was temporarily superseded by the challenge of resettling new refugees fleeing armed conflicts, especially the war in Syria. Seemingly separated by region, history, and culture, the three cities we studied not only participated in interrelated restructuring processes but also, by the end of our research, had become interconnected by geopolitical events within the current historical moment.

We began our research in a hopeful period. Plans to bring prosperity to cities around the world sought to attract new flows of investment and build "new economy" industries within revitalized urban vistas. The spirit of the times, evident in both public policy and scholarship, emphasized a "metropolitan revolution," with cities serving as engines of development (Katz and Bradley 2013). Cities were portrayed as generating wealth and restructuring forms of governance and power in ways that would benefit the majority of urban residents (Florida 2002). If migrants and minorities[3] were referenced at all, their role was to provide local color as part of the city's diversity or inexpensive labor in service industries. At the same time, many scholars understood that these urban redevelopment narratives masked growing inequalities within and between cities and offered at best only a short-term fix for underlying structural failures (Brenner and Theodore 2002). They demonstrated that panegyrics to the rebirth of rebranded cities, saved from decline by "culture-led regeneration," failed to acknowledge neoliberal fault lines, disparities, displacements, dispossessions, and contestations underlying recent urban restructuring (Miles and Paddison 2005; Yeoh 2005).

However, there is still insufficient research and theory that explores the relationship between projects to rebrand and regenerate cities with different degrees of political, economic, and cultural power, on the one hand, and the everyday sociabilities and social citizenship practices of city residents, on the other. Initially, exploration of cities in the global economy, as well as critiques of urban rebirth through regeneration and rebranding, focused on cities such as London, New York, and Tokyo, which were seen as global centers of economic, political, and cultural power (Keil and Brenner 2006; Massey 2007; Smith 1996; Sassen 2001). Studies of migrant incorporation also have tended to focus on such cities (Cross and Moore 2002), but increasingly urban researchers have expanded the scope of their inquiries into "midrange cities," (Sassen 2002a; see also Ward and McCann 2011), "gateway cities" (Benton-Short and Price 2008), and "ordinary cities" (Robinson 2006). Meanwhile, ethnographers began to examine the lives and social relations of migrants outside urban centers of global power, although with few exceptions (McEwan, Pollard, and Henry 2008; Barabantseva 2016; Frykman 2015) interdependencies among processes of displacement, urban restructuring, and migrant emplacement have not been sufficiently explored.

Migrants and City-Making: Dispossession, Displacement, and Urban Regeneration addresses how globe-circulating, contemporary urban regeneration agendas were implemented in cities that were clearly not global powerhouses. We focus on the relationships between these cities and their migrants as these relationships became part of projects of urban transformation. When we began our research, city leaders in Manchester had just initiated a new period of city regeneration. In Halle/Saale a decade after German unification, city leaders sought ways to reposition their city within Germany and beyond. Meanwhile in Mardin, leaders were just beginning to address the need to repopulate the city and reposition it within Turkey, in the region, and globally.

Since that time, the leadership in each city has experienced periods of success and failure in their efforts to regenerate urban districts and reposition their cities within multiscalar networks of power. At times, each city seemed to gain prominence and significance, yet, by the end of our research, all three faced further disempowerment. Setting aside dichotomies between agency and structure, mobility and stasis, and migrant and non-migrant, which so often configure urban and migration theory and research, this book offers a comparative multiscalar analysis that explores the interrelated processes of displacement, dispossession, accumulation, and emplacement through which urban life is constituted.

Beyond Methodological Nationalism and the Ethnic Lens

The multiscalar analysis we offer rests on a critique of methodological nationalism and the ethnic lens. Methodological nationalism is an intellectual orientation that approaches the study of social and historical processes as if they were contained within the borders of individual nation-states (Amelina et al. 2012; Beck 2002; Wimmer and Glick Schiller 2002, 2003). That is, methodological nationalists confine the concept of society within the boundaries of nation-states and assume that the members of these states share a common history and set of values, norms, social customs, and institutions. Viewing migrants as culturally and socially discrete from "national societies," methodological nationalists assume that these populations require social integration into the nation-state where they have settled.

This perspective on culture and membership is a product of nineteenth-, twentieth-, and twenty-first-century nation-state building processes that legitimate a political ideology that portrays individuals as having only one country and one identity. Because of the predominance of methodological nationalism and its ethnic lens, researchers assessing the implications of migration across state borders have tended to see differences in national origin as the most significant social and cultural division within the population of a nation-state. Class, gender, and subnational regional and cultural differences pale in significance. Through a single discursive act—the delineation of those of migrant background from "natives"—those who are designated as native to the territory of a nation-state become participants in a shared and homogenous culture; those departing from one national territory to settle in another are not only differentiated as "foreign" but also understood to share a common homeland identity and culture.

As we previously wrote (Glick Schiller and Çağlar 2009, 184) "starting with Barth (1969), there is a voluminous historical and ethnographic literature that details the constructed nature of ethnic identities and ethnic group boundaries, and the diversity that lies within a population labeled as an 'ethnic group' (Modood 1997; Sollors 1989). However, despite the scholarship detailing the social construction of difference and the challenge to write 'against culture,' migration studies continue to approach migrants' relationships to economic, social and political forms of urban incorporation through an ethnic lens."

This foundational "binary of difference" (Glick Schiller 2012b) leads many migration scholars to approach all people of the same national or ethno-religious migrant background as homogenous in terms of their values, culture, religion, achievement, leadership, and transnational networks as well as identity, aspirations, and desire to live in tightly knit immigrant communities. As a result, scholars of migration often continue to use the concept of "ethnic community" as both the object of study and the unit of analysis in migration research. When migration researchers adopt a transnational perspective on migration but retain an "ethnic lens," they assume that migrants who share an ethnic identity form a transnational or a diasporic community that links homeland and new lands of settlement (Cohen 1997). The field of diaspora studies has perpetuated the problem by defining the unit of study as people who share an ancestry and a history of dispersal (Soysal 2000). Scholars of new migration and diasporas who use an "ethnic lens" obscure the diversity of migrants' relationships to their place of settlement and to other localities around the world as well as the commonalities between migrant and non-migrant populations (Glick Schiller, Çağlar, and Guldbrandsen 2006, 613).[4]

The challenge for researchers who are critical of methodological nationalism is to discard the binary between migrants and non-migrants and yet keep in focus the migration experience, with its multiple forms of displacement as well as barriers to and modes of emplacement. Because discourses about cultural, racial, and religious difference can both legitimate and obscure various forms of displacement and emplacement, there are occasions when an analyst must retain the terms "migrant" and/or "non-migrant." Therefore, we use these terms not to continue a process of categorizing and assuming cultural or religious difference but to counter assumptions of many public policy makers and national politicians that migrant newcomers stand outside the social system, constitute a threat to social cohesion, and require integration. In fact, we use the term "migrant" to challenge the assumption that the lives and practices of people who move to a city from other countries are subject to categorically different dynamics from the "majority" and/or "natives." Instead, we maintain that it is necessary to place migrants and those who see themselves as natives within the same analytical framework.

We argue that because so many researchers, influenced by methodological nationalism and its by-product, the ethnic lens, accept a deeply embedded binary between migrants and the mainstream of society, the crucial role of migrants within the city-making process often has been discounted within public and scholarly narratives (Glick Schiller and Çağlar 2009; Çağlar and Glick Schiller 2011). Migrants must be approached as social actors who are integral to city-making as they engage in the daily life of cities through different and varied forms.

Of course, the term "migrant" is a fluid signifier. It can apply to persons who move within as well as across international boundaries and whose legal status can vary from unauthorized to citizen. However, for the purposes of this book and the specific historical conjunctures it reflects and reflects upon, we use the term "migrants" to refer to those who have crossed international borders. We join contemporary political debates at a historical moment when too many political leaders cast aspersions specifically on cross-border migration and focus on categories of legal status: undocumented,[5] refugee, legal resident, or "naturalized" citizen (Glick Schiller 2016). In *Migrants and City-Making: Dispossession, Displacement, and Urban Regeneration*, we explore the city-making practices of people with all these legal statuses. While we place migrants and non-migrants in the same analytical framework, we pay close attention to the racialization and stigmatization of international migrants, which are aspects of dehumanization. Various forms of dehumanization serve to legitimate the processes of dispossession and displacement (defined below) that are at the analytical center of this book.

Building on Critical Policy Studies

In exploring the legitimation of dispossession and displacement by a range of institutional multiscalar actors who have been central to urban restructuring, we build on the work of scholars who have offered a critical policy studies (Shore and Wright 1997, 2011; Kingfisher 2013; Clarke et al. 2015). Several urban researchers have contributed to this field of inquiry by exploring why so many cities adopted similar restructuring strategies (Peck 2005; Peck and Theodore 2015; Gonzalez 2006). These scholars note that restructuring strategies had embedded within them a set of policies that were attractive to city leaders globally. As Jamie Peck's (2005) critical reading of Richard Florida indicates, city leaders striving to adequately compete with other cities for "creative" talent and capital were attracted to a set of creative-cities policies. These policies seemed to provide a guaranteed recipe of urban growth in the context of the implementation of neoliberal agendas globally and the formation of "neoliberal policy regimes" (Kingfisher 2013, 17). Leaders found that they could justify as necessary and urgent a range of bureaucratic and judicial changes in institutions, procedures, and regulatory mechanisms. The policies thus facilitated the allocation of public resources and the reconstitution of governance procedures from previous legislative mechanisms to new decision-making bodies dominated by corporate actors.

Peck (2005) emphasizes that this restructuring of governance and its concomitant growing disparities could be legitimated in relation to external national and global forces. These have compelled each city to compete for capital and urban prosperity in order to be situated higher in various city rankings and their comparative indicators. This competition naturalized the uneven distribution of wealth and power as part and parcel of the functioning and structure of the world order.

As critical policy scholars, such as Peck (2005) and Clarke and his colleagues (2015) have pointed out, actors who implemented neoliberal policies were subject to the discipline of capital mobility. Their research makes visible far-reaching networks of experts, academic institutions, urban development corporations, websites, and speakers developed to "support, sustain and profit from the circulation" of wealth, ideas, and technologies of restructuring in specific localities (Gibson and Klocker 2004, 431). These scholars highlight the significance of tracing networks of power.

Our perspective on multiscalar urban regeneration also is informed by the broader literature on critical policy studies, including the anthropology of policy. This literature connects policy formulation and implementation with networks of power that situate localities to broader processes. As Clark and his colleagues (2015, 6) emphasize, "The social in the making always takes place within a world of preexisting fields of power." These studies stress the multiscalar nature of these fields, which is so crucial to understanding local transformations. For example, Susan Wright (2011, 27) calls attention to how "the small details of social change that are observable in particular locations connect to wider processes of social, economic and political transformation." As Clarke et al. (2015, 23) note, "Transnational policy flows are never linear transfers from one place to another but involve 'multiscalar networks' (Jones, Jones, and Woods, 2004, 104) that organize space in ways that enable—and constrain—the movement of policy."

Earlier anthropologists of legal policies, such as Merry (2006), documented the ways in which policies become vernacularized when they travel. Critical policy scholars such as Kingfisher (2013) and Clarke et al. (2015), among others, extend this analysis by noting that globally circulating policies are translated and locally assembled to reflect the conjunctural intertwining of the differential power of local forces and broader national and international actors. They approach translation "as an intrinsically political and contentious process in which forms and relationships of power are always at stake, even if processes and technicalisation try to make them invisible" (Clarke et al. 2015, 189). The interplay of each of these forces within changing local configurations and contentions must be part of the analysis.

Multiscalar: Not Multileveled, Multisited, or Merely Everyday

With rare exceptions (Gardiner Barber and Lem 2012b; Sum and Jessop 2013), most social scientists speak of analytical levels in which the macrolevel of the world system, or globalization, stands above and beyond the microlevel of daily life (Marcus 1986; Neal 2013). In contrast, building on critical policy scholars, geographers, historians, and others who have worked to theorize multiscalar processes (Jones et al. 2004; Clarke et al. 2015; Braudel 1974), we utilize methods of multiscalar research and analysis that discard the notion of levels. We also discard a nested concept of scale as encompassing a fixed hierarchy of bounded territorial units such as neighborhood, city, province, and nation-state. Instead we trace social processes as they are constituted, noting their interconnections through both institutionalized and informal networks of differential economic, political, and cultural power (Glick Schiller 2012a, 2015b; Çağlar and Glick Schiller 2011). We use the term "multiscalar" as shorthand to speak of sociospatial spheres of practice that are constituted in relationship to each other and within various hierarchies of networks of power.

Although we build on several decades of debate about the concept of "scale" (Smith 1995; Swyngedouw 1997; Brenner 1999, 2001, 2009, 2011; Marston 2000; Marston, Jones, and Woodward 2005; Hoefle 2006), when we use the concept of scale in the term "multiscalar," our concern is somewhat different from those of urban geographers (Jessop, Brenner, and Jones 2008; Brenner 1999, 2011; Swyngedouw 2004). They have often preferred to differentiate scale, territory, place, and network and then discuss the relationship between these concepts. We share with those critical geographers an understanding of scales as locally, regionally, nationally, and globally mutually constituted, relational, and interpenetrating entry points for an analysis of globe-spanning interconnected processes. However, we work in dialogue with an understanding of multiscalar that is highlighted by Sassen (2013). She finds the term useful in recalibrating approaches to the study of cities and urban spaces by rearticulating their multiple, spatially articulated forms of power. Similarly, our approach to scale is a relational one that recognizes that structures of unequal power exist within multiple, but not nested, networked hierarchies.

What happens in a locality is constituted in relation to actors' reach and/or connection to multiple actors possessing different amounts of power, including the control of capital. For example, in a local project to redevelop urban housing, city authorities may act in relationship to national agencies with the power to provide grants and loans, but they may also be directly constrained by global financial markets and credit ratings, which positively or negatively evaluate the city's credit worthiness. This directly affects not only the housing project but also the economic prospects and well-being of city residents. Or local authorities might acquire some control over federal agencies through direct relationships with supranational institutions, such as the European Union (EU), by means of a different set of political agendas. This, in turn, has an impact on the scope and nature of a seemingly local housing project.

In our approach to networked processes, we define social fields as networks of networks, emphasizing that social fields entail multiple and intersecting networks in which actors, as individuals, institutions, or corporate entities, hold uneven power (Glick Schiller 2003; Kingfisher 2013). Networks and the social fields they constitute may be locally or regionally situated, or they may extend nationally, transnationally, or supranationally, as in the case of the EU, or may span the globe. In their daily reach, all interpersonal networks may not be transnational in the sense of cross-border connections or be multiscalar, that is, linked to actors based in multiple distinct domains of power. However, in our daily lives we all participate in social fields that extend beyond the local.

Many researchers, particularly in anthropology, use "transnational" or "translocal" to follow personal networks across borders but decline to connect the personal to the institutionalized power embedded in scalar relations. The field of transnational families is marked by these limitations (Olwig 2007; Mazzucato and Kabki 2009). In contrast, we stress that we are all part of social fields that are multiscalar. In short, the social fields in which we are embedded link in some way to institutions of differential power based in many places. The concept of multiscalar social fields enables us to address and capture aspects of social relations through which broader social forces enable, shape, constrain, and are acted upon by individuals. By using the term "social," we specify our interest in links between people without neglecting the fact that these links are mediated through a growing range of technologies.

The migrants whose lives we follow in this book form multiple new social relations and maintain others as they settle in specific places. The networks in which they live contribute to the remaking of the institutional nexus of city-level, regional, national, supranational, and globe-spanning actors. These processes cannot be reduced to various modes of capital accumulation that interact within specific places and times, but they also cannot be understood without understanding the dynamics of these modes. A multiscalar global perspective provides a reading of capitalism that does not reduce it to anonymous economic forces but rather approaches relations of capital as multiple unequal social relations constituted within social fields of power (Kalb and Tak 2005; Clarke 2014; Hart 2001).

Our multiscalar global perspective allows us to approach cities not as units of analysis or as bounded territorial units but as institutional political, economic, and cultural actors positioned within multiple institutionally structured scales of differentiated but connected domains of power. Cities are useful entry points because they generally have their own governance regimes, economic and spatial development plans, and powers (Glick Schiller and Çağlar 2009). Each city's institutional structure shapes variations within its different local territorial districts and economic sectors. Enmeshed in globally articulated restructuring strategies, all cities are players in emerging public–private forms of governance (Brenner 2004; Syrett and Sepulveda 2012).

Multisighted, not Multisited

This methodology and mode of analysis deploys alternative "ways of seeing" (Berger 1972); research is multisighted rather than multisited. The relational and processual concept of rescaling challenges the concept of "multisited" analysis, which many anthropologists believe is the best, if not the only, way to study transnational migration and globalization ethnographically (Coleman and Hellermann 2011; Falzon 2009). Many anthropologists embrace multisited analysis because, despite their broad acknowledgment that the world is interconnected, they still claim an intensive study of a discrete "community," "neighborhood," or locality as their terrain (Ortner 1984). At the same time, many assert that such ethnographic study of a single site necessarily obscures "the ways in which closely observed cultural worlds are imbedded in larger more impersonal systems" (Marcus 1986, 166). If "up close and personal" ethnography can only describe bounded units of analysis, then it follows that ethnographers can only study interconnections by moving between sites and following flows of people, goods, and ideas. Researchers champion multisited ethnography because of their limited view of the local, maintaining that only by heeding George Marcus's (1995, 106–7) call to "follow the people" and "follow the thing" can they trace the ways in which people and places interconnect.

Our view builds upon a different lineage of scholarship. We agree that, with its attention to personal narrative and to the contextualized enactments of everyday life, ethnography offers an irreplaceable entry into the analysis of social practices and sociabilities and their shifting meanings. Yet, informed by the various strands of multiscalar scholarship, we hold that it is not only possible but also necessary for an ethnographer to observe in each location that "seemingly independent processes and locations are interconnected with each other" (Miraftab 2014). That is to say, no site can be understood apart from its interconnections through time and space, and these interconnections can be studied in a single site (Feldman 2011). The logic that Hannerz (2003, 206) describes as part of multisited research, namely, that "the sites are connected with one another" and "one must establish the translocal linkages, and the interconnections," holds true for the study of single sites as well.

Each research site is always multiscalar because all places are constituted in relationship to elsewhere as parts of intersecting networks linking multiple forms of disparate institutionalized power. Ethnographers past and present have been able to study these networks without moving (Gluckman 1940; Susser 2012a, 2012b; Müller 2016). For a single site, ethnographers can and must trace interconnections of unequal power to analyze processes and relationships and make visible the multiscalar power structures connecting different places (Feldman 2011). An urban space, whether a building, religious congregation, neighborhood, or city, is always multisited because it is simultaneously positioned in multiple interconnecting trajectories of power (Massey 2005). To speak about the multiple ongoing connected processes and relationships of urban restructuring, regeneration, and rebranding as they develop through space and over time, we use the term "city-making." Our approach challenges ethnographers of "everyday" life to situate their research within a framework of multiscalar city-making.

The Multiscalar Connection of Everyday Life

Many ethnographers of migrant settlement responded to reminders that "geography matters fundamentally" and that attention must be paid to "different conditions, at different scales, in particular places" (Berg, Gridley, and Sigona 2013, 352) by offering studies of "everyday life" that ignore the locality's multiscalar connectivities. Instead, they offered delimited ethnographies of neighborhoods, bazars and markets, public squares, or buildings (Vaiou and Lykogianni 2006; Watson 2009; Vertovec 2015; Eriksen 2010). Their research fails to explore how these sites are constituted by multiscalar networks of differential power. Because these ethnographers approach their research sites as not only units of study but also units of analysis, these spaces appear as self-constituting places. Many authors highlight the uniqueness of each city's everyday life and the historical specificity of its neighborhoods to counter what they see as an overly structural analysis of globalization and neoliberalism (Löw 2009, 2012; Berking 2008; Leitner, Peck, and Sheppard 2007). In so doing, they erode the theoretical basis for comparative urban and globalization research.

The result is that the literature on migrants' everyday life is confined to description and haunted by binaries of difference. Without fully assimilating critiques of the ethnic lens or adopting a multiscalar analysis that situates urban actors within various networks of power, this research continues to reflect national categories of difference. Much of this research remains focussed on the "ethos of mixing" in multiethnic neighborhoods (Berg, Gridley, and Sigona 2013, 355; see also Vertovec 2015). The penchant of many scholars to frame "'everyday' sociabilities" (Wessendorf 2013) or convivialities through a language of difference is shaped by the "double polarization" (Friedman 2004, 26) that has accompanied the implementation of neoliberal agendas. Political leaders, policy makers, prominent researchers, and funders in countries around the world have focused on the supposed threat foreigners pose to social cohesion. This threat is linked to the "lack of trust" foreigners are said to evoke wherever they settle (Putnam 2007). The scholarship of the everyday can be read as an effort by some scholars to respond to anti-immigrant narratives by stressing that people can and do form social ties across differences and that certain urban spaces present examples of "living with difference" (Nowicka and Vertovec 2014, 341). However, even as they work to combat contemporary anti-immigrant politics, these scholars unwittingly lay the groundwork for viewing migrants as dangerous strangers.

This book offers another response. We argue that, to address sociabilities forged on the basis of spaces and domains of commonality between migrants and non-migrants, researchers and policy makers need a global multiscalar analytical framework that can address common conditions of precarity and displacement that mark the lives of many urban residents. The challenge for researchers of urban sociabilities is to develop an analytical framework that traces connections between how city residents respond to their differential access to power, to their city's position in regional and global playing fields, and to their relationships to the ongoing restructuring and repositioning of the neighborhood places where they build their lives. Thus, to construct a multiscalar analysis of daily sociabilities is to place them within the specific conjunctural configuration of multiple institutional social fields of uneven power of globe-spanning, national, regional, urban, and local institutions. These social fields intersect and shape the possibilities of emergent sociabilities. In this way, we can understand the multiscalar constitution of localities as the ongoing production of all places and social relations that constitute them.

Migrants and City-Making explores several modes of migrant emplacement that contribute to city-making as a multiscalar process: nonethnic entrepreneurial activities; everyday life sociabilities and social citizenship through Christian claim making; and supranationally mediated processes of emplacement. We emphasize that processes of capital restructuring and competitive urban regeneration lead to similarities between cities that occupy comparable positions of power at conjunctural moments, despite different legacies and even as, within these similarities, domains of differentiation emerge. Yet in our emphasis on the active agency of migrants, the analysis we present differs from critiques of neoliberal restructuring in cities that have ignored the historical and continuing role of migrants in city-making.

We maintain that it is unsatisfactory to provide a structural analysis of neoliberal urbanism without attention to migrants' agency. Nor is it sufficient to offer ethnographic descriptions of everyday life in migrant neighborhoods, ethnic organizations, or other urban settings without considering the reconfiguration of multiple institutions and networks of power at each historical conjuncture. By tracing migrants' processes of emplacement and displacement in cities sharing similar positions within global fields of power, scholars and policy makers can see contradictions and tensions actuated by these dynamics. Our choice of cities and focus on migrant emplacement allow us to highlight claim-making practices, situations, sites, institutions, and social relations in which displaced people, migrant and non-migrant, build sociabilities that can form the basis for new kinds of political action. Therefore, our book responds both to the emerging social citizenship practices that underlie urban social movements and to a desire for and current interest in new approaches to sites and acts of being political (Isin 2002).

Placing Disempowered Cities

The studies of multiscalar processes in cities that lack adequate economic, political, and cultural power but are nonetheless shaped over time by regional, national, supranational, and global dynamics and forces can contribute much to our understanding of the relations between migrants and cities. As are more powerful cities, these cities are also caught up in globally competitive interconnected restructuring processes but experience them within positions more structurally disadvantaged than do global centers of power.

Therefore, we suggest the term "disempowered cities" to reference cities that responded to the pressures of neoliberal urban restructuring but entered the competition with a given configuration of limited assets. These are cities where leaders and residents can recall the loss of power while confronting the challenges to restructure and once again successfully compete. Acting within a revived historical memory of their city's past importance in their nation-state and beyond, city leaders demonstrate an explicit consciousness of the loss of power. They refer in their urban narratives to times in which their city and its residents shared greater prosperity and significance. Hence, when we speak of "disempowerment," we intend to highlight the entanglement of memories of the loss of power with neoliberal processes that underlie the regeneration of urban spaces and the restructuring of governance.

This past often remains inscribed in the material infrastructure. Such resources and the city's institutional repertoire, as well as references to its past glories, become the basis of urban developers' plans and aspirations for an urban regeneration that can restore general prosperity. However, the legacy of the past does not determine the choices city leaders take or the degree to which residents support urban regeneration; rather, it constitutes only one resource upon which restructuring efforts can draw. Thus, we are not talking about path dependency (Woodlief 1988), although a city's past enters our analysis. In the relational and historical perspective of this book, cities that do not have the reference point of past glories and previously greater relative empowerment have not, then, been disempowered. Thus, a disempowered designation entails both the objective loss of power and city leaders' subjective awareness of this loss. Cities that are simply down and out and whose leaders have not aspired to regeneration require further research and theorizing.

We note that our definition is not transhistorical but refers to the neoliberal competitive positioning of cities within recent historical conjunctures. The rise and fall of cities over the centuries and their histories of interconnections and competitions within changing historical conjunctures is a much broader topic and has been explored within several different analytic frameworks (Weber 1958 [1921]; Mumford 1961; Braudel 1974; Tilly 1990). Our comparative analysis of three disempowered cities within recent neoliberal restructuring and our historically specific approach to disempowerment certainly contribute to this broader discussion. Our comparison of three disempowered cities opens a dialogue about the relative outcomes of restructuring in cities that have sought to regain their lost power.

At the end of the twentieth century, disempowered cities around the world engaged with varying outcomes in urban renewal to generate wealth. Some cities such as Bilbao (Masboungi 2001) and Bogotá (Fonseca and Pinilla 2008; Venice Biennale 2006) were celebrated as exemplary cases of successful urban regeneration. The regeneration of other cities such as Detroit (Akers 2013; Smith and Kirkpatrick 2015) remained more problematic despite massive city center investment. We hope that the parameters we delineate, which we discuss below in the methodology section of this chapter and develop in chapter 1, will contribute to further and comparative discussion of a broad range of cases. We examine who benefits and who pays for redevelopment, document short-term successes and long-term further disempowerment and dispossession of different social groups, and trace that channeling of capital and resources mobilized for local redevelopment to various national and transnational centers of power. As critics of the celebratory narratives that surround certain urban regeneration projects stress (Ponzini 2010; Cifuentes and Tixlier 2012), it is important to move beyond a snapshot and a generalized view of success. Our comparison contributes to this dialogue and the emerging data on regeneration in such cities.

At the beginning of the twenty-first century, the leaderships of many disempowered cities, like those of more powerful cities, sought to regain their past stronger positions by generating wealth through urban regeneration and branding within globe-spanning efforts to attract capital, "creative classes," and supranational institutions. Migrants in a wide range of class positions have contributed to these efforts. Consequently, disempowered cities with often surprisingly migrant/minority-friendly narratives and policies have been featured in news coverage, as captured by this *New York Times* headline: "Ailing Midwestern Cities Extend a Welcoming Hand to Immigrants" (Preston 2013).[6] In Europe, with support from the Council of European Municipalities and Regions and the Committee of the Regions of the European Union, a network of cities, including some we designate as disempowered, recognized the role of immigrant entrepreneurs in the "economic growth of their local area" by offering services, products, and employment to "immigrants and the host population, and creat[ing] in many cities an important bridge to global markets" (Rath and Swagerman 2011). However, few scholars of either urban restructuring and or migration have acknowledged the multiscalar relationship between migrants and urban restructuring processes in such cities.

We emphasize the utility of studying migrants' relationships to disempowered cities because we believe that, in such cities, migrants' displacement and emplacement contribute to multifaceted aspects of city-making in ways that can be more readily studied and theorized. In addition, we argue that local leaders and policy makers in disempowered cities often become more aware of the importance of migrants and minorities than do similar actors in more powerful cities. This understanding emerges through their efforts within historical conjunctures to sustain and reconstitute their city. We realized the significance of studying displacement and emplacement in disempowered cities as we struggled to understand relationships between migrants and the three cities in which we worked. We wondered why our observations did not match claims from studies of cities that were powerhouses of corporate, financial, political, and cultural interconnection. In our search for answers, we began to examine the scalar repositioning of cities. This led to defining, identifying, and researching disempowered cities and to rethinking the role of migrants within the multiscalar processes that constitute cities with different configurations of economic, political, and cultural power.

The multiscalar theoretical framework of analysis of *Migrants and City-Making* highlights earlier work in urban history, historical sociology, geography, and anthropology that explored the generative role of city-making in broader social processes (Weber 1958 [1921]; Tilly 1990; Braudel 1974). It also underscores the significance of approaching city-making "within different conjunctions of the capitalist process" (Susser 2002, 3). Historical literature on relationships between cities, states, and empires makes clear that cities have played different roles based on their positioning within networks of power and that this differential embedding affected class composition and ways of life for all the city's residents.

In *Territory, Authority, and Rights* (2008), Sassen notes ways in which cities that are linked to a territorial base but look outward have in the past formed base areas for local people striving to forge new concepts of citizenships and rights. She also suggests that, within contemporary globalization, this process has begun again. But her theory building has generally been concerned with what she designates as global cities. *Migrants and City-Making* deepens Sassen's insights into contemporary processes by exploring how people live within and contribute to globe-spanning processes, even within disempowered cities. This book also counters disciplinary divisions between migration studies and urban studies that continue to obscure global processes of city-making.

Analytical Framework: Key Concepts

Having introduced what we mean by multiscalar analysis, we move on to define the key concepts that underlie and illuminate the multiscalar analysis of relations between migrants and the three disempowered cities that are explored in following chapters. These key concepts are: *accumulation by dispossession* as it relates to *displacement* and *emplacement, contemporaneity, historical conjuncture*, and *comparison*.

ACCUMULATION BY DISPOSSESSION, DISPLACEMENT, AND EMPLACEMENT

For us, displacement is not just another word for mobility, and emplacement is not just another way of saying integration. Displacement and emplacement are interrelated processes of the restructuring of space and social relations at given points in time. In the analytical framework of this book, displacement and emplacement take place as part of the accumulation of capital by multiple forms of dispossession. Capital is approached here in its Marxist sense as a set of unequal social relations organized within a range of cultural understandings for the appropriation of surplus value. As Thomas Piketty notes (2014, 20). "The history of the distribution of wealth has always been deeply political, and it cannot be reduced to purely economic mechanisms. . . . The history of inequality is shaped by the way economic, social, and political actors view what is just and what is not, as well as by the relative power of those actors and the collective choices that result. It is the joint product of all relevant actors combined."

Marx (1967) used the term "primitive accumulation" for the dispossessive processes through which capital was initially accrued to fuel the development of industrial capitalism in Europe. Through dispossession, the "social means of substance and of production" were transformed into capital (Marx 1967, 714). This form of dispossession took multiple forms, ranging from the violent seizure of land and resources during conquest and colonization to the "parliamentary form of robbery," such as the enclosure of the commons in England (Marx 1967, 724). Critical development studies and geographers (Glassman 2006; Hart 2006) and anthropologists (Kasmir and Carbonella 2008) have recently taken up the debate about the historicity and scope of the process, reassessing issues initially raised by Rosa Luxemburg (1951) and revisited in the 1960s within debates about dependency theory.

Renaming these processes of accruing capital by appropriating the social means of subsistence as "accumulation by dispossession," David Harvey (2003, 2004) has argued that while always present after the initial expansion of Europe, dispossessions and their resulting displacements have become central to capital accumulation in the current conjuncture. Harvey (2004) includes among contemporary forms of accumulation by dispossession not only older practices such as the seizure of communal land, precious resources, and public spaces but also capital acquired through neoliberal "reforms" such as the privatization of public utilities, schools, housing, and hospitals. Also integral to contemporary accumulation through dispossession are new and revitalized instruments that financialize risk and debt based on markets in mortgages, student debt, and car loans. Harvey's concerns mesh with popular accounts of contemporary capitalism, including capital accumulation via "the shock doctrine" (Klein 2007), "disaster capitalism" (Klein 2007), and the struggle for the "commons" (Susser and Tonnelat 2013).

We agree with Harvey (2004, 2012) that contemporary efforts by capitalists throughout the world to deploy new forms of accumulation have been precipitated by capitalists facing a crisis of overaccumulation, which leads them to turn to other means of accumulation. Whether one accepts this understanding of the dynamics that underlie contemporary dispossessive processes, there is general agreement among observers of diverse political outlooks that massive amounts of wealth are now controlled by a handful of people (Oxfam 2015; Piketty 2015; Milanovic 2016; Sassen 2014; Durand 2017). Those controlling this concentrated wealth are finding other forms of investment more profitable than the production of goods, whether the goods are steel, cell phones, garments, or gizmos. In 2016, the weakness of the world economy appeared in fundamental sectors such as oil, steel, and commodities (World Bank 2016), which reflected reduced production as corporations cut back on goods people couldn't afford to buy. As a result, those holding concentrations of capital sought new and intensified forms of accumulation by dispossession.

Although significant contemporary processes of dispossession related to land revaluation and governance are not solely urban phenomena, some of the most useful scholarship on contemporary dispossession have been analyses of urban restructuring processes (Smith 1996; Brenner, Marcuse, and Mayer 2009; Künkel and Mayer 2011). Recent forms of urban dispossession are documented in the literature on slum or favela clearance or "rehabilitation" (Freeman 2012; Banerjee-Guha 2010; Lees, Shin, and Lopez Morales 2015).[7] As has been noted for India, slum designations "function as a central vehicle for facilitating the alienation of public land to private developers" (Ghertner 2014). Approaching accumulation through dispossession in this way challenges urban scholars to cease viewing the urban poor as a marginal, surplus population or outside the processes of capital accumulation. The poor must be understood as contributing to the processes of creating value in city land and property in several interrelated ways. In cases where cities become depopulated or abandoned by wealthier people, some neighborhoods remain viable because they are claimed by the poor. These areas and the property within them are often constituted within multiscalar city-making networks of migrant and non-migrant small businesses and religious, political, social, humanitarian, and charitable institutions that cater to the urban poor (Morell 2015). Within these networks, poor people contribute to processes of accumulation by putting a brake on abandonment, decay, and devaluation as well as through the social relations their activities generate. In many places in the world, squatters develop urban peripheries only to be expelled as this land is claimed by public–private interests for redevelopment.

Focusing on these processes allows us to understand why so much capital has been invested in urban regeneration schemes around the world. This perspective situates conditions of contemporary city-making within a broader analysis of dispossessive processes that place migrants and non-migrants within the same analytical lens. Confronting processes that underlie displacements requires acknowledging that migrants can no longer be considered a separate category of actors but must be seen, along with everyone else, within their multiple identities/disparate positionalities and within configurations of dispossession and subsequent social and physical dislocations. Moreover, this theorization speaks to possible bases for the emergence of globe-spanning social movements that can counter globally resurgent nationalisms (Glassman 2006).

Processes of dispossession produce a range of physical and social displacements. The term "displacement" has transhistorical connotations and relates to processes of capital accumulation in specific places and times. In its transhistorical sense, "displacement" refers to the city-, state-, and empire-building processes that have stripped people of land, resources, and their means of livelihood and forced them to reposition, reorder, or relocate their lives and relationships. Often violent, these displacements were accompanied by new forms of emplacement, including class formation, slavery, intensified gendered hierarchy, and colonization (Wolf 1982).

However, we highlight a second meaning of displacement that is linked to the accumulation of capital by dispossession. In this second usage, displacement is the outcome of people losing their access to various social means of subsistence. This displacement has taken many forms. Sometimes the dispossession that leads to displacement occurs through neoliberal "austerity" measures and "reforms" and the restructuring and privatization of public land, housing, employment, and benefits. These transformations have led to downward social mobility as large numbers of people lose their social positions. Sometimes the dispossessive processes are violence and warfare linked to broader struggles for land and resources within geopolitical contentions, which cause people to flee their homelands. Because of these processes, the lives of increasing numbers of people around the world are becoming precarious. Precarity is *not* a synonym for poverty (Fassin 2015). In this book, we use it to refer to a state of insecurity and unpredictability brought about by neoliberal restructuring of both the terms and the conditions of working and living. However, we recognize that precariousness is basic to capitalist cycles of accumulation. In cities, the displaced are becoming urban precariats (Standing 2011): people who have never moved but have nonetheless been socially dispossessed, and displaced and people who have migrated either within or across borders only to face another cycle of displacement and insecurity within urban regeneration.

The people from whom wealth is extracted are increasingly cast out or cast aside as worthless, regardless of legal status within the country where they live. In the past and at present, such appropriations are ultimately maintained by force but simultaneously legitimated culturally by narratives of national, racialized, and gendered difference (Harvey 2005; Quijano 2000). That is to say, accumulation through dispossession is justified by the categorization of those who have generated value as less than human. To highlight this integral aspect of the process of dispossession, Butler (2009) notes that the powerful cast the displaced as the "ungrievable other." In this process, the construction of cultural, religious, or racialized difference, or the judgment that such people are "deplorable" or criminal elements who lack the necessary values or work ethic, may serve to justify displacement. In urban regeneration processes, after inhabitants of poor neighborhoods, whether categorized as "native" or migrant, are stigmatized as violent and dangerous, they are first deprived of urban services and then evicted. Dispossessions following these otherizing processes strip people not only of their housing and businesses but also of their social, political, and economic networks and concomitant social capital, deepening the negative effects on their livelihood of their displacement.

Within our analysis of three disempowered cities, we explore forms and processes of dispossession and displacement, which we understand as aspects of the worldwide neoliberal competition between cities with different degrees of economic, political, and cultural power. We ask how, when, and with what consequences dispossessed and displaced people, both migrants and non-migrants, reconstruct their lives within these urban restructuring processes in these cities. By understanding these processes within the dynamics of multiscalar city-making, we link displacement and dispossession with modes of emplacement, which include claims for social citizenship and the development of sociabilities that can underlie movements for social justice. In chapter 1, we provide a comparative analysis of Manchester, Halle/Saale, and Mardin that establishes the basis for further discussion about the momentary successes and the failures of restructuring projects of other disempowered cities.

Our concern is with emplacement as well as displacement within neoliberal restructuring. We define emplacement as the relationship between, on the one hand, the continuing restructuring of place within multiscalar networks of power and, on the other, a person's efforts, within the barriers and opportunities that contingencies of local place-making offer, to build a life within networks of local, national, supranational, and global interconnections. The concept of "emplacement" serves as both a useful analytical tool with which to understand city-making in diverse urban settings and as an evidence-based concept. Central to our analysis, the concept of emplacement allows us to situate all residents of a city within transformations of space over time. Restructuring, as it continually changes over time, reconfigures and re-represents social and political spaces and the social forces that produce them (King 1996). As a processual concept that links space, place, and power (Smith 2002; Massey 2005; Harvey 2006), emplacement must be understood within specific geographic and temporal spaces and power fields.

We use the term "emplacement" because, unlike the terms "integration" or "assimilation" or the discourse that targets migrants as threats to social cohesion,[8] the concept of emplacement both invokes a sense of place-making and allows us to focus on a set of experiences shared by people who are generally differentiated by scholars and policy makers as either migrant or native. By speaking of emplacement, we can situate migrant and non-migrant displacements within globe-spanning, but locally and temporally situated, neoliberal processes of the destruction and reconstitution of capital. In the framework we present, non-migrants as well as migrants must seek emplacement.

Chapters 2 through 5 examine several different processes of emplacement, all of which we found salient within the disempowered cities we studied. Those include entrepreneurship, sociability within shared spaces of residence, work and institutional settings, and social citizenship facilitated by religion, or supranationally facilitated place-making. Highlighting intersecting pathways of migrant and non-migrant displacement, emplacement, and city-making represents a much needed direction in comparative urban and migration studies and argues for an emerging displacement studies (Feldman Biano nd).

CONTEMPORANEITY AND CONJUNCTURE

Temporality as it relates to concepts of contemporaneity and conjuncture is an important but insufficiently discussed topic in urban and migration studies. By using the term "contemporaneity," we emphasize the need to conceptualize that those seen as migrants and those categorized as natives are coeval. These actors must be understood as sharing the same time/space, although with unequal access to resources and power. Too often the dynamics of migrant practices, whether glossed as traditional or transnational, are thought of as situated within other places and at other times. Migrant practices and their dynamics are often approached through "typological time" (Fabian 1983) and therefore conceived of as categorically different from the practices and dynamics of non-migrants (Çağlar 2013, 2016). By situating migrants as contemporaries of all other urban residents and by analyzing their practices as coeval, it becomes clear that all city inhabitants (migrant or not) build their lives within processes of displacement and emplacement.

To address the changing trajectories of forces within which city-making, displacement, and emplacement occur, it also helps to conceptualize time in relation to changing configurations of intersecting multiscalar networks of disparate power. To do this, we speak of historical conjunctures, a concept once used broadly and taken for granted among Marxist-influenced scholars. Over the past few decades, some authors writing about displacement, globalization, and crisis have made passing reference to "the current historical conjuncture" (Malkki 1995), or the "current conjuncture" (Lee 1998; see also Gill 1992; Susser 2002; and Castells 1977). But with a few important exceptions, mainly concentrated in a cultural studies project that builds on Gramsci's use of the term (Denning 1996) and Hall's subsequent writings (Hall et al. 1978), little effort has been made to define the term or systematically deploy the concept.[9]

However, John Clarke (2010, 6) has recently argued for "thinking conjuncturally." He writes that conjunctural analysis is not a theory but an orientation that offers "a way of focusing analytical attention on the multiplicity of forces, accumulated antagonism and possible lines of emergence from particular" intertwinings of relations of power and contradictions (Clarke 2014, 115). To make a conjunctural analysis is to assess "the forces, tendencies, forms of power, and relations of domination" that at any moment in history can lead to regional and local political, economic, and social arrangements that differ from each other yet are interdependent (Clarke 2014, 115). By making a conjunctural analysis, we can situate the significance of different modes of capital accumulation in relationship to different forms of governance, discourse, kinship, identity, belonging, policing, mobility, and activism over time and in particular places. Hence, an analysis of each unfolding conjuncture denaturalizes views of social order and challenges the hegemonic, common sense of a point in time.

The concept of the historical conjuncture challenges the widespread methodological nationalist tendency to discuss migration and urban dynamics within separate national institutional histories. This orientation provides social analysts with a means of examining transformations across places and times and the interrelations of these changes. A conjunctural analysis examines the multiscalar, globally extending relationships of places to processes of accumulating wealth and power, to constructions of meaning and affect, and to the ways in which modes of social, political, and economic life are organized and reproduced. Such an analysis brings together intersecting global transformations that condition the growth of different organizational forms of industry and agriculture; the growth of nation-states and national movements; the content, meaning, and role of religion; the nature and articulation of crises; the dynamics and success of movements for social justice; and the efficacy and forms of capital accumulation. Differing specific iterations of institutional structures and policies in specific states and regions reflect as well as contribute to transnational or global transformations and affect modes of life, production and social reproduction, and ideologies of self and society everywhere.

Although they generally did not use the term "conjuncture," those who wrote about globalization in the 1990s were attempting to analyze a global historical conjuncture as its transformative dynamics became apparent (Mittelman 1996). The transnational migration paradigm of the 1990s that made transnational lives visible was the product of that historical conjuncture (Glick Schiller 1999; Kearney 1995). By the 1990s, transformations begun two decades earlier in response to crises of previous arrangements of capital formation had made visible the high degree of global interconnectivity, the transnationality of migrants' lives, emerging forms of flexible accumulation, new urban dispossessions, and gentrification, as part of the intensifying implementation of neoliberal agendas for economic and political restructuring (Sassen 1998). Crises took different forms and intersected in different and nonlinear ways with various national and local histories from the 1970s to 2008. Within that conjunctural moment, cities became recognized as convergences of new arrangements of governance involving corporate, educational, and public actors.

Implementations of neoliberal agendas and the struggles against it, including anti-globalization and right to the city movements, are producing a world that is becoming increasingly different from that of the period between the 1970s and 2008. Of course, there is uneven development, and conjunctural forces play out differently in different places. Nevertheless, these forces extend around the world, and when a new reconfiguration of multiscalar networks and their imbricated processes of capital formation emerge somewhere in the world, there are ramifications elsewhere. The global economic crisis of

2008 both echoed and magnified cracks in the system of accumulation that had prompted an Asian debt crisis in 1997 and the dot-com crash at the turn of the millennium. It also marked the emergence of a new conjunctural configuration. We are just beginning to assess the implications of these further transformations for the multiple forces of dispossession, including war, the intensification of racism, deportations, restrictions on migration and resulting displacements, disempowerment, city-making, and struggles for social justice. Our data traced the situation until 2016, but each of our chapters ends by noting the implications of our observations for future developments. In our conclusion, we address the changing historical conjuncture and the politics of transformation.

COMPARISON AS A MULTISCALAR METHOD

We work within a renewed dialogue among urban scholars, primarily geographers, about the merits and methods of comparing cities (see, for example, Nijman 2007, 2012; McFarlane and Robinson 2012; see also Robinson 2004; Dear 2005; Ward 2008, 2010; Ward and McCann 2011). Until recently, many urban scholars had abandoned their earlier interest in comparative perspectives, and those remaining failed to delineate the variables being compared (Cross and Moore 2002). Distrust of comparison has been particularly potent among urban anthropologists, who tend to see each city as displaying its own logic and unique differences (Berking 2008; Löw 2012). We argue that despite their varying historical legacies, it is possible and useful to compare those cities that participate in ongoing struggles for positioning within multiscalar networked hierarchies of economic, political, and social power. Locality and local history matter but only in relation to the dynamic multiscalar reconstitution of place within which the sense of the local is constituted.

One reason urban scholars had abandoned comparative studies was that they distrusted any methodology that entailed "by necessity some degree of reductionism as a step in preparing empirical observations for comparative assessment" (Pierre 2005, 447). Scholars in many disciplines adopted postmodernist narrative strategies that emphasized the uniqueness and path-determined nature of each place, a perspective that negated the possibility of comparison. Others, influenced by Deleuze and Guattari's (1988) theorization of decentered rhizomic networks and Latour's (2005) actor-network theory, focused on the dynamics of interconnectivity. However, as John Law notes (2009, 141), "the actor network approach is not a theory. Theories usually try to explain why something happens, but actor network theory is descriptive rather than foundational in explanatory terms. . . . Instead it tells stories about 'how' relations assemble or don't." Influenced by this kind of postmodernist approach to globalization, some urban scholars have described multiple spatialities of place-making, networking, and urban social movements without paying sufficient attention to the questions of unequal power that shape the nature of networking and sociospatial positioning (Smith 2001; Leitner et al. 2007).

We maintain that a focus on interconnectivities without a comparative theoretical framework with which to identify hierarchies of institutionally based power at given conjunctural moments leaves analysts with no conceptual space to address important questions about dispossession, displacement, and emplacement in various cities. Hence, those concerned with horizontal networks of interconnection are ill-equipped to explore why cities differ in their reach to networked institutions of power at particular times and in their relationship to migrants, situating them differently within narratives and policies of regeneration.

Recently, several edited volumes have begun to make comparative claims. Books have categorized cities as "port," "secondary," or "gateway" (Kokot et al. 2008; Price and Benton-Short 2008; Chen and Kanna 2012). However, these books offer few actual comparisons beyond introductory remarks by the editors, which focus on categorizing types of cities. Urban anthropologist Setha Löw (1999, 8) provided an overview of typological thinking as a mode of comparison by identifying twelve different "images and metaphors" used by researchers to characterize cities, including "divided," "contested," "ethnic," "sacred," "traditional," "global," "informational," and "postmodern." Such representations fail to articulate underlying dynamics that make cities similar at particular conjunctural moments.

However, building on new work in comparative urbanism as well as debates about scale, some scholars have called for a "relative comparative approach" to urban studies (Ward 2008; Glick Schiller 2012a) that incorporates transnational studies and understands cities as "strategic nodes of financial flows, migration, policy formation, [and] the practice of state power" (Ward 2008, 408; see also Schneider and Susser 2009). Efforts to develop a new, comparative urban research agenda involve rethinking our assumptions of causality and questioning our units of analysis (Robinson 2011, 2).

Of course, the interest in causation as well as in locating instances of similar cases in which one can explore variation is several centuries old in western social thought (Mills 1882 [1843]). In our comparative study, we continue this dialogue by engaging in a critical reading of Charles Tilly's method of "variation" finding. According to Tilly, "variation-finding" strategies "establish a principle of variation in the character or intensity of a phenomenon by examining systematic difference amongst instances" (Tilly 1984, 83). It is important to note that, despite its emphasis on differences, this approach first identifies similarities. Comparative urban analysis begins by questioning "why separate places can be very similar in certain respects" (Nijman 2007, 1) and then studies variations within characteristics defined as similar.

Rather than inscribing the cities we have been studying—Halle/Saale, Manchester, and Mardin—into the global South or the global North, we present five parameters through which the similarities of these cities can be analyzed, despite their different national histories and geographies. We utilized a set of variables that occurs in each of the cities: disempowered positioning, plans and projects for urban restructuring, references to migrants within rebranding narratives, the degree of investment in services for migrants, and opportunities for migrant emplacement within multiscalar regeneration processes. Within this comparative framework, we examined variations in migrant and non-migrant processes of displacement and emplacement.

A Word on Methodology: Toward an Ethnographically Informed Analysis of Multiscalar City-Making

Our research combines ethnographic participant observation; in-depth interviews with people differentially positioned in the social, cultural, and political life of the city; and the collection and analysis of urban economic, political, and cultural development documents, initiatives, and regeneration programs.[10] In Halle and Manchester, we worked with teams of students; attended public meetings, religious services, and events that concerned migrants; and shopped in businesses owned or run by migrants. We also visited informally with local non-migrant residents and with some of the migrants, including their family and friends whom we had interviewed, and joined them in various festive occasions. In Mardin, we attended official meetings related to urban regeneration; participated in cultural events; and talked to Syriac Christian returnees as well as to those who had never emigrated, to religious leaders, to shop keepers, to cultural operators, to nongovernmental organization (NGO) workers, to directors of cultural institutions and industrial zones, and to entrepreneurs whose businesses range from small to large and powerful.

In all cities, we interviewed municipal officials, urban developers, and political leaders involved with urban regeneration as well as officials and leaders of civil society organizations, who were particularly concerned with the presence of minorities and new migrants. We drew from the local, regional, and supranational websites connected to each city and from institutional offices, civil society organizations, and newspapers. From these multiple sources, we collected relevant statistical information about trade, unemployment, labor, investment, institutional structures and profiles, budgets, development plans, allocations, population composition and change, and local narratives about each city and its migrants.

We note that in considering trajectories of urban restructuring, it is important to neither overestimate nor underestimate city narratives. We demonstrate that these narratives can neither be taken as a description of actual policies and practices nor be discarded as inconsequential. Narratives facilitate or impede action, even as they are affected by the changes a city experiences. They reflect and contribute to changing understandings of urban development and branding. Our analysis underlines the importance of using a variety of sources and not simply relying on city narratives to assess the outcomes of urban restructuring. We highlight the discrepancies between the urban narratives about successful regeneration and the data on growing debt, inequality, and displacement that the various planning documents of each city, as well as our observations and interviews, made apparent.

We also explored how migrants or minorities sought to settle in the city, built transnational connections and relationships with non-migrants, and, in building networks, became entangled with and participated in the construction of specific urban narratives and policies about migrants, belonging, and urban generation. When we began our research, migrants, including legal immigrants, people without legal papers, refugees, and international students, made up 8 percent of the population of Manchester (US Census 2000b) and 3.1 percent of the population of Halle (City of Halle 2016). Syriac Christian returnees to the city of Mardin and surrounding villages were a tiny fraction of the population of Mardin province. Though the size of the migrant/minority population is important for different aspects of displacement and emplacement, our research demonstrated that, within urban regeneration projects and narratives, the presence of migrants and their capacity to access networks of power do not necessarily correlate with the size of their population.

Despite small numbers, the significance of migrants in city-making in Manchester and in Halle became clearer to us after we considered the case of Mardin. Syriac Christians had fled the area in the 1990s to live in different parts of Europe. Only in 2002 did very small numbers of Syriac Christians begin to reconnect and return to the city and its surrounding villages.

These numbers were contested, but the proportion of Syriac Christians in all of Mardin province was not more than 0.06 percent of the total population. However, new returnees, together with the Syriac Christians who had never left, acquired a special significance in Mardin's city-making process at the conjuncture under consideration. As we show in chapters 1 and 5, they became very important to the city's access to various supranational multinational institutions such as the EU, the United Nations Development Program (UNDP), the World Bank, and the United Nations Educational, Scientific and Cultural Organization (UNESCO), which in turn played an important role in efforts by Mardin's leaders to restructure, rebrand, and re-empower their city.

We began intensive research in Halle and Manchester in 2000 and continued until 2007, making periodic updates until 2016. In Halle, our exploration of the possibilities of migrant emplacement led us to interview several snowball samples totaling eighty-one migrants of all legal statuses. Most interviews were with respondents from the Democratic Republic of Congo (DRC), Nigeria, Russia, Bosnia, Vietnam, Iraq, Turkey (Kurdish), and Syria. Intensive participant observation was conducted in two born-again Christian congregations, and ties with one of these congregations continued until 2015.

In Manchester, an initial series of snowball samplings also connected us to migrants of diverse backgrounds and all legal statuses. A subsequent focused sample concentrated our interviews with respondents from the Democratic Republic of the Congo (DRC), Nigeria, Russia, Bosnia, Vietnam, and two Latin American countries (Colombia and Mexico). In total, we interviewed 115 migrants not only from those countries but also from Sudan, Sierra Leone, Liberia, Rwanda, Uruguay, Romania, Taiwan, China, Iraq, and Greece.

In Mardin, research began with a focus on hometown associations in Europe in 2007 and continued through ethnography in Mardin in 2014–15. However, our collection of secondary material extends our data to 2000, the beginning of our research period. In Mardin, our research became multilocal and transnational in that we followed network ties to Istanbul and Vienna. In all, we conducted twenty-nine interviews with city officials, project leaders, and businessmen of various backgrounds and with Syriac Christians from Mardin who were businessmen and religious leaders and members of hometown associations.

Introducing the Chapters

Our exploration of the relationships between migrants and city-making begins in chapter 1. This chapter establishes the comparative framework through which we approach the three disempowered cities we researched. The following similarities emerged among the seemingly disparate cities of Manchester, New Hampshire; Halle/Saale, Germany; and Mardin, Turkey. City leaders initiated urban regeneration hoping that through neoliberal restructuring their city could regain some of its past significance and power. Redevelopment strategies, rebranding, and urban marketing sought to use public funding to attract private investment that would transform each city in a center of knowledge, tourism, and high-tech industries. Economic and social disparities increased; public coffers suffered. Migrants and minorities were welcomed in narratives that identified each city as diverse and welcoming. However, almost no city resources were invested in migrant-specific services or ethnic organizations. Nonetheless, in the context of welcoming narratives, migrants and minorities entered the economic, social, religious, and political processes of the city and became city-makers.

Four ethnographically informed chapters follow, chapters 2 through 5. Building on our comparative approach to multiscalar urban regeneration in all three cities, we reexamine a series of questions about the relationship between migrants and cities that not only have been prominent in the academic literature over the past few decades but also have been the focus of public policy. Each chapter highlights the dynamics, tensions, and dialectics of different forms of emplacement at changing conjunctural moments.

Using Halle as a case in point, chapter 2 explores the emplacement and displacement of small migrant businesses as part of city-making processes in disempowered cities. The chapter critiques literature that reduces migrant businesspeople to "ethnic entrepreneurs," focuses on neighborhoods with high densities of an immigrant population, and accords explanatory power to the cultural repertoires of certain ethnic groups. Instead, we build on the work of those who have approached migrant businesses as business, tracing the growth and decline of small migrant businesses according to changing conjectural configurations of networked urban, regional, national, European, and global institutionalized power. Migrants, we emphasize, participated in building and reconstituting these networks. Central to the chapter's analysis are the urban redevelopment programs and actors that transformed Halle's economy, population, and the city districts where migrants' businesses were located or where they moved after being displaced. Chapter 2 links the emplacement, dispossession, and displacement of migrants' businesses to the multiscalar restructuring processes that reconfigured the lives of all residents and small retail businesses.

Chapter 3 builds upon Simmel's understanding of "sociabilities," which emphasizes domains of commonality rather than difference in social relations. We explore the daily sociabilities through which migrants or non-migrants sought their place in the cities in which they resided. Drawing from our Manchester data, we focus mainly on different types of sites (i.e., proximal, workplace, and institutional) through which newcomers and non-migrants in Manchester established sociabilities. We link the emergence of these sociabilities to conditions that all residents confronted within the ongoing multiscalar processes of capital accumulation and to the precarities and impoverishment resulting from the dispossessive processes of urban restructuring and regeneration.

We begin chapter 4 by addressing the issues the concept of social citizenship raises and the theoretical space it offers to approach citizenship as both performative act and social process. We then examine the claims born-again Christians organizing in both Halle and Manchester made to their city. This chapter demonstrates that the theology, practices, and identities deployed by born-again Christian migrants constituted a form of social citizenship that challenged the established notions of rights to territory and belonging articulated within state-centric concepts of citizenship. Our analysis critiques debates about rights to the city that neglect a multiscalar analysis.[11] In the course of our comparison of the born-again practices and beliefs in the two cities, we demonstrate that forms of social citizenship are shaped by, as well as made more visible by, the structural disempowerment of these cities within conjunctural changes.

In chapter 5 we examine how in Mardin Syriac Christians and the places associated with them acquired value within the multiscalar urban restructuring processes precipitated by the Turkish government's efforts to both join the EU and reposition itself within the reconfiguring Middle East. Local leaders' efforts to rebrand and present Mardin as safe and friendly to business and investment and to obtain EU funding for urban regeneration depended on the visible presence of Syriac Christians, especially return migrants from Europe. The presence of Syriac Christians validated Mardin's self-presentation, to global investors and funding institutions, as a city with a peaceful multifaith heritage. The data in this chapter refutes those studies of hometown and migration and development that ignore the significance of structurally linked conjunctural factors. We maintain that researchers must assess such factors to understand when and how migrant transnational actors join development projects. We link returnees' emplacement in Mardin to the reconfiguring global networks of power, including global warring at a historical conjuncture.

In our conclusion, we combine our multiscalar analysis of the mutual constitution of the local, national, regional, supranational, and global not as different dimensions of experience but as interpenetrated domains of power and agency. The conclusion links our data and analysis to emerging intellectual and political debates. We include a cautionary proviso to those who, rather than providing a global perspective on uneven power within which urban contestations and migrant sociabilities arise, argue either that mobilities spark cosmopolitan openness (Hannerz 1990) or that they inevitably provoke conflict, nationalism, and anti-immigrant racist movements (Kymlicka 2015). Our conclusions neither celebrate nor deprecate mobilities. We highlight the growing threat posed to all struggles for social justice by the expansive powers of national security states and supranational institutions of border control.

CHAPTER 1

Introducing Three Cities

SIMILARITIES DESPITE DIFFERENCES

"Mardin," said the deputy district mayor in 2015, is a "city of Jews, Yazidis, Chechens, Hungarians, Kurds, Arabs, Syriacs, and Chaldeans." Sitting with Seda, a member of our research team, the deputy district mayor spoke about the historical significance of Mardin and its diverse population. In delineating this diversity, he clarified that he was not talking about a concept of tolerance, which would have cast populations such as the Kurds as outsiders whom Turks, defined as natives, could choose to include or exclude. The deputy district mayor's remarks reflected his own engagement in Kurdish/Turkish politics and commitment to his city's regeneration as a historical multifaith and multilingual city. This renewal involved forging a narrative that highlighted Mardin's past glories and civility. In this narrative, people of diverse backgrounds, rather than contributing "difference," constituted the local population of the city and region (interview March 23, 2015).

For the first fifteen years of the new millennium, Mardin rode a wave of urban regeneration. The reinvention of the city was the product of many intersecting networks of power—the Turkish state, the European Union, the United States, various governments in Europe and the Middle East, militaries, and commercial interests—at a historical conjuncture. These intersecting and contending forces all recognized that Syriac Christians—the city's ancient Christian community, most of whom had fled the area decades before and were beginning to return to claim their lands—were key to Mardin's rebirth as a multilingual city composed of many religious communities.

Nina began her interview in 2001 with Frau Haüssler, lord mayor of Halle/Saale, by explaining that she had previously studied migrants' relationships to institutions in New York and was now interested in the role of migrants "in a small city." New York City at the time numbered more than 8 million people, compared to the approximately 243,000 people in Halle (City of Halle 2016). The mayor's response was immediate and emphatic: Halle was *not* a small city, she told Nina. She also emphasized that "there were always foreigners in Halle" who "contribute to the development of the city" (interview H., November 22, 2001). Twelve years later, Nina interviewed the city's new lord mayor, who came from a different political background and a younger generation than Frau Haüssler. Their conversation touched upon Halle's urban regeneration progress and plans and the election of a Senegalese-born German citizen to represent Halle in the federal parliament. The mayor declared: "Every foreigner is part of Halle" (interview W., May 21, 2013).

In 2002, Nina made her way to the office of Mayor Baines in the city hall of Manchester, New Hampshire, in the United States. When asked about the role of migrants in Manchester, the mayor referred Nina to his second inaugural speech, delivered a few months earlier. As had the lord mayors of Halle and the deputy mayor of Mardin, Manchester's mayor had spoken of his city's regeneration by referencing its past significance and the integral role diverse populations played as city-makers, both past and present. He portrayed migrants in the past as important to making the city a global player and welcomed newcomers for their "profound and positive impact on the City's future." Moving beyond binaries of difference, Mayor Baines said: "They are us—or, it might be more appropriate to say that we were them—because we are all the offspring of immigrants" (Baines 2002).

Placing Urban Narratives: A Comparative Approach

City boosting is an age-old art. What is today called city branding can be read in archeological sites of the first cities and persistent tales of the seven wonders of the ancient world.[1] Today, competitive city branding is the stuff of city websites and Facebook pages, of applications for government grants and loans, and of political leaders' speeches. The urban narratives we found within each city's cyberspaces and our interviews with city leaders and politicians sounded in many ways as if they came from a global playbook on city redevelopment within contemporary neoliberal restructuring (McCann and Ward 2011). However, when we compared the empowerment outcomes in our research cities to those of global cities such as New York, Berlin, or Istanbul, clear differences emerged that made Halle, Manchester, and Mardin more similar to each other than to more powerful cities within the same country.

Deploying the variation-finding strategies we outlined in the introduction, we delineate in this chapter the domains of contemporary structural similarities brought about by processes of disempowerment in Halle/Saale, Manchester, and Mardin. The three cities differ in terms of their historical trajectories and recent population sizes: Manchester, 110,229; Halle, 238,321; Mardin center, 163,725 (greater Mardin, 796,237) (US Census 2017a; City of Halle 2016; TÜRKSTAT 2016). However, by the turn of the twenty-first century the residents of each city, including their political and economic leaders, were confronting the same structural dilemma and seeking similar solutions. The similarities among the three cities that we identify in this chapter are not timeless but reflect their shared disempowered positioning within a particular historical conjuncture of neoliberal capital accumulation through urban regeneration. Within these similarities, the leaders and migrants of each city engaged in mutually constitutive processes of displacement and emplacement that contributed to the reshaping and repositioning of their city.

We compare the three cities according to five parameters that both reflect and form the core of our research methods. These parameters require a constant dialogue between our multiple forms of inquiry: interviews; participant observation; websites; and documents and statistics culled from local, national, supranational, and global sources. They also require a form of analysis that approached each city not as a bounded unit but as a multiscalar social field of interconnection.

The five comparative parameters are:

(1) Whether there are indicators of the city's relative declining positioning over time that can be operationalized in terms of objective and subjective factors. Objective factors include a decrease in the scope or potency of past or current multiscalar economic, political, and cultural social fields. Spaces of abandonment serve as one indicator of the loss of potency. Subjective factors include leaders' awareness of their city's past and its current relative loss of potency.

(2) Whether the city embarks on a strategy of rebranding and regeneration and the outcomes of such an effort in terms of private investment, public benefit, public debt, and the relative global positioning of the city at the end of our study.

(3) The way in which city leaders position migrants or minorities within their regeneration narratives.

(4) The degree and kind of resources and services the city provides for migrant settlement and migrant and minority access to services.

(5) Evidence of synergy between city regeneration narratives and policies, on the one hand, and the multiscalar modes of emplacement of migrants and minorities, on the other, including whether their transnational networks emerged as assets in city-making.

Comparing the Three Cities

MANCHESTER, NEW HAMPSHIRE, USA

(1) The city's relative declining positioning over time operationalized in terms of objective and subjective factors.

Just fifty-three miles north of Boston, Manchester, by the beginning of the twentieth century, had become the largest city in the US region known as northern New England (Maine, New Hampshire, and Vermont). One hundred years later, it still held that distinction, although its population of 107,006 was relatively small (US Census 2000b). The city is centered in a city-region generally known as "greater Manchester," which at the turn of the twenty-first century numbered 198,378, and in Hillsborough County, which then had a population of 380,841 (US Census 2000b; Intown Manchester 2005; New Hampshire Employment Security 2017).[2] The city-region and Hillsborough County contained both wealthy exclusive suburbs and working-class towns, with some industrial production and unused structures marking generations of industrial labor.

Named after Manchester, England, and aiming to rival its namesake's global reach, Manchester, New Hampshire, was economically important in the nineteenth and early twentieth centuries. Its growth as an industrial powerhouse came about through a small circle of Boston capitalists who bought up the city's existing textile mills, incorporated them as the Amoskeag Company in 1831, and developed them into an industrial complex. They also bought land in the city center and laid out a planned company town, which directly influenced the character of the city and the growth of its paternalistic system of labor relations. At various times, the corporation also produced rifles, sewing machines, fire engines, and locomotives, augmenting Manchester's regional reputation for the manufacture of shoes and machine tools. But it was through its textile production that the city gained worldwide fame (Eaton 2015; Blood 1975).

In 1922, responding to dramatic wage reductions, Amoskeag workers

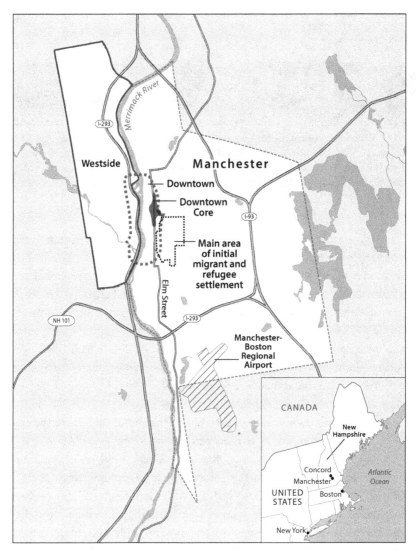

MAP 1.1 Map showing Manchester city center, city boundaries, and the location of the city within the northeastern United States. Cartography: Jutta Turner. Base maps: openstreetmap.org; Manchester Planning Board, 2009: Masterplan for the City of Manchester. © Jutta Turner.

FIG 1.1 Panoramic view of the cotton mills in Manchester, New Hampshire, by Alphonso H. Sanborn, 1903. In 1903, the productive capacity of the mills of Manchester, New Hampshire, made the city significant nationally and globally. Image courtesy of the Library of Congress Prints & Photographs Division, LCCN 200766256.

struck. Unconstrained, since they were not local actors, the Boston-based company owners sought a more docile workforce who would be satisfied with lower wages during a conjuncture marked by both growing national and global competition, on the one hand, and depression and crisis, on the other. They sold the mills in 1936 and relocated their cotton manufacturing to newer textile mills in the nonunionized US South. From that point on, the people of Manchester faced ongoing deindustrialization. Smaller concerns took over some of the old mill buildings, but ultimately these proved unable to compete with cheaper labor and the more technologically advanced facilities located elsewhere (Hareven and Langenbach 1978).

Some discussions of deindustrialization in the United States date the end of "Fordism," unionized, large mass production, to the 1970s (Amin 1994). However, the disempowerment of cities and regions through the loss of industry began much earlier. As the history of Manchester illustrates, deindustrialization need not be equated with the total loss of industry: the process may include downsizing, loss of unions, and periodic reinvestment and disinvestment. Greater Manchester, with its mix of machine tool and electronics shops and weapons manufacturing, continued to provide industrial employment in the post–World War II period. But by the mid-twentieth century, most textile and shoe production had shut down and the city center had become a backwater of enormous abandoned mills. The city center business district and surrounding neighborhoods were left desolate by growing postwar suburbanization and the growth of shopping malls. Failed US urban renewal attempts during the 1960s to revive and modernize Manchester's city center were painfully evident after "some of the historic mill buildings" had been leveled, the strip mall that replaced them rapidly abandoned, and Manchester left "with the general reputation as a 'lost city'" (Langenbach 1969).

Downtown abandonment became even more apparent in 1991, when federal authorities closed seven New Hampshire banks, four of them headquartered in Manchester, on the same day as a consequence of overextension in real estate speculation (Federal Deposit Insurance Corporation nd). Peter Ramsey, an actor in the efforts to regenerate Manchester's city center around 2000, described the situation that city leaders had faced almost a decade earlier: "There were rumors about how people wouldn't come downtown anymore. There were empty businesses up and down the streets" (Broussard 2015).

However, despite this grim picture of Manchester's city center, deindustrialization, accompanied by the abandonment of industrial sites and depopulation, was not linear or uniform across the city-region. In the 1990s, after a severe economic downturn, as neoliberal economic restructuring took hold regionally and nationally, the city and its surrounding region experienced a brief manufacturing effervescence. Employers were attracted to the Manchester city-region by low nonunion wage labor, inexpensive industrial space, and proximity to the belt of high-tech industries developing around Boston. The greater Boston area experienced a growth of high-tech, defense, and knowledge industries, and the Manchester area was incorporated into new, complicated, and flexible supply chains fueled by foreign investment (Gittell 2001). Unemployment that in 1993 had approached 8 percent in Manchester fell to 2.4 percent in 1999 (US Bureau of Labor Statistics 2016).

However, at this point, the economy entered a sharp and punctuated decline, owing first to the "dot-com" downturn of 2000 and then to the financial shock waves in 2001 from the September 11 bombings that reverberated through the United States' and world economies. Unemployment climbed, and plant layoffs and closings resumed. Increasing numbers of manufacturing sites in the Manchester area reduced their workforce or closed. The percentage of Manchester's workforce employed in manufacturing declined. Between 2000 and 2005, when developers issued a new set of redevelopment plans, manufacturing dropped from 12.7 percent of the workforce to 9.3 percent (US Department of Labor, Bureau of Labor Statistics 2012).

Manchester was never the political capital of New Hampshire, nor were its leaders ever significant actors within regional centers of power, which remain in the neighboring city of Boston, Massachusetts. Boston has always been the residential and institutional site of a social, intellectual, and political elite who have been national actors. Yet amid the vicissitudes of ongoing economic restructuring, as regional, national, and global investors played major roles in the changing fortunes of their city, local leaders were aware that

Manchester retained a peculiar national and even global prominence. New Hampshire hosts the first US presidential primary election. As the most populous city in the state, Manchester, every four years, is repeatedly visited by all aspiring presidential candidates, and city leaders and ordinary people are consistently featured in media coverage. As a local reporter emphasized in 2015 (Hayward 2015), "We're the crucible": "Yes, it's a statewide event, but . . . Manchester becomes . . . the focal point for the New Hampshire primary."

City boosters also harkened back to the city's former industrial glory. They claimed that by the beginning of the twentieth century, Manchester's Amoskeag mills, including mill number 11 with its four thousand looms and seventeen thousand workers, was "the world's largest textile mill complex" (Millyard Museum 2015; Intown Manchester 2005, 2). In Mayor Baines's second inaugural speech, one could hear both an acknowledgment of Manchester's lost global significance as a textile manufacturing hub and a desire to retrieve some of its past importance. The mayor looked forward to a time when, once again, "what Manchester, New Hampshire, says today, the rest of the world may indeed say tomorrow" (Baines 2002).

> (2) Whether the city embarks on a strategy of rebranding and regeneration, and the outcomes of such an effort in terms of private investment, public benefit, public debt, and the relative global positioning of the city at the end of our study.

It was within an assessment of past glory and continuing episodic political importance that Manchester city leaders contemplated the possibilities of reinventing their city. In 1993, they developed a master plan through a series of projects that justified various forms of public investment. This strategy sought to convince regional, national, and international corporations to situate their production facilities and offices in Manchester. Five years later, city leaders endorsed and publicly funded 85 percent of the necessary land acquisition as well as the construction of the new civic and sports arena situated in the city center (Lincoln NE City Government 2008, 96).[3] Investment in the arena was deemed the foundation for redevelopment. City leaders and developers saw the city's "downtown" as a "prime area for expansion and revitalization" (City of Manchester 2006).

Between 2000 and 2015, the stance that Manchester's leaders and the urban planners they commissioned adopted toward urban regeneration and the city's public narrative altered several times; after 2009, no new master plan was offered (Angelou 2005; Intown Manchester 2005; Manchester Office of Economic Development 2009). The changes in part reflected the politics and

FIG 1.2 View of regenerated downtown Manchester with sports and entertainment arena. Photo via Good Free Photos.

personalities of different mayors and the changing membership of the city council. But the twists and turns also reflected, and spoke to, shifts in national political trends as well as reconfigurations of the national and global economies. These conjunctural forces directly affected the possibilities of repositioning the city.

By 2000, Manchester had experienced a period of local industrial expansion as well as major regional and local bank failures that were a result of the first stage of overextension in the housing market. Local politicians, including the mayor, still saw industry as a significant component of the local economy but also began to confront the need to plan for "new economy jobs." The initial narratives of redevelopment called on international businesses, already present in manufacturing, to invest in the city, situate headquarters there, and bring in a new highly skilled workforce for what, in 2002, the mayor called "the new economy, whatever that is" (Baines 2002; see also Angelou 2005).

As the millennium progressed, Manchester redevelopers oversaw construction of a minor-league baseball stadium on the edge of the city center and facilitated the regeneration or development of hotels, parks, high-end housing, and office buildings. They also worked to help finance the redevelopment of the historic mill buildings that had been left standing in earlier failed efforts at urban renewal.

Bolstered by growing public investment and loan capital, industrial investment, especially in the defense industry, did grow for a time regionally as well as in city center districts. Some increases in employment followed from the regeneration strategies, although most were temporary. As we traced the presence of national and international corporate offices and production facilities in the city center and in greater Manchester over our fifteen-year study, the transience of much of this development became apparent. Many firms initially established in Manchester with the assistance of tax breaks, loans, and public expenditures, which were heralded in the press, downsized or left a few years later. The international military industrial complex proved to be a significant partner of rapid investment and disinvestment in the city, region, and State of New Hampshire (Anderson 2012; Donahue Institute 2015; Cousineau 2015).[4]

City leaders developed a trajectory of redevelopment and a local institutional structure to facilitate it. In 2005, the master plan was revised and expanded with funding from a key local player in redevelopment, the Manchester Development Corporation, and two US federal agencies, the Economic Development Administration and the Department of Housing and Urban Development (HUD) (Hillier Architecture 2006). The planning was facilitated by a new transnational actor, Hillier Architecture. Based in Princeton, New Jersey, and promoting itself as the "third largest architectural firm in the United States" with an international clientele and ties to key public-funding institutions in Washington, DC (Studio Hillier nd.), Hillier Architecture was hired to revise Manchester's redevelopment plan. Its Downtown Strategic Development Plan for Manchester noted that the city had "successfully guided development" to become "consistently rated one of the most livable cities in the country for the past decade" and worked to "foster its transition from a struggling post-industrial community into the 'place to go' in New England" (Hillier Architecture 2006).

City branding and planning reports described a thriving city center with high-end businesses whose employees would occupy new high-rise condominium apartment buildings and fuel a vibrant consumer economy. A 2005 report of Intown Manchester, an agency tasked with leading central city development and funded by a tax on commercial property, heralded the city's "economic renaissance" (Intown Manchester 2005). By this time, the city center was portrayed as a vibrant area of recreation and entertainment. The goal of such portrayals was attracting and retaining the youthful, highly educated workers, who were considered necessary to draw new "creative" technology industries to the city.

By 2014, leaders had moved from the hope of attracting high-paying new economy employment to targeting the logistics industry as a way to boost the city-region. They tried to attract "hundreds of jobs . . . including truck driver and warehouse worker positions" to new shipping and processing facilities at the airport tax-free zone. As did the various corporate offices and high-tech facilities attracted to the city, these logistics industries also came and went. Moreover, as part of a foreign trade zone and as an economic recovery area, none of these facilities were within the boundaries of the city and therefore did not directly contribute money to local coffers (Guilmet 2014; Delay 2014).

After they invested in the new civic and sports arena and rehabilitated a historic theater, Manchester leaders continued to rebuild the city center using a combination of public and private financing. However, the bulk of the regeneration, including support for corporate facilities relocating to Manchester, was fueled by public monies. The city auditor's 2013 report of the Manchester Economic Development Office (MEDO) provides a revealing list of Manchester's financial "resources for Economic Development" (Office of the Independent City Auditor 2013, 4, 6).[5] This list included five federal programs, eight State of New Hampshire programs, two city programs, and three bank-facilitated programs (one through a state program). The financing mechanisms and other subsequent related problems with these projects suggest the contradictions that emerged from rebuilding efforts.

Public money was channeled into the regeneration process in a host of ways: US Government Housing and Urban Development grants and loans were provided to redevelop housing; city funding was backed by guaranteed tax revenues; city purchases of land were sold to private developers at below market prices; the city made provisions of infrastructure for private development; and state tax abatements were offered for corporations located in the city center. Private developers reaped benefits from the public financing of projects that they subsequently owned or managed. Privately owned construction companies profited as well from related demolition and construction costs (Applied Economic Research 2010; City of Manchester 2012; Guinta 2009; US Department of Housing and Urban Development Archives 2011).

Housing redevelopment and construction in Manchester was imbricated in this transfer of funds to corporate pockets. In 2006, the city leadership used refugee flows to justify further regeneration activities and the need for expanding the Neighborhood Revitalization Strategy Area, funded by HUD (City of Manchester 2010a). Refugees, together with low-income residents of the city, became an asset that facilitated access to federal funds. Applications for funding claimed that the public programs would provide housing and services both for the impoverished local population and for refugees who were concentrated in the downtown and surrounding neighborhoods. The public housing authority, which had been reconfigured as the Manchester Housing and Redevelopment Authority (MHRA), worked closely with private developers to obtain massive amounts of federal money. Much of this money served as a tranche of capital for city center regeneration. The MHRA invested public funds in private development projects, calling its activities "instrumental in shaping the skyline of the city" (2016). They invested public money in an arena, office buildings, a shopping mall, a bank building, two industrial parks, a business park, and a hotel and convention center.

At the same time, various federal programs reached out to low-income clients to assist them in obtaining flexible rate mortgages, many of which were subprime and fed into global financial industries' mortgage packaging and sales (Buchannan 2002). In the years leading up to the subprime mortgage crisis, housing prices were dramatically inflated, housing became scarce, and Manchester's working- and middle-class were squeezed by high rents or mortgage payments, low wages, and periodic job loss or layoffs linked to dramatic fluctuations in defense-related industries. After the crash, rates of impoverishment increased, and city applications referenced this poverty in applications to federal authorities for additional development funding from the Community Development Block Grant Program. In 2013, 52.2 percent of the city's households earned less than 80 percent of the median income as compared to 43 percent in 1990 (City of Manchester Planning and Community Development Department 2014). The poverty rate increased from 10.6 percent in 2000 to 13.7 percent in 2007 (before the subprime crisis) and reached 19.5 percent in 2016 (City Data 2018).

Tax policy was central to the "business-friendly" regeneration strategy. Neither the State of New Hampshire nor the City of Manchester have income or sales taxes. City planning documents in the first decade of the millennium advised marketing Manchester by emphasizing its attractiveness to high-tech industries and professionals. These documents highlighted that "moving your business here is a non-taxing decision. Our state has no personal income tax, no sales tax, and very low business taxes" (City of Manchester 2014). Municipalities collected only property and commercial taxes so, unless corporations or individuals physically resided within the city, they paid no taxes to it.

In effect, regeneration did little to maintain a steady base or growth in employment, and this redevelopment strategy did not expand Manchester's tax base. The city center streets and storefronts were gentrified, the population grew, and a small stratum of young professionals settled in the rebuilt city center. The redeveloped mill yards were occupied by small businesses, a few corporate headquarters, a branch of the public university, and a museum dedicated to the city's industrial and immigrant history. There were efforts to jump-start high-tech through fostering start-ups (Solomon 2012). However, postmillennium development projects generally were not successful in substantively improving the local economy.

After 2007, the failure of subprime loans and associated banks and financial institutions dramatically disrupted whatever progress had been achieved. The worldwide capitalist crisis heralded a new conjunctural configuration and a new wave of unemployment and dispossession in the city.

(3) The way in which city leaders position migrants or minorities within their regeneration narratives.

Immediately after the attacks on September 11, 2001, federal authorities used them and the subsequent Patriot Act[6] as justifications for the increased surveillance of all migrants. Houses were entered without warrants and migrant individuals and their families were scrutinized. However, in Manchester, local authorities and community-based organizations took various measures to counter anti-immigrant currents and protect residents from unwarranted policing (field notes, 2001–2). Manchester's general narrative remained one of welcome. As the city took its first steps toward regeneration, various leaders coupled their welcoming greetings with efforts to recover Manchester's immigrant past, a theme they emphasized in numerous ways after 2000. The welcoming narrative was present in city politicians' public statements, in documents, on websites, and in interviews we conducted with the mayor, police chief, head of city welfare, city planning officials, aldermen, social and medical service workers, and clergy in 2001 and 2002.[7]

References to new immigrants on websites and in speeches in those years are interesting in light of the relatively few migrants who had settled in Manchester. The foreign born numbered 2 percent in 1990 and 8 percent at the millennium (US Census 2000a).[8] Although the percentage was greater than in the rest of the state, the "foreign born" constituted a relatively small sector of the city's population, and some had arrived in the United States decades earlier. In the 1980s, Vietnamese refugees settled there; in the 1990s, the largest group of refugees came from the former Yugoslavia. However, toward the end of the twentieth century, Manchester began to welcome a diverse settlement of migrants from Asia, Africa, the Middle East, and Latin America (New Hampshire Center for Public Policy Studies 2015, 8). At the same time, energetic international recruiting by a local private university brought a scattering of students from the Middle East, South Asia, and Africa, some of whom settled in the city after their studies. By 2015, 13.1 percent of the population were foreign-born (US Census 2017b).

As the mayor and city council sought to retain and attract industrial investments, migrants, including refugees, came to be valued as part of the workforce. Major Baines summarized how migrants were seen at the millennium: "Their presence will have both a profound and positive impact on the City's future" (Baines 2002). City officials publicly acknowledged that low wages might prove an incentive to employers and saw migrant newcomers as keeping wages low in times of low unemployment.[9] A section of Manchester's website that addressed businesspeople looking to relocate listed the presence of immigrants and refugees in the city as a positive aspect of the city's profile (City of Manchester 2004).

In 2006, city planners saw immigrants as vital to increasing the density and diversity of the downtown population: "The vibrancy of the downtown core is enhanced by the density and diversity of the local community. Manchester is an immigration center, which is increasing the ethnic and racial composition" (City of Manchester 2006). This narrative was part of an effort to rebrand the city in order to reposition it as a competitor for multinational investment. By this time, city officials supported the celebration of past waves of immigrants as well as contemporary cultural diversity. The city's immigrant heritage was highlighted and past assimilationist trends repudiated. Local leaders more readily claimed their Greek, Irish, and French Canadian ancestry, and the Millyard Museum, founded in 2001, profiled workers from all over Europe whose labor had made Manchester's mills internationally significant.

City marketing employed various public events that featured the migrant roots of the population—from St. Patrick's Day parades and Greek Glendi to Caribbean and Latino festivals—to give Manchester a multicultural ambiance. But on occasion, and strategically, migrants were also depicted as part of the urban poor. As we have already noted, federal housing and redevelopment grants and loans could be accessed by crafting a narrative in which migrants, especially new impoverished refugees, were in urgent need of public services.

By 2009, Manchester's political and corporate leaders, and the urban developers with whom they worked, had been pulled in different directions by competing sets of interests. Consequently, two different narratives about the city's relationship to migrants emerged. City business leaders continued to support diversity celebrations to create an urban lifestyle attractive to investors and the "creative classes," whose presence was felt necessary to gentrify and reinvent the city. These festivals have always served as a place of political networking for local politicians and those aspiring to office, both with and without migrant backgrounds.

In 2011, a newspaper article noted, "Manchester embraces its diversity on [the] city website" (Tuohy 2011). The story features "a smiling Mayor Ted Gatsas," who, with "a mouse click turns the script into Chinese, or Spanish, or any of 59 languages on the Google Translate toolbar atop the City of Manchester's website." The article quoted the city's director of information systems, who announced, "We are a city of diverse backgrounds and cultures."

However by 2009, the only reference to immigrants in the city budget was an item of $48,000 from federal Community Development Block Grant funds to "facilitate assimilation of Manchester's newest immigrants and refugees into the community" (Guinta 2009, table 2, 3). An increasing number of public officials had begun to portray refugees as a burden on local public and social services, which came under increasing pressure as federal monies receded and tax monies increasingly were channeled into public–private partnerships that were used to develop entertainment, hotels, and office complexes. Efforts by the local Islamic Society to build a mosque in Greater Manchester were blocked by people in a local township in the city-region. By 2012, local and state-level Republican Party members who served as aldermen, the mayor, and state representatives were taking increasingly anti-immigrant stands.

By 2014, as regeneration faltered and federal and state funding for urban programs dried up, the city faced debt, a reduced tax base, and public services they could not fund. Manchester's poverty rate stood at 15 percent, which was higher than the New Hampshire average, 8.9 percent (US Census 2014). When a local movement against refugees, spearheaded by a city council member, came to dominate the city's political leadership, Mayor Gatsas joined other elected officials in targeting migrants as a drain on the city: "These are not immigrants like I remember my grandfather sponsoring from Greece, where they had to have a job to come. We have 1,000 homeless in Manchester" (Siefer 2014).

Yet voices of welcome still could be heard. Saying that the mayor was sending "the wrong message about Manchester," Alderman Long supported efforts to settle unaccompanied minor children in the city, including children from Syria. He noted, "They're coming to the United States as a million people have, as refugees" (Siefer 2014). In 2015, despite growing political polarization in which US national and New Hampshire political parties sought legislation barring the entry of Syrian refugees or Muslims, the Manchester city council rejected a resolution banning the settlement of Syrian refugees (Feely 2015).

(4) The degree and kind of resources and services the city provides for migrant settlement and migrant and minority access to services.

At best, the city government of Manchester provided token amounts of money to organizations that highlighted diversity or celebrated cultural heritage and offered very little institutional support for services specific to migrants. At a time when the city was promoting its immigrant past and diverse present, funding for a cultural diversity coalition that promoted celebrating immigrant roots through commemorating national holidays received only several hundred dollars a year (field notes, 2004). For many years, the city partially funded a Latin American Center, which functioned as the preeminent association providing services to new immigrants and refugees. Finally, the center became attached to Southern New Hampshire Services, originally a federally funded community action program to empower the poor that became a private nonprofit organization.

The lack of institutional resources to sustain ethnic associations and organizations that highlight ethnic communities was apparent in the trajectories of these organizations over time. Organizations claiming ethnic specificity were ephemeral and tended to be the personal projects of aspiring educated migrants with political ambitions, locally and transnationally. Founded by migrants, ethnically specific organizations at best received very small amounts of public or charitable funding. Most either became umbrella organizations for refugees and immigrants from very different parts of the world or made it their mission to provide services to low-income groups. For example, the Somali Bantu Community Association, founded in 2006, transformed in 2011 into the Organization for Refugee and Immigrant Success (ORIS 2017).

The city did not fund services specifically for refugees, and city welfare funds appropriated for refugees were insignificant. By and large, while federal grants, as we noted, referenced the poor in the city center and areas designated for redevelopment, urban regeneration, including federal housing money, benefited wealthier populations. From 2000 to 2015, the poor, in whose name the money had been raised, were gradually pushed out of the city center as housing in that area became increasingly expensive. Because city regeneration was fueled by various forms of public investment and debt, amassing money for city center development led to increasing city impoverishment and reductions in public services. Manchester failed not only to provide transportation, affordable housing, and institutional support for impoverished populations but also to provide these services for the majority of its residents, who faced reduced possibilities in terms of education and health and whose lives became more precarious.

(5) Evidence of synergy between city regeneration narratives and policies, on the one hand, and the multiscalar modes of emplacement of migrants and minorities, on the other, including whether their transnational networks emerged as assets in city-making.

Responding to, as well as acting to expand, the opportunity structures they found in Manchester, migrants were engaged in the multiscalar social fields within which the city's regeneration efforts were situated. Often, they served as unacknowledged assets in rebuilding and rebranding the city by creating institutions and personal networks of support and emplacement in close relationship to people considered natives within this setting. In a subsequent chapter, we highlight the migrant leadership of born-again Christian religious and political networks that engaged mostly white non-migrants in transnational, born-again Christian networks that extended to centers of power, including the Bush White House and the Republican Party.

At the same time, these organizations and networks created national and transnational linkages for the city. These included not only Christian organizations but also a Buddhist temple and a mosque. The Buddhist temple brought transnational connections through a Buddhist network that stretched to headquarters in San Francisco and another that connected hundreds of cities around the globe (interview T., July 21, 2003). Similarly, the Islamic Society of Greater Manchester not only functioned as a mosque but also linked immigrants, refugees, and local professionals to the private university, to a range of business activities in the city and region, and to aspiring professionals inserting themselves in politics on the city and state levels (field notes, January–April 2004)

Local, national, and transnational connections not only linked local migrants and non-migrants to employment, politics, and needed services but also provided them with a sense of empowerment in the face of continuing precarity (Glick Schiller, Çağlar, and Guldbrandsen 2006). Migrants emerged as actors in the economic dimensions of multiscalar city-making. They were actors in processes of regeneration—as city residents who redeveloped property, stabilized neighborhoods, took out subprime mortgages, and suffered foreclosure and as members of a workforce in the rapid rise and fall of dot-com bubbles and fluctuations of the defense industry. They became owners and workers in businesses filling city center storefronts, worked as social workers and city planners, and became political representatives of Manchester who celebrated the urban regeneration narrative through public–private ventures and participation within both the Democratic and the Republican Parties. While city leaders searched for high-power transborder connections to bring investments and new businesses and profiled their city to attract global talent, migrants of various legal statuses quietly engaged in transnational city-making. Only occasionally and peripherally were these processes apparent to various urban developers and political officials.

By 2015, businesses established by a range of migrants helped fill regenerated city center storefronts with needed services for the entire population, including for the new, richer inhabitants of the city center: tailoring, shoe-making, and hair and nail styling. Some businesses in the city center and the larger city-region connected Manchester to transnational business suppliers.

Migrants also became part of transnational processes of real estate development, the international banking industry, and the subsequent foreclosure wave and collapse of the property market between 2007 and 2012. They filled the roles of real estate agents, bankers, and mortgage brokers and served as employees of local community-based, federally funded organizations that provided support and loans to first-time home buyers. Others, by purchasing houses, contributed to the spiral of rising prices for the city's aging housing stock, including in impoverished neighborhoods. Migrants bought inflated real estate because of the lack of affordable rentals, the need to house large families, and the discrimination they faced as renters in the housing market. That is to say, migrants in Manchester stabilized neighborhoods and created value even as they contributed to a mortgage crisis of unsustainable, inflated property values with national and global ramifications.

Refugee resettlement and the personal activism and crossborder ties of specific migrants who sometimes acted as "community" leaders also linked the city to broader networks of national and global power. Some refugees whose emplacement in Manchester linked them to federal refugee resettlement agencies and the United Nations used their institutional and crossborder ties to become agents of social and political activism as part of various organizations based in Manchester and elsewhere (field notes, 2015). For example, Manchester's narrative, which linked the "rebirth" of the city to its being a place "where people from all ethnicities and religious background come together to form a new and exciting community" (Baines 2004), created opportunities for migrants who were educated, ambitious, and eager to participate in the local political process.

As the city launched its regeneration efforts, the local Republican Party welcomed two new activists who went on to become members of the New Hampshire State Legislature: Carlos Gonzalez, born and educated in the Dominican Republic, and Saghir Tahir, born and educated in Pakistan. Both men gained a degree of local prominence from migrant-based organizing, but careful examination of their networks reveals that each man had political and economic connections that linked Manchester to elite US institutions, to the US federal government, transnationally to their homelands, and to powerful corporate actors.

When Gonzalez joined the local Republican Party in the 1990s and was warmly welcomed by Manchester's Republican mayor, Ray Wieczorek, he was not a political novice. He began his political career in the Dominican Republic, where he grew up, working for the Dominican president and for the US Embassy (Ballotpedia 2017). After he settled in Manchester, Wieczorek encouraged him to become politically active, saying, "Carlos, I'm of Polish descent. And this city is a city of immigrants. And you might very well be tomorrow the next mayor of the city" (Fabian 2012). Gonzalez was affiliated with several Hispanic local and regional organizations. But as he noted in an interview with UniVision, a major Spanish-language media company, "I represent a very big district and there are hardly any Hispanics. That means I am very accepted and respected. It's not about being Hispanic. It's about the quality of my personality, as a professional and a politician" (Fabian 2012). Gonzalez was not only a political professional but also a mortgage specialist trained at Harvard under a Fannie Mae fellowship that was organized to improve "affordable housing opportunities in communities across the country" (PR Newswire 2001).

When Saghir Tahir was elected to the New Hampshire House of Representatives in 2000, he became the second Muslim in the United States to be elected to a state legislature. In Manchester, he had been a real estate investor and an independent construction contractor for Fortune 500 firms (Dutt 2006). He was also a civic leader, chair of the Manchester Republican Committee, a member of the local Elks club and Kiwanis club, and president of the New Hampshire chapter of the American Muslim Alliance (AMA). Although the war on terror and the growth of the US national surveillance regime focused on Muslims, Tahir continued to be re-elected, serving until 2011. His activism and advocacy through transnational organizations such as the Overseas Pakistanis Foundation, which he also headed, linked Manchester and New Hampshire to national and international debates over Islam, the US relation to Pakistan, and the Kashmir conflict. After September 11, 2001, Tahir led a delegation to Pakistan to promote better relations between the United States and Pakistan. The US State Department and the Pakistani government both offered to fund his work. In 2003, as a result of Tahir's advocacy and networking, the NH legislature became the first state government in the United States to ask Congress to open an inquiry into the situation in Kashmir.

The careers of these two Manchester activists were not unique. During this period, several other people of migrant background gained political positions in situations in which regeneration processes focused on housing and urban redevelopment intersected with the city's migrant-friendly narrative. Through this organizing, migrants entered into political networks that helped launch their political careers as elected officials or political party activists who represented Manchester. Meetings held to organize cultural festivals—Latino, Caribbean, and African—were often central to this emplacement process.

At the same time, migrants joined with natives in different struggles for social justice. At times, these struggles resonated throughout the city, whose iconic role in the national US political process potentially gave them broader significance. As the conjuncture began to change, so did the goals of organizations that highlighted festivals of cultural diversity. Many activists and organizations increasingly embraced a social justice agenda, emphasizing civil rights, anti-racism, and social justice rather than cultural diversity. Commonalities, not cultural differences, came to dominate the narratives of most of these organizations (field notes, 2010, 2013).

The city had hosted Martin Luther King Jr. celebrations at a time when the State of New Hampshire refused to recognize the official holiday. After the state legislature adopted the holiday in 2000, these celebrations continued. At one such celebration in 2003 attended by the city's mayor and held at a Greek Orthodox Church, the keynote speaker, Reverend Canon Edward Rodman, a black Episcopalian pastor noted, "The stories of different groups in America should be told, so that we all understand each other's suffering, which will give a basis for common compassion and allow us to live in harmony" (field notes, January 20, 2003). This theme of addressing particular injustices while maintaining a position of opposition to all injustices was highlighted by the Ujima Collective, an organization that aimed to "combat the social isolation and cultural alienation" of people of African descent. By 2016, members of the collective had developed an explicitly anti-racist stance (field notes, 2002; Ujima Collective 2016). Meanwhile, Latinos Unidos de New Hampshire, which initially sponsored a Latino Festival, by 2013 had reimagined the African/Caribbean Celebration and the Latino Festival as the "We Are One Festival" (*Union Leader* 2015) with the purpose of bringing "together cultures and communities."

In 2002, activists established the Immigrants Rights Task Force, which rallied for the rights of and opportunities for all migrants and saw this struggle as everyone's concern. The task force brought together peace advocates, union organizers, lawyers, health-care activists, and representatives of faith communities, some of migrant background and some not, to organize on city and state levels and take on national issues. The task force was part of a coalition of state forces that successfully opposed state-level anti-immigrant measures to limit drivers' license access and impose racial profiling. In 2007, the organization became the statewide New Hampshire Alliance of Immigrants and Refugees. In 2015, they won a $25,000 grant from the prestigious New Hampshire Charitable Fund "to strengthen efforts to welcome immigrants and refugees to their neighborhoods" (Robidoux 2015) in a clear rejection of regional and national calls to halt refugee resettlement and of the increasing targeting and criminalization of migrants.

HALLE / SAALE, SAXONY-ANHALT, GERMANY

(1) The city's relative declining positioning over time operationalized in terms of objective and subjective factors.

A historic center of economic activity and learning, Halle was a powerful presence in regional and transnational networks from medieval times

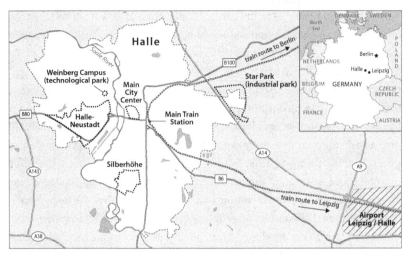

MAP 1.2 Map showing Halle city center, city boundaries, and the location of the city within Germany. Cartography: Jutta Turner. Base maps: openstreetmap.org; Stadt Halle (Saale) 2012: Fakten zum Wirtschaftsstandort Halle (Saale) © Jutta Turner.

through the German Democratic Republic (GDR) period. As in Manchester, the efforts of Halle's leaders to improve its competitive position drew from and referenced its past. The mayor's statement that Halle was *not* a small city, and the city's regeneration plans and narratives, recalled its greater historical significance and influence. Located on the river Saale in central Germany, Halle/Saale now combines remnants of castles and a medieval walled city with a modernist, prefabricated socialist era "new city" (Halle-Neustadt). In 2013, its population numbered 233,552 (Löbner 2013); after years of depopulation, the city registered small population increases beginning in 2010. As with Manchester, the region around the city also has a significant but much older history of trade networks. They originated in a medieval salt industry and later were fostered by Halle's membership in the Hanseatic League. In the nineteenth century, as a result of Prussia's, then Germany's, growing industrialization and the development of coal mining in the region, Halle became the center of significant chemical and machine tool industries. Its historic university, founded in 1694, had for centuries been part of intellectual and scientific movements in Europe. In the industrial era, the university facilitated Halle's rise to scientific and technical prominence.[10]

In the postwar GDR, Halle continued as a petrochemical and intellectual center that fostered transnational connection through trade networks and international student recruitment with socialist and nonaligned states. In the first years of our research, some of the political leaders we interviewed had worked in scientific fields before unification. Some of the taxi drivers born in Halle spoke of their previous employment as international sales representatives of local petrochemical factories and of Halle's links with the Middle East, Africa, and Asia. Many older migrants noted that they had arrived in Halle as students during the GDR period.

Halle lost its importance and many of these transnational connections as a result of the 1990 German unification, a process of disempowerment that affected all of the city's residents. In the first years after unification, the city witnessed dramatic deindustrialization, massive unemployment, and out-migration as factories were privatized, downsized, or abandoned. In 2002, 19.8 percent of the city's apartments were vacant (City of Halle Stadtplanungs-samt 2011, 31). When people speak of the abandoned and desolate landscape that areas of the city presented in the early twenty-first century, they continually harken back to massive layoffs at the nearby Leuna and Buna oil refineries and petrochemical plants. These facilities employed forty thousand workers at the time of unification. After the subsequent privatizations, technological upgradings, and automation, the local petrochemical industry and refineries once more provided some employment possibilities for workers from the region but not on the same scale.

A decade after unification, Halle continued to face high levels of unemployment. In 2000, 11 percent of its residents (27,378 of 246,450) were officially unemployed, youth unemployment was much greater, and there was intense competition among residents even for low-paid work (Löbner 2013). Disempowered, Halle offered few opportunities for employment or social mobility either for those seen as natives or those described as foreigners or of migrant background. Large numbers of city inhabitants sought employment in western Germany or elsewhere in Europe, where they were often treated as low-wage labor, whatever their education or experience. Even after the unification of Halle-Neustadt and the historic city, Halle suffered an ongoing population loss; eighty thousand people left between 1990 and 2005.

In the wake of the political reorganization of administrative structures that accompanied unification, neighboring Magdeburg became the political capital of the newly formed state of Saxony-Anhalt. Only twenty-two miles away from Halle, Leipzig, the largest city and an administrative center in the neighboring state of Saxony, had strategic advantages in the competition to become the region's economic and cultural hub. Among these advantages was its strategic position adjoining the Leipzig/Halle Airport.

In evaluating the need for urban regeneration, city leaders confronted not only their political disadvantages but also the city's negative national and international reputation. The penchant of urban planners, scholars, and artists to highlight the deserted landscapes of "shrinking cities" was a significant global phenomena after the millennium and Halle was singled out as a prominent example for "post socialist" eastern Germany (Endres 2010; Richardson and Nam 2014). People elsewhere in Germany spoke of Halle as an undesirable place to live or work. It was envisioned as despoiled by past industrialization and by a current landscape of crumbling factory structures and abandoned, rotting buildings (Postkult 2015). This bleak image persisted, despite renewed historic and Art Deco neighborhoods and green foliage-filled vistas that replaced much of the brown industrial film that once coated trees, rivers, and buildings. The narrative of abandonment created a perception of Halle that city leaders had to challenge if the city was to be marketed in Germany, Europe, or globally, and thus attract private capital.

Even more damaging was the national and international reputation that Halle gained in the media as a racist city where migrants, whether well-paid professionals or impoverished asylum seekers, faced the threat of attack from neo-Nazi youth. As a result, few migrants voluntarily came to Halle; however, German authorities sent asylum seekers to the city and region. The migrants who remained included asylum seekers whose mobility in Germany was legally limited, students, migrants who married or had children with members of the local German population, and the elderly who came as refugees, Jewish settlers, and "ethnic Germans"[11] mostly from the Soviet Union and who didn't believe they would be employable elsewhere in Germany. In 2000, migrants constituted 3.1 percent of Halle's population (City of Halle 2015), with the largest number of migrants coming from the European Union.

In point of fact, neo-Nazis periodically attempted to organize in Halle and attacked people racialized as different. However, these attacks were neither concentrated in nor peculiar to Halle but were part of a broader phenomenon of racist, anti-refugee assaults that turned murderous in a number of German cities beginning in the early 1990s.[12]

(2) Whether the city embarks on a strategy of rebranding and regeneration and the outcomes of such an effort in terms of private investment, public benefit, public debt, and the relative global positioning of the city at the end of our study.

When Halle's political leaders looked to rebuild the economy and reputation of their city, their aspirations intersected with a range of institutional actors in Germany, the European Union, and around the world who saw economic opportunity in the city's terrains of abandonment. As in Manchester, in Halle many city leaders—political, economic, cultural, and academic—embraced a vision of regenerating the city through building new economy industries fueled by international investment. They were convinced that a critical factor in this new urban growth would be highly skilled international personnel, including "foreign scientists," who would repopulate the city and provide the necessary workforce and critical mass of consumers to support new high-tech industries, research institutions, upscale businesses, and gentrified inner-city districts.

Rather than one comprehensive plan, different plans were devised for redeveloping Halle's different territorial spaces and economic sectors. Vast amounts of public monies were channeled into these projects from several sources, including EU structural funds, German federal and local state (Länder) funds, and, in some cases, matching funds or loans from the city itself. One thrust of redevelopment centered on rebuilding housing stock, infrastructure, and storefronts with the retail ambience of urban shopping districts. Between 2000 and 2013, the EU Structural Fund allocated €55,492,926 for urban redevelopment in Halle (IBA 2010, 5). A large investment for reconfiguring Halle-Neustadt came from federal and Länder funding through the framework of Urban Redevelopment East (Stadtumbau Ost).[13] This program funded the demolition of large numbers of long-abandoned buildings, many of them prefabricated socialist housing (Plattenbauen), and at the same time supported the renovation of buildings and reconstruction of housing. It provided funds to both private landlords and publicly owned housing companies for renovating their properties and substantially reconfiguring urban districts in terms of value. These rebuilding projects were framed within a narrative that vast public investment in rebuilding could help Halle overcome its reputation of abandonment and attract international investors.

In fact, rebuilding enhanced the social spatial inequalities of the city. Areas of the city began to differ markedly in rates of unemployment, income levels, and youth gangs and crime, and they gained very different reputations (Baum, Vondroušová, and Tichá 2014). As property was redeveloped, rents rose for renovated apartments while the stock of unregenerated and more affordable apartments was reduced. As the city was transformed, sectors of the population continued to lose not only their jobs but also their neighborhoods, local institutions, social spaces, and spatially situated networks of support. Meanwhile, social agencies placed concentrations of refugees and troubled families in the former workers' districts of Halle-Neustadt and Silberhöhe. These former socialist residential districts were then stig-

FIG 1.3 Poster promoting and rebranding Halle, located on abandoned socialist housing on street connecting the central railroad station to the city center. Photograph by Nina Glick Schiller.

matized as places of poverty, unemployment, crime, and youth gangs (field notes, 2014). As Halle's city center and neighboring districts, with their gracious early-twentieth-century apartment buildings and storefronts, were renovated and its historic churches, towers, and public buildings were restored with EU, federal, and Saxony-Anhalt funds, these districts attracted a small, new middle class.

Over time, the visible dispossession of residents who hadn't migrated and yet were being physically displaced justified a further round of rebuilding within the city, which generated additional processes of dispossession and displacement. The links between displacement and gentrification were made clear in a report evaluating regeneration: "In Halle urban redevelopment means the demolition of housing. However, as specified by the program Urban Redevelopment East, this always takes place in conjunction with urban gentrification in other districts" (IBA 2010, 15). When Länder, federal, and EU funding for disadvantaged city areas could be raised by acknowledging interconnections between regeneration and impoverishment, applications followed suit and highlighted the growing disparities. For example, a report assessing some of the city's regeneration projects, "Balancing Act: Dual City," described the "old city" as "stabilized" and as having "secured its future" and argued that redevelopment was now needed in outlying areas to achieve "a new balance in the ratios between the two poles of the dual city" (IBA 2010).

At the same time, city leaders sought economic development in multiple directions. From the millennium to 2015, they persistently referred to "business, science and culture" as "the basis for the success of Halle (Saale)—the 'City of Handel.'" They claimed that "as Germany's greenest city, Halle's potential is demonstrated by its flexible and adaptable economic development which profits from state-of-the-art infrastructure and transport links to Europe's major cities and economic centers" (Business and Science Support Centre 2015, 2). Each of these claims accompanied considerable public investment, but the outcome in terms of repositioning Halle and developing a vibrant local economy was, as we show below, negligible.

After 2000, as cities around the world began to compete to become centers of science, Halle's city leaders believed they could reposition their city by emphasizing its former international prominence in science. The federal government helped initiate these efforts by locating two Max Planck Institutes, a Max Planck International Research School and the Leopoldina, the German National Academy of Sciences, in Halle. City leaders built on this momentum by investing in a new urban zone, the Weinberg campus, dedicated to attracting profitable science and technology corporations. The European Union principally funded construction of cutting-edge research facilities and necessary infrastructure (interview May 24, 2015). However, as a member of the Business and Science Support Centre of Halle (Dienstleistungszentrum Wirtschaft und Wissenschaft) noted, land was sold to corporations at below market rates, leaving Halle's impoverished taxpayers to pay the difference between the sale and market price (interview May 24, 2015).

At the same time, Halle looked to attract various forms of industry by constructing and promoting seven industrial parks and upgrading tram, rail, and roadway infrastructure—further incentives for businesses to locate their headquarters, personnel, and research, development, and production facilities in the city (Business and Science Support Centre 2015). Investors were promised "an entire city to support your economic potential" (Business and Science Support Centre 2015, 2). Halle's leaders also spoke of development through culture industries and tourism. Its art school was celebrated as a center of design. Drawing on its past, Halle called itself "the City of Handel," because George Fideric Handel was born in Halle, in 1685. Looking to its future, the city funded a state-of-the-art multimedia center and marketed its facilities for "film sound mixing" worldwide (Business and Science Support Centre 2015, 2, 15). A city report in 2015 claimed, "Around 1,000 companies in the dynamic industry of information and media technology operate here, employing around 4,500 people" (Business and Science Support Centre 2015, 14).

In fact, the results of all this redevelopment were decidedly mixed. According to a city official charged with economic development, many projects brought prestige rather significant private investment (field notes, July 12, 2015). The Weinberg Center, for example, attracted many start-ups, but most were small and provided relatively little employment given the sums invested. The petrochemical works nearby in Leuna once again became significant, employing nine thousand people by 2015 (Werkfeuerwehrverbandes Saxony-Anhalt e.V. 2015). While, in a 2015 report, the mayor claimed to have secured investment from Russia, China, and Norway, many corporate investors initiated projects that proved transient, despite receiving public subsidies (Halle Saale INVESTVISION Entwicklungs- und Verwaltungsgesellschaft Halle-Saalkreis GmbH. 2015). The largest industrial park, the "Star Park," was so underutilized that in a 2015 speech the mayor hailed as a great achievement the opening of a logistics center there, which paid its 130 workers only slightly more than the minimum wage (Pohlgeers 2015). The head of Saxony-Anhalt also noted that "Halle had recognized the trend of online trade quickly and provides an important locational advantage of the good transport links via the motorway and the airport Leipzig-Halle" (Pohlgeers 2015).

In fact, in a trajectory such as that of Manchester, the city was more successful in attracting low-wage logistics and call centers than "new economy" high-wage industries. Drawing on Halle's nineteenth- and early-twentieth-century history as a rail transshipment point for central Germany, Deutsche Bahn, the German railroad corporation, invested 700 million euros in 2014 to develop a rail transshipment facility next to Halle's central train station. However, Leipzig, with its proximity to the airport, also worked to establish its reputation as a logistics center.

Saxony-Anhalt, including Halle, emerged in 2013 as a significant location for call centers. According to the Federal Employment Agency (Budesagentur für Arbeit) in 2013, of all federal states, Saxony-Anhalt had the second highest percentage of its population employed in call centers—1.6 percent, compared to the national average of 0.4 percent (Bendick and Tempel 2014). The Länder had six thousand call center jobs in 2013. Call centers in Saxony-Anhalt paid the lowest wages of all federal states in Germany (Call-Center-Agent 2015). Nonetheless, by 2015 these centers were cutting jobs or closing down and moving to locations with even lower wages.

FIG 1.4 Regeneration of Marktplatz Halle and promotion of short-lived Dell call center. Photograph by Nina Glick Schiller.

Regeneration projects produced neither the increased tax revenue nor the greatly diminished unemployment that were the goals of the redevelopment. Unemployment, while lower than in 2000, was still sizeable in 2013, at 12.5 percent (Business and Science Support Centre 2015, 6). Figures for the long-term unemployed and the increasing rate of unemployment among people over fifty-five are significant in that regard. In 2013, 21 percent of the unemployed had been unemployed for two or more years and, although unemployment in the city was dropping, an increase (1.6 percent) in the long-term unemployed occurred between 2012 and 2013 (City of Halle 2013, 121). Until 2015, wage rates in the east were legally maintained below those of western Germany and there was no national minimum wage. Moreover, during the period of urban regeneration we are considering, residents' standard of living was also reduced because of the introduction of the euro in 2002 that drastically increased the daily cost of living.[14] The dispossession and impoverishment of the city and region's workforce, working below their qualifications and experience, were then used to attract industries in search of tractable low-paid labor such as call and logistics centers. While there was some influx of highly paid professionals and young people into the region, it was obvious by 2015 that Leipzig was attracting more of them. They preferred the shopping and housing possibilities established in Leipzig's regenerated city center and neighboring districts. Rail and tram investments made commuting between the two cities easier. Even high-income people who settled in Halle began to shop in Leipzig.

By 2015, the most significant demographic change in Halle was the growth of its student population. With these students came a kind of economic regeneration. Students created a market for bars and inexpensive restaurants. Rather than attracting large-scale private investment as a center of science and industry, Halle, through its research and university core, gained a reputation as a university city. Yet even this form of redevelopment was constrained by the city's lack of political and economic power. Halle faced ongoing disinvestment by the Länder in various departments of the university, and between 2010 and 2015 the university's international ranking fell precipitously (Center for World-Class Universities 2015).

At the same time, Halle faced the debt repayment incurred during redevelopment, which placed significant strains on funding public services such as education. What has become clear is that the national and EU projects of reclaiming the eastern region of Germany through large-scale investment of public funds initiated processes of capital accumulation in Halle. These accumulation processes proved lucrative for national and international construction companies and multiscalar corporate and financial interests. However, these processes dispossessed and displaced significant sectors of the local population and put future city development at risk. As in Manchester, the implementation of urban regeneration in Halle obscured the complex intertwined processes of regeneration, dispossession, and displacement taking place in the city. Inequality increased, and the city as a financial actor became more impoverished, even as some transnational corporate actors and local public–private partnerships continued to generate private profits from their activities in the city.

(3) The way in which the city leaders position migrants or minorities within their regeneration narrative.

Halle city leaders of different political outlooks repeatedly worked to craft a migrant-friendly narrative as part of the city's regeneration profile. They were aware of the city's reputation as racist and sought to combat this notion by emphasizing migrants as an integral part of the city. In interviews in 2001, city council members of various political parties and local religious and civic leaders all stressed that, whatever their legal status, migrants belonged in the city. At the time of our interviews, half of the newcomers had some form of asylum-related status, but only 10 percent had full asylum with the right to stay permanently and work. In the context of Halle's competition with other cities and its need to combat its racist reputation, these migrants, along with highly educated professionals and technicians, became members of the same team, so to speak. The thirty-one leaders we interviewed in 2001 were committed to changing the city's image not only in Germany but worldwide. The mayor, officials, and organizational leaders we spoke to between 2013 and 2015 were equally concerned and continued to emphasize Halle's embrace of foreigners as integral to its character.

Although after German unification many city residents and some leaders spoke of minority religions and migration as new to Halle, efforts to rebrand the city sometimes acknowledged certain aspects of the city's diverse past. For example, an online magazine about Halle noted that "the history of Jews in Halle is as old as the city" (Seppelt 2014). Other sources traced Halle's transnational industrial ties to the seventeenth century, when French Huguenot refugees arrived (*Halle Spektrum* 2014). In 2002 and for several years afterward, a wreath was ceremoniously laid at the statue of an African couple in front of a university administration building to honor Anton Wilhelm Amo, an African who studied law and became a university professor in the eighteenth century. Representing the city in 2003, the vice mayor spoke at this ceremony. In 2013, Lord Mayor Bernd Wiegand supported a city council resolution to name a street after Amo. The resolution read: "This renaming connects the university with the future history of this cosmopolitan city of science" (Prasse 2013). These activities highlighted and celebrated the historic African presence in the city.

The actual historical diversity of Halle was broader and grimmer than the dimensions acknowledged by city boosters. The city's historic population included people displaced by various wars (*Vertriebene*), people coming as labor migrants, and people brought there as forced labor. Toward the end of World War II, Halle's population included forced factory laborers confined in an offshoot of the Buchenwald concentration camp (van der Zanden 2014). All contributed to Halle's wealth, to the rich cultural and intellectual mix of the city, and to its regional, national, and transnational networks.

Under the leadership of Dagmar Szabados, lord mayor from 2006 to 2013, the city officially addressed all newcomers, including asylum seekers, as "new residents of Halle." In the "Door-opener" section of the city website, Lord Mayor Szabados invited all newcomers "to use the possibilities that Halle (Saale) has to offer": "Halle is a cosmopolitan, family-friendly city. It has a rich history with many traditions. For example, the first African student to receive a doctorate in Europe was awarded this degree at the University of

Halle in 1727. The city loves its traditions, but is also glad to accept changes and improvements. I sincerely invite you to work with us towards the goal of enriching our city's social, cultural and community life with new ideas and thoughts" (City of Halle 2015).

In 2013, under the tenure of the next mayor, who positioned himself politically as more business-minded than his predecessors, the open-door policy continued under the rubric of "a welcoming culture." However, by 2016, the city website had scaled back its inclusive welcome of all newcomers (City of Halle 2016). No longer were "foreign citizens/ asylum seekers" among the welcome newcomers. The page on the website devoted to them merely listed the three weekdays during which the relevant office was open, without providing interactive links to actual sources of information.

(4) The degree and kind of resources and services the city provides for migrant settlement and migrant and minority access to services.

While Halle maintained a welcoming narrative from 2000 to 2015, few resources or services were allocated to newcomers, whatever their legal status or education. We were told in the interviews we conducted with city council members in 2001, as well as during interviews and informal discussions with city officials and economic development experts in 2013 and 2015, that the city had little or no resources to invest in services to attract, emplace, or retain newcomers or to assist refugees. When it could, Halle accessed various bits of funding from the EU, the federal state, and the Länder to assist new residents. For example, the "Door-opener" on the city website, which provided information about settling in the city and its available health, education, and social services, was partially funded by the European Refugee Fund (ERF) and the Youth Action Program of the European Commission.

The massive amounts of public funding for regeneration provided resources or services to newcomers only when their needs were linked to impoverished neighborhoods that required restructuring. For example, public funding designated to address the growing "social polarization" in the city (IBA 2010, Löbner 2013) included migrant services. In 2008, the city council decided to expand the scope of its Social City (Soziale Stadt) program by working to provide employment opportunities on the periphery of Halle-Neustadt and support "quartier management" there.[15] Programs were developed in the areas of "economy, culture, education, and sports." As in Manchester, public and charitable funding was generally made available to clients in terms of their "special needs" rather than their cultural difference. Integration programs geared toward newcomers, including asylum seekers, remained relatively small scale and dependent on small and short-term grants and volunteer services, compared to the much greater institutional support available to the impoverished. While the "Door-Opener" offered information in German, English, French, Arabic, Vietnamese, and Russian, most organizations provided services and information only in German, with no translators or translations available.

The city council's welcome to newcomers included the appointment of an official, the commissioner for integration and immigration, who was responsible for addressing the needs of migrants. In 2000, this commissioner had little public credibility with migrants, the city council, or the public. Later on, a new commissioner played a more visible role as a liaison between the city government and an ever-growing number of local organizations that interacted with migrants, including asylum seekers. The commissioner was also tasked with consolidating the Advisory Committee for Foreigners of the City of Halle, which represented "the interests of all foreign residents of Halle and rouse[d] public understanding for their needs and problems" (City of Halle, Door-Opener n.d.). From 2006 to 2013, Karamba Diaby, a German citizen of Senegalese background, led this committee. Without adequate staffing or resources, neither the commissioner nor the Advisory Committee could offer much to migrants. Most available programs were funded by short-term grants and many were staffed partially or entirely by volunteers. Only in 2015 did the city hire a coordinator to assist the commissioner for migration and integration with the task of bringing together the many volunteers who provided services to newcomers, including asylum seekers.

After a relative hiatus in refugee settlement, by 2013 a new wave of asylum seekers were arriving in Halle, part of an increase in displaced people fleeing war, disruption, and political upheavals in Syria, the horn of Africa, Iraq, and elsewhere. Several new, privately owned asylum homes were organized with the understanding that, after a short period, newcomers could seek private apartments in the city. The city's Office for Migration and Integration mobilized local institutions, including some long involved in service provision for asylum seekers and refugees and others newly or more intensively engaged with the recent influx of asylum seekers. While a broader network of institutions was seemingly involved in the provision of services for migrants, once again much apparent support was simply the continued regular function of local institutions. Many of these institutions organized volunteer services with the limited funds the city provided.

By 2015, the number of organizations providing services to migrants had grown. Their efforts were nominally coordinated, or at least connected, by the

Office for Migration and Integration. However, the services provided by these organizations still came from specific short-term grants. Often services were situated within larger organizations that provided counseling, education, or health care to impoverished residents of the city. Generally, neither staff nor volunteers were knowledgeable about migration law and entitlements.

Nonetheless, in their efforts to be migrant friendly and demonstrate that people of all backgrounds were part of the city, Halle defied national policies and provided services to migrants, including asylum seekers. The city contributed to minimal salaries for teachers giving German lessons to asylum seekers and supported programs of volunteer teachers. In some years the city gave asylum seekers access to apartments, rather than insisting they remain in shelters or refugee camps (field notes, 2005, 2015). For many years, the city also funded the One World House (Eine Welt Haus), a center that provided migrant-specific services as well as cultural programs, and supported a community center dedicated to foreign-native interaction. However, Halle could fund very few migrant-based and migrant-led organizations of the kind that serve as a base for socially mobile migrants to emerge as "community" leaders.

As a result, most migrant organizations that were initiated and primarily funded by the migrants were generally short-lived. These organizations, identified in terms of the nationality of the members, appeared only on festive occasions when funding or support for public events was available. These organizations lacked the political clout and professionalism that could attract support from public or charitable sources. Although in 2006, there was a push to create an umbrella organization that would bring the various migrant-based groups into an Association of Immigrant Organizations, little enduring organizing ensued. Halle's Door-Opener website listed eighteen members, but the lack of ethnic organizing in the city at that time was evident in the fact that members of the Association included "clubs, initiatives and individuals." Member associations participated in local activities and celebrations, such as Intercultural Week, African Week, International Week against Racism, and the Human Rights Conference, and were invited to discussions, celebrations, and exhibits. Despite this prominence, the trend of providing at best token support for immigrant organizations continued.

(5) Evidence of synergy between city regeneration narratives and policies, on the one hand, and the multiscalar modes of emplacement of migrants and minorities, on the other, including whether their transnational networks emerged as assets in city-making.

As in the case of Manchester, the ongoing regeneration of Halle, including the city's migrant-friendly narratives, both created opportunities for migrant emplacement and posed new hazards and barriers as conditions changed. In the swirling currents of city-making, migrants' transnational networks served to create new multiscalar connections for various city residents and organizations. Some connections, such as those of transnational scholars and students contributing to the city's research and intellectual capacity, were recognized and encouraged by city leaders and developers, while others, such as born-again Christian networks organized by migrant religious leaders, contributed to efforts to reposition the city and rebuild its reputation but were not publicly acknowledged or fully understood.

Urban developers and the city leaders publicly acknowledged their desire to rebuild Halle and its university as an international hub of science. They noted that scholars working in various research institutes foster valuable transnational connections. Through well-funded academic conferences, hiring, and research collaborations, individual scholars and research institutions brought international researchers to Halle, inserting the city in transnational networks of intellectuals and institutions and making it visible on the international academic landscape. Halle's academic institutions not only benefited from but also, to a limited extent, contributed to reconstituting its tourist-oriented restaurant and hotel industries.

However, these transnational networks did not meet expectations that science and academic institutions would change Halle's demographic and consumption patterns by attracting permanent residents drawn from a global pool of "creative talent" and high-tech workers. The city center did begin to fill with highly skilled international migrants working in various start-up and other international businesses, but these businesses and their workforces were transient. Their increased presence in the city and relatively high salaries of their employees provided a market for upscale rentals, restaurants, travel, and services and contributed to the gentrification of the old city center. Described by urban planners as "project workers" (van Winden 2010), these newcomers constituted a mobile workforce. Flexible and precarious employment conditions made it difficult for many highly skilled workers to settle in Halle.

The student body of the university and the Burg Giebichenstein art school added to an increasingly mobile mix of residents. By 2015, university enrollment had reached twenty thousand, double its number in 2010, and included more than one thousand international students as well as students from all over Germany. During the years of our research, students contributed to a countercultural, transnationally connected ambience that included a changing musical scene, often staged in unregenerated buildings. They also participated in anti-racist movements that worked with asylum seekers. A more urbane mix of bars and restaurants developed rapidly in the regenerated streets of the old city, reflecting changes in the student body. While the student presence connected Halle to political, social, and cultural movements, the city had difficulty retaining educated youth. Its relatively inexpensive cost of living attracted students initially but characterized a faltering local economy and limited local job market that could not provide sufficient employment and career opportunities (interview R., 2015).

Even academics and highly skilled professionals with long-term, well-paid employment often encountered barriers to settling in the city, and their discontent detracted from urban branding efforts. While Halle offered excellent childcare, it did not offer migrant professionals and technicians other desirable services, such as an international school for their children, public services accessible in English, or sufficient entertainment and shopping. Consequently, some professionals commuted from Berlin or further afield, as they had before regeneration, while others chose to live in Leipzig.

Meanwhile, and generally unremarked by Halle's leadership and urban developers, some asylum seekers and members of refugee populations responded to city narratives and became city-makers as they found opportunities for emplacement locally. They built multiscalar networks of local and transnational actors, which engaged in a range of economic, political, and social activities. For example, during the first fifteen years after unification, migrant businesses begun by individuals who were not defined by the city as desirable for the "new economy" nevertheless became part of the central city street scene.

Political leaders interviewed in 2001 observed that migrant businesses were one way that migrants settled in the city. The migrant-inclusive narrative certainly facilitated businesses founded by new Vietnamese, Kurdish, and Nigerian residents. By the time Halle's "Door-Opener" guide to newcomers was posted on the city website (shortly after 2006), an array of local migrant businesses were listed as a matter of course among shopping opportunities in the city. While in their regeneration plans political leaders and redevelopers saw migrant businesspeople as an asset in their overall efforts to develop a new image for Halle and reposition the city globally, they did not consider the multiple ways migrants contributed to remaking the city.

As we note in chapter 2, the first stages of city center regeneration featured small retail migrant businesses selling clothing, fresh food and vegetables, and fast food to financially weakened city populations. They occupied empty spaces or newly rehabilitated but empty storefronts in the city center. At a critical point in regeneration efforts, these businesses brought commercial life to city center streets that otherwise would have seemed abandoned. Thus, they played a crucial role in maintaining and restoring value to this property at a time when the city was struggling against its shrinking image.

Migrant businesspeople, sometimes with local German partners or staff, reached out to transnational networks to access inexpensive goods, drawing on a combination of personal and regional wholesale networks that connected Halle to Leipzig, Dessau, Berlin, and a range of crossborder locations such as the Netherlands, Vietnam, and China. These businesses were built on multiscalar networks that included ethnic ties but were often multiethnic. China emerged as an important production and distribution location for packaged goods and inexpensive household items. In subsequent years, as the student population grew, clusters of inexpensive migrant-owned restaurants near the university also grew. However, after 2005 as the city center entered a second stage of rebuilding, expanding gentrification and increasing rent for storefronts and housing displaced the small businesses that served the poorer populations of the city. These businesses, both migrant and non-migrant, were replaced by international chain stores and department stores and other small businesses such as nail parlors oriented to higher-end clientele (Tempel 2014).

Migrant businesses that served the poor became increasingly concentrated in Neustadt, increasing the sense of street life in this region of the city. Thus migrant-owned small businesses continued to contribute to the city's economic life and international connections, even after many were pushed out of the city center during the gentrification process.

Similarly, in the first years of the millennium, a range of newcomers to Halle, including asylum seekers, refugees, students, and professionals, built religious networks that connected the city nationally and transnationally in ways that raised its visibility and prestige. However, Halle's leaders and developers did not acknowledge city-making through religious networks, even as city boosters worked to win international prominence by obtaining global recognition as a historic center of the Protestant Enlightenment. In 1998, applicants initiated the process for the Franckesche Stiftungen, the origin of Halle's Pietist movement in 1698, to become a World Heritage Site. Despite intensive efforts in 2015, in which Halle invested more than 100,000 euro and

Saxony-Anhalt provided 230,000 euro, the city's application was criticized so severely that the bid was withdrawn (Eger 2016).

Such religious emplacement in Halle, as we note in chapter 4, constituted a form of social citizenship that engaged migrants and natives within the city and around the world. These networks placed the city within multiscalar social movements and institutional connections that supported refugees and asylum seekers as well as globe-spanning born-again Christian networks. Pastors originally from Nigeria and the Congo led congregations of African and German believers to develop born-again networks that became increasingly present in the city, in the region, and in the lives of its inhabitants. These networks connected those experiencing different forms of dispossession— refugees, East Germans who had lost their country and economic position due to German unification and "postsocialist" reforms, and German youth facing precarious employment—with powerful, globe-spanning Christian networks that extended into US imperial projects and European missionary activities.

By placing Halle as a node on the global mapping of cities claimed for Jesus, migrant believers not only made claims to belonging to the city but also contributed to raising the city's visibility and prestige. A young white German from Bavaria active in organizing one of the born-again congregations explained this dynamic in an interview in 2015. After researching the matter, she moved to eastern Germany to join the Miracle Healing Church in Halle because of its reputation for sincere religiosity. However, we note that both she and that congregation's pastor, a migrant from Nigeria, lived in Leipzig.

The political ambience of Halle after unification, which continued into the turn of the century, also contributed to an opportunity structure that facilitated forms of migrant emplacement in the city. At the same time, migrants' entry into mainstream politics and progressive political movements connected the city to broader audiences in a way that countered Halle's negative racist image. After German unification, the same political forces in Halle, which during the GDR period had opposed repression from the secret police through a left-wing Christian social movement, continued to give the city a core of left political activism. Migrants with histories of political activism in their homelands felt more at home in this setting. Several became German citizens and party activists. When we began our research, two were members of the city council and one held a city office. They became public representatives through gaining seniority and influence in their political parties, not through serving as representatives of ethnic populations.

FIG 1.5 The office of Karamba Diaby, a representative to the federal parliament for the Social Democratic Party. Photograph by Robert Schutz.

At the same time, several other individuals of migrant background became public actors, occupying a niche in the city of a "public foreigner." These people also had histories of being active in Halle's public life. They found themselves drawn into a series of activities that conflated the city leaders' need to forge an anti-racist image with broader anti-racist or multicultural representations emerging on the national scene in debates about changing Germany's migration laws and policies. Halle's "public foreigners" were prominent in annual festivities, leading discussions, participating on panels, and sitting at information tables that celebrated Intercultural Week and African Week.[16]

Karamba Diaby emerged as one of the most prominent of these personages and began to occupy a changing role within the city and its narratives. Born in Senegal, he arrived in Germany in 1985 to study for an advanced degree and obtained a PhD in chemistry (interview D., December 18, 2001; Cottrell 2013). A longtime resident of Halle and a German citizen married to a white German, for many years Diaby functioned as a public foreigner in discussions of migration and integration and as a political actor within multiple German venues. For example, as an employee of the Heinrich Böll Stiftung, the Green Party Foundation, Diaby linked the Green Party to activities such as African Week in Halle. As Halle's regeneration proceeded, Diaby's role changed, and he became a Social Democratic Party (SPD) activist. As a member of its electoral lists, he was elected in 2013 as one of the first black German members of parliament.

In the months before the election, Diaby's blackness was highlighted and his candidacy scrutinized in the national press. In evaluating Diaby's chances, *Der Spiegel*, a prominent German national news magazine, portrayed Halle as so racist that Diaby was unable to campaign in certain neighborhoods of the city (Hengst 2011). In response, various sections of city leadership defended Diaby. It was in reference to Karamba Diaby and the *Der Spiegel* story that the mayor told Nina in 2013: "Every foreigner is a part of Halle" (interview W., May 21, 2013).

By 2015, in the context of intensifying new conjectural crises that brought increased numbers of refugees into Halle, the networks that linked local migrant activists with city institutions, including mainstream Protestant and Catholic churches and institutions, grew in extent and density. Increasing numbers of citizen volunteers were drawn into the nexus of multiscalar connections. Ironically, while city developers had stressed connecting Halle through networks formed by academic and research institutions, the city's international connections were intensified within broader networks of humanitarian aid, refugee support, and anti-racist struggle. For instance, Catholic institutions forged links within the sanctuary movement that offered protection to migrants without legal papers.

Anti-racist social movements that involved an array of ordinary citizens and local political leaders were not new to Halle. In 1998, Halle was among the first German cities to formulate a civil courage initiative to halt the election of neo-Nazis to the Saxony-Anhalt parliament. Later, this initiative organized citizens to act against neo-Nazi activities and to protect migrants under attack. Over the years, many anti-racist projects were supported by federal funding and supplemented with volunteer staff.

In 2015, Halle continued to have its share of racist attacks, including a major arson attack on asylum seekers in a neighboring village and racist demonstrations in the city center. At the same time, within the changing historical conjuncture of increased racism globally and in Germany, Halle's anti-racist movement participated in the Federation Against the Right/Halle Alliance for Diversity (Bündnis gegen Rechts/Hallianz fuer Vielfelt), a well-funded federal initiative that included political leaders such as Halle's mayor. In Halle, as in Manchester, some city leaders struggled to maintain a welcoming profile for the city in the face of strong anti-immigrant currents. But disparities of wealth and power, heightened by intensified processes of accumulation by dispossession, also made political polarization an aspect of life for all the city's residents.

MARDIN, SOUTHEASTERN TURKEY

(1) The city's relative declining positioning over time operationalized in terms of objective and subjective factors.

Mardin is an ancient hilltop city in southeastern Turkey overlooking the Tigris and the flat Mesopotamian plains. Located at the crossroads of the historic (eastern) Silk Road connecting India and China to Europe, it was a powerful center of trade, commerce, and the arts and of religious learning and education. Unlike Manchester and Halle, Mardin has never been an industrial center. Its disempowerment processes, while not indexed to the loss of industries, have been related to the loss of power and wealth. This loss extended across a much longer time frame than the disempowerment processes we addressed in Manchester and Halle. Mardin's loss of significance and power started in the seventeenth century with the clear peripheralization of the Silk Road, the rise of the Atlantic economy, and the emergence of a European world economy (Wallerstein 2011). As trade routes and transportation systems were restructured beginning in eighteenth century, the situation worsened. Mardin declined further when it was not incorporated into Europe's international nineteenth-century division of labor (Özcoşar 2006, 2009). However, until World War I, Mardin was still a key regional node of commercial and economic networks to Aleppo, Damascus, Beirut, Mosul, and Bagdad.

Before the twentieth century, Mardin had a religiously, linguistically, and ethnically diverse population. Its Christian population was composed mainly of Armenians, Syriacs, and Chaldeans. However, in the early twentieth century, massacres and displacements within the Ottoman Empire began to transform the population. Beginning in 1915, genocides of local Armenian and Syriac Christians decimated their numbers in the city, depriving Mardin of valuable human capital and skilled labor. Following the fall of the Ottoman Empire, the founding of the Turkish Republic in 1923, and the establishment of national borders with Iraq and Syria, Mardin was cut off from important regional economic, social, and cultural connections, including its Aleppo-centered economy and Caucasian networks. Mardin was reduced to a marginal border city between Turkey and Syria.

Although illegal border trading replaced the commercial activities that once generated wealth in the city, Mardin continued to be impoverished and

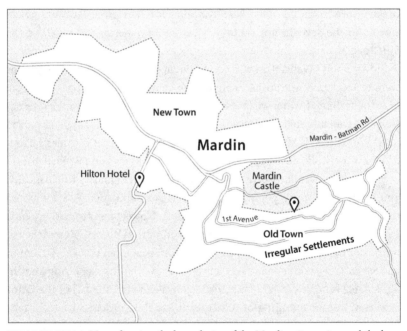

MAP 1.3 AND MAP 1.4 Maps showing the boundaries of the Mardin city-region and the location of Mardin on the Turkish border and border-crossing routes to Syria and Iraq.

disempowered throughout most of the twentieth century. Despite inclusion in a large-scale irrigation and energy production development project (the Southeastern Development Project [GAP] in the 1970s [Yüksel 2014]) at the end of the twentieth century, Mardin remained one of the least developed cities and regions in Turkey, with a growth rate of less than half of Turkey's average. Mardin's loss of power and underdevelopment became more striking when compared to the city of Gaziantep (202 miles away), which, after the founding of the Turkish Republic, emerged as a crucial regional center in Southeast Anatolia, with flourishing textile, food, and machinery industries.

Mardin's historical strength had been based on its position as a crucial node within several Christian and Islamic religious networks. The province was home to monasteries, churches, religious missions, mosques, and influential madrassas and educational institutions of Catholic, Orthodox, Protestant Syriac, Armenian, and Chaldean Churches. Like many cities on the Silk Road, Mardin was a crossroads of intellectual and religious exchange and learning and a hub for science, languages, art, and crafts. From the thirteenth century to the 1930s, the seat of Syriac Orthodox Patriarchs was in Mardin.[17]

Early in the twentieth century, Mardin also began to lose this source of power. The genocides of the Armenian and Syriac populations in 1915 left churches without congregations. After the departure of the Patriarchate, many of the Eastern Orthodox churches and monasteries were shut down and left to decay.[18] In their abandoned condition, the unique and world-renowned architecture of these religious sites, together with the forsaken vineyards of monasteries and the ruins of Syriac Christian villages, stood as an epitaph to the massacres, displacements, lootings, and confiscations of property that took place in Mardin province. At the beginning of the twenty-first century, these remains of displaced Christian populations were vividly present in the collective memory of the Syriac minority in and from Mardin. Defined as "abandoned property" by the Enval-i-Metruke law, this property, including houses, ateliers, and churches of the massacred and displaced Armenian and Syriac Christian populations, was appropriated by the state and often was left to decay (Polatel 2010; Biner 2007).

The demographic composition of Mardin continued to change during the Republican period. After successive discriminatory measures and attacks, the remaining Christian population left in successive waves, including significant emigrations in the 1940s and in 1974, after Turkey's invasion of Cyprus (Biner 2007). In the 1950s, while local elites of all religious backgrounds left the city center, migrants from nearby towns and villages settled in the city (Biner 2007). Beginning in the 1980s and extending over several decades, Mardin increasingly functioned as a home and an important gateway for internally displaced people (IDP), mainly dispossessed Kurdish peasants from the countryside who fled their villages. Population fluctuations continued, spurred by conflicts between the Turkish armed forces and Kurdish Labor Party (PKK). These conflicts led to massive village evacuations enforced by the Turkish state.[19] For a decade (1987–96), and for the third time in the twentieth century, Mardin fell under martial law (State of Emergency Governorship).[20] As a result, by 2000 the city was strongly associated with political instability, poverty, and terror.

Although Mardin's population reached 705,098 in 2000 (TÜİK 2013), in the previous decade, the number of people migrating from Mardin had almost doubled the number of people immigrating into the city.[21] The high rates of out-migration slowed only after 2009. Still, according to projections of the Turkish Statistical Institute in 2012 (TÜİK 2013) Mardin's population was expected to grow at a slower rate than that of neighboring cities.

In Mardin, the depopulation of the city-region, out-migration from the city center, and economic stagnation went hand in hand. Throughout the history of the Republic, an important part of Mardin's local economy had been built upon the agricultural production of cereals. When the central government deregulated agriculture and disrupted this production, it was not replaced by the growth of industry. Although Mardin's governorship established an Organized Industrial Zone (OIZ) in 1976, which offered attractive infrastructure and lucrative business conditions such as tax rebates, subsidized electricity, and services, it failed to attract investments for three decades after its establishment.[22] In its president's words, despite all efforts, the OIZ "only took off after 2007" (interview F., March 1, 2015).[23]

(2) Whether the city embarks on a strategy of rebranding and regeneration and the outcomes of such an effort in terms of private investment, public benefit, public debt, and the relative global positioning of the city at the end of our study.

In the face of Mardin's centuries of decline, including the violent disruptions and economic stagnation of the twentieth century, city leaders sought to re-empower their city. Beginning in 2000, they embarked on an organized effort to change Mardin's reputation from a place of terror and poverty to a prosperous, peaceful, multifaith, multiethnic, multilingual center of historical culture, tourism, and industry. Despite different historic and geopolitical circumstances, Mardin's city leaders resembled their peers in Halle and Manchester in their struggle to reposition their city more competitively within regional, national, and global networks of power by attracting flows of capital and skilled labor.

As the political and economic conjuncture in the Middle East began to change after the Gulf War (1991), Mardin's leaders saw new opportunities for their city. The unilateral truce between the Kurdish PKK and Turkish armed forces beginning in 1999 and the so-called democratization process in 2009, which entailed settling the "Kurdish issue" (the escalated conflict between the Turkish State and Kurdish groups), provided a period of relative stability and enabled the city to set aside its conflict-ridden image. City leaders agreed that a conflict-free and safe environment was crucial if they were to attract capital to re-empower the city. In the words of the president of Chamber of Industry and Commerce, "For the development of Mardin, and for attracting investments by foreign or by Turkish industrialists and businessmen in the OSB [OIZ], the region should be primarily peaceful and safe" (Avuka 2015).

Speaking about the terror-filled years of the 1980s and 1990s, the president of the OIZ stated during an interview that, in those days, the region's association with armed conflict was so strong that Mardinites were not even trusted as businessmen. Often their checks were not accepted because Mardin businesspeople were seen as terrorists (interview F., March 1, 2015). To change this image and attract private investments, Mardinite businessmen "invited journalists, people from the media and from the two biggest newspapers to Mardin . . . and asked them to write about Mardin" (interview F., March 1, 2015).[24] Similarly, Mardin's businessmen paid the production costs of a TV series popularizing Mardin and its unique architecture, sponsored cultural activities and cinema festivals, and invited powerful businessmen to Mardin from Istanbul and Ankara, including the president of the most powerful business association in Turkey, the Turkish Industrialists' and Businessmen's Association (TÜSIAD). They organized important annual meetings of business federations and associations in Mardin and hosted leaders of major holdings in Turkey (interview F., March 1, 2015).

A campaign to revive and restore memories of Mardin's past glories and historical connections was a key component of this effort at repositioning the city. City leaders sought to brand Mardin as a multireligious, multilingual city marked by a historical legacy of the peaceful coexistence of "civilizations." Beginning in the 2000s, city leaders and developers sought to address the city's lost power, placing the motto "Searching its Future in its Past" on the city website (a theme that we explore further in chapter 5). They framed projects of urban restructuring and regeneration as attempts to "retrieve" the city's prestigious former economic and cultural power (Biner 2007). By using a "renaissance of Mardin" narrative, city leaders highlighted the city's multi-faceted cross-border economic, cultural, and historic trade and commercial ties to regional markets. These narratives highlighted the city's locational advantage in relationship to Middle Eastern markets, which were important for seeking industrial and logistics investment in the city. References to the city's history also served to emphasize its diversity of languages and cultures, underscoring Mardinites' linguistic competency in Arabic and Kurdish, which was useful for intensified cross-border commerce.

In the context of the new regional dynamics and investment and trade opportunities unleashed by the Iraq War, projects to restructure and rebuild Mardin gained ground (Tepav 2011). Meanwhile, starting in 2001, the prospect that the Turkish Ministry of Culture would nominate Mardin as a candidate for the UNESCO World Heritage list further incentivized city leaders to embark on city branding and urban regeneration projects. Companies were hired, grants were acquired, travel guides were commissioned and written, and the entangled processes of rebranding Mardin began with programs to restore the historical built environment and projects to restructure urban spaces (interview P., February 24, 2015).

Urban restructuring in Mardin embraced several intertwined regeneration projects. All these projects (Mardinar, the Mardin Urban Regeneration and Rehabilitation Project, the Historical transformation Project, and the Mardin Sustainable Tourism Project) focused on rehabilitating the historical texture of the city and regenerating the old town, the city center. While leaders spoke of "re-establishing the honor and dignity" (iade-i itibar) of the city,[25] a project representative of the governorship stated, "The aim here [with these projects] is not to simply develop the cultural heritage. These are not renovation projects. . . . In fact, at the core of this project lies economics, which will also serve for social development" (interview T., February 23, 2015).

The city's leadership first focused on development of the "old town" and on the abandoned or decaying historical core of the city. According to Mardin's governor, the plan was to restore "the historic city of Mardin to the way it looked around a century ago." Restoring the city's historical profile entailed demolishing (completely or partly) 1,430 buildings in the old town and large numbers of buildings on its outskirts (Ana-Mardelli 2011).

These buildings had been primarily inhabited by peasants who had been evicted and/or had fled from their villages. Since their dispossession and displacement, these people had been living in buildings constructed after 1969 in the old town at a time the area had been declared an Urban Conservation

Site (sit Alanı), which prohibited new construction. Proclaiming such buildings "illegal," or "risky," the regeneration process dispossessed and displaced this former rural population once again. Some of the displaced were offered apartments in buildings constructed on the fringes of the old town, while others were provided with places in newly built mass housing areas outside the old town, in the new city (Edis 2012).

The twenty-first-century regeneration of Mardin was a significant multiscalar transformation in which displacement and emplacement involved multiple, differentially powerful actors. A national Turkish agency, the Housing Development Administration (TOKİ), was a major force in the city's massive urban regeneration project.[26] Under direct rule of the prime minister, TOKİ was empowered to seize public lands, transform them into private property, enforce evictions and demolitions, and develop profit-oriented housing as well as infrastructure projects. It established companies for this purpose. Beginning in the 2000s, TOKİ worked closely with Mardin's municipality and governorship. The European Union also provided funding, including 85 percent of a 9 million euro Mardin Sustainable Tourism Project (2013–15), for which the central government provided the remaining funding. The Sustainable Tourism Project sought to increase the city's competitiveness by rebranding and increasing tourism. City leaders and all involved in this project saw it as part of an effort to enhance Mardin's chances at being included on the UNESCO World Heritage list, which was important for the global repositioning of the city.

In addition to the rebranding and publicity campaigns, the Turkish state offered a broad range of subsidies and tax incentives to encourage national and transnational corporate investment in Mardin. Extensive incentives (some linked to listing Mardin among the least developed Turkish cities) included customs duty and value-added tax exemptions, tax rebates (reaching up to 90 percent), interest rate support, income tax rebates, and social insurance premium support for investing companies. These incentives lowered an investor's cost of labor to 38 percent of what it would have been in the most developed region of the country (DİKA, Mardin Yatirim Destek Ofisi 2014, 15–16). As did urban developers in Manchester and Halle, promoters attracting capital investment to Mardin highlighted the low cost of labor, achieved in Mardin through subsidies and incentives that public money provided to corporate capital (DİKA, Mardin Yatirim Destek Ofisi 2014).

Following the crisis in 2008, demand in Europe stagnated and European corporations sought opportunities in expanding Middle Eastern markets, especially in Iraq. As a result, trade through Mardin flourished. The only route to Iraq and Syria (in fact, to the Middle East) from Europe went through the Mardin city-region (see Map 1.3, p. 74). Thus, the volume of trade in Mardin increased 46 percent between 2008 and 2009 (DİKA 2010b, 2010c; interview F., March 1, 2015). Incentives over time produced some new corporate investment in Mardin, including by international companies. While the manufacturing sector started to grow in Mardin in the early 2000s, the main increase came in the next decade.

Between 2004 and 2012, the number of workers doubled, with the largest growth coming from construction-related production, such as cement, and from food industries, such as flour processing (DİKA Mardin Destek Ofisi 2010; Tepav 2012). Because of regeneration activity, construction became the third most important employment sector, according to the president of the Organized Industrial Zone (interview, March 1, 2015). The major Istanbul-Çanakkale-based industrial holding company (Kale Group) made a substantial investment in the city-region. In 2013, it opened a $2.5 million factory (Kalekim) to produce thermal insulation material for the construction sector (Kale 2013). In 2014, 30 of the 160 investors in OIZ were from outside Mardin. Meanwhile, in 2013, Hewlett Packard (HP), which aimed to "enter the Middle Eastern and European advertising markets and make Mardin one of the digital printing centers of the world," announced a $100 million investment in a digital advertising printing facility in Mardin city-region. Despite the projected large investment in the project, only two hundred jobs were promised (*Today's Zaman* 2013). The discrepancy between the large investment and the small number of jobs anticipated highlights the problematic nature of this urban regeneration strategy. Overall, the number of jobs created in the new facilities was often modest. For example, in 2011, a Turkish flour factory employed thirty-five workers (İlhan 2011).

The volume of trade also increased dramatically, so much so that Mardin ranked eighteenth out of eighty-one city-regions in Turkey in 2010 (interview F., March 1, 2015). Because the cost of transportation from Mardin to economic centers in the Middle East was lower than shipping initiated from other places in the region, Mardin increasingly acquired importance in the logistic and transportation sector. Reflecting Turkey's desire to become an economic and political player in the Middle East, Mardin was chosen as a site for one of the nineteen planned Turkey-wide logistics centers. In Mardin, the logistics center was envisaged as the storage and distribution depot for iron, steel, construction material, and military equipment (Erkeskin 2013; DİKA, Mardin Yatirim Destek Ofisi 2014).

If one looks at the flow of investment into the Mardin city-region in the form of production and logistic facilities, the increased volume of exports (150 percent between 2003 and 2015), and the redevelopment of housing and infrastructure in the city center and surrounding districts, the city leaders' project to rebrand and regenerate Mardin would seem to have been a success in the years between the millennium and 2015 (DİKA 2010b; interview F. March 1, 2015). However, less than half (43 percent) of the exported goods and none of the iron and steel were produced in Mardin (DİKA 2013). While a Free Trade Zone was established in 1995 and located within Mardin OIZ, it had only a 30 percent occupancy rate (DİKA 2010d). Overall, the rate of industrial employment in 2006 was only 20 percent, and most of the workers were unskilled and working in food-processing industries (DİKA 2010b).

As we have seen in Manchester and Halle, public monies and multiscalar regeneration funds went primarily to public–private partnerships, construction firms, and real estate interests. Public subsidies and tax breaks led to a reduction of public wealth, including lower revenue for the city. This process was intensified through the sale of public and/or treasury land to private developers and companies at below market prices and through public subsidies to private corporations from land redevelopment.

Although Mardin was celebrated as a hotspot of tourism—with increasing tourism-based development between 2011 and 2014, some world-class hotels, a shopping mall, and plans for an aqua park by the US-based Bridgestone Corporation—tourism did not bring high-paying jobs or greatly expand employment. Nor did the city's emergence as a globally prominent tourist destination reassure well-paid professionals employed in these new industries that the city was a safe or attractive place to live. Some firms active in Mardin remained reluctant to relocate their headquarters there, and many employees chose to reside nearby in economically stronger Gaziantep, staying in Mardin from Monday to Thursday (field notes, 2015). Similarly, some of the relatively high-income faculty of the newly established university in Mardin commuted from major cities in Turkey rather than have their primary residence in Mardin.

Regeneration did little to stimulate growth in employment, and most of the jobs created were in the low-wage sector. More than half of the jobs in 2008 (54.5 percent) were in the service sector, especially tourism-related services like hotels, restaurants, and transportation. In 2012, the share of the service sector in Mardin's economy increased to 64.9 percent (İŞKUR 2011, 2014; Mardin Tourism Strategic Plan 2014). At the same time, rates of labor force participation and employment generally remained lower than Turkey's average. Unemployment rates fluctuated. While they decreased between 2008 and

FIG 1.6 Mardin old town viewed from the outskirt settlements. Photograph by Seda Yuksel.

2010 and the 2010 rate of 9.1 percent situated Mardin's unemployment below that of the other cities in similar socioeconomic regions (TRC3) and in Turkey (11.9 percent), in 2012, Mardin's unemployment increased (Tepav 2012).

Meanwhile, redevelopment not only displaced the urban poor but also inflated housing and real estate prices and the overall cost of living in the city. Livelihoods of people whom TOKİ evicted from the outskirts of the old town and irregular settlements became more precarious once they lost their spatially situated networks of support. The IDP in the city, together with the local impoverished population, became a cheap labor pool. Furthermore, the tourism sector (which failed to deliver anticipated profits and public benefits) increased the demand for historical buildings in old town, which tripled real estate prices.[27]

Despite private sector investments, per capita income in Mardin (DİKA 2010a) remained at almost half the average in Turkey. In its 2010 report, the Tigris Development Agency (DİKA) highlighted the increasing poverty and the income gap as the most important threats to the region (DİKA 2010c). In 2013, an organization to fight poverty, established in Mardin, voiced concern about the large numbers of IDPs and argued that unrestrained, neoliberal urban regeneration projects were the major causes of the increasing impoverishment. The entangled dynamic processes of urban restructuring, capital accumulation, the strengthening of private corporations and their profits, especially in construction and real estate businesses and service sectors, and the dispossession, displacement, and increasing impoverishment were very clear in Mardin, as they were in Halle and Manchester. In 2011, despite a massive influx of capital and city boosterism, Mardin remained disempowered. It ranked seventy-second out of eighty-one provinces in Turkey in terms of socioeconomic development (Özceylan and Coşkun 2012).

(3) The way in which city leaders position migrants or minorities within their regeneration narratives.

Mardin's religious and ethnic minorities came to the fore in multifarious ways in narratives that reinvented Mardin as a peaceful, multifaith, multiethnic, and multilingual city. Despite their small numbers (altogether three thousand people), Mardin's remaining Syriac Christians occupied a central place in discourses, projects, and imaginaries about Mardin's past and future and in city renewal narratives circulating in several media outlets. Between 2000 and 2015, media presentations constantly underscored the presence and heritage of Syriac Christians in Mardin as proof of the city's unique multifaith and multilingual heritage and as a future asset.

Given Syriac Christians' long history of persecution since the turn of the twentieth century, the sudden revaluation and the disproportionate weight they were accorded in city narratives was striking.[28] In 2001, the prime minister's office reached out to Syriac Christians primarily from Mardin in Europe and to their religious leaders in and outside of Turkey. The prime minister invited those in Europe to return to their ancestral homeland, promising that they would be welcomed.

The welcome of religious minorities was not presented within a multiculturalist framework centered on questions of accessing resources through collective cultural and/or religious rights. Nor were welcoming narratives of the city leadership about identity politics. Instead, the new foregrounding of persecuted Syriac Christian minorities (and returnees) in city narratives was very closely tied to the conjunctural moment of Turkey's EU accession negotiations. Minority governance and the protection of minority rights play an important role in EU institutions' understanding of its political space and the verification of democracy within that space (Cowan 2007a). EU policies and organizations monitor applicant states' efforts and programs for evidence of the democratization process. They search for indicators of the installation and implementation of democratic political and legal frameworks to secure and guarantee minority rights.

Following recognition of its candidacy, Turkey increasingly came under pressure to demonstrate progress in securing human rights. Christian minorities, particularly persecuted Christian minorities such as the Syriacs, acquired a special importance in the evaluation of Turkey's observance of minority rights. Thus, Syriac Christians' presence in and return to their ancestral home of Mardin and improvements in Mardin's safety and stability became an index of Turkey's observation of minority rights. While public enactment of the first was crucial for accessing supranational, including EU, funds and institutional programs, the second was crucial for attracting capital and investment to the city, as we have shown. Both performances were very closely related to Mardin's urban regeneration and repositioning within multiscalar networks of power.

Multifaith heritage and a narrative welcoming to religious minorities found its expression in the city's built environment and contributed to its revaluation. As Mardin came to be promoted as the City of Stone and Faith,[29] architecture that proclaimed this centuries-old multifaith legacy and the built environment signifying this heritage gained prominence in branding narratives and the promotion of tourism. The presence of monasteries and churches next to mosques and medrassas became a critical asset for urban regeneration narratives and projects. Mardin's built environment became crucial for accessing the supranational funds (such as those from the EU, UNESCO, and UNDP) required for large-scale urban regeneration projects aimed at facilitating the growth of tourism.

The remarks of the deputy of Mardin's co-mayor, which we referred to at the beginning of this chapter, indicated that returning Syriac Christians were greeted not as members of the labor force or as newcomers in city narratives but as the "original" inhabitants of the city. However, although Kurds made up the majority of Mardin's inhabitants and despite an emphasis on the equal significance of all city inhabitants' heritage in constituting the city's culture, Mardin's branding and urban regeneration narratives and projects did not acknowledge the Kurdish legacy in the city. They were strikingly absent in these accounts and redevelopment activities.

A set of new institutions, including Mardin City Museum, Artuklu University, and the Mardin Biennial (whose development we examine in chapter 5), was closely entangled with city leaders' regeneration efforts. These institutions not only helped revive the cultural sector but also played an important role in the revaluation of Christian minorities. They portrayed the various religious and cultural heritages as integral to the city and visible within its built environment and everyday life. "Syriac wine" made its way onto the refashioned menus of new cafes and restaurants that opened around the university campus as part of the regeneration of the area and added an "ambience" of this heritage (interview L., May 19, 2015). The new city museum displayed, celebrated, and popularized the city's acclaimed tolerant cultural, religious, and linguistic heritage and its minorities (interview E., February 21, 2015).

Mardin's minorities, especially its Syriac Christians, were accorded prominence in international events such as the Mardin Biennials (Mardin Biennial 2010, 2012, 2015), which sought to situate Mardin within the global contemporary art world, a crucial element of the campaign to reposition the city.[30] As one of its first organizers recalled, "Aiming to be like Venice, we wanted to start a Biennial tourism" (interview B. and CM., June 6, 2015). Two of the most prominent culture/heritage tourism agencies in Turkey contributed to this goal by organizing Biennial tours to Mardin (interview CM., June 6, 2015).

While churches from different denominations, monasteries, medrassas, and old mansions hosted the three Mardin Biennials, restored, functioning, or abandoned Syriac Christian churches and historic Syriac mansions (such as Tokmakçılar Konaği) took central stage in these events. According to one member of the Biennial team, "If you enter the name of this mansion, or the monastery of Mor Efrem [a Catholic Syriac Monastery abandoned for about seventy years] into Google now, the first things that appear are about the Mardin Bienniale" (interview B., June 6, 2015).

Thus, Syriac Christians, whether they had remained or returned, became part of the value-creation processes in Mardin in multiple ways. Sites of daily life and real estate associated with Syriacs increased in value. As a deputy from Mardin, who was also the first Syriac in the Turkish Grand National Assembly, put it, "People once fled and left the land, now they are returning, and the land is regaining value. . . . In fact Syriacs themselves became a value" (Dora 2011).

(4) The degree and kind of resources and services the city provides for migrant settlement and migrant and minority access to services.

While Mardin maintained a welcoming narrative for returning Syriac Christian emigrants starting in the early 2000s, very few services were allocated to resettling these returnees. In fact, the discrepancy between Syriac Christians' concentrated presence in Mardin's city narratives and the actual emigrant/minorities-specific resources and services that city government offered was striking. All Syriac Christians in Mardin (returnee or not) and the Syriac religious and community leaders with whom we spoke complained about the lack of community-specific funds. Given the official invitations and the promises made to them, returnees were especially disappointed with the lack of funds for basic infrastructure in their settlements, including roads, sewage, electricity, and Internet connection (field notes, 2015). They also demanded institutional support for teaching Aramaic in Mardin.[31] Resettled Syriac Christians from Europe repeated these complaints to endless foreign delegations, ambassadors, and EU and human rights representatives who visited Syriacs in Mardin (field notes, 2015). The city provided no services to minorities as religious or ethnic communities. Although Aramaic was hailed as part of the city's multilingual and multifaith linguistic heritage, there was no support for teaching Aramaic in schools.

In fact, Mardin offered few resources or services to any of its inhabitants. In 2014, Mardin, a disempowered city, ranked very low among Turkish cities in terms of funds available for education and health (DİKA 2013; Yüksel 2014; DİKA 2011). The massive allocation of public funding, tax rebates, sales of public lands at below market prices, and other forms of financial support, which were central to Mardin's urban regeneration projects, resulted in a high level of city debt and limited financial resources. In 2009, Mardin ranked among the top 10 cities in Turkey for Social Security Insurance debt (*Memurlarnet* 2009).[32] In 2004, 2007, 2012, and 2016, municipal property was subjected to processes of debt-related sequestration, through which public property was sold to pay the city's debts. The city owed money to its employees; it even owed a large sum to its soccer team (Mardinspor) players (*Haberlermardinimiz* 2010).

The city government responded to the debt crisis by continuing its policy of depleting public resources that could have been invested in services to all inhabitants, including returning Syriacs. To generate income for the indebted city, more and more city and/or treasury lands were provided to private developers and companies or sold at below market prices. As the Mardin governor said in 2010, "Mardin failed to generate the expected income from tourism and the city government continued to develop plans to repay debts by selling public land for regeneration" (NTV 2010).

While returnee's need for services was generally ignored, in 2008 the Mardin city government held a special meeting with Mardinites, especially Syriac religious leaders and returnees, to announce a new regeneration project. TOKİ had decided to develop housing to meet the special "community needs" of potential Syriac returnees from Europe who wished to resettle in Mardin. These houses would be styled after old Syriac houses but would offer much-desired infrastructure, including electricity, sewage, and roads. This special housing project for returnees even included a church and a school (Toprak 2008). Ironically, this effort was to be done through a further wave of dispossession. Abandoned, confiscated, or treasury-owned lands were to be allocated to private developers to deliver the promised services to the much-desired returnee Syriacs.

(5) Evidence of synergy between city regeneration narratives and policies, on the one hand, and the multiscalar modes of emplacement of migrants and minorities, on the other, including whether their transnational networks emerged as assets in city-making.

Syriac Christians in Mardin, including the returnees, were inserted into the multiscalar city-making processes in many ways beyond their symbolic presence within city branding narratives. Their multiple transnational personal, social, political, and religious networks connected Mardin to places in Sweden, Germany, Switzerland, Austria, Iraq, and Syria and extended into several supranational and global institutions such as the Catholic Church, Caritas, Eastern Christianity networks, the EU, and UNESCO, thus embedding them within a multiscalar social field. This social field not only enabled them to contribute significantly to the city-making processes but also opened pathways of their emplacement in the economy and in the political and religious life of the city.

The returnees themselves became part of business networks that invested in Mardin, of global Christian agendas very much centered on reconfiguring power in the Middle East, and of political networks seeking historical justice, especially in relation to the 1915 genocides. Last but not least, they found partial political emplacement in the increasing social justice claims initiated by the Kurdish social and political movement in the city and the region.

Within the opportunities opened by urban restructuring, returnee Syriacs in Mardin found possibilities for emplacement by serving as brokers between potential investors from Europe and local business interests in Mardin. Some, but not all, of these investors were Syriacs, and not all Syriac investors were emigrants from Mardin. Syriac returnees mediated between the Tigris Development Agency, part of the investment and promotion agency Invest in Mardin,[33] and potential investors from Europe. According to the director of this development agency, some emigrants from Mardin who remained in Europe reached out to their former homeland to obtain business and investment opportunities. Such opportunities were a central interest of a twenty-five-person Swiss delegation that arrived in 2010. The emigrant group was interested in viniculture. However, the director's hopes were centered on three big Mardinite European investors, whose investments in the hotel business could triple the bed capacity of the city (*Hürriyet Daily News* 2010).

Another Syriac returnee from Switzerland undertook wine production in partnership with a Mardin businessman who was the nephew of the metropolitan bishop of the famous Syriac monastery of Mor Gabriel in Mardin.[34] In 2009, the partners invested in a wine production factory where, according to them, wine was produced following "5000–6000 years-old traditions in compliance with what was depicted in the Bible, Kuran and Old Testament." Named after a Syriac village and meaning "peace" in Aramaic, Shiluh was the only Syriac wine produced and distributed in Mardin. Due to its historical association with Christianity in Mardin, Syriac wine produced in Mardin had a strong symbolic value for Syriac Christians as well as for Mardin. The symbolic value and contested nature of wine production in Mardin becomes clearer when one considers that before Shiluh began to be made in Mardin, the last winemaker in the city was killed in the 1990s. The new winemakers planned to export Shiluh to Europe, "to reach out to Syriac Christians there from Mardin and Mesopotamia and to give all Syriacs hope for their return to their ancient homeland" (interview L., May 19, 2015, and field notes, 2015).

Both Syriacs and Kurds, who compose the majority of the population in Mardin, had strong historical connections across the border. Before the Syrian Civil War, 70 percent of Syriacs on the Syrian side of the border were estimated to have roots in Mardin province (Altuğ 2011, 18–19). These cross-border networks of Syriac Christians in Mardin both contributed to and were themselves enhanced by the increasing volume of exports from Mardin to Iraq and Syria. These historical and political as well as cultural and linguistic cross-border networks of Mardin's inhabitants, including Syriac Christians, became an asset for the city at a particular conjuncture of the political restructuring of the region and of the expansion of Middle East markets.

Furthermore, in the context of growing radical Islamic movements and war in the Middle East, the Christian minority in Mardin acquired renewed importance and value as part of global Orthodox and Catholic Christian networks. Given the decreasing Christian population in the Middle East and their increasing persecution, and in the face of rising radical Islam in this region, the continued presence of Syriac Christians and their well-being in the ancient homeland of Eastern Christianity[35] became important for global Christian institutions. As we detail in chapter 5, their voices found resonance even at the very top levels of the Catholic Church. This multiscalar political field was strengthened by collaborations between political and religious associations of Syriacs as well as Armenians and Kurds in different parts of Europe (Biner 2010). These networks enabled these minorities to reach even to the pope as part of the project to win international recognition of the Syriac and Armenian genocides at the beginning of twentieth century.

From 2004 to 2008, Turkey's EU membership candidacy and the heightened attention paid to concomitant policies on minority rights, democratic participation, and antidiscrimination opened local political spaces in Mardin for a broader range of actors. Together with other excluded and/or impoverished city inhabitants, Syriac Christians became part of the political forces and social justice movements in Mardin. Returnees found emplacement within Mardin's civic and political life in political associations with broad social justice agendas. They contributed to integrating the previously excluded Kurdish and Syriac languages into the public sphere, entered local elections, and became part of local political leadership with strong social justice claims.

In 2014, a twenty-six-year-old Syriac, Februniye Akyol, a graduate in Aramaic language and literature from the newly established Artuklu University in Mardin, ran in local elections for the pro-Kurdish Peace and Democracy Party (BDP), together with a well-known veteran of Kurdish politics, Ahmet Türk. Both became co-mayors of Mardin's metropolitan municipality with a broad antidiscriminatory agenda, rather than with a program dominated by ethnic and communal politics. The multiscalar positioning of Mardin provided Akyol with the opportunity to become the first Syriac Christian mayor in one of Turkey's metropolitan municipalities (and the first female mayor in Mardin). After their election, the Kurdish and Syriac languages, long excluded from state institutions in Turkey, acquired a public presence in Mardin. The trilingual (Turkish, Kurdish, and Syriac) nameplate installed on the Mardin metropolitan municipality building became a clear sign of this presence.[36]

Several returnees as well as members of some Syriac associations joined with other groups in Mardin in shaping politics in the city beyond ethnic and/or religious community agendas. A number of minority-based organizations clearly began to speak for and represent broader constituencies. The president of the Syriac Unity Association, who was also an alderman from the Peoples' Democratic Party[37] with a pro-Kurdish, left-wing, participatory, egalitarian, and minority rights–based agenda, spoke forcefully about this political movement's foundation in unity, emphasizing commonalities rather than differences between minorities: "What we need is to meet on our commonalities. In order to be able to live in peace, we need to set aside red lines and find our commonalities" (interview, May 19, 2015). According to him, there would be "no future for the Syriacs in Mardin outside of the future of political and social justice movements lead by Kurds with a broader constituency" (interview, May 19, 2015).

Similarly, the president of the Federation of Syriac Associations, who returned from Switzerland after residing for twenty-three years in Europe, described the city-making politics of the moment, to which many returnees contributed. He emphasized that the Kurdish political movement, which embraced civil society organizations, trade unions, different professional organizations, and human rights organizations, made clear to the people in Mardin the importance of establishing a common future in these lands (interview H., March 23, 2015). He vehemently differentiated this political and social justice–based vision of a common future from a future projected through general communitarian multicultural politics. He said, mockingly, that "this multi-lingual, multi-cultural, multi-religious talk is just irrelevant" for understanding and fighting discrimination and injustice and for building a common future in Mardin (interview, March 23, 2015).[38]

With the widening of the Syrian Civil War in 2015, the Turkish state's geopolitical desire to expand its influence in the Middle East, and the governing party's declining popularity, the government abruptly and violently ended its so-called peace process with Kurdish population. This policy reversal changed the power contingencies of the multiscalar social and political field within which the urban restructuring of Mardin was embedded. Narratives about the peaceful multifaith, multicultural, and multipolitical heritage of the city lost their relevance. Tourists disappeared, forcing world-class hotels, internationally prominent only a year before, to shut down. The planned new wave of investments failed to materialize. A court case was opened against the Kurdish co-mayor, and for the first time in the history of the Turkish Republic, a Syriac association (the Syriac Unity Association) was closed by the state. Many returnees, caught in escalating violence between military forces, once again started to leave Mardin.

In the context of its changing priorities, the Turkish state seemed to set aside its EU membership aspirations, which reduced the salience of Mardin's Christian minorities and their power to reach out to supranational institutions. With the initiation of the Syrian Civil War in 2012, a new stage of global warring was initiated in the Middle East, leading to a new phase of dispossession, displacement, and capital accumulation with altered valorizations and devaluations of people and sites. These processes changed the dynamics of emplacements, including the returning Syriac Christians in Mardin.

Comparative Analysis

This examination of our five comparative parameters revealed the following similarities between the cities:

1) Each city once had a more significant positioning, and a diverse population had been part of the networks of connection that made the city noteworthy. These connections were lost in processes of disempowerment relative to the region, the nation-state, and the world.
2) Within the recent millennial conjuncture, leaders in each city adopted a strategy of urban regeneration focused on transforming spaces of abandonment with the goal of improving their city's relational position. A quest to obtain significant private investment configured regeneration strategies, but none of the three cities could attract significant degrees of corporate and financial capital. Instead, city regeneration was shaped by a dependence on public funds, tax strategies, and the awarding of public resources to private development interests. Public revenue streams were not increased through regeneration, leaving these cities with fewer resources for public services.
3) To rebrand the city and thereby attract transnational flows of capital and new economy workers, city leaders developed migrant- and minority-friendly narratives to alter their city's negative reputation. City redevelopers also used the presence of migrants or minorities and impoverished residents to gain access to public funds, which were channeled into rebuilding efforts that ultimately benefited developers, multinational corporations, including construction companies, and wealthier residents. Public–private partnerships, especially in the form of housing corporations, played an important role in this process.
4) As accumulation through dispossession intensified within the conjunctural configuration that took hold after the millennium, migrants and minorities faced not only racism and exclusion but also opportunities for multiple forms of emplacement. Transnational networks of migrants or returnees, embedded in multiscalar social fields, emerged as assets in efforts to reach out to powerful global institutions, ranging from religious institutions to corporations, and rebuild competitively the city's economic, political, and social life. Increasing polarization between rich and poor both acerbated racist currents in these cities and produced changing possibilities for emplacement for

various transnational actors, from multinational corporations and NGOs to migrants who lived their lives across borders.

5) The outcome of regeneration efforts, resulting from the initial relative disempowerment of the city, continued to be entangled with processes of dispossession, displacement, and emplacement and to drain the city's public resources. Rapid alterations in the terrain of regeneration reflected changing regional, national, and global power configurations of the global restructuring of capital accumulation. The historical conjuncture of the millennium was one in which patterns of flexible capital accumulation became linked to neoliberal regeneration in various locations around the world, but it was also one in which disruptures reflected a new expansion of global warring and overspeculation.

Furthermore, our comparative analysis clarifies the importance of comparing processes of city-making rather than static snapshots of urban governance and policies. The relationship between migrants and minorities in each city reflected ongoing conjunctural changes that were multiscalar and processual. Our comparative research highlights the importance of drawing from a variety of sources and not simply relying on official city narratives, reports, policies, or interviews. In Mardin, the discrepancy between city leaders' narratives of successful growth, on the one hand, and the grim realities of public debt as revealed in the reports and statistics of various development agencies, on the other, is especially striking.

In assessing the outcomes of urban restructuring, city narratives can be neither accepted as accurate descriptions of a city's current situation nor discarded as inconsequential. These narratives affect other structural factors, even as they are affected by changes that the city experiences and by broader understandings of ways to initiate urban economic development and branding, which themselves change with the realignment of intersecting conjunctural forces. Thus, while we have utilized each city's narrative of renewal in our analysis, we have situated these narratives in relation to a variety of multiscalar parameters.

Our comparative analysis adds depth to the term "disempowered cities" and lends substance to the claim that cities are global in various ways. As we note in the introduction, the term "disempowered" does not apply to all impoverished cities. Disempowered cities are those that once boasted greater economic, cultural, or political significance, upon which these cities now strive to build. Although these cities lacked adequate economic, political, and cultural power, they were nonetheless global, not only in their multiscalar interconnections but also in their leaders' regeneration strategies. As we have noted, city leaderships comprise city officials as well as business leaders, chambers of commerce, bankers, real estate developers, and organizational and institutional leaders whose interests are closely linked to the restructuring and repositioning of their city. We also outlined the strategies city leaderships used to re-empower these cities and the consequences of these strategies for local and corporate coffers. In each case, we found that city leaderships are part of broader configurations of regional, national, and global power.

While in all three cities migrants and minorities were considered necessary components of urban restructuring, their agency and city-making possibilities and limitations in each case reflected the trajectories of different regional histories and the different institutional and discursive resources available for urban regeneration projects. However, this cautionary note does not reduce the significance of the fact that leaders of all three cities responded to the disempowered situation of their city and the challenge of restructuring by embracing a welcoming narrative that cast newcomers and returning minorities as crucial to urban development. Halle elected one of the first two citizens of African background to the German parliament; Manchester elected the second Muslim citizen to a US state legislature; and Mardin elected the first female and the first Syriac Christian mayor in Turkey. Moreover, the unfolding of the historical conjuncture in each city simultaneously led to, and was facilitated by, processes of political emplacement in which migrants and minorities together with non-migrants moved beyond idioms of ethnic and religious communities to participate in social justice movements. We underline this point because our comparisons demonstrate narratives of commonality that differ from widespread understandings of multiculturalism and tolerance, which urban policy discourses have highlighted. Our notion of historical conjuncture highlights the necessity for social justice movements that speak of common struggles and aspirations to confront changing configurations of power and the contradictions of violent force.

CHAPTER 2

Welcoming Narratives

SMALL MIGRANT BUSINESSES WITHIN
MULTISCALAR RESTRUCTURING

Between the steady ebb and flow of customers buying fresh herbs, staples such as rice, and dried, frozen, bottled, and canned cooking ingredients from Vietnam, Korea, Thailand, China, and various regions of Africa and Europe, Nina[1] spoke with Lan, the woman who owned the store. It was 2016, and the store seemed to be in an excellent location, on a traffic circle in a busy area intersected by three tramlines. The traffic circle had recently been redeveloped as part of Halle's new light-rail program at a cost of more than 4.7 million euro.[2] It was a sleepy August afternoon. Other storefronts on the circle—including a Mediterranean-style restaurant, a sports team clothing shop, and a cosmetics and sundry shop (the latter two owned by large multinational corporations)—had inviting renovated storefronts but infrequent customers. In contrast, in Lan's shop business was brisk, despite its location in the only unregenerated building on the circle and its makeshift appearance. Numerous men and women of all ages and from many countries made their way through her doors. Some were Vietnamese, like Lan, but others were from China, Syria, and various countries in Africa. There also was a steady flow of Germans. They came for a snack, ingredients for evening meals, or to pick up restaurant supplies.

But despite the pace of her sales that day and the strategic location of her business, enhanced by the multi-million-euro urban regeneration project literally at her doorstep, Lan said that her business had gotten much worse over the past five years. Some of the slowdown could be attributed to disruption caused by the recent infrastructure upgrade. However, Lan focused on other factors, and her account of the difficulties confronting her business resonated with the struggles small businesses were facing in many areas of the city.

From Lan's perspective, "Halle was going downhill," and therefore younger and more economically active people, including Vietnamese migrants, were leaving for the west of Germany. Compared to five years earlier, her business was down 50 percent and, although the shop looked busy, she was "just making ends meet." In addition to a loss of customers, her business faced competition from the increasing number of supermarkets located in the city. Though official statistics reported that Halle grew between 2008 and 2015 (City of Halle 2015), Lan's discussion of her shrinking customer base highlighted the out-migration from Halle of more educated young people, including people of migrant background, and the impoverished state of those who remained. Lan maintained her business by undercutting supermarket prices. Even though she relied on family labor—herself, her husband, and two sisters—profit margins were getting slim.

Lan's negative assessment of the state of Halle's economy after more than two decades of urban regeneration echoed frank assessments we heard in discussions with city officials between 2013 and 2015. What made her voice particularly interesting was that Lan and her small immigrant business represented exactly the economic sector that urban policy makers and journalists in Europe and the United States had been hailing as the savior of failing cities (Echikson 2000; Hesson 2015a; Wirtschaftsstandort Dortmund 2014; European Commission 2008). In the first decades of the twenty-first century, small businesses of migrant entrepreneurs were judged to be important contributors to the process of regenerating and reinventing cities.

This chapter connects emplacement and displacement processes evident within the rise, the struggles, and the demise of migrants' small businesses to efforts by urban leaders and redevelopers to neoliberally reconstruct, rebrand, and reposition cities globally. We find fault with the migration scholarship over several decades in both Europe and the United States that categorizes migrant businesspeople like Lan as "ethnic entrepreneurs" who build ethnic economies and "ethnic colonies." Instead, we offer a multiscalar conjunctural analysis of relationships between migrant businesses and city restructuring. Our approach not only sets aside the concept of ethnic entrepreneurs but also situates and critiques the celebration of migrant businesses within urban regeneration policies. Our analysis builds on authors who speak of "mixed embeddedness" to situate migrant businesses within national and local policy, regulatory and institutional structures, and the demographic and economic profiles of specific places (Kloosterman, Leun, and Rath 1999; Nonini 2012). Our work also resonates with those who situate migrant businesses within transnational flows of capital, location-specific opportunity structures and possibilities, and processes of globalization (Hsing 1998; Yeung and Olds 2000).

We conclude by developing the concept of emplacement, which we present in the introduction, and considering the differential positioning of a city in relation to national and supranational institutions, regulations, and policies in global fields of power. We demonstrate the utility of viewing migrant businesses as multiscalar modes of emplacement. This approach sheds light on efforts of both migrants and those considered non-migrants to build meaningful lives within reconfigured urban terrains. The chapter examines trajectories of migrant businesses in Halle/Saale, but insights came also from our research on migrant businesses in Manchester, New Hampshire, in the United States, and on minority businessmen and their relationship to the restructuring and destruction of Mardin.

Neoliberal Celebrations of Migrant Entrepreneurs

In 2000, the respected magazine *Business Week* called migrant business-people the "unsung heroes" of urban regeneration, a phrase taken up a decade later by the Cities for Local Integration Policy (CLIP) network (CLIP 2010; Echikson 2000), a coalition of research centers and local authorities. The CLIP network (2010, 5) regarded these entrepreneurs "as active agents, shaping their own destinies as well as revitalizing economic sectors especially in neoliberal times" (CLIP 2010, 5). In 2015, journalist Ted Hesson wrote an article in the *Atlantic*, a magazine featuring news and analysis, titled "Why American Cities Are Fighting to Attract Immigrants" (Hesson 2015b, 1). According to Hesson, "many metro areas with large foreign-born populations have thriving local economies. And now local governments all over the U.S. are trying to replicate their successes." His observations that "immigrants helped save Main Street" in Nashville, Philadelphia, and Minneapolis–Saint Paul "were substantiated by an Americas Society/Council of the Americas and the Fiscal Policy Institute study that found that nationally immigrants make up 16 percent of the population, but represent an outsized 28 percent of Main Street business owners" (Kallick 2015, 2).

These findings were reflected in a series of urban policy initiatives in Europe that looked to migrant businesses as instruments of urban neoliberal redevelopment, including strategies of self-employment (Ülker 2016). Migrant businesses were seen as contributing to the diverse ambience necessary to give cities a competitive edge in attracting a high-income workforce with "cosmopolitan" consumption patterns (Şahin, Nijkamp, and Rietdijk 2009). Meanwhile, the National League of Cities (2011), an organization of US cities, articulated a similar understanding of the synergies that develop between migrant businesses and urban growth and worked to develop similar policies at the local level. A report of the US Small Business Administration (Fairlie 2012) spoke to the national profile of these businesses and summarized what had become received knowledge: "The importance of immigrant entrepreneurs to the U.S. economy has been very well documented. . . . They contribute greatly to the economy, have high business formation rates, and create successful businesses that hire employees and export goods and services." The report also asked whether such entrepreneurs had distinctive culturally inflected forms of accessing capital and concluded: "Overall, the sources of startup capital used by immigrant businesses do not differ substantially from those used by non-immigrant firms" (Fairlie 2012, 1).

Nonetheless, some policy makers, in tandem with scholars committed to capitalizing on what they saw as the productive role of migrant businesses, have categorized migrant businesspeople as ethnic entrepreneurs, continuing a widespread tendency among scholars of migration research (CLIP 2010; Lüken-Klaßen and Pohl 2011; Rath 2011). In 2003, the UK government provided funding under the rubric "minority ethnic business support" (Dhaliwala 2008). Migrant businesses in various regions of Germany received support within policies that spoke of the "locational development of the regional potentials of the ethnic economy" [Standortentwicklung Untersuchung zu den regionalen Potenzialen der ethnischen Ökonomie] (Kayser 2008; Ülker 2016). Meanwhile, whether scholars call migrant businesspeople "ethnic entrepreneurs" or insist that a migrant business is just like any other business, they have generally failed to critically situate the celebration of migrant businesses by urban developers and city leaders within the multiscalar efforts and challenges of city making.

A Migrant Business Is a Business: A Critical Overview of the Concept of Ethnic Entrepreneurship

The concept of "ethnic entrepreneur" has been critiqued extensively over the years (Pieterse 2003; Pecoud 2000, 2004a, 2004b; Razin and Langlois 1996). As Rath and Kloosterman (2000, 666), summarizing research in the Netherlands but aptly critiquing much of the literature on ethnic businesses, argue, "Exactly what distinguishes ethnic entrepreneurship from entrepreneurship in general is seldom or never (theoretically) made explicit: does this adjective refer to the origins of the entrepreneur, his or her management strategies, personnel, clientele, products, or a combination of these? Most researchers just assume without any further reflection that there are real differences, just because they are dealing with immigrants. Explanations for every aspect of immigrant entrepreneurial behavior are directly related to ethno-cultural traditions, ethnic moral frameworks and ethnic behavior patterns, ethnic loyalties or ethnic markets."

Despite this potent critique, over several decades many migration scholars developed an analytical category of ethnic entrepreneurship and routinely conflated the terms "migrant business," "small business," and "ethnic entrepreneurship" without ever specifying what made migrant entrepreneurs different from other small businesspeople. These scholars continue to distinguish the activities, networks, and outlook of businesses and entrepreneurs they designate as "ethnic" from all others in the neighborhood, city, or national economy being studied (Eckstein and Nguyen 2011; Deakins et al. 2009; Kitching, Smallbone, and Athayde 2009; Laurence 2011).

Beginning with Ivan Light's (1972) seminal discussion of "ethnic enterprises," scholars debated for several decades which factors led to the cause and success of what they termed "ethnic small businesses." Light, and those who adopted his categorization of migrant businesses as "ethnic," initially stressed that migrant businesses were the products of entrepreneurial cultural histories or the cultural skill set of specific ethnic groups (Masurel and Nijkam 2004; Kaplan and Li 2006; Constant, Shachmurove, and Zimmerman 2007).[3] Others argued that migrants succeeded in business, whatever their cultural background, because of their ability to accrue ethnically based social capital (Bonacich and Modell 1980). They spoke of ethnically bounded networks of trust and solidarity from which migrants obtain access to goods, services, capital, and markets. In some cases, a migrant community was portrayed as an actor that gave ethnic businesses a competitive edge against native competitors. Roger Waldinger, for example, argued this position noting, "(a) they provide a mechanism of organizing an otherwise unstructured labor market; and (b) they provide a mechanism for mediating the strains in the workplace and providing a normative basis on which the rules of the workplace can be established" (Waldinger 1986, 269; see also Portes and Stepick's 1993 discussion of ethnic economies).

In response to critiques of the concept, Min Zhou (2004, 1043) argued that "the ethnic economy concept, with its dual aspects of co-ethnic ownership and employment network, is thus a neutral designation for every enterprise that is either owned, or supervised, or staffed by racial/ethnic minority group members regardless of size, type, and locational clustering" (see also Min and Bozorgmehr 2000). In fact, this designation of "ethnic" moves out of the domain of cultural difference and communal networks of solidarity and into an implicit structural category, situating the term "ethnic" as well as "minority" within racializing and differentiating structures of power. Yet the literature on ethnic businesses, while making reference to discrimination in terms of employment opportunities as a motivating force in migrants' decisions to establish their own business, continued to provide insufficient analytical tools to locate these entrepreneurs within multiscalar institutional constraints and the racialized structuring of opportunity. In short, the literature on immigrant businesspeople as "ethnic entrepreneurs" situated the actors "within an economic and institutional vacuum" (Rath and Kloosterman 2000, 666). Because of their assumption that migrant businesses are differentiated and shaped by the ethnicity of their owners or workers, many of the scholars who contribute to the ethnic entrepreneurship literature proved unable to connect their research either to the literature on the dynamics of small businesses, including sectoral dynamics (Nonini 2012), or to analyses of neoliberal urban restructuring.

Although researchers of the ethnic economy often conducted their research in cities, many have continued to approach cities simply as geographical locations (Dabringer and Trupp 2011), without a systematic examination of these cities' political economies, including structures of discrimination and class, ongoing multiscalar reconstructions, and changing configurations of power, within which all small businesspeople act and to which they contribute. On the other hand, even some of the scholars who framed their research in terms of an "ethnic economy" (Portes and Stepick 1993, Light and Gold 2000), "ethnic enclave" (Wilson and Portes 1980), or "*ethnische Kolonie*" (Heckmann 1998) repeatedly documented how migrants are part of larger economic and often transnational processes that reconfigure the places in which they settle. In many cases, without abandoning their references to terms such as "ethnic entrepreneurs," these scholars have specifically acknowledged the "changing opportunity structures confronting immigrants in Western capitalist societies as well as the distribution of resources and the terms on which they are available" (Waldinger, Aldrich, and Ward 1990, 14).

Meanwhile, urban developers (Wirtschaftsstandort Dortmund 2014) in impoverished cities became increasingly interested in migrant business as contributing to urban regeneration without necessarily adopting an "ethnic lens" (Glick Schiller, Çağlar, and Guldbrandsen 2006). Ironically, despite the flurry of interest among urban developers in the importance of migrant businesses to urban regeneration, with few exceptions (Aytar and Rath 2012), scholars of gentrification and urban restructuring in Europe and North America may have described but did not theorize the role of migrants (Holm 2006, 2010; Häußermann, Holm, and Zunzer 2002). Migrants as economic actors, including entrepreneurs, were at best marginally visible, remaining outside discussions and critiques of urban regeneration and research on urban social movements in relation to neoliberal globalization and the reconfiguration of state territoriality (Bodnár 2014; Brenner, Marcuse, and Mayer 2009; Mayer and Künkel 2012; Leitner, Peck, and Sheppard 2007; Mayer 2010).[4]

Those few urban researchers who included migrant businesses within their discussions of urban rebranding and "entrepreneurial cities" (Hall and Hubbard 1998) saw migrants as ethnic actors (Hackworth and Rekers 2005). In this literature, migrant businesses have generally been examined only within descriptions of "ethnic neighborhoods," which are viewed as destinations for tourism because of the availability of ethnic restaurants and shops selling "exotic goods" (Clarke and Gaile 1998; Novy 2011). As Barabantseva (2016) notes in her critique, when urban researchers have included migrant businesses in discussions of urban culture industries, they expect them to be confined to ethnic neighborhoods such as Chinatowns and Koreatowns (Zukin 1995; Pethe, Hafner, and Lawton 2010).

In contrast, an increasing number of migration researchers have begun to delineate an array of structural factors that foster or inhibit the growth of small businesses, including those of migrants, and shape the location and nature of entrepreneurial activity. Some ethnographies document the relationship between urban restructuring and neighborhood-based migrant businesses (Salzbrunn 2011; Aytar and Rath 2012). Taking the exploration of structural factors further, Kloosterman (2010, 167) has argued that "entrepreneurship and self-employment cannot be solely understood by focusing on the micro-level but [must] include the larger macro and meso structures that impact on these actors' choices." Many who address structural factors when examining migrant businesses use a concept of "multiple embeddedness" to highlight the significance of varying urban opportunity structures in the trajectories of migrant businesses (Kloosterman, Leun, and Rath 1999).

According to this perspective, migrant business dynamics are "the product of the inter-action of structural factors such as migration history and processes of social, economic and political incorporation in the mainstream, as well as their spatial variations" (Rath 2006, 5; see also Rath, Kloosterman, and Razin 2002). Without using the term "mixed embeddedness," other authors have analyzed the structural and sectorial factors that produce variations in migrant businesses in specific cities (Morokvasic 1993). More recently, Rath (2011) has highlighted the significance of city-making process, noting that local policies, histories, demographics, and the relative cultural and political power of a specific locality and economic sector structure business and employment possibilities for everyone living there.

However, these discussions of the factors that structure migrant businesses very rarely address the multiscalar networked institutions and actors that form part of the mutual construction of local, regional, national, and global institutional power. Scholarship on migrant entrepreneurs has often not adequately examined how the local economy and the opportunity structures available to residents are part and parcel of the movements of capital, people, and ideas. These scholars pay insufficient attention to the constant reconstitution of national, regional, supranational, and global institutions in which local people play a part.

Differences in national and local jurisdictions and shared cross-border regulations, such as those of the European Union (EU) and World Trade Organization (WTO), affect the economic insertion of all residents, including migrants, the availability of employment, the degree to which wages can be locally modified, and the regulations that confront small entrepreneurs. Therefore, as scholars of globalization have long noted, it is important to address the global reach and power of processes and actors that restructure various forms of capital (Rothstein and Blim 1992; Harvey 2012). Those interested in migrant small businesses must address urban variations within the multiscalar processes that affect a migrant's project of local emplacement through the development of a small business. At the same time, as small entrepreneurs are reconstituted as actors within these varying social fields, the positionality of a city matters.

To address and critique neoliberal celebrations of the power of migrant entrepreneurs to revitalize "failing cities," we provide a multiscalar example in a disempowered city. With this multiscalar perspective, we can understand why at the beginning of the twenty-first century urban planners began to acknowledge migrant businesspeople such as Lan as heroes in their narratives of urban regeneration and why such narratives are flawed. To fully appreciate Lan's challenges, we must assess the possibilities and limitations of her actions as she makes her way within intersecting networks of power. Our assessment must speak to changing historical conjunctures and their local configurations.

Migrant Entrepreneurs as Actors within Multiscalar City-Making: Halle as a Processual Example

To understand the positioning of migrant businesses, we must revisit the nature of the multiscalar networks of economic, political, and cultural restructuring that have reshaped the landscape and daily life of Halle. As we note in chapter 1, from the time of the 1990 Wende (unification of Germany), Halle/Saale has experienced a rapid process of first disempowerment and then ongoing urban regeneration. The first decade led to a massive political, economic, and cultural disempowerment of the city. It lost much of its industry and a significant proportion of its population, suffered defeat in the struggle for political power within Saxony-Anhalt, and gained the reputation of an undesirable wasteland (IBA 2010).

Consequently, in a dramatic contrast to other German cities with more economic, political, or cultural resources, at the millennium migrants constituted only 3.1 percent of Halle (City of Halle 2016). Neither natives nor migrants from within or without the European Union saw much of a future for themselves in Halle. The small number of migrants included a visible minority of people from several countries in Africa and the Middle East and from Vietnam. Paradoxically, however, as we will show, how processes of urban regeneration were configured in Halle, within the possibilities, stipulations, and program specifications of funding sources set by the EU, the German federal state, and Saxony-Anhalt, initially not only created conditions for displacing much of the local population from employment but also made it possible for migrants to become emplaced. Some migrants, especially those from outside the European Union, responded to the opportunity structures created through the restructuring of the local economy by establishing businesses. In subsequent years, these same multiscalar institutional forces, through the massive flow of reconstruction funds to Halle, displaced local Germans and migrants from their housing and from their business locations and were part of the development of new forms of emplacement and contestation.

As we indicate in chapter 1, the urban regeneration process in Halle was uneven across time and space. Plans and funding for regeneration focused on different parts of the city and different aspects of rebuilding between 1990 and 2016. Initial plans for regeneration included science institutes and parks that sought to bring world-class researchers together to create a local "new economy" powered by innovation and new technology. Although Frau

Haüssler, the lord mayor we interviewed in 2001, was clear that not all migrants were poor or uneducated, planners ignored the fact that the migrant population included multilingual people with professional degrees and international students who wanted to settle in Halle after graduation because they had local ties. Instead, planners focused on attracting desirable technologically skilled newcomers who could help rebuild the city. The city center (Mitte) was refurbished with new storefronts to make it more attractive for these newcomers, to meet their consumption needs, and to provide adequate frontage for German and international retail firms. Our review of plans to redevelop various districts in Halle indicated that even though development was undertaken with public monies, impoverished unemployed residents and migrants already living in Halle were, to a large extent, disregarded until an opportunity for further reconstruction presented itself, such as the one at the end of the 2000s, to combat inequalities in the "dual city" that urban regeneration had itself produced (IBA 2010).

Not until several initial redevelopment plans failed to produce or retain sufficient so-called high-end new residents did city policy makers take note of and reevaluate migrants' technical skills and eventually utilize them to some extent. For example, by 2015, refugees with medical training began to be integrated into Saxony-Anhalt's health-care system (field notes, 2015). However, from the beginning of the regeneration process, city leaders recognized that negative images of Halle as a racist stronghold were a major hindrance in attracting the global talent, corporate offices, and large-scale capital investment that were central to their redevelopment plans.

HALLE, THE WELCOMING

Consequently, faced with the necessity of rebranding and marketing Halle as open for business and open to the world, both within Germany and globally, city leaders began to forge a migrant-friendly narrative. The leaders we interviewed in 2001—city officials and members of political, economic, religious, and social service organizations with very different political affiliations—spoke about migrants through the lens of city positioning. Whatever their personal and party politics, our interviews revealed that these leaders included the migrant population as part of the city. Even when interviewees used the term "foreigner," they included these foreigners as part of the locality and emphasized how residents' provincialism could be overcome through interaction with these newcomers. That is, these leaders saw migrants from outside Germany as allies in their goal of repositioning Halle as a city of the world. City leaders also embraced migrants as an indication of Halle's openness. This public stance was badly needed to improve Halle's competitiveness, especially in attracting knowledge industries. As a city councilor commented when discussing the struggle of city leaders to reposition their city, "there are too few foreigners living here" (interview C.1, August 24, 2001).

Within a population that ranged from migrant professionals to failed asylum seekers, migrant businesspeople were singled out as helpful to developing the local economy. In 2001, the narrative highlighting the significance of migrant businesses for urban regeneration was just beginning to be developed in Europe and the United States. However, Halle's leaders recognized migrant businesspeople as economic actors who could become agents of city redevelopment. In discussing efforts to revive its small business sector, most city leaders included migrant entrepreneurs. They acknowledged that, after unification, empty storefronts would have lined the rebuilt city center without the shops and restaurants opened by migrants.

A representative of the Employment Bureau explained, "Foreigners who want to open a shop here . . . help the employment situation if they come here and also employ people who already live in Halle" (interview E., August 8, 2002). A city councilor stated that he was "comfortable with migrants who had made a place in the city through the establishment of small businesses" (interview C.2, August 30, 2001). These leaders emphasized migrants as businesspeople rather than as contributors of exotic marketable difference to the city's rebranding efforts. As urban regeneration continued and many migrant and other small businesses were displaced from the city center, Halle continued its migrant-friendly narrative, emphasizing that all newcomers should be considered part of the city. In the "Door-opener" offered on the city website from 2005 to 2013, Lord Mayor Szabados, who was married to a migrant, welcomed all newcomers, whether tourists or migrants, and provided information, including a list of shopping locations ranging from large supermarket chains to various small migrant businesses.

However, in the initial periods of redevelopment, the city gave no assistance to migrants who wished to set up businesses. There was no official source of advice or support in navigating the regulatory regime, nor were financial incentives offered. This changed only decades later when the Jobs Office offered unemployed people, including legal migrants, small business grants.

OPPORTUNITY IN THE CONTEXT OF DISPOSSESSION:
THE PARADOXICAL DEVELOPMENT OF MIGRANT SMALL
BUSINESSES IN HALLE

When we started our research, migrant small businesses were visible, even crucial, components of retail business in several areas of the city, including the center of the old city. Migrants from Vietnam, Nigeria, Ghana, Greece, India, Bosnia, Iraq, Sudan, Azerbaijan, Turkey, Syria, and Lebanon (including migrants from the last three countries who identified primarily as Kurds) started, or were employed in, these businesses. In all the cases we observed, the networks within which these businesses functioned comprised people from multiple backgrounds, migrant and non-migrant. Sometimes spouses native to Germany became partners in these businesses. Wholesale networks extended elsewhere in Germany, to several European countries, and to Vietnam, China, Thailand, and Nigeria.

As with many cities in Germany during the same period, migrant businesses lined the street from the railroad station to the city center. In Halle, their presence extended far beyond the neighborhood of the train station. Our 2001 survey identified seventy-five businesses owned by or employing migrant workers within streets that, over the next sixteen years, were absorbed into regeneration plans for the city center and its immediate periphery. Although only 3.5 percent of Halle's population had migrant backgrounds, 12 percent of the businesses in this sample were owned or operated by migrants. These numbers indicate only that migrants filled storefronts in key parts of the city. They do not account for the total number of migrant businesses in the city center or elsewhere in the city. In addition, *imbisses* (kiosks) did business in mobile trailers on empty lots or on unused land around the city center's periphery.

These businesses found fertile ground not because of official assistance but through the conditions that the city and its residents faced after unification. Local contexts included both a niche for the kinds of businesses that migrants could provide and conditions within which they could establish small retail shops. The city's official narrative welcomed migrant enterprises, and storefronts, many of them renovated, stood empty. Initially, rents were low. At the time of unification and the reintroduction of a local capitalist economy, migrants could compete with natives who also had little retail experience or access to wholesale networks. At that moment, all aspiring retail merchants faced the challenge of developing wholesale networks.

The legal regime immediately after German unification also encouraged

FIG 2.1 Storefront of a long-term migrant business near Halle city center. Photograph by Robert Schutz.

the establishment of migrant businesses. Many migrants who had come to the GDR as workers or students were able to maintain legal residency if they opened a business. This was true in other eastern German cities, but Halle had specific opportunity structures, including a city leadership that fostered a migrant-friendly narrative and policies. As a result, Halle offered opportunities to budding businesspeople. These included Kurdish refugees who lacked entrepreneurial backgrounds but could access wholesale networks (initially in nearby Berlin), migrants from Vietnam who had come to the GDR to study or work in factories and who had little retail experience and few commercial connections but some ties to Halle, and migrants from West Africa who brought some history of small-scale trading and long-distance trading networks in their homelands but no knowledge of retail sales in Germany.

The niche these migrants filled was certainly not an ethnic one, although local people might refer to these businesses in ethnic terms. In Halle, fruit and vegetable and *döner* (kebab) businesses were publicly identified as "Kurdish" (although in German cities such as Berlin they might be identified as Turkish) and in at least one instance included workers from Azerbaijan. So-called Vietnamese shops included stores selling fruits and vegetables and textile shops that sold inexpensive clothing and gifts.

With a large percentage of the local population receiving social benefits or reduced to low-paid employment, migrant businesses provided inexpensive food and clothing—an important service. In addition to factory closures, massive downsizing, and loss of jobs in government and public institutions, people were impoverished by currency transformations. First, for some people, savings accounts shrank in value when the West German deutsche mark replaced the GDR's currency. Then, in 2002, when the euro replaced the deutsche mark, local prices for food and other living essentials rose dramatically.[5] In the first years after unification, migrant businesses supplied low-cost fruit, vegetables, and staples such as milk, bread, and salt; inexpensive clothing and household items; and affordable fast food in the form of *döner* kebabs and noodle dishes. Only during a second regeneration phase, when the migrant population had become larger and more diversified and German desire for "ethnic foods" had grown, could a handful of specialized businesses become well established, such as Lan's, which began in 2004.

The success of migrants' businesses in the first ten or fifteen years after unification can be contrasted to the failure of many businesses operated by West German or powerful international chain stores, which briefly filled the city with relatively expensive consumer goods. Shoe stores were common. At that time, most city center consumers enjoyed window-shopping but had little money for high-end consumption.

Migrants established businesses in Halle within a conjuncture in which multiscalar forces had dramatically restructured the local cityscape, residents' livelihoods, and the business environment. We have highlighted the impoverishment of the local population after the Wende, the presence of renovated empty storefronts, and the challenge of linking local retail businesses to multiple and geographically dispersed wholesale networks. From the beginning of the restructuring, the local context was not simply the product of local or even national conditions.

MULTISCALAR EMPLACEMENTS OF MIGRANT
SMALL BUSINESSES

By examining the history of several businesses established by migrants within the first wave of urban regeneration, we can gain insight into the dynamics at play, which first made these businesses possible and then led to their displacement. Subsequent cycles followed in which migrant business again responded to reconstruction and its aftermath. It is important to note that multiscalar social fields—networks of networks within which displacement and emplacement processes were situated—included not only fields of interaction forged by the institutional actors reconstituting Halle but also networks forged by ordinary residents, both migrant and non-migrant.

We begin our analysis of the social fields constituted by migrant business-people in Halle by tracing the pathways through which Phuong Schmidt, a migrant from Vietnam, became a shopkeeper in Halle. Phuong Schmidt's network-building practices illustrate how migrants' efforts to obtain emplacement by building businesses intersected with the city leaders' project to improve the national and global positioning of the city in which they all lived. Migrants' transnational networks included people of multiple backgrounds. Stretching between other cities in Germany as well as cities in Europe and other regions of the world, including their homelands, migrants' family ties were entangled with multiscalar networks that contributed to the establishment of small businesses in Halle and linked the city to many other places. The small business sector in Halle, and the social fields within which it was constituted, helped recruit newcomers to a city that was generally deemed undesirable by Germans from the west and unwelcoming to foreigners, including "foreign scientists," whom city leaders were eager to attract.

Phuong Schmidt founded her clothing store soon after unification. Trained in law and pedagogy in Hanoi and the child of a university professor, Phuong Schmidt came to Halle after unification to visit her sister, who had a university degree but owned and worked in a clothing shop. This sister used distribution networks that stretched from nearby Leipzig back to China, initially the source of many of the inexpensive items sold in the shop. Through a Vietnamese woman who had studied in an elite graduate program in Halle, Phuong met Bernd, her future husband, a native of the city and of Germany. Their courtship took place in the meetings and conferences of an Esperanto club they both had joined.

Bernd was unable to find a job in the depressed local economy, so the couple decided to open a women's clothing shop. Bernd and Phuong drew on her sister and brother-in-law's entrepreneurial experience and networks and obtained a loan from Bernd's father, who had some savings. The shop also provided part-time employment for an experienced German shop assistant. Through her marriage and her business, Phuong started to identify with Halle and Germany as well as with Hanoi and Vietnam. She said that she "felt like a German because Halle was her 'second home'" (interview P., October 16, 2003). At the same time, she maintained strong family ties in Vietnam. However, the social field Phuong lived in cannot be encompassed by two national identities. Her Esperanto networks stretched to several countries, as did the networks she used to supply her stores. At the time of the interview, wholesale networks connected her not only to Leipzig but also to China through Budapest.

Phoung's pathway of emplacement, through a business built on her marriage to a man born in Germany and on the skills of a German shop assistant, was not typical of migrants of Vietnamese background or of migrants who began businesses in Halle. She also was not unique. Among the twenty-three business owners we interviewed during our research, five told us about their intermarriages. Moreover, we found German employees in businesses owned by people of Nigerian, Vietnamese, and Indian backgrounds. All these businesses were transnationally connected in different ways, but each contributed to and reflected the struggles of Halle's leadership to reposition the city within multiple networks of power. None of these businesses, in terms of clientele or multiscalar networks, could be understood as ethnic businesses, nor could their successes or failures be understood in terms of cultural background or ethnic networks. Rather, we suggest that the dynamics of these businesses must be understood within the configuration of the multiscalar structural forces shaping Halle's economy and the opportunities for and constraints on emplacement the city offered to all its residents.

The two businesses we consider next were begun by African migrants and located in unregenerated storefronts in two different districts that bordered the city center. Examining the history of businesses begun by African migrants highlights the utility of setting aside the ethnic lens in order to see the relationship between migrant businesses and multiscalar urban restructuring in disempowered cities. These migrants remained in business, with different degrees of success, until a new wave of regeneration affected their customer base and storefront locations.

Flora's business success was a product of the timing of her emplacement in Halle, the location she chose for her business, and the force of her personality. Arriving from Ghana as an asylum seeker, Flora gained permanent legal status by wending her way through the bureaucratic procedures necessary to open a legal business, with the help of her "best friend," a women migrant from Russia who spoke German (interview F., November 18, 2001). Her business was located on the edge of the redeveloped area near run-down housing blocks and abandoned or demolished factories. From conversations with Flora, as well as through participant observation in her shop, it became clear that her business served not only African asylum seekers and refugees but also local German residents in the neighborhood. There were no other Ghanaians in the city, but there were other English-speaking migrants, and Flora expanded her multilingual competence to include some German. At the same time, she skillfully marketed her diverse stock to her various clienteles. Impoverished Germans in the area came to her shop for soft drinks, beer, cigarettes, and snacks that she kept close to the checkout counter. In the bleak surrounds, Flora's shop was the closest source of these products for locals, and Flora sold them cheaply.

She also sold telephone calling cards, fresh and frozen food, and male and female beauty products familiar to customers from other African countries, including Nigeria, Congo, and Mozambique. In the front of the shop, a migrant from Nigeria sold hip-hop fashions produced in Asia. Food on the shelves included British and European products favored in West Africa and not available elsewhere in Halle. Her back room served as a meeting place where young men from diverse African countries could purchase cooked food, exchange information about how to settle in the city, and further develop their networks and connections to cities throughout Europe and North America. Next door to her shop, Flora set up a store with phone booths for international calls, but the advent of inexpensive calling cards and cell phones rapidly made this venture a dead end.

Another business established by an African migrant on another street skirting the city center sold similar products, including cooked food, and also catered to local residents and African migrants. However, this business was less successful. Owner personality played some role in this, but the second business also faced more competition. A Kurdish migrant in a nearby storefront also served food and drinks to local residents and operated until late in the evening.

As urban regeneration spread to the streets that bordered the city center, both these businesses started by migrants closed. Buildings and storefronts in those areas were renovated, and the population changed. Poor Germans were forced to relocate, and some African migrants were deported or left for other parts of Germany and Europe as Germany, within a changing conjunctural moment, altered its immigration laws to allow for professional migration while making refugee status increasingly difficult to obtain.

Structural Forces, Changing Times, and Business Failure

Beginning about 2002, a series of conjunctural forces began to change the physical appearance of the city, the demographic profiles of the various city districts, and the distribution and type of large and small businesses that occupied Halle's storefronts. The downturn in high-tech dot-com industries in the United States, including in Manchester, New Hampshire, was not directly visible in Halle, but small merchants began to talk about a poor local economy a few years after the millennium. These business owners faced displacement from the city center and the areas immediately adjacent to it in the wake of the inflation in rents and wholesale and retail commodity prices that accompanied conversion from the deutsche mark to the euro. Soon after these disruptive forces, they were confronted with further urban regeneration focused on gentrifying central neighborhoods of the city.

As we have seen in chapter 1, this process took several different forms. Private landlords received a combination of federal, land, and city money to renovate historic buildings constructed before 1948, first in the city center and, from 2007 and 2013, in various districts in southern and northern parts of the city. The Urban Redevelopment East program provided funds to private landlords as well as to publicly owned housing companies for renovating, conserving, and revaluing their property (Baum, Vondroušová, and Tichá 2014, 22–23). Private landlords (many of whom came from the west of Germany to reclaim family property after unification or to buy real estate for investment) initially received loans, tax abatements, and other forms of public funding to reconstruct Halle's early-twentieth-century apartment houses, town houses, and Art Deco decors. Seventy percent of the buildings in the southern district of the city center, where reconstruction was concentrated, were owned privately (Bundesinstitut für Bau-, Stadt- und Raumforschung 2015). Newly renovated buildings could charge higher rents for storefronts and apartments. Small businesses and poor people, both migrants and non-migrants, were forced out. As we note in chapter 1, a dual process of dispossession occurred here because the city of Halle provided one-third of the total funding to obtain German federal and Saxony-Anhalt monies. Poorer people, including migrants, not only lost their homes and the businesses that provided them with inexpensive goods but also were left with fewer services due to the impoverished city budget. International chains and supermarkets took the place of many local businesses, including some owned by migrants (Bendick and Tempel 2014). Kiosk businesses primarily run by migrants were pushed off the streets. Many migrant businesses in the area were unable to pay rising rents. Within a short period of time, even some of the international chains and upscale restaurants that replaced them failed.

During the first decade of the millennium, redevelopment of the city center was focused on making the city more appealing to the cosmopolitan tastes of "new economy" technical workers and scientists, the desired targets of regeneration. A gourmet food court was situated in an expanded department store in the Marktplatz and a new wave of businesses linked to international

FIG 2.2 Renovated storefront near Halle city center, abandoned by an international retailer and upscale restaurant. Photograph by Nina Glick Schiller.

corporations and franchises occupied storefronts in major business districts. The regeneration not only displaced the food and clothing stores of migrants that sold inexpensive goods to poorer residents (and who were increasingly displaced from regenerated housing in the area) but also forced the closure of several local businesses, migrant and non-migrant, that catered to wealthier clients.

Detailing the struggles of two businesses with wealthier clientele, Elite Foods and Beautiful Dream Gifts, makes clear that their failure did not reflect migrants' cultural differences. Rather, the failure of these small businesses reflected the ongoing restructuring of the city economy in the face of global economic downturns, higher rents on storefronts, and the absence of the wealthier populations who were the focus of the regeneration projects. Both businesses were positioned to sell to upscale cosmopolitan customers rather than to the urban poor. Their fate paralleled that of city center businesses owned by non-migrants that sold upscale gifts made by global craftspeople and fashions crafted locally.

Elite Foods was owned by Helga, a Halle native married to Kadri, a migrant from Turkey. In terms of assessing relationships between migrant-owned businesses and Halle's local structural context, it is important to note that, although his German was not fluent, Kadri was well emplaced within the local political and social fabric through his marriage to Helga. Helga had a fierce love of her native city and extensive local social networks. These were publicly visible when, many years after their relationship began, the couple married and wedding guests included city officials (field notes, January 2001–December 2002).

Helga and Kadri located their shop on an urban pedestrian mall, a section of a street in the city center dedicated as the "high street" by urban planners. However, when our research began in 2001, the most desirable section of the street hosted three other migrant-owned shops: two selling inexpensive clothing and cheap goods and a soft ice cream stand. In contrast to these businesses, Elite Foods met the upscale aspirations of the city planners. It featured expensive imported fruits, olives, and candies sought by consumers who desired high-end commodities. These high-quality imported goods, including those from Turkey, were priced too high to be accessible to the poor.

The second elite-oriented migrant business in our sample was Beautiful Dream Gifts, a shop filled with African jewelry and art that the owners wished to market to consumers who sought to validate their cosmopolitan tastes through such purchases. The shop's interior, its merchandise, and even its wrapping paper catered to this market. Beautiful Dream Gifts was owned by Evelyn, a woman from Nigeria, and her husband, Stephan, a retired businessman from Germany who grew up in a village near Halle (interviews E., June 8, 2003; July 7, 2004).

Unfortunately, at the turn of the millennium, businesses in Halle faced the ramifying effects of economic restructuring, currency transformations, and related speculations. In this climate, it was increasingly difficult for small businesses to compete with well-capitalized, corporate-owned businesses targeting upscale consumers, which, at the time, was a diminishing rather than a growing population in Halle. While Helga and Kadri held on to their valuable corner high street location for a few years after the downturn, eventually they were unable to compete with the gourmet food court of the upscale department store located down the street and on the square. Concurrently, their profit margin was destroyed by currency conversion; even their relatively upscale customer base could not support higher retail prices. Some migrant businesses in the city center selling inexpensive goods found new locations with cheaper rents on the city periphery. But Elite Foods and Beautiful Dream Gifts, poised for Halle's new cosmopolitan market in a central location, went out of business.

During the last days of their gift shop, Evelyn and Stephan sought new markets by participating in what they thought was an open-air crafts fair. To Evelyn's dismay, when they arrived they found that the event was a multicultural project funded by the Saxony-Anhalt office of the Heinrich Böll Foundation of the Green Party to celebrate migrants' cultural difference. The foundation's efforts reflected the German national policy of approaching migrant integration through multiculturalism and intercultural understanding. Evelyn and Stephen found themselves among booths sponsored by the few small migrant organizations in Halle, which were generally active only at such events. Some migrant families also had been contacted to display goods, foods, or crafts such as hair braiding that were seen as ethnic and exotic. Evelyn was discomforted by such marketing. She did not want to position her business or herself within an ethnic niche and vowed to avoid participation in such events.

While most inexpensive clothing stores and many inexpensive fruit and vegetable markets had been displaced from the regenerated streets near the city center and university buildings, a few migrant businesses continued, including small grocery stores that stayed open long hours and some of the long-established Asian and *döner* fast-food shops. Other migrant businesses, pushed out by growing disparities in the city, increasingly concentrated in Halle-Neustadt. They joined migrant businesses that had already made inexpensive retail commerce and restaurants part of the profile of that district's main thoroughfares, and they brought an intensified sense of street life to that region of the city. This contribution was slowly acknowledged in assessments of urban regeneration in Neustadt.

By 2010, the city center and surrounding districts became populated to some degree with offices and businesses linked to new economy industries that were becoming established in Halle, although not to the extent envisioned in the various redevelopment plans. Property management and small, struggling start-ups in technical and financial services became part of the commercial mix. Those benefiting from the new opportunities primarily represented an influx of people from other parts of Germany. The increased number of real estate sales offices reflected the growing tendency for Halle to become the residential base of a workforce who worked and often shopped in Leipzig. New types of small businesses catering to different, more affluent interests, such as nail parlors or restaurants with trendy menus, became part of the entrepreneurial profile in regenerated areas of the city center. Several Vietnamese restaurants added sushi to their menus.

While unemployment in Halle dropped to just under 12 percent in 2015

(City of Halle 2016), the city still had a higher unemployment rate than did other eastern cities. Employees generally earned lower wages than in other regions of Germany or even in nearby cities in eastern Germany. In response to the continuing disempowerment of the city and its people, by 2016 many upscale businesses, including fancier restaurants and bars established after the second wave of regeneration, had closed. Once more, many storefronts were empty despite having been renovated. Streets in regenerated areas reverted to marketing to low-income consumers, but now the customer base included increasing numbers of students as Halle became less a center of advanced science and more a university city, hosting twenty thousand students in 2015 (Federal Ministry of Education and Research 2015). Some new businesses were outlets of international chains, which had corporate headquarters based in Germany or the Netherlands and thousands of retail stores in a range of countries. These retail businesses, some known for low wages and long working hours, marketed inexpensive household goods and novelties.

Nonetheless, migrants began once again to initiate new fast-food restaurants, primarily Asian noodle shops, *döner* shops, and small grocery stores specializing in soft drinks, beer, and snacks. These businesses continued to be pressured by the scarcity of affordable storefronts in regenerated city districts. The owner of an Asian market noted the contradiction he faced in establishing a business in Halle. This man had begun his business during the second wave of storefront regeneration and found a customer base among the university students who had come in increasing numbers to the city. "Halle," he said, "is a good city for foreigners but it is hard to get a shop in the center."

The Halle of 2016, when our research ended, was not the Halle of 2000, when our research began and when we first became aware of the engagement of small business owners—migrant and non-migrant—in city-making. Conditions for all small businesses, including those begun by migrants, altered because of city restructuring, the dynamics of capital flows, the partial success of the city's knowledge industries, and the revaluation of urban spaces. These transformations and the reconstruction of some research and industrial facilities offered new possibilities and benefits for some people. However, by 2016, it also had become clear that despite massive EU and public redevelopment funding, public money would not be able to leverage private corporate investment in Halle's industrial, scientific research and technology parks and create well-paying jobs and prosperity in the city. This idea had been discredited in the eyes of many residents, including some city leaders. Yet new regeneration schemes continued in the city.

One such program had begun to rebuild key intersections, with light-rail federal, Saxony-Anhalt, and Halle funding. This was the program that had rebuilt the traffic circle in front of Lan's shop. The relationship between migrant businesspeople and city leaders and developers who wished to reposition Halle contributed to and reflected the realignment of trajectories of multiscalar institutional power after the reverberations of 2007–8 banking and loan debacle. This realignment exacerbated the city's difficulty in attracting private capital.

While migrant businesses in Halle remained prominent among small businesses that were not franchises or chains, and by 2016 their number had once again grown in Halle's regenerated districts, they, too, were drawn into the corporate networks through their supply chains. As had the initial migrant businesses in Halle, including the so-called Afro-shops, the newer or persisting migrant businesses in Halle were not "ethnic businesses" that marketed exclusively to or drew from the supply networks of migrants of the same national or regional backgrounds. However, the array of nationalities living and cooking in Halle became much wider, and local German clientele over time came to include not only bargain shoppers but also, as our description of Lan's customers indicated, a more internationally oriented consumer population seeking fresh ingredients and new flavors. In response, Lan included among her services cooking guidance and instructions for her German and diverse international clientele.

In a related development, while in 2000, the owners of the Elite Food Shop had personally bought imported and fresh produce each morning from Leipzig wholesalers, by 2016 businesses such as Lan's looked to a variegated supply chain that included multinational corporations as direct suppliers. Indeed, by 2016, Lan ordered much of her stock online, using a computer as well as earlier technology—a massive catalogue from a Dutch firm that marketed categories of "African," "Asian," and Caribbean "ethnic foods." Many "ethnic foods" in the catalogue were actually processed by US or European firms, but under labels familiar in migrants' countries of origin. Others came from firms in Vietnam, Thailand, and Korea. Large orders could be paid for online and delivered directly to her store. At the same time, Lan stocked live fish that her family purchased in Leipzig from a German wholesaler, frozen herbs from Thailand and Vietnam in the winter from Vietnamese connections in Poland and Thailand, and fresh Vietnamese herbs supplied in summer from small gardens in Halle. She also sold snacks—spring rolls and fried dough—made in her kitchen. Businesses such as Lan's grocery store highlight the role of migrants as multiscalar city-makers whose activities stimulate small-scale local producers, as they link their locality to the transnational networks of multinational corporations.

In short, in a restructured Halle that now contained several districts with lovely regenerated housing, new tramlines, and refurbished historical sites, businesspeople such as Lan contributed to efforts to more favorably reposition their city, even as these shopkeepers struggled to keep afloat. Lan's shop was not isolated in an ethnic enclave or neighborhood. Rather, through her actions, she linked her own kitchen, Halle, Leipzig, and massive multinational corporations connected through a wholesale firm in the Netherlands. However, she took these actions within the contingencies of structural forces that played out in Halle as they provided both opportunities and barriers for small retail businesses. Contrary to claims made by celebrants of migrant businesses, Lan and other migrant businesspeople could neither revitalize Halle nor be sure of secure emplacement for themselves and their families.

Conclusion

The analytical perspective on migrant small businesses that we develop in this chapter is very different from that offered within the literature on ethnic entrepreneurs. Not only do we highlight the reality that these businesses are not organized around migrants' cultural background and ethnic networks but we link the dynamics of business emplacement and displacement to multiscalar restructuring processes that reconfigured the lives of all residents and conditioned the growth and demise of businesses.

We argue throughout this book for a concept of "emplacement," which emphasizes that all individuals live within a nexus of unequal power comprising all with whom they connect and interact. To study how these migrants establish and maintain their businesses, migration scholars must explore the connections between businesses and the constant multiscalar conjunctural processes of restructuring a city—processes that shape all residents' livelihood opportunities and constraints.

The relative positioning of a city within hierarchies of uneven power can enable or impede pathways of emplacement for all businesspeople residing there. From this perspective, much can be learned from our study of migrant businesses in a disempowered city such as Halle. Some of the processes we highlight can be attributed to the disempowered positioning of the city and the constraints that all residents face in trying to earn a living. Severe limitations on opportunities make challenges to migrant newcomers especially pressing, and the development of migrant businesses must be examined in that light. Not only must our understanding of migrant emplacement examine how migrants constitute their life trajectories within the multiscalar forces through which they contribute to city-making but we must also examine how the nexus of these forces changes over time. We hope to alert researchers to the need to link specific pathways of emplacement to the varying opportunity structures of different localities, noting that both the localities and the pathways develop with, and are part of, global networks of power at a particular conjuncture.

At the same time, precarity must be understood as a widespread condition of small businesses in cities around the world. However, the ethnic lens, strengthened by researchers' propensity to confine their attention to migrant-dense neighborhoods and ethnic social networks in more powerful cities, often obscures more general structural features in much of the research on migrant businesses in those cities. Therefore, our data can serve as a stimulus for researchers to rethink their entire approach to migrant businesses. On the other hand, we also note the paradoxical nature of disempowered cities' opportunities and constraints for migrant businesses, which we demonstrate in relation to Halle. These cities may not provide migrant businesses with opportunities to be portrayed and emplaced as part of the "cultural" ambience of the city, which is a mixed blessing. Emplacement offered through the marketing of cultural diversity may offer business possibilities but may also impose racialized constraints.

By examining the relationship between Halle's leaders' efforts to reposition and re-empower the city, on the one hand, and migrants' efforts to secure emplacement in the city through small businesses, on the other, we are able to see that, from unification until 2006, Halle provided migrants with a particularly welcoming economic niche, when there were few other opportunities for emplacement. After 2006, given spiraling regeneration and conjunctural transformations, many small businesses, including those begun by migrants, were displaced, forced to close, or relocated. At the same time, regeneration created possibilities for businesses that could serve the gentrified city center or the outer margins to which impoverished residents had been pushed. That is to say, migrants' emplacement and displacement in Halle through small businesses were shaped by the city's restructuring over time and within circumstances constituted by political and economic actors and institutions in Germany, in Europe, and around the world.

The ethnic entrepreneurship literature often provides examples of success or failure without reference to changing economic structures and conditions locally or, when reference is made to such local sectorial dynamics, then without sensitivity to the temporal dimensions of global economic structures and corporate and financial actors that shape these dynamics. The variable of time, within ongoing globe-spanning processes, has proven central to an understanding of migrant businesses in Halle. Depending on the city's relative political, economic, and cultural positioning and its response to the global neoliberal agenda, migrant businesses can play different roles at different times not only in terms of emplacing migrants in the city but also in terms of the city's efforts to situate itself competitively within a global market. Migrants who initiate small businesses find themselves simultaneously positioned as active agents of neoliberal urban regeneration and among those dispossessed by these processes. However, in all cases, and often within networks of emplacement that are not visible through an ethnic lens, migrants participate in reshaping urban fortunes and in repositioning the city together with all those who confront and participate in processes of accumulation by dispossession.

In Lan's case, Halle's leaders' quest to regain their city's cultural prestige by confronting its racist reputation may have provided a supportive ambiance. But this ambiance did not extend a political voice to more than a handful of migrants. For Lan, Karamba Diaby, one of the first two people of African background to be elected to the German federal parliament, was neither a political representative nor a symbol of the struggle against racism. Rather, he was a frequent customer who appreciated her stock of yams, okra, and chilis. She had no relationship with local politics or social movements. In chapter 5, we look at how other migrants joined with local people to use Christian churches and networks to make social citizenship claims in the face of their multiple displacements.

CHAPTER 3

They Are Us

URBAN SOCIABILITIES WITHIN
MULTISCALAR POWER

In 2003, Hubert and Helene were sitting in a Catholic church in Manchester, waiting for the French mass to begin, when Nina came into the church, sat nearby, and introduced herself. This meeting initiated networks that stretched from Manchester, New Hampshire, to Washington, DC, in the United States, on to Goma, in the east of the Democratic Republic of the Congo (DRC), Kampala, Uganda, and Geneva, Switzerland. Hundreds of people became connected through a campaign to reunite the couple's seven children with their parents.

Hubert and Helene had come that day to pray for their children, aged six to sixteen. They had been forced to leave their children behind in the care of a cousin in Goma, who was later brutally murdered. Warring militias linked to Rwanda or to the Congolese government—with reputed ties to Canadian mining interests and US government funding—roamed the eastern Congo, raping, looting, and capturing children to work as enslaved labor or as soldiers (Ismi 2014). The worldwide demand for rare metals and other Congolese resources had unleashed a regime of the violent forces of accumulation by dispossession.

Hubert—beaten, mutilated in front of his family, and left for dead because of his work countering the recruitment of child soldiers—felt it was imperative to flee the country. Soon after this, the whole family won the US immigrant visa lottery, but Hubert and Helene could not afford all their plane tickets and requisite processing fees.[1] Borrowing enough money from close friends already settled in Manchester to cover their own plane tickets and fees, Hubert and Helene planned to come to the United States, earn enough money to pay back their generous friends, and bring their children to safety. But when they arrived in Manchester, they learned that their children were trapped in the DRC. By not flying with their parents, the children lost their rights to the lottery visas and had to "wait their turn"—at least five years—to legally join their parents in Manchester.

Nina had come to the church in search of newly arrived migrants to interview. When she asked Hubert and Helene for an interview, they agreed but had their own request: "Please help us bring our children to America." To help, Nina and her undergraduate students created the Committee on Rights and Justice (CORAJ). CORAJ learned that the children could come rapidly if they were granted "humanitarian parole," an immigration status requiring a special act of the US Congress. This could happen only if sufficient political pressure was brought to bear. In addition, they needed to raise about twenty thousand dollars for travel costs and immigration-related fees. To try to bring the children to safety, Nina and her students took the initial steps of what emerged as a new multiscalar transnational social field.

A network of networks developed that involved hundreds of people: pro bono lawyers from a prestigious Manchester law firm, a freelance journalist from a small New Hampshire town, a Democratic Party activist who was a former University of New Hampshire trustee and New Hampshire legislator, three Republican US congressmen from New Hampshire, a congressional staff member based in Manchester, the US consul in Kampala, a local nonprofit organization, rotary clubs in New Hampshire, the International Red Cross in Geneva, the president of the University of New Hampshire, a local supermarket, a family foundation based in Boston, a Manchester Catholic parish, a local born-again Protestant pastor, and many individuals throughout New Hampshire. These were the days before social media, so word of the struggle and the need for funds spread via coverage by the *University of New Hampshire Magazine*, New Hampshire Public Radio, the Associated Press, regional television stations, and newsletters of the New Hampshire Bar Association and New Hampshire Business Review.

Each of these network ties represented personal actions taken by individuals. For example, junior Republican congressman Jeb Bradley called the US Consul in Kampala from his home phone. Two years after their parents left them behind, the children arrived in Manchester in September 2004—a reunion broadcast on regional television. The massive outpouring of support raised enough funds and resources not only to process the necessary papers and fly the children to the United States but also to provide the family with clothes, furniture, a donated freezer filled with food, a used van to transport them around Manchester, and a down payment on a subprime mortgage for a large dilapidated house.

FIG 3.1 Hubert and Helene, launching the campaign to bring their seven children from the Democratic Republic of Congo to Manchester. Photograph by Lisa Nugent, courtesy of *UNH Magazine*.

In this chapter, we explore the daily sociabilities that lie behind the surges of public support for migrants that have periodically emerged in both Manchester and Halle. We link them to shared sensibilities and aspirations. Tom Holdreth, Hubert and Helene's lead lawyer, explained the domain of common feelings that led him to work tirelessly to bring children he had never met to Manchester. "Hubert and I are about the same age. We both have young families. I could immediately understand the anguish that Hubert and Helene lived with every day that they were living apart from their children" (Rorick 2004). Identification with Hubert and Helene as parents bereft of their children was expressed repeatedly throughout the campaign. In this chapter, we link the sociabilities engendered by such sentiments to conditions that the residents of Manchester confronted within the dispossessive processes of multiscalar urban restructuring and the regeneration that city leaders initiated beginning around 2000.

Building on our research in Manchester, we argue that to understand the full range of urban sociabilities—for all urban residents, migrant and non-migrant—we need to explore how, where, why, and within what structural contingencies city dwellers build domains of affect, mutual respect, and shared aspirations. To find a way to speak about the bonds that underlie such sociabilities beyond the idioms of community, we use the terms "domains of commonality" and "sociabilities of emplacement." This chapter focuses on sites where these sociabilities were initiated, including the shared physical spaces of apartment buildings, city streets, workplaces, and urban institutions. We explore the situations in which displacements engendered by urban regeneration in Manchester, New Hampshire, give rise to domains of commonality between migrant newcomers and people seen as local. When migrants and non-migrants seek their place within restructured urban sites, they always do so within conditions of ongoing multiscalar processes of capital accumulation.

In the years following Hubert and Helene's children's arrival and emplacement in Manchester, local and national US media and some New Hampshire and Manchester political leaders increasingly focused on anti-immigrant politics. Migration has become a partisan issue, with the Republican Party taking the lead in rallying anti-immigrant public opinion (Scott 2015). Meanwhile in Germany, refugee housing has been attacked and some burned, including a 2015 arson in Saxony-Anhalt (*Der Spiegel Online* 2015). But networks of volunteers who wished to welcome newcomers also persisted in Halle and elsewhere in Europe, as they did in the United States, including in Manchester.[2] Even as the historical conjuncture changed, the US Conference of Mayors continued to welcome migrants, including Syrian refugees (US Conference of Mayors 2015). Media reports provided little insight into the social basis for social movements that support migrants, and social theory built around "binaries of difference" (Glick Schiller 2012b) also offered little to explain the continuing outpourings of support or the daily sociabilities that unite migrants and non-migrants.

While this chapter focuses on sociabilities of displacement and emplacement in Manchester, we found similar sociabilities in Halle. Our research helps us to identify a crucial component of the larger puzzle of what brings migrants and non-migrants together in relationships of mutual support around the world. To date, when scholars address how migrants build their daily lives as they settle in a new place, they too rarely examine what Hage

(2014, 236) calls a "space of commonality." As Hage notes (2014, 236), this domain of commonality characterizes "any desirable intersubjective relation. We do it all the time with people we care about despite being differently positioned in hierarchical structures." Yet most of the literature approaches relationships between natives and migrants as one in which newcomers are tolerated through the bridging of differences. Those outside the national community are classified as "strangers," to whom we respond with a different dimension of affect, one of "humanitarianism" or assistance, compared to the shared solidarity that accompanies a shared national origin (Kymlicka 2015, 4).

Migration Theory and Migrants' Social Relations

The emphasis on difference in social research and in policy seeking to respond to migration is not surprising. For more than a century, the question of living with difference has pervaded Western theories and imaginaries of the city. Initially viewing urban vistas as characterized by "mutual strangeness," Simmel ([1903] 2002, 15) posited that city dwellers formed situational, utilitarian, and illusive social ties devoid of the overlapping unities of kinship, neighboring, and cultural commonalities that knit together rural communities. The classic rural–urban dichotomy (Tönnies [1877] 1957; Wirth 1938) envisioned a rural folk society unified by multiple dense social ties, while urban dwellers were thought to live detached, alienated solitary lives. When urban ethnographers began to contest this dichotomy (Miner 1952), they adopted the anthropological penchant for studying territorially situated cultures and selected locations that they thought shared common class or ethnic traditions (Whyte 1943; Young and Willmott 1957; Gans 1962; Liebow 1968). They portrayed cities as composed of multiple neighborhood-based communities (Apparicio 2006; Baumann 1996; Stack 1974). When the rural-urban continuum (Redfield 1940) was repudiated in social theory, many researchers continued to understand social solidarities as built on shared territory, culture, and culturally or religiously inflected forms of identity.

Debates about multiculturalism, diversity, and mixity have been imbricated with this flawed social theory. Researchers begin with the methodological nationalist assumptions that nation-states are culturally homogenous and that homogeneity produces social cohesion. They also assume that both the "native" local communities and the national cultures are homologous. That is to say, if you study a neighborhood, you can say something about the social cohesion of the nation-state. This approach defines all migrants not only as introducing difference but also as inherently threatening the social fabric of community and state. According to Robert Putnam (2007, 139), a seminal researcher in the contemporary study of social cohesion who has been widely quoted as well as critiqued, "immigration and ethnic diversity tend to reduce social solidarity and social capital."

Both scholars and policy makers who oppose diversity and multiculturalism and those who seek to valorize multicultural difference have tended to equate migrants with concepts of diversity (Huntington 1996; Gilroy 2004; Grillo 2005; Johnston, Poulsen, and Forrest 2010; Eriksen 2010). Putnam argues that "new evidence from the US suggests that in ethnically diverse neighborhoods residents of all races tend to 'hunker down.' Trust (even of one's own race) is lower, altruism and community cooperation rarer, friends fewer" (2007, 138).[3] For Putnam and others engaged in integration polices who see the value of immigration, "fragmentation," which they see as caused by migration, may not be inevitable "in the long run." It could be "overcome . . . by creating new, cross-cutting forms of social solidarity and more encompassing identities" (2007, 138). A view that nation-states constitute discrete societies that must maintain social cohesion to prosper and be secure informs metaphors of bridging difference and crosscutting solidarities, which have been central to discussions of migrants in cities.

Most ethnographers of migrants in cities continue to study neighborhoods or sites such as markets and festivals or ethnic or ethnoreligious organizations because they are perceived as locations where "differences" can be overcome or mediated. Often scholars who study migrant sociabilities within migrant neighborhoods also situate migrants and non-migrants within differential temporalities. A neighborhood imaginary invokes time as well as space. To envision spaces as imbricated by traditional cultural difference is also to convey a different temporality that denies migrants' coevalness.

Contemporary urban ethnographers, committed to countering political narratives that define migrants' cultural difference as problematic, argue that diversity and difference are assets central to everyday urban social life (Vertovec 2007). They stress that multiple intersecting and fluid diversities are found in everyone's lives, including those who face racialization, discrimination, and differentiation (Vertovec and Wessendorf 2010). These scholars of everyday lives and urban sociabilities of people of migrant background build on pioneering work by Baumann (1996) and Back (1996), which contests the utilization of an ethnic lens.

Yet despite this foundation, scholars of the everyday highlight cultural and religious "diversity" (Berg, Gidley, and Sigona 2013), "superdiversity"

(Vertovec 2007) or "living-with-difference" (Nowicka and Vertovec 2014) and search for how ethnoreligious differences are "bridged" (Wise and Velayutham 2014). Paul Gilroy (2004) links his conceptualization of "convivialities" to "multiculture." Amin (2012, 5) insists that although convivialities emerge, "a slew of personal and collective labeling conventions—inherited, learnt, absorbed and practiced that flow into the moment of the encounter" are central to social life. A vast body of literature identifies organizations built around ethnoreligious differences as the primary venues of migrant incorporation into the social, political, and cultural life of countries and places of settlement (Pries 2007; Pries and Sezgin 2012).

These organizations are seen as the primary vehicle of migrant settlement as well as transnational connection (Portes, Escobar, and Radford 2007; Portes and Fernández-Kelly 2015; Waldinger 2015). Most research examines the role of these organizations in the claim-making processes of migrants who seek recognition as a collective representative of what they project as a unified ethnic or religious community within the city of settlement or the national society (Glick Schiller 1977; Sökefeld 2006). Setting aside whether, where, and when these organizations represent the migrants for whom they claim to speak, confining research to the activities and leadership of these organizations keeps us from studying migrants' multiple sites of sociabilities. Moreover, these kinds of organizations generally persist to the extent that they become part of organized state–"minority" relations and receive some type of public funding.

Generally, urban ethnographers researching migrant neighborhoods have persistently disregarded the broader multiscalar structural forces within which patterns of inequality, opportunity, residence, and sociability are constituted and restructured (Kalandides and Vaiou 2012) or have relegated them to "context." It is insufficient to relegate structural issues to what Leeds (1980) and Brettell (2003) call "the city as context" (see also Cadge et al. 2010) without connecting them to multiscalar value-creation processes taking place in these cities. Only by setting aside neighborhoods or migrant organizations as the primary and often sole units of study and analysis can urban sociability researchers make visible processes of displacement and emplacement shaped by the structural positioning, regeneration possibilities, and limitations of a city.

Over the years, a potent critique of the literature that sees economic disparities as threatening to social cohesion has developed. A number of researchers have found that lack of social cohesion in economically restructured cities is related to social inequality and disparities of wealth (Kearns and Forrest 2000; Ratcliffe 2011). In addition, important bodies of research document that worksites and social movements continue to be significant loci of urban dwellers' sociabilities and social networks, despite neoliberal restructuring of urban life (Amin 2012; Leitner, Peck, and Sheppard 2007). However, much of this research on solidarities ignores the presence and participation of migrants, despite the fact that migrants, whatever their legal status, occupy key niches in neoliberal service economies and have become again, as they were in the past, significant actors in social justice movements.

Theorizing and Studying Sociabilities of Emplacement

In summary, the social theory upon which research on diversity, superdiversity, and bridging diversity is built leaves no room to observe and analyze sociabilities. Research on the relationship between cities and migrants requires a concept of the social that is built on domains of commonality, as they arise within the multiscalar constitution of place and time (Glick Schiller 2012b, 2015a, 2016; Eckert 2016). It may well be that the penchant in anthropology for the study of signification (Geertz 1973) and, since the 1980s, for research on identities of difference and identity politics left little conceptual space for theories of relationality, which are only now reemerging. We suggest that a useful step in theorizing relationality is to distinguish between sociality and sociability.

The term "sociality" denotes the entire field within which individuals are embedded in a "matrix of relationships with others" (Strathern 1996, 66). Much of what is described as living with difference, encompassing relationships of "commonplace diversity" and the "ethos of mixing" (Wessendorf 2013) as well as conflicts and hostilities made visible in terms of difference (Rogaly and Qureshi 2013), is best understood as sociality.

In contrast, "sociabilities" can be defined as social relations that provide pleasure, satisfaction, and meaning by giving actors a sense of being human. In this definition, we build on the Latin origins of the term "social," which refers to fellowship and companionship (Isin 2008; Brodie 2008; Çağlar 2015), and return to the concept of sociability offered by Simmel. He defined "sociability" as relations in which "one 'acts' as though all were equal, as though he esteemed everyone," exactly because these interactions are *not* about difference (Simmel [1910] 1949, 257). For Simmel, the stringent demands of "real life" ([1910] 1949, 255) impose limits on situations in which this form of social relationship is possible. However, beginning with the path-breaking work of Lofland (1985), urban researchers began to document multiple forms of daily sociabilities based on shared affect and demonstrated that urbanites frequently turn casual informal meetings into ongoing affective relationships linking them to urban spaces (Pink 2012).

Our research explored sociabilities that developed even though the people who came together had unequal access to resources, including information, skills, and institutional networks. We examined social bonds that emerged from a perhaps limited but potent shared set of experiences, emotions, and aspirations: "a desire for human relationships" (Glick Schiller, Darieva and Gruner-Domic 2011, 415; see also Glick Schiller and Irving 2015). Such interactions can be fleeting or can persist and develop over time (Lofland 1985). Our respondents used the term "human" to refer to the domains of commonality that emerged from some of their interactions.[4] Some used the word "friendship" to encompass sociabilities that combined mutual support and positive affect.

Our research took place in Manchester, where, aside from the historic east end / west end division dating from French Canadian settlement, named neighborhoods were generally not units of self-identity, service provision, or governance.[5] Distinctive neighborhood cultures were not part of the contemporary ethos of the city, although the city did have areas associated with richer and poorer residents and areas that could be considered multiethnic, with migrants from diverse countries. However, people of migrant background lived throughout the city. This research challenges the neighborhood bias of urban ethnographies drawn from "global" or primary cities. Rather than operating with an assumption that cities consist of neighborhoods whose residents identify with each other and share an experience of community, we need to explore whether neighborhoods become important sites of sociability and, if so, under what conditions, when, and through what kind of relations.

By developing a global, relational perspective on all potential sites of sociability, including neighborhoods, our research in Manchester raises broader questions about the nature and sites of migrants' sociabilities in all cities. We join with authors such as Kearns and Forrest (2001, 21–25) who critique the reemergence of "the neighbourhood . . . as an important setting for many of the processes which supposedly shape social identity and life-chances." Our goal is to address the multiple hierarchies and institutionally networked structures of power within which these spaces and their conditions are constituted (see also Gijsberts, van der Meer, and Dagevos 2012).

All residents must build their daily sociabilities and the socialities of their lives within their city's multiscalar political and economic restructuring and its concomitant narratives about itself and its residents (Smith 2002). Relationships of urban residents to each other are shaped by these processes, which in turn contribute to the restructuring of each city and the construction of its narratives. To address, particularly in cities, what sites and what kinds of sociabilities emerge between people categorized as native or local and newly arrived migrants, we suggest that our units of study become the social relations formed by people as they encounter each other. The ethnography in this chapter indicates that from 2000 to 2008, the period of most of our participant observation and interviewing, migrant newcomers of various legal statuses in Manchester, including the undocumented, were able to build urban sociabilities in similar ways.[6] The sociabilities we describe were sociabilities of emplacement. They connected migrant newcomers and local people who together built aspects of their livelihood and social belonging in Manchester within the context of opportunities and constraints of a particular historical conjuncture.

Restructuring and Sociabilities of Emplacement

The relations of sociability we found in Manchester must be understood as part of residents' responses—migrant and non-migrant alike—to the city's redevelopment strategies and their outcome. As we indicated in chapter 1, to confront conditions Manchester faced, including its negative reputation as deindustrialized, backward, and having an abandoned and dangerous city center, city leaders and developers, around the millennium, crafted a migrant-friendly narrative. This narrative made a difference to the way migrants related to Manchester; indeed, a representative of the Office of City Planning (interview O., September 2002) insisted that migrants "were not a drain" on the city but, to the contrary, vital to its redevelopment. The mayor at the time forcefully conveyed the message that migrants were welcome. In 2002, he called on his fellow citizens "to continue to make Manchester a welcoming threshold to New Americans" (Baines 2002). Newcomers could settle in an environment where they were not politically targeted.

However, as we documented in chapter 1, Manchester was similar to Halle and Mardin in that it provided few resources for settlement. Without well-funded institutions and voluntary organizations, all newcomers, migrants as well people arriving from elsewhere in the country, generally depended on personal networks for support in their processes of emplacement. Our data revealed that, to learn the routines of local daily life, find work, shop, and access schools and medical care, migrant newcomers often forged relationships of mutual support and positive affect with people seen as local.

Our respondents searched for individuals who might help them: in many cases, migrants took the lead in establishing forms of sociability. Doing so transformed their lives as well the lives of those with whom they interacted. As Leila, an Iraqi refugee, recalled: "The people are friendly. Not at first, you have to talk to them. . . . My neighbor had a bad attitude toward me, but I made her cookies and now she is nice" (interview L., March 10, 2002).

Our research revealed that newcomers in Manchester established sociabilities in three types of sites: proximal, workplace, and institutional. In all three sites of emplacement, relationships based on domains of commonality, not differences or common cultural backgrounds, were pathways of emplacement for newcomers and locals alike. Emplacement opportunities and new displacement situations arose within the regeneration processes that altered spaces and conditions of daily life, including housing, employment, and the organization of civil society.

PROXIMAL RELATIONS

While Manchester's city center redevelopment, documented in chapter 1, had some "success" in that the city center became repopulated and local retail activity increased, its dispossessive aspects—the revaluation of land, housing, and storefronts—increased the precarity of the city's less wealthy population, both migrants and non-migrants. Urban regeneration and its accompanying revaluation of land and real estate during the years of our research produced a situation in which Manchester's population became more impoverished as redevelopment proceeded (City of Manchester nd). The poverty rate increased from 10.6 percent in 2000 to 13.7 percent in 2007 (before the subprime crisis) and to 14.2 percent in 2013 (City Data 2015). The cost of living index in Manchester was higher than the national average (City Data 2015).

Housing costs rose as housing prices inflated through gentrification processes, leading to a rise in rent and to very low vacancy rates after 2000.[7] Investors who bought rental property charged higher rents, and new owners faced large mortgage payments. Property owners also found that the assessed value of their property rose and, with it, their property taxes. City coffers had been emptied as Manchester borrowed money for regeneration. The redevelopment of the city center was made possible by public financing of 85 percent of the 65-million-dollar cost of land acquisition and construction (Lincoln

NE City Government 2008, 96). These debts had to be repaid from tax revenues. This required increasing property taxes and decreasing public services.

At the same time, during relatively high employment—with rates fluctuating in relationship to the 2000 and 2008 financial crises—the wage rate remained relatively low. Many residents faced higher housing costs but not rising incomes. This situation affected the social relations of many migrants and non-migrants in Manchester. Many of our respondents shared a sense of precarity, which they expressed in numerous conversations with members of our research team. Tenants shared concerns about being forced from a neighborhood by higher rents or job loss. Homeowners simultaneously faced difficulties paying taxes and mortgages. They also feared deterioration in the quality and security of local neighborhoods in the wake of cuts in public services and the inability of some neighbors to maintain their property. While this sense of being at risk was common in poorer neighborhoods, respondents generally did not have a sense of the neighborhood as community in the forms depicted by social cohesion researchers.

We did find that migrants and non-migrants sought support, solace, and a sense of commonality with certain neighbors who lived close by. Most of our migrant respondents found themselves initially in dilapidated rental housing near the city center, in areas where some of the buildings had been constructed to house workers, immigrant and nonimmigrant, during Manchester's long, slow industrial decline in the first half of the twentieth century. These streets also contained stately large houses that over time had been converted into multifamily dwellings. Interspersed were three-story apartment buildings built between the 1950s and the 1970s. Through random encounters with someone living nearby, or within the shared proximal space of an apartment building or apartment complex, newcomers found supportive and sympathetic people who became key to their emplacement in Manchester.

Kate, a refugee and single mother from Sierra Leone, was one of many people whose ability to become settled in the city was linked to someone she met in her first place of residence, a three-story building with several apartments on each floor. The building housed refugees from different countries as well as people native to Manchester or to the region. Kate explained: "The people on the first floor were 'black and white' and were friendly with me. Roz lived on the first floor. She is very good. She is . . . unable to walk. She helped me read and played cards. After that building was sold, she had no apartment near me and moved to Maine [the neighboring state]. But she brought her friend Karen . . . [who still comes to visit and brings her daughter]. . . . Roz still visits me and I like her" (interview K., April 14, 2002).

Kate's memories of the conflict in her homeland were often too painful for her to readily talk about, but Roz, her neighbor, was initially able to approach Kate's traumatic experiences through her own disability and its accompanying social barriers. Soon after they met, both were displaced by the city's regeneration processes and the redevelopment of property in their neighborhood. Roz was not only forced from her home but also from her neighborhood, city, and state. She was not able to find the housing and support services she needed in Manchester. However, Roz and Kate maintained their relationship, and, through Kate, Roz continued to be linked to social networks in Manchester.

Several respondents reported that they "found" people who proved to be significant in their lives on streets where they lived. These strangers, who became companions, sometimes offered immediate help, ranging from food to a telephone calling card and survival English. Such local, serendipitous relations often linked a newcomer to work or to local institutions without the mediation of communitarian structures and narratives. On the street where he initially settled, Emrah, who fled from what is now Bosnia, found not only informal employment but also someone he liked and trusted.

Emrah recalled that "the first two months I was here I got to know a black man, Dave—an American. I was watching him from across the street. He was mowing the lawn and . . . I said 'I can help.' He offered me a job working with him. This was my first job, although it was informal. I consider this man to be like a brother. I still see him, although now I have moved" (interview E., February 6, 2002). In understanding this social bond, it is helpful to note that Dave was no stranger to precarity, although he was a local with more knowledge about how to get by in Manchester's low-wage economy. Manchester offered few opportunities to any of its residents, and even fewer to African Americans.

After Emrah managed to buy a house, he moved from his initial location. In the short term, the ability of Manchester's working poor to access subprime mortgages mediated some of the high costs of local housing. They could buy houses, but many buildings needed repair and were bought at inflated prices and with loans that had adjustable interest rates. Migrants were targets for these loans and their subsequent dispossessive processes. Local real estate brokers told a team member who was studying migrant home buying that loans backed by the Federal Housing Authority were granted even when mortgage costs were 50 percent of the borrower's income (Buchannan 2002). Until 2008, a widespread strategy of migrant newcomers was purchasing a multifamily house that could shelter not only their family but also tenants or relatives, who could contribute to mortgage payments. Our interviews with local real estate agents made clear that local lenders were more willing to give mortgages to migrants who bought multifamily homes.

Proximal relations between migrant landlords and migrant tenants sometimes led to new sociabilities that furthered the emplacement of both families. When Hubert and Helene bought a two-family house, the ground floor apartment was rented for a while by another migrant family from Vietnam, with whom they shared information about Manchester as well as informal social relations. When one of Hubert and Helene's children graduated from high school, these tenants were among their guests. After a few years, Hubert and Helene faced foreclosure. They were forced to move when the house's aging plumbing required tens of thousands of dollars just as their variable mortgage rate ballooned to something they could not afford. Their tenants were also forced to move, and the relationship weakened, though it did not fully break.

Proximity did not automatically lead to sociability. Migrants who saw themselves as superior in class to their neighbors might keep their distance, despite being ethnically similar. Boris, a Bosnian refugee, initially related to his neighbors in "a good part of the city" where his family first rented a house. The commonality of class he felt with his neighbors made him feel at home: "Neighbors were talking and . . . visiting, it was good. Some Vietnamese, but mostly Americans we were visiting." This experience evoked his sense of home. "My home is where I find myself comfortable and that I can live . . . to be free, to be safe. Anywhere in the world. Just, I want like peace, I want to live in happiness. So it doesn't matter if it's Bosnia or here, just I want the peace, you know, human rights, a normal life." However, the multifamily house that his family later bought was in a poorer neighborhood. Boris avoided his neighbors because "they did not lead respectable lives" (interview B., June 6, 2003).

Sometimes proximity precipitated hostility. In the same building where Kate made her first friend in Manchester, she also encountered hostility. On the second floor, one "white woman . . . turned her back to me whenever I passed." Kate challenged her, saying, "Did I do something bad to you, you don't say hi?" The woman answered, "Maybe I don't want you here." However, like other respondents who described threats or conflict, Kate emphasized that this incident did not characterize her reception. Instead, she said, "I like Manchester. . . . My children and I are getting help and I meet nice people" (interview K., April 14, 2002).

In some instances, a concern for protecting the street and its property values could turn hostility into mutual support. In several instances, migrants and non-migrants came together out of a need to respond to conditions in a neighborhood that had been marginalized, criminalized, and devalued, usually through the processes of dispossession and repossession. The Nuhanovich family, who came to Manchester as refugees from Bosnia, bought the two-family house that they had been renting and began investing their time and labor in renovating it. Their renovations bound them to neighbors who at first kept their distance but over time began to help and exchange labor and supplies with the family (field notes, March 9, 2003). After housing prices dropped dramatically as a result of the subprime mortgage crisis, Hubert and Helene bought a house on a street that previously had no migrants. They were warmly welcomed by one neighbor who continued to be a source of information and support, but another neighbor was openly hostile, to the point of waving guns. Still, after several years of not only living in their new house but also clearly keeping it in good repair, the hostile neighbors came to see Hubert and Helene as local residents and warned them about a gang coming into the area and breaking into cars (field notes, April 16, 2015).

Our respondents' generally positive view of their reception in Manchester was supported by city statistics that recorded only one violent incident in 2008 and three in 2009. Although these statistics are inadequate measures of racial or religious slurs and other forms of discrimination or attack, Manchester had a very low incidence of "hate crimes" "compared to other multiculturally-dense communities nationally" (City of Manchester Health Department 2011).

We have designated the sites of these sociabilities as proximal rather than neighborhood-based for several reasons. First, as we indicated above, Manchester's neighborhoods were generally not units of self-identity, service provision, or governance. Second, relationships with neighbors did not necessarily develop on the basis of communal identities, be they cultural, ethnic, religious, or neighborhood-based. Third, participants in proximal relationships did not seek to initiate neighborhood-wide, territorially based solidarities. If any broader localized collective identity emerged, it was identification with the City of Manchester. Identification with the city was widespread among the newcomers we interviewed.

Residential proximity in itself did not produce sociabilities. What brought people together was not simply shared space but the fact that each, in very different ways, drew from their own history of social or spatial displacement and their own precarities to seek new social relations of emplacement in the city. Although residential proximity was one means through which domains of commonality were facilitated, the sociabilities of our respondents were not confined to relationships with those who lived nearby. Migrants moved through the city and the region, forming relationships in different sites of sociability.

Workplaces have long been sites for the study of social relations. Some of this literature developed within studies of labor history, labor relations, or work councils in various contexts, including that of colonial rural labor migration (Kapferer 1972), domestic workers (Gutierrez-Rodriguez 2010), and workplace teams in scientific projects (Amin 2012). Our interest here, however, is how newcomers to a city participate in sociabilities of emplacement within multiscalar processes that are shaped by urban regeneration. In this regard, it is important to note that, given the precarity of the local economy, not only the workers but also the managers, professionals, or even owners were in relatively insecure positions. Many sociabilities we traced remained confined to the workplace; others extended into social relationships that continued outside of and after workplace encounters.

In addition to restructuring conditions of settlement that had been actuated by property redevelopment, rising land and real estate values, and mortgage markets, city structuring also produced changing conditions and possibilities of local employment for migrants and non-migrants in Manchester. Waves of investment and disinvestment in local industries and businesses marked the multiscalar restructuring of the city and region. City developers sought new industries by advertising that Manchester offered good workers, including immigrants and refugees, for relatively low wages; employers who moved their businesses to Manchester tended to pay relatively low wages. Many of the new jobs, whether they were for high-paid professionals or for low-paid workers classified as low skilled, were short lived. The industries and new businesses, generated by the city's redevelopment and tax policy came and went, leaving behind newly rebuilt and rapidly abandoned buildings and sites. Although patterns of layoffs and business closures did not constitute a lineal downward trend, manufacturing in New Hampshire declined from 13.4 percent in 1998 to 9.5 percent in 2004, and much of the decline centered around Manchester (City Data 2015).

Initially, many newcomers found work in the shrinking manufacturing sector. Factories offered very low wages, benefiting from the arrival of refugees whom US policy required to take the first job they were offered. Working conditions were hazardous, unions were generally nonexistent, and paternalistic personalized management policies functioned to forestall workers' struggles for improved working conditions. Hiring was often through personal networks of managers and workers, and more experienced workers were expected to informally train and discipline newcomers.

Given that Manchester didn't contain concentrations of people who shared a common ethnicity and that most workplaces had relatively few employees, migrants relied on coworkers with different cultural backgrounds. Armando, educated as an architect in Colombia, had to master assembly line and kitchen skills as an undocumented worker in Manchester. He explained the need for assistance and the significance of workplace sociabilities: "The moment I begin at the factory, I start to be a dependent person. . . . What I need to do, I don't understand. Jose, my Puerto Rican friend, said 'don't worry. . . . I made that [mistake] a lot of times.' . . . This guy was a really remarkable friend" (interviews A., May 24, 2003; October 10, 2003).

The welcome extended to newcomers often went beyond sharing workplace knowledge. Armando continued: "So Jose says to me, 'Hey. Are you hungry? . . . Take my food! Enjoy!' And I say, 'But it's not my food, you are supposed to eat.' He says, 'You don't know my wife. She's doing a lot of food for me, and don't you see how fat I am? . . . So please eat it.' That was for almost 18 months, the same situation!" (interviews A., May 24, 2003; October 10, 2003).

Armando and Jose were helped by their common knowledge of Spanish and their mutual understanding that, although Armando was an undocumented newcomer and Jose was a native-born citizen, they shared the insecurities that came with racialization as Hispanic. But, in many accounts, sociabilities emerged between individuals who did not share language, racialization, or gender. While commonalties of practice brought people together, our respondents' descriptions of their workplaces were not those of a "community of practice" (Amin 2012, 39). Rather, they described significant affective and supportive interpersonal relationships, often forged within precarious employment situations.

For example, Emrah, the refugee who first found work through someone he met on the street where he lived, next worked in a local electronics factory owned by a multinational conglomerate. The refugee resettlement agency required him to take the position without training, even though he worked alongside "people from Vietnam, Puerto Rico, Mexico, Ukraine, Russia, Romania, and Americans" and could speak to none of them (interview E., February 6, 2002). However, Emrah was able to find a place for himself through a new friend. "From the beginning my closest friend at work was an American woman, Linda, of about forty-five. I worked with her for about three years. She . . . helped me from when I first came by explaining things to me. When I started I spoke Bosnian and she spoke English but somehow we understood each other and she would explain what the supervisor wanted." What Linda did not explain, and both Emrah and Linda experienced together, was the precariousness of earning a living through industrial work in twenty-first-century Manchester—a precarity that was part of the multiscalar restructuring of disempowered city. Emrah and Linda shared experiences of reduced hours, layoffs, and persistent rumors of factory closure, which came to pass several years later.

Not all factories offered conditions that encouraged these kinds of supportive relations, and at some workplaces open racism greeted the newcomers. At the beginning of our research, a meat processing plant, which was one of the larger employers in Manchester until it closed, began to employ increasing numbers of refugees and immigrants. During this period, managers at the processing plant began to delegate the most difficult jobs to Sudanese refugees, and, according to many workers encouraged or at least tolerated racial slurs against them. With the support of a local immigrants' rights coalition, the local union, previously quiescent about defending workers' rights, began to challenge the health and safety conditions in the plant. It also initiated an active membership recruitment. As part of the union drive, some workers, both non-migrants and migrants of various backgrounds, joined together to support the union and to discuss racism at the factory.

As our research began, we noted the effects from the dot-com crash in 2000, which decimated the "new economy" high-tech industries recently established in the region. These were the industries that urban developers in Manchester and around the world had heralded as the new economy that would revitalize cities and justify new waves of public investment in city center redevelopment. This dramatic downturn affected Manchester's migrant professionals and their networks and had myriad ramifications for displacement and emplacement. For example, Hubert and Helene's friend Marcel, who borrowed on his credit card to help them fly to Manchester and to whom they had looked for financial and emotional support, was laid off from his technology firm, which then closed permanently. Unable to find other permanent professional employment in Manchester, Marcel finally left the city.

Similarly, as a result of the high-tech downturn around the millennium, Rajesh and Nagamalla found themselves opening a restaurant and living within an entirely different social network of emplacement than during their first years in the city. Rajesh had been sent by his family in India to study at the local private university and then became a permanent resident working for a computer programming company. However, after he was laid off, he opened an Indian restaurant with his Pakistani friend, Nagamalla. Nagamalla had worked at a technology firm for more than three years, had bought a house and a car, and had settled into a middle-class life, only to find himself unemployed when his technology firm folded (field notes, April 4, 2003). The restaurant the two friends founded provided employment not only for both partners but also for several workers, including Raul, the dishwasher.

A carpenter from Uruguay who came to Manchester on a visitor's visa in search of greater prosperity, Raul formed a strong friendship with Nagamalla. Soon after, the partners fired Raul because he lacked legal permission to work and because, in the wake of the September 11, 2001, US global war on terrorism, the Muslim partners were afraid that their business would face additional scrutiny. Raul moved on to work in a Chinese restaurant, but he stayed close friends with Nagamalla (interview R., May 21, 2003). Migrants such as Emrah, who had official refugee status, and Armando and Raul, who were undocumented workers, were able to forge workplace sociabilities. In their workplaces, newcomers with varying legal statuses, languages, and religions found, in Armando's words, "at least one great friend" (interviews A., May 24, 2003; October 10, 2003).

Newcomers also forged workplace sociabilities of emplacement with managers or employers, forming social connections that were sometimes life-altering. For example, Tuan, one of the first Vietnamese refugees to settle in Manchester, asked John, a white engineer and a native of New Hampshire, if he would sponsor Tuan's family's application for resettlement. Impressed by Tuan's drive and job commitment, John and his family cosponsored Tuan's parents, several siblings, and their nuclear families. Tuan obtained a college degree, found a better job, bought a house, and became a leader at the local Buddhist temple. Over the years, he and his extended family continued to include John in family celebrations. Then John lost his engineering job through neoliberal corporate restructuring and confronted the fact that Manchester offered limited opportunities for professionals or entrepreneurs. He tried running a small business but was unsuccessful. At a Buddhist dinner, Tuan's extended family offered John a Christmas card that contained warm wishes and hundreds of dollars (field notes, 2003).

Similarly, friendships between the Indian and Pakistani restaurant owners and Raul, the dishwasher, cut across divides between employer and worker, legal statuses, cultural and religious backgrounds, and languages and lasted beyond their common employment. Raul told us, "I have good friendships with the people from the restaurant. They've felt like a family to me, they've never made me feel bad, I always feel comfortable with them. . . . I've been to visit Nagamalla's family, a birthday or something. They always invite me. When they have a get together in his house, he always invites me. I think they're very good people" (interview R., May 21, 2003).

While many of these sociabilities had as their context the mutual precarity of Manchester's transforming economy, in some cases other forms of social dislocation, such as aging or disability, formed the context of the relationship. Mijo, a young Bosnian refugee, formed a long-term relationship with the elderly veterinarian who had employed him as an assistant and who "became a good friend." Mijo recalled that "at first he seemed totally different from me. He was a businessman, materialistic, patriotic Republican but he wanted to learn more. I think I changed him." Increasingly isolated as he approached retirement, the veterinarian had never left the United States until he traveled to Bosnia and became part of Mijo's transnational kinship networks (interview M., January 28, 2002).

Pierre, a college-educated refugee from Rwanda, managed to gain a US college education by caring for Albert, who was severely disabled. Serving as the low-wage caretaker for severely disabled people was one of the jobs available to new migrants in Manchester. Albert's parents came to be among the people Pierre felt closest to in Manchester. He reported, "If I ever have a problem, I call them" (interview P., March 14, 2002). While Albert's parents provided advice and support, Pierre gave them confidence that their son was being cared for with respect—a respect that was evident during the interview we conducted in the apartment Pierre shared with Albert. As in many of the sociabilities we explored, although the relationship was unequal in terms of social, economic, and cultural capital, both sides found sources of satisfaction. Both also, although unequally, brought to their interactions their experiences of feeling out of place. Albert's parents' openness to Pierre was mediated by their disabled and stigmatized son's social positioning.

Social service jobs such as caretaking became increasingly frequent forms of employment in the fifteen years of our research. The new economy that the urban regeneration of the city center and surrounding neighborhoods brought to Manchester involved "an expanding service sector," which, as Manchester's Office of Economic Development (City of Manchester 2009) conceded, "generally provide[d] lower wage jobs." "These are suitable for entry part-time employees seeking supplementary income, but cannot generally support a livable household income" (City of Manchester 2009). Health and human services emerged among the largest employers. The employment trajectories of Hubert and Helene and of their children reflect this history. Although he was a former banker and she was a teacher, both husband and wife initially found employment in a small textile factory in the greater Manchester area. This factory, owned by a multinational conglomerate that did most of its production in China, closed and then reopened, employing for a time Hubert and Helene's eldest daughter. By 2015, Hubert had worked for several years as a low-paid human services worker, and Helene worked as a hospital cleaner. Their college-educated sons could find only managerial jobs in fast-food restaurants.

Many of the industries that stayed on in the greater Manchester region were tied to the "defense" industry. New Hampshire, including Manchester, had a concentration of military production facilities, but they featured rapid employment fluctuations, with hirings followed by layoffs (Coughlin 2010). The defense industry highlights the need for multiscalar analyses of the conjunctural forces within which Manchester residents experienced precarity and displacement that engendered sociabilities of emplacement. The various factors that constituted the ephemerality of armament-related workplaces included the growth of the US and European engagement in Afghanistan and Iraq after September 11, 2001, and the related massive increase of foreign and domestic surveillance industries. Beginning in 2011, US federal austerity programs, which heralded a "defense industry downturn," exacerbated the restructuring of this industry in a massive way and contributed to loss of employment. In 2015, Manchester reported a loss of industrial jobs, down 1.3 percent from the previous year (US Bureau of Labor Statistics 2016). However, the following year, employment in the defense industry expanded once again.

SOCIABILITIES INITIATED IN INSTITUTIONAL SPACES

Manchester's disempowered positioning was exacerbated by regeneration accompanied by tax abatements for local industries and new high-end residences, leaving the city with even fewer resources than before for maintaining vital city services, including education, health, and transportation. The severity of the situation became well known in 2015 after two major credit agencies downgraded city bonds, making borrowing more expensive (Fitch 2014; Moody's 2015). But those who worked in health and human services were aware of the city's economic precarity well before this disclosure because funds for these services, never ample, were further reduced. Meanwhile, social service organizations[8] that provided support for initial migrant settlement or self-organization, also never well-funded, were reduced at best to token funding, although political leaders in Manchester maintained their migrant-friendly narrative through 2009 (Greater Manchester Chamber of Commerce 2009). As we note in chapter 1, in the following years, the city became divided on the question of refugees. During the same period, federal funding continued its decades-long downward trajectory, with reduced funding for housing and support for the poor. Moreover, public funds were channeled to private investors and service providers, which prioritized profit-making activities.

The lack of public funding for ethnic organizations in Manchester even during the decades of the 1970s and 1980s, when such activities received public support in cities such as New York and Boston, and Manchester's continued disempowered positioning produced a different configuration of migrant organizing than in other more powerfully positioned locations of settlement. In Manchester, some ethnic or panethnic organizations have been short-lived or have transformed over time into multiservice corporate entities in which professionals administer short-term grants that reflect ever-changing priorities. As we note in chapter 1, the most enduring migrant organization, the Latin American Center, was transformed over the years into a multiservice agency within a consolidated broad-based nonprofit corporation, Southern New Hampshire Services, serving residents in sixty-five towns and three cities in Hillsborough and Rockingham Counties (Southern New Hampshire Services 2016). In discussing how they found a place for themselves in Manchester, our respondents, except for an occasional mention of the Latin American Center—especially their English classes—generally did not speak about the few existing, if rather transient, ethnic or panethnic organizations.[9]

However, our respondents mentioned other kinds of organizational activities that provided migrant newcomers with the possibility of forming relationships based on domains of commonality other than culture. They spoke of an array of city institutions that provided some services to the poor, including migrants: a refugee resettlement agency, a multiservice center, Catholic parishes and mainstream Protestant churches, schools, a library, and public housing. However, generally these institutions served as spaces of encounter rather than agents of integration that either provided assistance in emplacement or "bridged differences." Exceptions to this pattern were born-again Christian churches, Seventh-day Adventist Churches, and the multi-ethnic mosque that provided not only organizational platforms for network building but also direct mechanisms of support and emplacement. We discuss religious emplacement in chapter 4. Newcomers generally used these institutional spaces to form informal interpersonal connections.

Some of the local people whom our respondents met in institutional spaces were volunteers; others were paid staff and clients. Although begun in these institutions, the relationships that ensued extended far beyond institutional mission statements or the professional obligations of staff members or what these institutions expected from volunteers. This finding about the role of these individuals in forming sociabilities of emplacement with newcomers highlights the need for researchers to distinguish between institutionally organized processes of settlement and institutional sites that offer initial spaces of encounter through which individuals may endeavor to find their place in a city.

For example, Leila, an Iraqi refugee, met Fran in the office of the local public housing authority where Fran worked. A native of the city, Fran not only assisted Leila in obtaining access to Manchester's very limited amount of public housing but also provided her with emotional support, networks to other institutions, and ongoing friendship, none of which was in Fran's job description. Fran brought to the relationship her own sense of Manchester's inadequacy in providing opportunities for her own professional skills, her broader social and political horizons, and her aspirations for social justice (field notes, March 6, 2003).

Armando, the undocumented worker from Colombia, walked into a public library looking for support and met Tom. Tom, a middle-level manager forced to retire early because of corporate restructuring, found solace in the public library, as did other similarly displaced local people. Armando explained how he met Tom: "One day I request for help in the library and the librarian tells me that 'the person sitting over there is looking . . . for a person who needs help.' And I present myself and Tom and I start to be really really friends. He was protecting me, teaching me, showing me the new life of the US. . . . So, he was one of the important points in my life in the US. He sometimes calls me, 'Hey, what are you doing now? . . . I received a beautiful and unique bottle of wine and I want to enjoy one glass with you.' We are friends now for, say, almost 12 years" (interviews A., May 24, 2003; October 10, 2003).

Devout Catholics, Hubert and Helene met Nina at a Catholic church, but their relationship was not organized around the church or shared religious beliefs but reflected their shared commitments to social justice. Local parishes offered an African mass, and for a short period Helene sang in the choir organized for that mass. Their parish organized a one-on-one campaign to link nonimmigrant parishioners to new migrants, but its publicity depicted local people as culturally competent and migrants merely as recipients of their good will, rather than as individuals. This program failed to recruit Hubert, Helene, or many other migrants into the parish organization, despite migrants' need for services and their search for networks of support. Instead Hubert befriended Pastor Robert, a born-again Protestant pastor, after visiting his church. While Robert and Hubert maintained their religious differences, over the years Pastor Robert provided Hubert's family with material assistance and advice as part of an ongoing sociability built on mutual respect.

While we have been highlighting sociabilities initiated in institutional spaces, though not as part of the institutions' organized activities, other institutions, including local political parties and organizations linked to social movements, provided individual migrants with opportunities to constitute sociabilities of emplacement. As we indicate in chapter 1, in Manchester as in Halle, migrants could become activists within local political parties and form close relationships, including sociabilities of emplacement, based on a shared outlook and political aspirations. For example, when Saggy Tahir, an Indian-born migrant from Pakistan and chair of the Manchester Republican Committee, hosted an annual barbeque in his backyard, with New Hampshire's governor, state senators, the county sheriff, and aspiring mayoral and city council candidates as guests, he was forging personal sociabilities of emplacement as well as political solidarities (Manchester Republican Committee Newsletter 2003).

At the same time, sociabilities of emplacement were forged by migrants who participated over the years in various progressive organizations that were combatting racism and attacks on migrants. For example, chanting "No Human Being Is Illegal," Marcel, the migrant who facilitated Hubert and Helene's arrival in Manchester, participated in a demonstration in 2005 against using local police forces to arrest undocumented migrants. Marcel had become a member of the local immigrant rights organization and forged personal ties with some of its members. Despite his own increasingly desperate struggles to find work, he maintained ties that were not only political but sociabilities based on common commitments to social justice (field notes 2005).

Analytical Conclusions

The sociabilities we trace in various locations in the city were forged within insecure, rapidly changing settings of urban regeneration constituted by multiscalar actors within regional, national, and multinational networks of power. Increasingly, these regeneration processes impoverished the city, amplifying economic disparities, reducing economic opportunities, and dispossessing and displacing migrants and non-migrants alike. The dispossessed included individuals of various class positions.

This chapter has offered the opportunity to rethink debates about the nature of society and sociability as it is lived in specific cities, sites, and moments of time. In such a reexamination, it is important to set aside all communitarian approaches to society and social life that envision bounded communities as the building blocks of society, whether they be neighborhoods, organizations, cities, nation-states, religions, or cultural groups. Much of the angst about deteriorating national social fabrics and the supposed threats migrants pose to social cohesion are fueled by these assumptions (Arapoglou 2012). Once these assumptions are set aside, the questions become, first, on what basis is social life built and, second, how, where, and within what structural processes do sociabilities and domains of commonality emerge within a world of increasing precarity? To begin a different conversation, we have examined relationships among migrant and non-migrant displacements, sociabilities of emplacement, and city-making processes.

In proposing the study of sociabilities of emplacement and domains of commonality, we want to emphasize that it is always necessary to keep in focus the construction, imposition, and naturalization of categories of racial, ethnic, and religious difference and their use in legitimating exclusion, criminalization, and hyperexploitation. These categories were certainly present in Manchester, and newcomers were well aware of their use in justifying or excusing the low wages and dangerous working conditions, high rents, and poor housing they confronted. They also faced interpersonal discrimination; Kate was only one of many respondents who described instances of racism in Manchester. Armando and Jose bonded in part because they experienced racialization as Hispanic, a category sometimes understood locally as criminal and poor. As new conjunctural forces once again reconfigure Manchester, incidents of racism and antimigrant rhetoric have increased. Leila and her children encountered intensified Islamophobia. Once at home in Manchester, they began to feel friendless. Hubert and Helene's sons—by 2015, hardworking college graduates—encountered the police surveillance common to black youth in New Hampshire.

At the same time, within domains of commonality, migrants and nonmigrants in Manchester continued to organize against injustices at home as well as abroad. Natives and migrants, including the children of some migrants whom we met in our research, have joined organizations to combat racism and anti-Islamic politics and to support the struggle for social justice. We think our research provides insights into how sociabilities of the displaced emerge and constitute building blocks of the fluid constellations of urban social movements that seek economic and social justice (Mayer and Boudreau 2012). It is from sociabilities established by people, who construct domains of being human together despite their differences and who aspire for social justice, that struggles against the growing disparities and displacements of global capitalism can and do emerge (Susser 2012a).

We suggest that shared sensibilities, which underlie the daily sociabilities explored in this chapter, help explain the sudden outpouring of support that greeted refugees who defied barbed wire and guards on the eastern border of the European Union and began to walk into Europe in the fall of 2015. Press reports documented the wave of support for the newcomers but had difficulty explaining how public opinion seemed to change overnight from xenophobia to welcome (Kermani 2015).[10] Based on the discussions we had in German and Austrian cities at the time, we conclude that the people who greeted the refugees seemed to have been motivated by a commonality, an identification based on shared aspirations for safety, justice, and family life. The ranks of young and old, workers and professionals, social movement activists and those who had never joined a political movement literally embraced the newcomers and showered them with gifts. Halle/Saale and its surrounding villages were among many places that prepared to welcome refugees (field notes, 2015).

Unable to explain the depth and breadth of welcome given to the refugees in Europe, the press quickly returned to a xenophobic status quo, reporting, for example, that "migrant attacks reveal dark side of Germany" (Hill 2016). Certainly, in the emerging conjuncture, nationalist political parties with antimigrant platforms are gaining in strength throughout Europe and have claimed the US presidency and congressional majority. In many cities in the United States and in Europe, including Germany, attacks on migrants have increased significantly (Hill 2016). At the same time, volunteer networks and programs to welcome refugees, including the ones we observed in action in Halle, continued to function. Gallup public opinion polling in the United States in 2016 revealed that 76 percent of Republicans and 84 percent of the population as a whole favored paths to citizenship for undocumented immigrants and that two-thirds opposed deporting them (Jones 2016). Various polls also revealed that these sentiments were linked to experiences of daily sociability rather than to hospitality to strangers. Transatlantic Trends (2014), a survey conducted in the United States and eleven European countries, including Germany, reported that "majorities in both the United States (69 percent) and Europe (58 percent) said that they had at least a few friends who were born in other countries."

CHAPTER 4

Social Citizenship of the Dispossessed

EMBRACING GLOBAL CHRISTIANITY

In the storefront church, on a street replete with weatherworn buildings, some of them empty, almost all the congregants were white. Their clothing and their battered faces bore witness to struggles with unemployment, alcoholism, and precarious lives. Godsword and his wife, Elizabeth, both refugees from Nigeria, sat off to the side, not as guests but as leaders of the congregation.[1] They were dressed in their Sunday best, he in a suit and tie and she in a good dress and churchgoing hat. A white minister conducted most of the service, accompanied by a small group of musicians, one of whom was from Ghana and had a Harvard degree and a good job. When it was time for the sermon, Godsword preached to his fellow congregants, calling on them to step forward and pray that their bodies be purged of all evil spirits so that believers could be healed. Many did so, and at his touch they silently fell to the floor in a state of trance (field notes, March 4, 2003).

Nina and several students had gone to the storefront church assuming that because Godsword was a refugee from Nigeria, the members of his home church would be African immigrants. While Manchester had few migrants of Nigerian background in 2001, the year our research team first visited that church, there were enough immigrants and refugees from Africa to form a congregation with an African identity. In fact, a local Catholic parish had recently initiated an African mass. Most literature on migrants' congregations at the time portrayed them as ethnoreligious organizations (Warner 1998). However, as soon as we walked in the door of Godsword's home church, we realized that we had to set aside this ethnic lens in order to discover what this congregation could tell us about relationships between migrants and non-migrants and processes of dispossession and emplacement.

Over the next few years, Godsword formed an umbrella organization that united his home church with more than twenty congregations in the greater

Manchester area in a Resurrection Crusade to "take the city for Jesus." The Resurrection Crusade, whose central leadership comprised Godsword, a few non-migrants, and migrants from several different countries, was part of a multiscalar social field that stretched from Manchester to Texas, through various other US cities, and on to Israel, London, England, and Port Harcourt, Nigeria. It linked congregants to the Bush White House and to US imperial war making (Resurrection Crusade 2004; Glick Schiller 2005b). As we learned more about the reach and vision of those who joined the Crusade, we began to approach this practice of born-again Christianity as a pathway to social citizenship for the dispossessed, migrants and non-migrants alike.

In Halle in 2001, Nina began to participate in prayer meetings at the Miracle Healing Church. Over the next fifteen years, under the leadership of Pastor Joshua, a migrant from Nigeria, the church brought increasing numbers of non-migrants and migrants together to claim the city in the name of Jesus. To further their city-claiming project, Pastor Joshua connected his congregants to a multiscalar social field that extended into other German cities and across many national borders and linked the Miracle Healing Church to the same "world ministry" admired by Pastor Godsword in Manchester. This ministry wages "spiritual attacks against [the] forces of darkness" by "building God's victorious army" (Cerullo 2002, 2016).

In chapters 1, 2, and 3, we describe the multiscalar neoliberal restructurings and urban regeneration of Halle and Manchester and the intertwined multiple dispossessions and displacements of migrant and non-migrant residents of those cities. In this chapter, we examine the relationship between the determination of born-again church members and organizations to reclaim their disempowered cities for Jesus and the restructuring processes that were transforming their lives. The chapter situates our analysis of claim-making and related religious practices of born-again Christian congregations in these cities within debates over the nature and potency of social citizenship (Isin and Nielsen 2008).

Our focus is not on the entire belief system of what many scholars of religion characterize as Pentecostalism[2] (Robbins 2004) but on the territorialized narratives, forms of sociability, and struggles for empowerment of its congregation members and networks. Hence, our examination of this form of Christianity incorporates a multiscalar analysis that adds concepts of place, power, and historical conjuncture to Ruth Marshall's (2014, S352) call to think comparatively "about . . . [Pentecostal Christianity's] social and political effects across a range of very different contexts as well as the ways, if any, in which these Christians can be understood as forming a global community." Marshall writes: "One of the things that makes Pentecostals and charismatics distinctive and so successful is their development of an extremely robust paradigm for thinking globally, which is to say 'global spiritual warfare.' Intimately associated with the project of global evangelism, it is increasingly enacted through the growing phenomenon of reverse mission."

There is now an important body of scholarship that deploys the concept of social citizenship to examine claim-making practices of people who, either through legal means or through constructions of gendered, religious, racialized, or class-based difference, are excluded from the body politic (Çağlar 2015; Haney López 1998; Isin 2008; Lister 1997; Marshall 1964; Shafir 1998). Generally, discussions of social citizenship examine how those who are excluded use forms of discourse and social relations, organizations, and movements of inclusion to establish themselves as social and political actors. Most of that research focuses on classic domains of claim making in spheres of political action, including ethnic politics or secular social movements (Nuijten 2013). This chapter explores a less frequently queried site of political claim making, namely, religious congregations taking as their charter of citizenship the biblical promise that the Lord will guide a wandering people to a new land, promising them "ye shall possess it and dwell therein."

Religiously based claims to membership and belonging made by migrants and natives in disempowered cities shed new light on political energies generated by those stigmatized as different—racially, culturally, religiously, or because of their poverty. Even as city leaders and promoters framed these congregations as sites of cultural and religious difference, born-again congregation members told a different story through their sociabilities, solidarities, and moral economy. In Halle and Manchester, members of these born-again churches responded to various experiences of stigmatization and dispossession though acts and narratives of social citizenship, contesting disempowerment by political authorities by affirming that "there is no power except for God."

Social Citizenship Defined and Expanded

The word "citizen" is now generally understood to mean a full member of a modern state who has all possible legal rights, including the right to vote, to hold political office, and to claim public benefits. Citizens of states also have certain responsibilities that vary from country to country (Bauböck 1994; Shafir 1998). However, the clear-cut textbook-style definition gets very muddy in practice: in different nation-states, people practice and conceive of citizenship somewhat differently.

Conventional liberal understandings of citizenship focus on the rights of the nation-states to grant or deny membership and its accompanying rights and obligations. These approaches formulate citizenship as a legal relation between the individual subject and the nation-state, which grants membership and belonging to a political community. This community is envisaged as the nation that limits membership to those granted rights and responsibilities. As scholars of citizenship have noted, not all people who are legal citizens receive the same treatment from the state, nor can they all claim the same rights. Formal membership status is neither necessary nor sufficient to guarantee and generate an array of civic and socioeconomic rights.

There are often categories of people who are legal citizens according to the laws of a state yet face various forms of exclusion and denial of civil rights because they are not considered to be truly part of the nation. Those categorized and racialized as not belonging to the ethnoreligious nation are placed outside the legitimate body politic (Hamilton and Hamilton 1997; Haney López 1998; Lister 1997; Marshall 1964; Yuval-Davis 1997). As the past and present struggles for women's rights, gay and transgender rights, or welfare rights have indicated, full civil and property rights, including the protections of family law, may also be denied to people who are racialized as members of the dominant population but who contest normative definitions of gender, sexuality, or dominant middle-class values. These kinds of exclusions operate within systems of law and within civil society.

In a range of countries at the end of the twentieth century and the beginning of the twenty-first, struggles arose to contest categories of difference that denied legal citizens their civil rights and expanded the definition of national culture to include cultural and religious diversity. These movements deployed concepts of cultural citizenship and cultural rights to validate as equal members of the state those marked as culturally different from the dominant national culture. As defined by Rosaldo and Flores (1997, 57), cultural citizenship refers to "the right to be different with respect to the norms of the dominant national community, without compromising one's right to belong." This approach to citizenship was a product of struggles against assimilationist policies that limited full members in a polity to those who conformed to dominant cultural practice and values. Advocates of cultural citizenship sought to ensure that the multiple cultural heritages contained within a single nation-state would be recognized and respected; they wanted the practice of cultural difference to be accompanied by the assurance of equal opportunity (Glick Schiller 2005a).

Therefore, the concept of cultural citizenship focused on multiple identities and the diversity of cultural practices and norms. Advocates of cultural citizenship did not address how persons who are not legally citizens or not recognized as citizens participate in the common social, economic, and political life of a specific locality and nation-state and claim rights in these multiple quotidian domains. Their incorporative forms of participation and the claims that they generate move beyond the politics of difference and the cosmology of identity politics. These individuals contribute to shaping institutional practices and ideas about the state and governance within nation-states. To address their practices and claims, scholars have begun to speak of social citizenship, which foregrounds belonging and participation.

The concept of social citizenship shifted discussions of citizenship and belonging from legal arrangements to enactments (Isin 2002, 2008). Arguing for an approach to citizenship that was practice-centered, Clarke et al. (2014, 12) move beyond the concept of citizenship "as a legal/juridical and political status as corpus of rights and obligations and responsibilities." This scholarship arose and reflected a certain historical conjuncture as the trajectories of neoliberal capitalist agendas and their emphases on individualism, fluidity, and mobility made inroads in public discourse and forms of political struggle in Euro-American terrains. In the context of increasing access to social and civic rights in Europe from the 1970s to the 1990s, Soysal (1994) emphasizes that although migrants and their descendants lacked formal membership in the host nation, human rights regimes and their own claim-making practices give migrants various social, economic, civil, and cultural rights. In their quest to understand the social dynamics of participation in social and political processes of state making, and aware of the limitation of the formal status of membership, many scholars of citizenship began to speak of the practices and performance of citizenship rights, rather than merely the formal status of membership. Social citizens substantively assert rights to citizenship through social practices rather than through law. When people claim to belong to a state by collectively organizing to protect themselves against discrimination, when they receive rights and benefits from a state, or when they contribute to its development and the lives of its people through practices of political claim making, they are said to be social citizens.

This approach to citizenship, which is concerned with the moral and performative dimensions of membership beyond the domain of legal rights, defines the meaning and practices of participation and belonging as it is displayed within the public sphere (Holston and Appadurai 1999). Rather than a static view of citizenship inscribed into formal laws, which portrays rights as possessions, the concept of social citizenship offers a processual, contextual, and relational understanding of citizenship, emphasizing its "unfinished" nature (Balibar 2003). Social citizenship differs from legal citizenship because of the misalignment between formal citizenship and the actual exercise of rights, benefits, privileges, and voice.

Social citizenship practices emerge from social relationships. Often social citizenship is discussed in relation to social rights and benefits that facilitate the participation of citizens and noncitizens in a polity. As we note in our discussion of sociability in chapter 3, the term "social" stemmed from concepts of fellowship and companionship. Isin and his colleagues (Isin et al. 2008, 12; Brodie 2008) argue for a concept of social citizenship built on this understanding. In this sense, social citizenship refers to "the dense fabric of relations that constitute humans as social beings who coexist with their fellow beings in and through conflict and cooperation that undergird norms, laws and customs" (Isin 2008, 282). This important point of entry addresses sociability that binds people together beyond their legal status in a nation-state or locality.

When the excluded, the undocumented, the refugees, or the poor claim or demand their rights as valid members of the society through informal, unofficial, and/or illegal venues, they are practicing what is called "insurgent citizenship" (Holsten 2008; Varsanyi 2006). Isin and Nielsen (2008, 5–6) refer to such insurgencies as "acts of citizenship." This concept allows us to capture the moments when subjects constitute themselves as those making claims, asserting rights, and imposing obligations beyond the ones granted them by law (2008, 5–6). According to Isin and Nielsen, acts of citizenship "contest" habitus and citizenship practices by grounding their legitimacy and entitlements not in existing legal and social frames but in unfamiliar or new grounds. They introduce "rupture" to the given order. By instantiating a crack in the institutionalized order of things, claimants become part of contentious politics (Çağlar 2015, 2016a).

However, tracing the course of the initial access and more recent denial of rights to migrants who are not legal citizens reveals not only the discrepancy between formal and substantive citizenship rights but also how the relationship between the formal and substantive is related to contingencies of social forces and modes of capital accumulation within a given conjuncture. Several decades after Soysal (1994) and Sassen's initial statements about "post-national" citizenship (Sassen 2002b), their arguments appear dated, whether they were theorized from the spaces of Europe or from the "global city." The weaknesses of those conceptualizations of social citizenship highlight the need to situate discussions of citizenship within changing trajectories of power at different conjunctural moments. Over time and within the contingencies of different localities, multiscalar displacement and emplacement processes have been transforming access to formal or substantive rights within and beyond nation-states. As the intensive accumulation by dispossession and neoliberal restructuring have begun to take their toll around the globe, and as new restrictions on the legal rights of noncitizens are increasingly widespread in many regions of the world, both the limitations and the political possibilities opened by the practices of social citizenship are coming more clearly into view.

At the same time, contemporary conjunctural transformations have made it more apparent that citizenship creates, and is created by, its relationship to those excluded from its domain of privilege within the power geometry of a given historical and political context. The presence and the practices of the excluded and the modes of their exclusion are central to the constitution and the transformations of formal citizenship (Isin 2002; Balibar 2003; Sassen 1998; De Genova 2013). People who fall into the category of excluded—the undocumented, refugees, and migrants—come to the fore as major constituents of citizenship (Isin 2002; Holston 2008; Varsanyi 2006; Rajaram and Arendas 2013; Çağlar and Mehling 2012).

The concept of social citizenship complements this relational and conjunctural approach by drawing attention to the complex processual and contentious inroads into rights and belonging that practices of social citizenship may initiate. The processes of social citizenship challenge the binary of exclusion and inclusion, which restricts rights and membership to those who hold legal status. Responding to an understanding of citizenship in which margins are essential to constituting the whole, Clarke et al. (2014, 49) call for a "recentering of citizenship around spaces, sites and practices that are often described as marginal." They argue that citizenship is defined at its margins, because inclusion of the excluded leads to a rearrangement of the existing structures and a disruption of taken-for-granted assumptions upon which the hegemonic understanding of citizenship is based.

In this broader understanding of citizenship, the emphasis is on people's everyday acts of citizenship, on the formation of their subjectivities, and on their political agency through their claim-making processes within a given historical and political context (Neveu 2005; Nuijten 2013). This processual perspective allows us to see how the insurgency of such practices has transformative capacity. This analysis identifies processes by which claim making and social practices lead to the granting of rights to the excluded, resulting in the formation of new categories, laws, and political subjects—in short, in the remaking of citizenship (Clarke et al. 2014, 171).

However, the social citizenship perspective, with its emphasis on emplacement and belonging through everyday life, has important weaknesses, especially when it neglects an analysis of institutions of power, including the power of states, and fails to address changing configurations of power over time. It is true that without active social citizenship, formal, legally protected rights may exist only on paper, may be abrogated in practice, or may be rescinded. However, when activists and scholars emphasize practices and related claims at the expense of attention to the translation of claims into formal legal rights, claimants are left vulnerable and ultimately unprotected (Varsanyi 2006).

Scholars of social citizenship also have tended to canonize certain sites such as plazas or public parks as inherently productive of acts of social citizenship. Sites of claim making can in fact be variable, and in which sites people chose to act performatively reflects contingencies of time and place and the alignment of conjunctural forces, tensions, and possibilities. Therefore, researchers must identify claim-making sites based on empirical research, not on a priori categorization (Çağlar 2016a). These sites might range from religious organizations to dance associations. Any site may offer possibilities for social citizenship that function beyond formal citizenship venues (Hamidi 2003). As Clarke et al. (2014, 5) aptly underline, "citizenship always takes specific forms that are outcomes of sets of processes and are related to specific political projects, particular social contexts and distinctive cultural configurations."

The enactment of social citizenship brings together multiple sources of notions of rights, entitlements, claims, and political practices. These sources do not reflect the citizenship rights, notions, or practices of a single nation-state. Instead, those who enact social citizenship often draw from the citizenship practices of multiple states as well as their personal transborder networks and multiple embeddings in far-ranging transnational social fields. They bring together experiences of human rights regimes as they are differentially implemented in various states and regions and in globe-spanning social media narratives and debates about rights and belonging.

In this chapter, we turn to social citizenship claims based on global born-again Christianity. To explore the tensions and possibilities opened through social citizenship practices, we situate these claims within particular places, at particular historical conjunctures, and within multiscalar networks of power. While increasing attention has been paid to transnational networks of Christians and their transborder projects and identities, scholars of religion and migration have had less to say about how religious belief and practices can foster social citizenship (Levitt 2003; van Dijk 2011; von Vasquez and Marquardt 2003). Yet, based on what they see as their God-given rights, migrants moving within a transnational social field endeavor to act upon the institutional, legal, and societal processes of the state and locality in which they have settled to claim place-based rights and identities.

Building Born-Again Organizations

In Halle, we participated in two different born-again churches initiated by refugees from Africa who saw themselves as Christians claiming the land in the name of Jesus. The first, the Miracle Healing Church, begun by African asylum seekers in 1996, started to grow in 2001 after Pastor Joshua became pastor. Originally from eastern Nigeria, Joshua had a well-paying factory job in western Germany at the time he assumed leadership of the congregation. He was fluent in German as well as English and had permanent residence through his marriage to a white German woman from Leipzig. By 2003, the church had enough money from tithes and Sunday offerings to lease a small, one-story industrial building. Pastor Joshua led bilingual English and German prayer and healing services from this church, and this unpresupposing structure became the headquarters for his growing transnational ministry. By 2005, the Miracle Healing Church had approximately 150 members. Twenty percent of the congregation was white German. Most African members were Nigerian, but other West African countries were also represented. Over the years, a growing number of the migrant members learned to speak some German and obtained permanent legal status by marrying Germans. German partners, especially women, became church members and attended services with their children. Increasingly, white Germans from the region around Halle who were not married to members also joined the church.

After a schism reduced its membership, a core of activists rebuilt the ministry. These activists included migrants from Africa, local non-migrants, and young white Germans from western Germany who migrated specifically to work with Pastor Joshua. The reconstituted congregation reconstructed the church's website and gave its ministry an active Facebook presence. By 2015, the approximately seventy-five congregants worshipping on a warm sum-

FIG 4.1 Halle residents pray for healing as part of their Christian missionizing in Halle. Photograph by Nina Glick Schiller.

mer Sunday included almost as many white Germans as migrants. Over the years, Pastor Joshua inserted the Miracle Healing Church within a wide, intricate web of Pentecostal prayer and healing networks and their texts, music, and ritual practices. Visiting pastors circulated within a social field that connected Germany, Europe, Africa, Asia, and the United States.

The L'espirit de Signeur congregation, led by Pastor Mpenza, numbered about thirty members when we began our research in 2001. Its congregation remained primarily African and did not grow over the years. During the first five years of our research, most core members were young men from the Congo region and other parts of Francophonic Africa or Angola. However, several women from these regions and a few white German partners of African migrants participated in the choir or other church activities. Worship was in French, with translation sometimes into Lingalla, a Bantu language of the eastern Congo region, parts of Angola, and the Central African Republic. Initially, only a few African members spoke passable German, although this changed over time.

Pastor Mpenza and his wife had been granted refugee status with permanent residence, but most members were asylum seekers with only temporary rights to stay. For a number of years, the congregation struggled to maintain itself, as people central to the group lost their final appeal for asylum and fled to western Germany or France in the face of imminent deportation. After years of transient membership, and although the congregation remained primarily migrants from Francophonic or Lusophonic Africa, its core members eventually obtained rights to live in Halle as partners of German citizens, as parents of children born in Germany, or as students. Pastor Mpenza had led a church before migrating to Germany and arrived as part of a Pentecostal network based in Africa. He utilized his ties to connect his congregation to born-again networks in western Germany and elsewhere in Europe.

The asylum seekers who initially founded both born-again churches in Halle were quite poor, since German laws initially forbade them from working. Even those with legal rights to work had trouble finding formal employment. As we indicate in chapters 1 and 2, unemployment in the city was high and a legal preference was given to Germans and EU citizens. Over time, those migrants who stayed earned a subsistence income from temporary employment outside of Halle or through informal trade in imported goods such as cosmetics, clothing, and hair products. Several opened businesses near the city center, including the Beautiful Dream Gifts, whose rise and fall are described in chapter 2. By 2015, the socioeconomic composition of the Miracle Healing congregation had broadened to include educated Germans with white-collar jobs and a handful of well-paid professional researchers of African background who worked in Halle's prestigious science institutes.

In Manchester, we participated in various healing conferences and prayer breakfasts led by Pastor Godsword of the Resurrection Crusade, met with the Crusade's core members, and attended several services within its networked churches. Arriving from Ogoniland in Nigeria as an English-speaking refugee already embedded in Pentecostal networks that linked Nigeria, the United Kingdom, and the United States, Pastor Godsword created a religious organization that united a multitude of independent, born-again congregations in a campaign to bring the word of God to the people of Manchester. At its height, more than twenty congregations in the Greater Manchester area participated in the Crusade. Most of these congregations were predominantly non-migrant white. The Crusade included two congregations that prayed in Spanish and one African American congregation, but all churches participating in the Crusade espoused a born-again Christian, rather than an ethnic or racial identity.

From 2002 to 2005, migrants from all over the world increasingly joined the churches that made up the Crusade. The number of migrants in its core group also increased. By 2004, about 20 percent of the participants in conferences, prayer breakfasts, and prayer events sponsored by the Crusade were migrants of African, Caribbean, Latin American, and Asian origin. The Crusade was more than an organizational nexus. It had its own individual activists, including people of migrant background, racialized minorities, and non-migrants. These believers drew their family, friends, and coworkers into an expanding global field of Christian activity with multiple connections to different ministries and religious networks in the United States, Europe, Africa, the Philippines, and Latin America.

Migrants in member churches and the core of the Crusade ranged from factory workers to professionals, but most held working-class jobs. Non-migrants in the activist core included a factory foreman and an office worker. Similarly non-migrant members in church networks varied widely in occupation and income. They ranged from the unemployed and retired to owners of small businesses whose prosperity was linked to the condition of the local economy.

In 2005, Godsword and the Crusade initiated the Regional Prayer Center, renting space in a small office building in the regenerated city center. The Regional Prayer Center began to host visiting pastors, Sunday Bible study, and weekly women's groups cosponsored by the Crusade's member churches. However, the Prayer Center was less successful than the Crusade in attracting support, perhaps because it seemed to resemble a new church and competed for funds and activists with its member congregations.

In the wake of the 2008 subprime mortgage crisis and major recession, a new wave of dispossession afflicted the Manchester city-region. Members of the Crusade and its constituent congregations lost homes, jobs, and confidence. The Prayer Center closed, and the Crusade ceased activities in Manchester. Godsword had quit his job for full-time Christian organizing when the Crusade began and was among the many migrants in Manchester who had bought an old dilapidated house with a subprime mortgage. He continued his activities within his multiscalar born-again Christian social field but moved the base of his proselytizing and healing conferences to Ogoniland, Nigeria.

Urban Regeneration, Religious Difference, and Subordinated Emplacement

As we saw in chapters 1, 2, and 3, leaders in Halle and Manchester began efforts to re-empower and globally reposition their respective cities by projecting an image of their city as culturally diverse and open to the world. Embracing this image and its promise of urban renewal and development, they initiated regeneration projects, and political officials, city planners, and heads of cultural, religious, and social institutions welcomed migrants as members of the urban community. In 2000, this welcome was inclusive: it extended to legal residents, students, refugees or asylum seekers, and the undocumented. However, in their representations and positioning of migrants, city leaders subordinated them. In these representations of migrants, even as they enveloped migrants in a narrative of inclusion, city leaders positioned migrants in ways that failed to acknowledge their multiple forms of city making. Those who designed, articulated, and led Manchester's regeneration projects failed to acknowledge migrants' multiple forms of city making even as they welcomed migrants as belonging to the city. Disregarding migrants' city-making activities and capacities, they embraced the globe-spanning mantra that only investment capitalists and global talent could revitalize a city and usher in a new era of prosperity. Migrants were reduced to the embodiments of cultural and religious diversity that were necessary to attract the desired agents of urban regeneration.

Given this mind-set, official and publicly funded institutions in both Halle and Manchester included born-again Christian organizations in their listings of local organizations that embodied cultural diversity. For example, in 2003, an Africa Week in Halle program, sponsored by the city's Office of Culture and Office of Foreigners of Halle and by a range of local institutions and civil and religious NGOs, listed an African Worship Service hosted by Pastor Mpenza and L'espirit de Signeur congregation.[3] Eine-Welt-Haus, an organization to promote intercultural understanding funded by the city government as well as by Saxony-Anhalt, the EU, and political foundations, included both the Miracle Healing Church and L'espirit de Signeur in a listing of the city's multicultural activities. Approaching the Resurrection Crusade with a similar mind-set, the mayor of Manchester initially called it an organization that highlighted the "colorful mosaic" that the twenty-first century brought to the city. In a letter of support for a Wind and Fire Prayer Conference organized by the Crusade, he wrote, "We celebrate the diversity of Manchester and embrace the fact that people from all over the world come to our wonderful city" (Baines 2004).

As we document in chapters 1 and 3, despite their policy of welcoming migrants, officials in Halle and Manchester provided few resources and services for migrants' settlement and support. As tax revenues became increasingly constrained, officials prioritized investing public funds in urban regeneration, although they did provide born-again religious organizations that were viewed as migrant organizations with access to regenerated spaces. These allocations not only situated what city leaders saw as cultural diversity within revitalized spaces but also enlisted migrants as placeholders, ensuring that underutilized rebuilt spaces were filled until they generated higher market values. It is interesting to note that, in both cities, religious organizations begun by migrants were also provided with virtual space in the form of public airwaves where the city's religious diversity was highlighted.

As part of his institution's "multicultural integration consultancy," the head of the Bauhof, a youth training center supported by the Evangelical Church,[4] allowed the Miracle Healing Church to hold prayer services in a building restored with German federal state funding. L'espirit de Signeur was given space to pray in a regenerated factory specifically designated as a meeting center for foreigners and Germans. This center and a neighboring park served to anchor prospective development in Riebeckviertel, a historic industrial area near the central railroad station. City planners designated the area for new economy industries, which planners envisioned rising from the rubble of early industrial- and socialist-era workplaces but which had not yet arrived (City of Halle 2004). However, for most of the decade after the millennium, the meeting center's regenerated space continued to stand amid abandoned factory buildings.

While the Resurrection Crusade in Manchester was not given office space, it was provided with public space within the regenerated city center to lead celebrations during the National Day of Prayer. On that occasion in 2005, the mayor provided the Crusade with the Aldermanic Chambers of Manchester City Hall so that pastors and intercessors could pray for the city. The historic city hall building was completely restored in 1998 as one of the first steps in revitalizing the main street of the city center. The Crusade was also given access to a public park in the city center dedicated to war veterans. Several hundred people, including military veterans, participated in a "major prayer rally" heard over city loudspeakers.

Although they accepted and welcomed these various forms of public support, leaders and members of the Miracle Healing Church, L'espirit de Signeur, and the Resurrection Crusade understood their relationship to the cities in which they were located very differently than did city leaders. Born-again Christian migrants created a counternarrative and set of practices that grounded their claims to rights, belonging, and city making on Christian theology and global Pentecostal Christian doctrine. In formulating their claims, migrants joined with non-migrants who also sought recognition, rights, and citizenship outside of and beyond the legitimacy of government officials and institutions. Below, we discuss three different aspects of how migrants and non-migrants who were members of these born-again organizations narrated their feelings of being disempowered and set aside and their quest for emplacement and re-empowerment.

"In the Name of Jesus": Born-Again Multiscalar Social Citizenship

CLAIMING THE LAND

Migrant and non-migrant leaders and members of each organization claimed rights to land, access to power, and moral authority in the name of Jesus. According to Pastor Mpenza, of the L'espirit de Signeur Church, who came to Germany as a refugee from the Congo, the Bible's message was clear: "Every place whereon the soles of your feet shall tread shall be yours" (Deut. 11:24).

These organizations deployed born-again Christian discourses and doctrines to set aside categories of native and foreigner, black and white, and seek instead domains of commonality in their shared commitment to bring the word of God to inhabitants of the city. Therefore, they did not build their churches around ethnic terms, national identities, or cultural identities. Speaking to a prayer conference in Manchester, Pastor Godsword said, "No longer is it about black or white issues in America. It is not about racism. It's about bringing the word of God" (field notes, March 22, 2004). When Pastor Mpenza explained his presence in Germany as well as his insistence that his church be understood as Christian, not Congolese, he said:

> I have told you about my origin. I have come from Congo where I met my Lord, where I worked for the Lord. And now I am here in Germany where I had the feeling that the inhabitants were in need of the same message. So I've clearly said that this church is not a Congolese church. I've clearly said it is a church of Jesus. In other words, it is for the Germans, for all nationalities; I can also say, in this church we have Germans, we have Angolans, we have Ivories, we have people from Togo, we have Burundians, we have all possible nationalities. (Interview M., 2003)[5]

According to believers, their rights to the land and its fruits came with responsibilities. All congregation members took the stance of missionaries tasked with claiming the land for the Lord and winning its inhabitants for Jesus. As Pastor Joshua of the Miracle Healing Church emphasized, "We consider it our duty to fulfill the commandment of our risen Lord and Master Jesus Christ as it is written in Matthew 28:19–20, 'Go ye therefore, and teach all nations, baptizing them in the name of the Father, and of the Son, and of the Holy Ghost: Teaching them to observe all things whatsoever I have commanded you: and, lo, I am with you always, even unto the end of the world. Amen'" (field notes 2016).

Similarly referring to what "the Lord told me," Godsword, leader of the Resurrection Crusade and its prayer network in Manchester, New Hampshire, stated that his mission was to "bring change" to the city and make it a "place of God." Positioning himself as a messenger of the word of Jesus, he explained that his Crusade had grown because "God brought people around me" so that "the Kingdom of God will come to the City" (interview, April 30, 2004).

While all three pastors and the core members of their organizations shared an understanding of their evangelizing mission shaped by a global and centuries-old project of Christian proselytization, their specific methods reflected vistas of dispossession, displacement, and restructuring in the city where they were located. Their missionizing also reflected how Christianity was perceived locally and nationally and the personal talents and resources they could muster. Therefore, the three organizations differed in the size of their congregations, the composition of their membership, the extent and composition of their networks, and their means of evangelization.

When members of L'espirit de Signeur learned that their choir was in demand at public occasions such as summer folk festivals or the annual Intercultural Week celebration, they began to participate in these activities. As a result, during their first ten years, the church and choir developed weak but multiple ties to various local cultural and political institutions. To the pastor and his congregation, choir performances in Halle "took place within the frame of evangelization. There is evangelization by means of language, and there is evangelization by means of music" (interview PM., 2003).[6] Given this congregation's meager resources and limited German language skills, church members sought to use music to bring the people of Halle, both migrant and non-migrant, to God.

With a pastor and key members who spoke German, and with core members established as legal residents by 2004, Pastor Joshua and the Miracle Healing Church congregants increasingly evangelized by organizing healing services beyond the space of their own building. In 2005, the Miracle Healing Church led a five-day healing conference at a hockey rink in Halle that attracted several hundred people, two-thirds of them German. With assistance from his congregants, Pastor Joshua also began to hold healing services for German congregations in neighboring cities. The church produced videotapes of these services and sold them through their website and at church services. In 2005, their website featured Pastor Joshua praying with a young blond white woman and a caption proclaiming that the church was "the place of miracles, signs, and wonders. Here . . . the sick get healed, the blind see, and many are delivered from bondage of sin" (field notes 2005). The goal of these healing services was to exorcise the evil spirits of sickness from the bodies of the sick and from the city and to defeat the Devil, so that God could rule the city and its people.

As did migrants in the born-again churches in Halle, the migrants who built the Resurrection Crusade in Manchester claimed to be spiritual intercessors whose God-given mission was to rid the city, state, and country from evil spirits and claim it in the name of Jesus. Godsword brought in a wide range of pastors from the region, the country, and internationally to hold healing ceremonies. His Prayer Center trained "prayer intercessors" in "strategic or city level spiritual warfare" against the Devil, who assigns his "territorial spirits . . . to rule geographical territories and social networks" (Smith 1999, 23).

In both Halle and Manchester, these evangelizing activities legitimated these born-again organizations' claims that their members not only belonged to the city but were its spiritual leaders. By defining the current state of the world as a battle between God and demonic forces, migrants and non-migrants in these born-again organizations took on the role of global "spiritual warriors" for Jesus.

In their literature and on their websites, the global evangelizing networks associated with the religious organizations we studied spoke of the need to wage spiritual warfare to root out the evil within each locality. Interestingly, both the US Prayer Center, the powerful right-wing Texas-based network with which the Crusade was affiliated, and the Organization of Free Churches (Bund freikirchlicher Pfingstgemeinden), to which both L'espirit de Signeur and the Miracle Healing Church belonged, specifically encouraged each congregation to claim the territory in which they were located. By emphasizing a Christian universalism that divided the world into the saved and the unsaved—namely, those on the side of God and those on the side of the Devil—rather than ethnic particularism or a stigmatized local identity, migrants and non-migrants who joined this religious movement could become incorporated as local and global actors on their own terms.

In both Manchester and Halle, migrants, especially those racialized as nonwhite, felt highly visible because of their small numbers. Migrants who joined born-again churches found a setting that did not highlight their public differentiation and brought them together with non-migrants as the saved.

Non-migrants in Halle could shed the stigmatized regional identity of being from the east in a unified Germany. In Halle and Manchester, non-migrants faced urban regeneration that served the needs of "new economy workers" and left members of the white working class and an increasingly precarious middle class feeling like "strangers in their own land." They gained a political voice, cultural legitimacy, and social citizenship as they organized to put "God in command."

POWER: PLACING JESUS IN COMMAND OF THE STATE

In all three born-again organizations, prayers, sermons, written text, websites, individual testimonies, and our interviews with congregants contained frequent references to the term "power." In 2005, the Miracle Healing Church's website explained the source of healing miracles: "There is Power in God's Word!!" In a letter to the people of Manchester from the Resurrection Crusade, Godsword made it clear that "only the power of prayer can change lives in our city, state and America" (Miracle Healing Church 2005).

In invoking the concept of power, members of these born-again organizations challenged political leaders to subordinate their authority to the word of God. Through much of the twentieth century, Pentecostal Christians had tended "to shy away from 'hard' political acts that they consider[ed] immoral, such as working for parties, criticizing public officials, or running for office" (Robbins 2004). This changed at the end of the twentieth century, when many Pentecostals took a more activist and critical stance toward secular government. Distrusting existing governments and political leaders, organizations such as the Christian Coalition, composed of well-funded nationalist right-wing pastors and political operatives, began to speak of "putting God in command" of governments and politicians and calling for "the Lord and his anointed to subdue all nations."[7]

To asylum seekers in Halle, the state was unreadable and mercurial. It granted one person asylum while another seeming to have more valid claims faced deportation. To counter the insecurities of their tenure, pastors in both churches preached that migrants had God on their side and that God held all power in the world. Pastor Joshua reminded migrants of Daniel, "who was in a strange land like you and me and never gave up. He only paid attention to what God said. It will come to pass. . . . Nothing will be impossible" (field notes, June 2003).

In her testimony to the congregation of the Miracle Healing Church, Evelyn, who became the owner of Beautiful Dream Gifts (see chapter 2), shared her confidence that God was in charge. Striding up to the front of the congregation, she said:

> I have found a German man who wants to marry me. . . . The problem is the paper. I have been told that I have to send to Nigeria for a paper. But there has been a two-month strike of public workers there and no one is filling out any papers. . . . I went to speak to the lady in the office [of the Germany immigration authority] about the strike. The woman refused to listen and said that the marriage could not happen without the paper. . . . I told the lady that "I believed in God and I did not need the paper." She said, "Who is this God?" I said, "He is all I need and not you or your paper," and I left. . . . Because I know there is no power except for God (field notes, November 2, 2001).

Many non-migrants who joined the Miracle Healing Church, such as the ones we interviewed who sought healing at a 2005 healing conference held at the ice hockey arena, had already attended churches in the villages surrounding Halle. Ranging in age from teenagers to pensioners, they came seeking moral support and empowerment that they felt they could not find elsewhere. Pastor Joshua and the spiritual warriors of the Miracle Healing Church prayed that "the door of power" would be opened to them at the conference (field notes, May 12–16, 2005). Almost all the non-migrants, who included teachers, counselors, and the unemployed, had more economic resources and legal rights than the migrants at the conference. However, they brought to the conference their own histories of precariousness and dispossession. Their lives were marked by the disruption of local certainties that accompanied the Wende. German political leaders had assured Halle's population that unification and local urban restructuring would yield a prosperous and secure future. As these promises became increasingly discredited, many began to distrust established political authority and sought new sources of transformative power.

By 2013, efforts to restructure Halle as a center of science and knowledge by recruiting "foreign scientists" had changed the composition of the Miracle Healing Church as more students, researchers, and professionals came to the city from other parts of Germany and around the world. The changing composition of the congregation was reflected in the contents of their prayers. Rather than pray for "papers" that would allow them to marry or settle, those who testified more often spoke of the precarious economy and their fears of businesses failures and layoffs. Within the continuing disempowerment of Halle, both migrants and non-migrants in the congregation continued to link their search for security and prosperity to the power of God.

Both the Miracle Healing Church and the Crusade specifically called out congregants and individuals to ensure that God took charge. At a healing conference in Manchester, Alice Smith, a white American preacher from Texas, joined Godsword on the pulpit to pray for the "spirit of God to take the mayor so he could turn over the city to God" (field notes, 2004).

The Resurrection Crusade called for "America to Pray for America's 2004 elections." "God is very jealous over the nation of America and deeply interested in her forth-coming election. . . . America is pregnant with her destiny. . . . We as her midwives must help her . . . not to have a stillbirth but to deliver a glorious male child." "Key Prayer Points" for the election included the following directives: "Unseat all wicked rulers in America and enthrone the righteous. . . . Pray that God's will and counsel will prevail. . . . We need great men and women after His heart to occupy every position from the least to the greatest. . . . Pray for President Bush's protection [George W. Bush was running for re-election]" (Resurrection Crusade 2004). In 2005, the Miracle Healing Church in Halle issued a flyer calling on the "Jesus Army" to pray for "the influence of the spirit of God upon the coming German elections" (Miracle Healing Church, 2005).

The political dynamics in Manchester and in the United States that empowered members of the Resurrection Crusade, including those who had arrived as migrants within a multiscalar social field of power, seem at first very different than those that confronted the two born-again churches in Halle. In Manchester, political and business leaders were receptive to public displays of religious fervor. In this setting, the Crusade built local networks that linked their members to city- and state-level Republican and Democratic politicians. The New Hampshire governor in 2004, a conservative Republican and strong Bush supporter, personally attended a Resurrection Crusade prayer breakfast. Robert Baines, the Democratic mayor of Manchester, not only attended the breakfasts from 2003 to 2005 but also developed an ongoing relationship with the Crusade. Initially, Baines had approached the Crusade as an immigrant church, but he soon took a prayerful stance and publicly acknowledged the power of God. Although he was a Catholic, he testified in 2005 to those assembled at the annual prayer breakfast that his granddaughter had been miraculously healed after members of the Crusade had prayed for her (field notes, April 30, 2005).

The two born-again organizations that we followed in Halle could not use the salience of Christian legitimacy in Germany as an entry point into local politics. Most people in the former West Germany held official membership in a recognized church and paid taxes collected by the state to support Church activities. However, many saw born-again churches as sects rather than legitimate congregations. Furthermore, in the former socialist East Germany, most people did not belong to any church.

Although Pastor Mpenza's church and its choir came in contact with local politicians and officials at public events, church members as invited guests were never in a position to set the agenda of the meeting. Given this situation, Miracle Healing Church members generally declined to participate in these events. In the face of their distance from local political power in Halle, members of born-again organizations turned to a multiscalar social field—a network of networks linked to powerful institutions and political leaders— as a means of challenging the locus of power. The Resurrection Crusade also drew on its relationships within a multiscalar Christian social field. These ties validated not only members' faith but also their claims as social citizens to assume political authority.

Our ethnography revealed that congregation members were connected to individuals, including powerful political leaders, and to social and political institutions through the global Pentecostal social movement. For example, when they held their citywide healing conference in Halle in 2005, the Miracle Healing Church responded to a call originating at the pan-European Pentecostal conference in Berlin in 2003 to bring religious revival to Germany. Several members of the Miracle Healing Church congregation had attended the Berlin conference (field notes, June 17, 2003). In organizing their healing conference two years later, they drew on a repertoire of knowledge about Pentecostal revival and healing protocols popularized by the globe-spanning networks and intertwined websites to which they were linked.

Through the arrival of visiting pastors, each local organization's connections to these broader networks became visible to local congregants. An Indian pastor based in western Germany visited the Miracle Healing Church and convinced congregants to support his missionary work in India by sending funds on a regular basis. Through a global Mennonite ministry linked to Mennonite missionaries in Halle who helped organize the 2005 healing conference, Joshua himself joined the preaching circuit and made visits to India and Korea. The Miracle Healing Church also participated in the Morris Cerullo World Evangelism organization and sent funds to Cerullo's efforts to convert Jews in Israel to born-again Christianity. Cerullo's ministry placed the church in a multiscalar social field connected to political leaders of many countries, whom Cerullo knew personally. By 2014, Pastor Mpenza had joined this network, proclaiming his ties to the Cerullo ministry on his Facebook page.

Godsword was also a great fan of Morris Cerullo. He had attended one of Cerullo's conferences, and he filled the Crusade's bookshelves with Cerullo's books. The Cerullo ministry was only one of multiple Pentecostal networks to which the Crusade was linked through its own networks and those of the twenty local churches affiliated with the Crusade. Its member churches varied in size and in institutional and denominational affiliations, but each had their own national and transnational networks. The range and diversity of the Crusades' networks were on display at "Power Night," organized in 2005. Among the speakers were pastors from churches with small networks of five congregations (three in New Hampshire, and one each in Maine, Kenya, and India) and others with more extensive networks, such as the Revival Church of the Nations, with twenty-nine congregations in Massachusetts, two churches in Portugal, and websites in Portuguese and English (Power Night Flyer 2005, in files of N. Glick Schiller).

Moreover, the US Prayer Center, which was formative in the political stance and claim making of the Crusade, was connected to various forms of institutional power that extended into the Bush White House. In 2005, the US Prayer Center recruited worldwide under the slogan "Disciplining the Nations" and boasted a membership that included four thousand pastors. These disciples were encouraged to identify with the United States, even as they espoused a Christian identity (US Prayer Center website 2004). In a sermon on the "power of networking," Godsword portrayed President Bush as someone who speaks directly with the Lord and as "God's right hand" (field notes, April 30, 2004).

The right-wing political organization Focus on the Family, which had taken over leadership of the National Day of Prayer celebrations, was an additional and even more powerful network within the Crusade's multiscalar social field. By linking his local political contacts, including the mayor of Manchester to Focus on the Family, Godsword enmeshed city officials in the implementation of the values and narrative of highly political right-wing evangelical Christian organizations, the National Day of Prayer Task Force, and Focus on the Family. According to the National Day of Prayer organizers, "several million people participate every year in this call to prayer for our nation, its leaders and citizens" (National Day of Prayer Task Force 2015). Focus on the Family claimed that its daily radio program was broadcast in more than a dozen languages and on more than seven thousand stations worldwide and was reportedly heard daily by more than 220 million people in 164 countries (Amazon 2016).

Thus, the Crusade's network became part of a larger public–private social field that enmeshed city officials in the implementation of values and a narrative crafted by a set of political operatives with corporate ties who operated through extensive born-again Christian networks.[8] Rather than being outside of the political life of the city, this social field was part of powerful corporately funded state and national political processes. In this social field, city officials who controlled access to public space had merged with migrants and non-migrants who claimed to belong to the city as representatives of Jesus, actors in powerful US political, private religious networks, and corporately funded operatives, lobbyists, and political action committees. Private religious actors such as Focus on the Family, together with the Resurrection Crusade, began to contribute to public political discourse about moral values as well as to ideas about how and when to pray and what to include in public prayer.

CLAIMING THE MORAL HIGH GROUND

In Halle and Manchester, congregants spoke to us about their concerns for religious unity, and stronger families and churches. The morality preached and modeled by members of each of these born-again organizations reflected moral values developed within a nongovernmental highly politicized Christian social field that sought to shape public moral economies throughout the world. However, their efforts to seize the moral high ground and invocations of Christian morality to assert social citizenship varied in different localities. These variations, we suggest, reflected the confluence of local historical circumstances and the relative positionality of each city, including its multiscalar reach and the degree and types of displacement and dispossession processes, which reconstitute the locality.

While marriage and the family were celebrated throughout the multiscalar social field of born-again Christians, these social values resonated in eastern German contexts, where young couples often didn't get married. Members of the Miracle Healing Church entered into contestations over whose authority should define public morality by making marriage and the family a central ethos of the congregation. As marriages between black Africans and white Germans became more commonplace, attending prayer meetings of the born-again congregations became a form of courting. Migrants who were church members often involved their partners in church services to demonstrate their own good character and to convince their German partners of the necessity of getting married.

During these services, potential German spouses could see that, while they might find their partner's religious behavior strange, the congregation was part of a broader and powerful movement that had presence and legitimacy, if not in Halle, then globally. Partners also learned that heterosexual marriage was necessary to be a church member in this movement. The desire of their African partner to marry became not a simple utilitarian effort to obtain a passport but a promise to both partners of health, prosperity, and fulfillment, with the assurance of divine assistance. In these marriages, migrants not only preached and practiced born-again Christian morality, which condemned homosexuality and abortion, but also shaped the citizenship practices and beliefs of non-migrant residents. Once married, migrants often found their spouses' family networks welcoming. Although the families of German spouses were often poor, they could provide forms of direct assistance such as childcare and local knowledge about accessing governmental offices and benefits. This local knowledge enhanced the ability of migrants as social citizens to claim rights, participate, and move toward legal residence.

In Manchester, Christian marriage was the norm, but born-again believers, whether migrant or non-migrant, viewed their shared values of heterosexuality and heterosexual marriage, patriarchal authority, and the condemnation of abortion as under threat from the larger society. Daily life activities that joined migrants and non-migrants were built on domains of commonality and around a shared fundamentalist biblical reading of Christian values as well as the everyday activities of marriage, family, and child-rearing. The migrant and non-migrant activists who served as the core members of the Crusade developed sociabilities of emplacement, a concept we explore in chapter 3. They worked together to organize prayer meetings, conferences, and breakfasts; helped people in need; and acted as prayer "intercessors" for the city and country. The Crusade's local networks connected migrants to people who could and did provide resources: supervisors who helped migrants find employment, middle-class housewives who furnished apartments for newcomers or provided clothing and furniture for newborn babies, and public officials who provided prestige, social acceptance, and access to public resources. The Crusade's activities established and expanded networks of trust that encompassed both migrants and non-migrants. Within the limited opportunity structure of greater Manchester and in the face of multiple dispossessive processes, local people who were not Crusade activists but who attended their own church as well as Crusade prayer breakfasts, conferences, and days of prayer found themselves part of the Crusade's multiscalar networks of power and the social and political capital they contained.

This is not to say that our analysis of born-again organizations in Halle and Manchester ascribes pragmatic goals to the social citizenship practices of these congregants. Believers saw each concrete manifestation of political and social power as imbricated with the power of God and the presence of Jesus. They saw their local practices as constituted within God's globe-spanning power. Moreover, in the context of the ongoing disempowering of Halle and Manchester and the social and economic displacements that were part of daily life for so many residents, born-again Christian networks became sources of hope.

Scholars who debate the distinction between formal and substantive citizenship by focusing solely on relations between the individual and the state miss a highly significant yet little-noticed aspect of social citizenship. They ignore the transversal relationships forged between many migrants and non-migrants that entail substantive ties to "fellow" citizens (Offe 1994, 1999; Çağlar 2004). Christianity, as a set of practices, networks, and ideology, provided the basis and discourses for such horizontal networks. In this way, born-again Christianity forged multiple ties of solidarity in and beyond Halle and Manchester. By joining with migrants, non-migrants active in the born-again churches found new possibilities of forging ties locally and transnationally around their shared aspiration for a new Christian public morality and spirituality.

Multiscalar Analysis and Multiple Spheres of Emplacement

Although in this chapter we highlight how migrants joined non-migrants in emplacement within multiscalar religious networks through which they made social citizenship claims, our respondents participated in social networks that linked them to multiple spheres of life. For example, Evelyn, an active member of the Miracle Healing Church over several years, first enters this book in chapter 2 when she and her husband opened the Beautiful Dream Gifts in Halle. Initially from Lagos, Nigeria, Evelyn's business plan was to open a shop that offered new consumer options to sophisticated new economy workers. These were the very people whom Halle's city leaders, urban developers, and German and EU funders had in mind when they invested structural funds and scarce public funds in revitalizing storefronts and infrastructure in the city center and surrounding neighborhoods. Therefore, Evelyn's small business activities situated her in multiscalar networks of economically and politically powerful institutions that connected massive flows of public capital, banks, multinational construction companies, and construction workers from western Germany, all of whom benefited from urban restructuring. However, Evelyn's gains from this set of networks were minimal: access to an initially inexpensive storefront rental and a government-funded, formulaic training program to provide new entrepreneurs, including migrants, with retail skills. On the other hand, Evelyn benefited from her supply chain, which involved her in a range of other multiscalar networks that accessed individuals and corporations of different degrees of power: family members purchasing craft items in Nigeria; wholesalers in Europe, big and small; and producers of goods, including so-called African crafts manufactured in China.

Though only peripherally involved in Halle's political networks and public welcoming narratives at one point Evelyn came in contact with Karamba Diaby, as we mention in chapter 1, the migrant from Senegal who became one of the first people of African background elected to the German parliament. Hoping to find new ways to market her imported goods, Evelyn and her German husband found themselves in the midst of a multicultural fair organized by Diaby and sponsored by the Heinrich Böll Foundation (linked to the German Green Party). However, although Evelyn's contacts with Diaby were minimal, through her social citizenship claims as a longtime activist of the Miracle Healing Church, she entered into a far-reaching political field. As treasurer of the Miracle Healing Church, Evelyn facilitated the congregation's network to the Morris Cerullo World Evangelism organization, which linked her not only to multiple world leaders but also to Godsword, the pastor in Manchester, New Hampshire, and to his multiscalar networks.

Godsword, organizer of the Resurrection Crusade in Manchester, New Hampshire, was also a member of the Cerullo network and of many other multiscalar born-again Christian networks that connected migrants and non-migrants to powerful political actors in the City of Manchester, the State of New Hampshire, and the US government as well as in Europe and Nigeria. In addition to his simultaneous insertion in both religious and political multiscalar social fields, Godsword participated in processes of urban regeneration in Manchester through his personal network. His position and personal connections facilitated his access to capital to purchase a house despite his lack of formal employment or savings. When we traced his multiscalar networks to Manchester's subprime mortgage brokers, we found him linked through mutual acquaintances to Carlos Gonzalez. As we note in chapter 1, Gonzalez arrived in Manchester with transnational political networks stretching back to the Dominican Republic and the US Embassy there. He became a mortgage broker connected to networks of financial capital through the US public–private mortgage-lending corporation Fannie Mae, an important actor in the subprime mortgage bubble in Manchester and nationally. As a member of the local Republican Party and eventually a New Hampshire legislator, Gonzalez hobnobbed with many state-level Republicans who knew Godsword.

Conjunctures, Contradictions, and Born-Again Social Citizenship Theory

The Christian social citizenship claims explored in this chapter reflect and resonate with the political project of the leadership of the United States between 2000 and 2008, when most of our ethnographic research in the three born-again organizations was conducted. Only by keeping in mind the prominence and power of these networks can we assess the significance of local congregants' social citizenship practices. They made it possible for participants in born-again Christian networks, whether migrant or non-migrant, to be part of a potent political and moral project that stretched from congregation members who were asylum seekers to the US president. They provided venues to access power via electoral processes, as we have seen in the case of Manchester; assisted members in acquiring status as legal permanent residents, as pastors, or through spousal rights; challenged local public morality by insisting on the necessity of marriage; and expanded members' social capital through networks based in different localities.

Forms of Pentecostal Christianity grew throughout the world in the twenty-first century, and believers became increasingly engaged directly in questions of politics and citizenship. The processes of flexible capital accumulation and its multiple dispossessive forces, coupled with the specific regional and local forms of implementing neoliberal "reforms," have generated both a reduction of the security of social welfare programs and a generalized anxiety about "the direction of our country" and our world. Increasing numbers of the dispossessed found answers, new forms of social support, and a new sense of empowerment in global Christianity.

Many of the members of the born-again Christian organizations we came to know, joined not only to improve their individual spiritual and material well-being but also because of their aspirations for a world of social and economic justice. In the three organizations in which we worked, these aspirations led most members to endorse the explicit anti-racist stand of their pastors in public statements. Members claimed unity and equality on the basis of their common project: spiritual warfare against the Devil in which the born-again of all nations and backgrounds stood together on the side of God. Yet their beliefs entwined them within imperial social fields that fostered and profited from global warring and neoliberal dispossession. It is important to note that there is no single born-again movement but only a series of overlapping organizations, each with its own priorities. However, the social fields in which the organizations and their members were embedded served to support US actions around the world.

Connections with US foreign policy, which brought war, dispossession, and displacement in its wake, were both ideological and organizational. Key US foreign policy makers and the president of the United States at the time were members of the born-again globe-spanning social field described in this chapter. Focus on the Family and its related organization, the Family Research Council, became mainstream players in the Republican Party and in the White House. Their ability to turn out the vote was made clear by the Republican congressional victories in 1994 and directly contributed to George W. Bush's ability to take the White House in 2000 and 2004.

Key to linking US imperial power with a more global born-again Christianity was Christian networks' increasing engagement in projects in Israel. Participants affirmed the world leadership of the United States as a protector of Israel. For example, Evelyn, who had testified that she needed no authority but God's to marry her man and live legally in Germany, summarized her understanding of the God-Israel-US nexus as follows: to be "on the side of Israel is to be on the side of God. The US is on the side of Israel." Members of this social field, through their various and disparate networks, also rallied in support of the US and European invasion and occupation of Iraq. According to Evelyn, the "United States must be doing the work of God in Iraq because it is a country with so many strong Christians and because it is a friend of Israel's" (field notes August 20, 2003).

It is widely acknowledged that, in the past, missionaries served as ideological agents of imperial rule, legitimating the right of colonial states to transform belief systems of the colonized and impose the values, standards, laws, and interests of the colonizers. The evangelizing organizations and networks of born-again Christians among whom we worked followed a similar process globally in legitimating the exercise of imperial power. Their endorsement of imperial projects was intimately connected to their support for missionary activity elsewhere as well as to their local role as self-defined missionaries to the disempowered cities in which they worked.

The concept of changing historical conjunctures is crucial for an adequate analysis of the role that transnational Christian social fields played in the emplacement practices we describe in this chapter. In the context of continuing and expanding US and European war making after 2008, globe-spanning Christian networks continued their efforts to influence political outcomes in the United States and worldwide, though these efforts took on a different resonance. The transformation had several dimensions. The relationships between the Obama White House (2008–16) and these social fields differed from those of George W. Bush. Under Obama, right-wing Christian organizational networks undermined the presidency while increasingly making their presence known in the US Congress and at the level of state legislatures and city politics. Born-again Christian discourses also became more firmly entrenched in various globe-spanning culture wars. Meanwhile, migrants became increasingly visible as "reverse missionaries" bringing Christian readings of apocalyptic end times to American and European landscapes of intensified accumulation by dispossession.

This missionizing not only brought about versions of Christianity that can be called fundamentalist in terms of scriptural invocations of public morality but also gave prominence to ones that had become openly Islamophobic. At the same time, growing nationalist and openly racist rhetoric targeting immigrants, whom political leaders around the world blamed for the vast inequalities wrought by contemporary forms of capital accumulation and the attrition of social welfare programs, challenged the social citizenship claims of migrants, including born-again Christians.

By noting how migrants' social citizenship claims were challenged under changing conjunctural conditions, this chapter makes clear that struggles for social citizenship require a multiscalar conjunctural reading of city-making. This approach to city-making highlights the millennial conflation of the public and the private as well as the state and the civil society that we witnessed in Manchester and Halle. It is a reminder that, in our analysis of social citizenship, we need to be attentive to both enabling and constraining co-optive workings of the neoliberal state as it has been configured within multiple globe-spanning networks of power.

By activating the leadership of religious networks in domains that previously had been considered the province of the state, relationships between public and private and state and civil society became differently entangled. Moreover, our account of born-again Christian networks' endorsement of the war in Iraq also illustrates how these church congregations seemed to function independently of the neoliberal state but in effect became part of a broader governmentality that included that state. Contrary to the perspective of much of the social citizenship literature, which posits a binary relation between the formal state and the everyday politics of empowerment from below, a careful reading of the networks of the three congregations we studied indicates a different relationship. When these congregations endorsed the US-led war in Iraq in their prayers, they seemed to be acting as an independent grassroots force. However, a careful analysis of the multiscalar networks of these congregations links their perspective on the war directly to the White House and the neoconservative strategists who planned and executed the war.

As we have noted, the concept of social and urban citizenship highlights the ways in which legally or socially disempowered people come into political life by making claims to rights and power. There is an implicit assumption in much of the literature on social citizenship that such political motion contributes to struggles for social justice. Our research within born-again Christian organizations that brought migrants and non-migrants together indicates that we need to look further into the claiming of social citizenship by the dispossessed. On the one hand, we show that people who were experiencing multiple forms of dispossession and displacement forged sociabilities of emplacement through claiming rights and political voice as members of born-again Christian organizations. Moreover, these sociabilities often united people in explicitly anti-racist organizations and spoke to their aspirations for a more just world. On the other hand, we explore the *limits* of citizenship claims when religious practices and identities are situated within multiscalar networks linked to imperial power. Even as born-again Christians within these networks expressed their distrust of government and political leaders, they legitimated global warring, neoliberal governance, inequality, and nationalist attacks on migrants.

CHAPTER 5

"Searching Its Future in Its Past"

THE MULTISCALAR EMPLACEMENT OF RETURNEES

On May 16, 2015, Seda and Ayşe sat with the Mukhtar[1] of Kafro, his wife, and his teen-aged son on the verandah of his impressive stone house, located near the entrance of the fifteen-family settlement of Kafro. Facing vineyards and idyllic gardens in the comforting heat, they talked about the Syriac Christians who had emigrated from Mardin to Europe and had recently returned to their ancestral homeland. In 2006, Mukhtar Demir and his family had returned from Switzerland to live in Kafro, in the Midyat district of the city-region of Mardin (sixty kilometers from Mardin city center), and had been living in the meticulously built village since then.

They sat on the very same verandah shown on the website of the Kafro Tahtoyto (Kafro Development Association-Kafro Hometown Association [HTA]). This website depicted the visit on September 29, 2014, of a five-person delegation from the German parliament (Deutsche Bundestag) and an international human rights organization. Ayşe knew from the website that participants at that meeting discussed minority rights, land survey problems, mother-tongue schooling, and, above all, the future of Christians in the Middle East.

After finishing their coffee and conversation, Ayşe and Seda strolled along empty, elegantly manicured garden paths to talk to another returnee, this one from Germany, who was responsible for the finances of the Kafro Tahtoyto. Ayşe recalled pictures, dated September 19, 2014, on the HTA website of the Swiss ambassador to Turkey walking on the same garden path with his wife and the returnee to whom she and Seda were going to talk. The visitors in 2014 had spoken about Turkey's accession to the EU and the injustices Syriac Christians faced in Turkey and in the Middle East. In the guest book that Mukhtar's son asked Ayşe to sign as they were leaving, she found the names and good wishes of these representatives next to the wishes of officials from

FIG 5.1 Swiss ambassador to Turkey visiting Syriac Christian settlement at Kafro, in Mardin city-region in September 2014. Photograph by Sabro.

several foreign embassies in Turkey and of representatives from numerous international organizations, including churches all over Europe.

Yet Kafro was the very settlement that the American consulate in Adana called "Potemkin Village-like" in a confidential communiqué (June 8, 2005) sent to the American Embassy in Ankara (Wikileaks 05ANKARA3191). In evaluating "the prospects of greater religious freedom in the foreseeable future in Turkey," of guaranteeing the property (land) entitlements of Syriac Christians, and of ensuring Turkish authorities' sincere and serious attention to the return and well-being of Mardin's Syriac Christians, the communiqué articulated substantial skepticism. It concluded: "Aside from occasional Potempkin Village-like displays by Turkish authorities in the Tur Abdin region, Ankara has been conspicuously indifferent to the slow death of a Christian community with almost two millennia's presence in this corner of modern-day Turkey" (Wikilieaks 05ANKARA3191).

As did the numerous, powerful international signatories in the guestbook, this confidential US Embassy communiqué gave center stage to the Syriac Christian returnees. The state of Syriac Christians in Mardin and the possibilities of their return were also the subject of reports written by powerful US government representatives in the late 1990s. Their prominence stood in striking contrast to the few Syriacs in Mardin and to the empty roads and pathways of the lightly populated Kafro.

Syriac Christians are by no means a unified ethnic or religious group. People who designate themselves and are referred to by religious and state authorities as Syriac Christians are divided by linguistic differences, by geographical borders, and by Catholic, Orthodox, and Protestant Church divisions. However, within the geo-religious politics and the efforts by multiple actors, including city leaders, to revitalize Mardin at the beginning of the twenty-first century, Syriac Christians took on a new salience and singularity.

Mardin, a city located on the slope of a rocky hill on the Turkish–Syrian border and facing the Mesopotamian plains, has for centuries been home to different religious and ethnic groups: Orthodox and Catholic Christians, Sunni, Alevite Muslims, Zoroastrians, Kurds, Arabs, Armenians, Yezidis, Turks, and Syriacs. Displacements of Syriac Christians from Mardin have a history that dates to the early twentieth century (Özçoşar 2009, 2006). The last major exodus of Syriac Christians from Kafro occurred in the 1980s and 1990s. In the midst of increasing pressures and armed conflict between the Turkish military and guerillas of the Kurdish liberation movement, the Kurdish Labor Party (PKK), inhabitants of Kafro left for different parts of Europe. Kafro literally stood abandoned after 1995. Then, following more than two decades with no connection to their "ancestral land," displaced Syriacs in Europe started to return to Kafro. Despite their small numbers,[2] during the first decade of the twenty-first century, Syriac emigrants' return to Mardin, their "ancestral land," became of interest to many national, international, transnational, and supranational actors as well as to the city leadership in Mardin. The multiscalar social field within which Syriac Christians were embedded is apparent in the US consulate's communiqué to the US embassy in Ankara. In this chapter, we argue that to understand the dynamics of hometown associations such as Kafro Tahtoyto, the return of displaced Syriac Christians to Mardin, and their valorization in city narratives, we need to situate their emplacement in Mardin within a multiscalar social field constituted by multiple and intersecting social, political, and religious networks and institutions, including the EU, UNESCO, the US State Department, and the networks of Eastern Christianity. Actors in this field included several other Syriac Christian HTAS in different places in Germany, Sweden, Switzerland, Austria, and Turkey.

Building upon the distinctions we made in the introduction between transnational and multiscalar social fields, we argue that although the literature on hometown associations in migration scholarship acknowledges transnational or translocal personal and/or ethnic or religious community relations, it fails to connect these relations and their efficacy to multiscalar institutions and their fields of power at given conjunctures. This chapter demonstrates that the prominence accorded Syriac Christian returnees and the reach of their HTA to institutionalized power within this multiscalar field emerged in relation to powerful intersecting forces which, at the beginning of the twenty-first century, sought to revitalize Mardin. This revitalization was part of the changing positioning of Mardin and Turkey within regional and global processes of political and economic restructuring at that historical conjuncture. Returnees became city-makers in this context.

Hometown Associations and Returnees within a Multiscalar Field

Studies about hometown ties and hometown associations contribute to the rich body of migration scholarship. This literature variously positions HTAS as (1) part of transnational ethnic community-building processes through ethnic associations and organizations (Bada, Fox, and Seele 2006; Orozco and Garcia-Zanello 2009; Sezgin 2011); (2) an important aspect of transnational politics (Portes, Escobar, and Radford 2007; Landolt, Autler, and Baires 1999; Østergaard-Nielsen 2010); (3) part of sending-state policies and remittance markets (Levitt and de la Dehasa 2003; Levitt 1998; Orozco 2000b; Sørensen 2008); (4) agents of local and grassroots politics (Smith and Guernizo 1998; Goldring 1998); and (5) agents of international development (Orozco 2000a; de Haas 2012; Iskandar 2011). While some of this scholarship celebrates HTAS as new actors of international development policies and grassroots local politics (Orozco 2000b), other authors highlight these organizations' entanglements with state institutions and rightly question the utility of situating HTAS within the state–civil society binary (Çağlar 2006; Iskander 2011; de Haas 2011; Faist, Fauser, and Kivisto 2011). Although there is a critical literature urging scholars to situate HTAS and migrant hometown ties within new global labor regimes (Glick Schiller 2009, 2010; de Haas 2012), most of the studies fail to embed their analysis of migrants' hometown relations and associations within a multiscalar field composed of institutions of varying scope and power shaped by temporal dynamics. When the temporal dynamics of HTAS and migrants' hometown ties have been addressed, it is generally because of dramatic political changes in migrants' countries of origin, such as in the case of the rising power of the People's Republic of China (PRC). For example, the HTAS of diaspora or overseas Chinese in Southeast Asia, Cuba, Mexico, and Panama have been studied in relation to the changing political economic strength and the global positioning of the PRC (Siu 2007; Nonini 2015; Hearn 2016). Although these studies note the conjunctural positioning of nation-states, they do not address how the economic and political restructuring of regions and localities affects the potential for migrants and their hometown associations to become salient actors of city-making processes in a specific conjuncture.

Even studies of HTAs that highlight the increasing importance of remittance industries and their entanglement with powerful global organizations such as the World Bank, the IMF, and the EU (Orozco 2002a, 2013) fail to examine the degree to which the reach of migrants and hometown associations to these global institutions varies in relation to the power contingencies, including that of different home countries and hometowns in various historical conjunctures. The temporality of these dynamics escapes these researchers' analytical lenses; moreover, they generally fail to analyze how the ongoing reconstitution of specific places vary within conjunctural forces.

In contrast, in this chapter, we focus on the dynamics of the HTA, Kafro Tahtoyto, the return of the displaced Syriac Christians to Mardin, and the way they became desirable and therefore of value to a variety of powerful state and nonstate actors. We situate the analyses of Syriac Christians' hometown ties and associations in relation to the transformations over time of multiscalar processes of capital restructuring and to the interrelated reconfiguring of multiple institutions and networks of power in Mardin. Syriac Christians did not establish HTAs such as Kafro Tahtoyto until 2002 and did not resettle in Mardin until 2006, despite the policies and explicit attempts of the Turkish state and local city leaders to reach out to Syriac Christians starting at the end of 1990s.

We were able to make sense of the Syriacs' increasing prominence in city narratives and in the reports and programs of supranational and global institutions, despite their small numbers, only through a conjunctural analysis. In this way we could address the position of Mardin and the region within the reconfiguring of multiple institutions and networks of power at the turn of the twenty-first century. Such an analysis requires an examination of the broader dynamics of city-making and value creation, including the valorization of places and population groups in Mardin.

Great Expectations: Historical Conjuncture and Mardin's Repositioning Efforts

An underdeveloped region, as described in chapter 1, Mardin was included in a comprehensive, state-led infrastructural development project in Turkey that aimed to overcome the socioeconomic gap between more developed regions and the Southeast (Özok-Gündoğan 2005). However, in 2000, despite subsidies and large-scale development programs, Mardin's desired socio-economic development had yet to be achieved. On the contrary, with decreasing exports, a lack of investments, high rates of unemployment, and war and conflict, Mardin's economy stagnated between 1990 and 2000. In 2000, as in 1990, Mardin's share in Turkey's gross domestic product was only 0.4 percent (DİKA 2010; 19), and the proportion of its labor force in the industrial sector remained between 2.3 and 2.4 percent (Ekinci 2015). Although the Mardin city-region's high fertility rates led to an increase in population, which reached 705,098 in 2000, between 1990 and 2000 as noted in chapter 1, almost twice the number of people emigrated out of the Mardin city-region as immigrated into it. High rates of out-migration continued during the 2000s.

Part of this stagnation was due to the First Gulf War in Iraq, which drastically constricted Mardin's economy. After Turkey joined the coalition forces against Iraq in 1991, border trade ground to a halt. The only border-crossing to Iraq on the direct land route between Europe and the Middle East, the Habur Gate, 230 kilometers away from Mardin city center, was closed. Largely dependent on this cross-border trade, Mardin's economy also suffered from international sanctions imposed in 1990 on Iraq, which were observed by Turkey. Though some sectors, such as cement production, eventually benefited from rebuilding the areas in Iraq destroyed by the war, Mardin's economy continued to deteriorate until the early 2000s.

Despite offering profitable tax and labor conditions for investment, business, and trade transactions, even Mardin's Free Trade Zone failed to attract investment and capital. Trade volume dropped drastically between 1998 and 2001. Furthermore, in 2000–1 (at the same time that the United States and Manchester faced a severe downturn), Mardin and Turkey experienced their worst financial crisis since World War II. As stocks tumbled, banks went into crisis, and the Turkish lira was devalued, the economic situation worsened everywhere in Turkey. Mardin, still struggling after more than ten years of a conflict-ridden social, economic, and political environment and the after-effects of the Gulf War, certainly felt the effects.

Indeed, not only the Gulf War but also the US invasion of Iraq in March 2003 contributed to the further deterioration of Mardin's economy. At first Mardin's border positioning seemed to benefit the region as the war expanded. The US military leased industrial sites in Mardin's Industrial Organized Zone (IOZ) to provide a base for about sixty thousand soldiers as well as trucks and equipment (Migdalovitz 2003; Birch 2003). The US State Department and military expected Mardin to become the logistical support center for the US invasion force. However, contrary to US plans, the Turkish parliament rejected (March 1, 2003) the resolution that would have authorized the deployment of US troops to Turkey to invade Iraq from the north. Although Turkey granted the United States access to its airspace for air strikes shortly after the start of invasion and "agreed to provide food, fuel and other non-lethal supplies," Turkey-US relations suffered. Turkey lost revenues and billions of dollars in US aid and loans. Though the war opened opportunities for certain sectors in Mardin, trade with Iraq completely collapsed. Following the 2003 invasion, Mardin's local economy suffered severely and trade volume in the Free Trade Zone showed steep declines. With only twenty-three of its seventy factories in operation, the IOZ was producing at 10 percent of its capacity in 2003 and unemployment hovered above 50 percent (Collins 2003).

Yet, amid the economic and political dynamics that began in 1991 with the US invasion of Iraq in the Gulf War, which subsequently has led to continuous warfare in the region, in 1999 the European Union accepted Turkey's official candidacy for membership. This introduced a new set of conjunctural factors that shaped city-making possibilities and the relationship between Mardin and the city's minorities. Turkey's candidacy meant access to several EU funds, aspects of its institutional assets, and power, but to qualify for "accession negotiations" a series of conditions had to be met, including legal and institutional reforms.

Both the funding mechanisms and the required reforms had an important impact on various social, political, economic, and cultural power configurations, including the positioning of minorities such as Mardin's Syriac Christians (returnee or not) vis-à-vis the Turkish state and supranational institutional forces. Their EU candidacy gave rise to great expectations in Mardin after ten years of extreme economic stagnation, armed conflict between the PKK and the military, and warring in Iraq. Syriac Christians' "project of return" and the city leadership's efforts to reposition Mardin regionally and globally were situated within increased hopes of accessing the powerful EU networks that had entered into the conjunctural moment in the region.

"Return as a Project": Globally Mediated Emplacement

At the same time, in the wake of the arrest of the PKK leader in 1999 and a cease-fire brokered by the Turkish military and the PKK, although war was being waged in Iraq, relative peace emerged in Mardin. At that point, the national government sought to improve social and political conditions in southeastern Turkey through a series of development programs, especially in places where the population had been subject to severe displacements. One such regional development program, the Return to Village and Rehabilitation Project (RVRP), initiated in 1998 by the Turkish prime minister, targeted twelve cities, including Mardin. RVRP was formulated to attract displaced people with a series of monetary and/or in-kind incentives and to revive economic life in depopulated areas by creating favorable conditions for investment (Ayata and Yükseker 2005, 23).[3]

Syriac Christians abroad did not initially react to Turkish government programs designed to repopulate Mardin by reaching out to displaced populations. Then, in 2001, the prime minister specifically and directly addressed the displaced Syriac Christian population in Europe. According to the Mukhtar of Kafro, himself a returnee from Switzerland, Syriac Christians began to consider "the return" only after this 2001 call. Returnees or not, all Syriac Christians we talked to in Mardin, Istanbul, and Vienna emphasized that this renewed call addressed Syriac Christians as the original inhabitants of Mardin (burası [Mardin] Süryanilerindir) and, most importantly, promised to secure their religious and property rights (field notes, January–May 2015). Plans to "return" to their historical "homeland" and return-oriented HTAs like Kafro Tahtoyto began to emerge. Neither Kafro nor the Kafro Tahtoyto HTA was unique, although they were the most prominent town and organization in Syriac Christians' return narratives. In Europe, Syriac Christians from Mardin started to plan returning to other places in the Mardin city-region as well (such as Yemişli, Gülgöze, Altintaş, Anıtlı, Oyuklu, Sariköy).[4] They established numerous HTAs crisscrossing Europe and Mardin.

The abbot of the Mor Gabriel Monastery, the governor of Mardin, the Turkish deputy of the Syrian Catholic Patriarchate in Istanbul, and Mardin's local bishop of the Syriac Orthodox Church were all involved in conveying the 2001 call to return to recipients in Europe. In fact, after the call, the bishop and the Syrian Catholic Patriarchate immediately contacted Mardin's Syriac Christian expatriates in Europe, including the ones from Kafro, to mediate and facilitate the resettlement process (interview H., December 7, 2015).[5] By the autumn of 2001, Syriac Christians in Germany and in other parts of Europe had already been contacted. Like several other Syriac HTAs in Sweden, the Netherlands, Belgium, and Austria, the Kafro HTA began in Switzerland in January 2002 and was formed in the wake of such meetings.

As we indicate in chapter 1, Mardin's population, and especially its Christian population, has been subject to different streams of dispossessions, displacements, and emplacements (Gaunt 2006). Although Armenians suffered most from massacres and forced displacements, Syriac Christians also had these experiences, including what they refer to as the Syriac genocide (Seyfo, "the sword") in 1915. The highest toll of the Syriac massacre was in Tur Abdin, the historical homeland of Syriac Christians; Mardin city-region is part of Tur Abdin.[6] The Armenian genocide and the Seyfo reduced Mardin's Christian population from 36,000 in 1914 to 11,000 in 1927 (Aydın et al. 2000, 370).[7] The memory of these massacres and the complicated alliances and hostilities between religious and ethnic groups and Ottoman military forces that emerged during these events continue to affect the political and social dynamics in Mardin and in the Syriac Christian "diaspora."[8]

Throughout the history of the Midyat district of Mardin city-region, Syriac Christians had densely populated the district where the village of Kafro is located. Until the 1930s, Midyat was the only district in Turkey where Christians outnumbered Muslims (Oktik and Nas 2005). After the establishment of the Turkish Republic (1923), Midyat, like many other places in Turkey, began to lose its Christian population.

Faced with state Turkification policies and the suppression of religious and linguistic rights during the Turkish Republic, the Syriac Christians who survived the massacre left Mardin in large numbers. As mentioned earlier, Syriac Christians were the only non-Muslim minority in Turkey whom the Lausanne Treaty did not grant the limited rights accorded to other non-Muslim minorities (Jews, Greeks, and Armenians) that safeguarded their language and religion. Changes in military-service laws permitting conscription of non-Muslim citizens for indefinite periods of service and the introduction in 1942 of a capital tax that levied higher taxes on non-Muslim citizens of Turkey triggered further dispossession and displacement of Syriacs from Turkey and from Mardin. During the Cyprus crisis in 1964 and the Turkish invasion of Cyprus in 1974, which was a Greek and Turkish island, anti-Greek sentiment played an important role in Syriac Christian displacements. Associated with the Greek Orthodox population in the popular imaginary, Syriac Christians were threatened with lynching and looting (Aydın et al. 2000; Özmen 2013; Biner 2011). This fueled additional out-migration from Mardin.

Armed conflict between the PKK and the Turkish Army led to a massive displacement of Syriacs in the 1980s and 1990s because they faced economic and physical insecurity.[9] In fact, Mardin witnessed the displacement of two different groups during the years of conflict, which changed the demographic composition of both Mardin's city-region and its old town. In southeastern Turkey, the Turkish military evacuated thousands of villages, ordering their inhabitants to leave their property behind. Other villages were abandoned as inhabitants fled for their lives. Approximately 2 million people (mostly

Kurds) had been forced to leave their villages. By 1996, Kafro had been evacuated by the Turkish Army and declared a prohibited area. It remained completely abandoned until displaced Syriac Christian inhabitants started to return in the mid-2000s.

Evacuations and forced displacements resulted in an influx of dispossessed peasants into urban areas. In Mardin city-region, many of these dispossessed villagers settled in district centers and on the fringes of the old town in Mardin's city center, becoming a cheap labor pool.[10] Meanwhile, most Syriac Christians from Mardin fled to Europe. Simultaneously, the local elites and upper middle classes also left the city. In Mardin's city center, which used to be predominantly Christian, only seventy-five Christian families were left by 2000. All Mardinites we spoke to, including returnees, still have vivid memories of these difficult times, particularly the periods of martial law.[11] As we have shown in chapter 1, periods of martial law and states of emergency were strongly associated with violence, terror, and poverty in the eyes of all Mardin residents, including Syriacs.[12]

After a century of displacement, 3.5 million Syriac Christians (often referred to as the "Syriac diaspora") are estimated to live in Europe, the United States, Australia, Brazil, Iraq, Syria, and India. Many Syriac Christians who fled Mardin in the 1960s settled in Europe as "guest workers"; in the 1980s and 1990s, they came as refugees. However, despite the multiple religious and political networks and institutions interconnecting these places of settlement, until the beginning of the 2000s, Europe's Syriac Christian population kept few if any ties to their hometown. On the other hand, they had established complex and changing forms of alliances and relations with other displaced minority groups from Turkey living in Europe.[13]

In 2002, following the Turkish prime minister's call to return and the initiation of the EU accession process, about ninety Syriacs from Mardin who lived in different parts of Europe organized a visit to Mardin to assess the conditions there firsthand. Initially, many were hesitant even to visit Mardin, but they were reassured by various commitments made to them. As a returnee to Kafro put it, "After being in touch with several institutions and authorities in Mardin and in Europe, we were encouraged that we could return and claim our abandoned land" (interview A., May 16, 2015). A Syriac Christian businessman who was very active in Syriac politics in Midyat saw Kafro as "a model village, which we have been organizing for several years. We wanted that village to give hope to the frustrated and displaced Syriacs abroad" (interview L., 2014). Along similar lines, another returnee recalls that their "organized return" was carefully orchestrated and transnationally planned. He reported, "We [displaced Syriacs from Mardin in Europe] had twenty-three meetings in different places in Europe before we actually returned" (interview B., May 13, 2015). After much preparation, including beginning the construction of Kafro's stone houses in 2004, seventeen Syriac Christian families from Zurich, Augsburg, Trulliken, and Goppingen returned to Kafro in 2006 (Güsten 2016). Ninety-one families from Europe resettled in the Mardin city-region.[14]

The guarantee of Syriac emigrants' property and religious rights, which was crucial in their decision to return, embedded the returnees' emplacement in Mardin within a social and political field composed of networks of powerful Christian institutions, religious foundations, and supranational institutions such as the EU. In the early 2000s, land registries in Turkey were being modernized as part of the required legal and institutional reforms that were conditions of Turkey's EU accession. Within this registration scheme, unless owners registered their titles for abandoned and/or expropriated land, they would lose all legal entitlement to their property. Thus, these reforms would have a substantial impact on landownership and on the legalization of land grabs. Those living abroad who had fled persecution, poverty, and war were particularly affected.

Many displaced Syriac Christians were confronted with losing their legal entitlement to most of their land in several ways. According to Turkish law, land left untilled for twenty years is counted as "abandoned" and was claimed by the state treasury. Similarly, although it had been private property, land classified as "forested" can be seized and transformed into the property of the state forestry ministry. Moreover, special clauses stipulated that those who were not registered as village residents were prevented from owning village land. Displaced Syriac Christians' property was subject to all these forms of land grabbing and expropriation.

Absent Syriac Christians were dispossessed from their land because they were not able to find ways to till their land and pay the property tax. Such properties were transferred to the state treasury as abandoned land. Abandoned vineyards and fruit orchards, which had provided livelihoods for Syriac Christians before they fled, were burned down by the military to prevent guerilla fighters from hiding there in the 1990s. Thus, many Syriacs and others who fled or were evicted from this war-torn region lost their property to the state treasury or forestry through formally "legal" expropriations. As shown in chapter 1, property transferred to the state treasury later became an important resource in restructuring Mardin.

Most displaced Syriacs were subject to another form of land grabbing that specifically targeted the minorities who were forced to abandon their land (Güsten 2015). Many emigrants from Mardin ended up losing their land to squatters from nearby villages, in most cases to their (Kurdish) neighbors, who simply registered the abandoned Syriac land to their own names or seized it by force (Griffith 1999, 2000, 2001). Since the 1990s, Mardinite Syriacs in Europe no longer resided or had a legal presence in Mardin, so they lacked the power to counteract this expropriation (Güsten 2015, 2016). Thus, the physical return and settlement of Syriacs in Mardin Kafro was crucial to claiming rightful ownership of formally or informally seized property. Although by 2015, returnees to Kafro, like those in other parts of Mardin, had been able to register only 20 percent of their land as their own property, they all said that, had they not returned, they would have been legally dispossessed of all the property they abandoned when they were forced to flee (field notes, December 2014–May 2015).[15]

As indicated by Kafro's guest book entries, which we refer to at the beginning of this chapter, global and supranational institutions and forces loomed large in the Syriac Christians' vision of their "project of return" and emplacement in Mardin. All the returnees we have spoken to referred to their return as an orchestrated resettlement involving a broad range of actors and institutions. Syriac returnees' designation of their resettlement as "return as a project" or as an "organized return" denoted the multiscalar social field within which their HTAS and their return were embedded. Indeed, a closer look at their return reveals a surprisingly broad range of global, supranational, and religious state and nonstate actors concerned with and involved in the return and emplacement of Syriac Christians in Mardin. As the reports and communiqués written by representatives of powerful global institutions manifest, Syriac Christians' "collective return" and their continued presence in Mardin were of concern to all these institutions.

These concerns came together at the nexus of several different but intersecting, political, economic, and religious agendas. The project to revitalize Mardin was the meeting point for multiple institutional networks of power. These included globe-spanning financial and corporate institutions bent on the accumulation of capital through urban restructuring and tourism; the EU, with its own complex mission of capital formation and geopolitical influence; the United States and NATO, with related but not identical imperial projects entangled with military interests; and global Christian institutions, with their religious missions. Beginning in the 1990s, representatives of several religious missions in Europe and the Middle East; representatives from the embassies of the United Kingdom, Australia, the United States, Holland,

Switzerland, India, Canada, Korea, Slovenia, and Germany; and the US Defense Attaché, the chairman of the secretary of state's Advisory Committee on Religious Freedom abroad, and representatives of UNESCO all visited Mardin and met with several representatives of local churches and monasteries and with Mardin's governor. Each visitor expressed interest in the region through queries framed about the welfare, condition, and especially the religious rights and freedom of Christians in the area. Their reports repeatedly assessed the possibilities of Syriac Christians' return (Griffith 1999).

Tourism Industries, Urban Regeneration, and the Valorization of Syriac Christians in Mardin

The meeting points between the project of urban regeneration, assistance from EU institutions, and a variety of funds, on the one hand, and the project of Syriac Christian return, on the other, were the heritage tourism industry and Turkey's EU candidacy. City leaders looked to this nexus to attract investment and capital to the city, to generate wealth, and to alter Mardin's regional and global connectedness. Attracting investments and capital became more viable with the opportunities opened by the context of the relatively peaceful environment following the cease-fire with Kurdish guerillas, the emerging markets and the changing global power dynamics in the Middle East. Heritage industry–induced urban regeneration and pre-accession EU funds and institutions established an axis of efforts to reposition Mardin within a multiscalar field. It is within these processes that Syriac Christians, returnees, their HTAs, and the spaces that came to be associated with them acquired value in Mardin. All these value-creation processes became entangled with and constitutive of each other.

During the early 2000s, heritage tourism industries came to the forefront as sectors through which wealth could be generated. The goal was to attract capital, resources, and subsidies to reposition the city regionally and globally. In 1999, in order to develop domestic tourism, an airport opened in Mardin and an international airport was planned for 2014. At the same time, mayors, governors, and businessmen in Mardin put forth a coordinated effort to promote the city-region through heritage tourism and cultural and art events. City-promoting documentaries and promotional material "commissioned" by Mardin businessmen appeared on domestic and international media, incuding numerous TV channels (TRT, NTV, Show TV, BBC, Al Jazeera, Hungarian TV), and were featured in Sunday and travel newspaper supplements. In the tourism sector, cultural institutions and activities were developed to transform Mardin's image from a fortified, dangerous, violence-ridden site to a city with a centuries-old legacy of the peaceful cohabitation of religions, languages, and ethnic groups. Mardin's Syriac Christian minority became central to these branding narratives.

To brand Mardin as a city with a multifaith heritage, city leaders, project directors, and businessmen organized and launched several promotional campaigns. They agreed that Mardin should be branded for "niche tourism, with culture and heritage tourism . . . because it is classified internationally as the place of birth of civilizations" (interview P., 2015). According to the program director of the Sustainable Tourism Project:

> The advantage of Mardin compared to the other cities in the region is that it is not a simple religious tourism. . . . Mardin is culture and heritage. . . . A tourist goes to see a monument, it is a pile of old stones. . . . You have to give meaning to the pile of stones. . . . If I mention three cities to you internationally and ask you the one thing that is famous about them—if I say London you would say Big Ben or if I say France you would say Eiffel Tower. What would you say about Mardin? The Deyrulzafaran Monastery in Mardin. . . . [It] is the oldest monastery operating in the world. . . . The Deyrulzafaran Monastery is a Syriac institution, it is presented very well. . . . This is a Syriac tourist attraction (interview P., 2015).

Branding and regenerating Mardin through culture and heritage tourism acquired considerable momentum in the second half of the 2000s through several tourism and urban development projects. Large projects were needed to market the city globally. One of the most important sources of funding for tourism infrastructure and urban regeneration projects in Mardin was the EU. Since Turkey was not a member state, it was not entitled to full EU development and structural funds. However, as an accession country, beginning in 1999 Turkey became eligible for financial assistance through Instrument for Pre-Accession (IPA) funds. These funds provided EU candidate countries with assistance in their transition to membership. At the same time, this funding required the EU to monitor a country's progress in fulfilling membership conditions. The monitoring process focused on the development of legal and political frameworks that specified the rights and obligations of EU governments and citizens, and these concerns shaped how the return of the Syriac Christians was narrated within the city's regeneration processes. Turkey received its first IPA funding in 2002.

At the same time, several of the initiatives that sought to situate Mardin within the tourism-heritage industry were also closely entangled with urban regeneration. The old city center and its historical buildings as well as the multireligious, multiethnic, multicultural built environment in the Mardin city-region had to be renewed and restored. As the presence of Syriac Christians was vital to verifying the multifaith nature of this heritage, restoring Syriac (as well as Catholic and Orthodox) monasteries and churches in situ took pride of place in accessing funds and institutional support for restoration projects. Funds came from different global institutions.

The Mardin Participatory Urban Rehabilitation Project (Mardinar Project) initiated the restoration and renovation processes in the city. Financial support came from the government of Switzerland through the United Nations Development Programme (UNDP), and the project was supervised by Istanbul Technical University. The state-sponsored South East Anatolian Project (GAP-Gidem) channeled project coordination for the Mardinar Project to local actors and organized a civic platform (Local Agenda, Yerel Gündem). This was turned into a civic organization called City Council, with support from the UNDP, the World Bank, and İstanbul Technical University as well as from the local governor, the municipality, and other local actors. According to one of its founders (interview K., 2015), those involved in the Mardinar Project were enchanted with "the idea that such a project would permit [us] not only to preserve the historical assets of Mardin and promote them to the world but also convert them into marketable commodities. . . . Mardin will be promoted to the world!! These assets will be preserved and promoted to the world. But also these assets will become our bread." The Mutual Aid and Education Foundation of Mardinites (MAREV) in Istanbul and the City Council platform played a critical role in the implementation of this project.[16] Another large (9.2 million euro) project that sought to promote the city globally by improving Mardin's tourism infrastructure focused on renewing the main street (1st Avenue) of the old city center by refurbishing building facades and standardizing signboards, shutters, and sunshades.[17]

According to a member of the civic platform City Council, to create Mardin as a tourist attraction for cultural tourism, they tried to attract the funds of cultural agents such as the World Bank, the EU, and cultural funds of certain countries. Within the IPA framework, twenty-six projects in Mardin received a total of 3,194,910 euro. Additionally, projects developed by different Turkish ministries and associations were also supported through EU funds. One such project, the Mardin-Cultural Tourism Project, aimed to improve the infrastructure of the tourism industry and the city's marketing activities.[18] These funds also helped regenerate the old town. In addition to contributing "to the social and economic development of Mardin" by strengthening

FIG 5.2 Mardin city center, before renovation. Photograph by Ayşe Çağlar.

FIG 5.3 Mardin city center, after partial renovation. Photograph by Ayşe Çağlar.

its tourism sector, the Mardin-Cultural Tourism Project's main aim was to develop and execute a branding strategy for the city (GOPA Worldwide Consultants 2012).

Moreover, 6,795,809 euro were allocated to eight projects in Mardin through the Financial Support Program for the Development of Competitive Sectors and Financial Support Program for Industry, Tourism and City Infrastructure via the regional Turkish development agency DİKA, established in 2010 as part of the reforms introduced to bolster Turkey's EU candidacy.[19] The development of tourism infrastructure and urban regeneration was closely connected in the deployment of these funds. Because of this support for tourism and urban regeneration projects, domestic and international (especially heritage) tourism substantially increased in Mardin. After the mid-2000s, the city witnessed steady domestic and international tourism, and organized tours and flights to Mardin increased. The number of tourists visiting Mardin increased from 54,870 in 2001 to 203,000 in 2010. At 270 percent, growth was double the average in Turkey (Egresi, Kara, and Bayram 2012), and between 2009 and 2012, the total number of visitors to Mardin increased 44 percent. Consequently, employment in tourism-related areas (hotel, restaurant, food and beverage services, transportation) as well as in the culture and entertainment sector also increased in Mardin (Mardin Tourism Strategic Plan 2014; İŞKUR 2011).[20]

The ambitious urban rehabilitation project carried out by the municipality, governorship, and the Housing Development Administration (TOKİ), which we refer to in chapter 1, aimed to regenerate the old town by returning "the historic city of Mardin to the way it looked around a century ago." In announcing the massive renewal project, the governor of Mardin emphasized the city leaders' regenerative vision: "We constructed the city's past from the perspective of its future" (Star Gazete 2011). According to him, "Mardin possessed an extraordinary cultural heritage, and as therefore, ancient churches belonging to the city's Süryani [Syriac Christian] community were pegged next for restoration. . . . We are doing what suits a city known for its tolerance" (Ana-Mardelli 2011). The construction sector and related subfields became local economic drivers in the context of these massive rehabilitation and regeneration projects.

Syriac Christians also took central stage in the emerging cultural institutions that were established in Mardin after the mid-2000s. On the one hand, these institutions and their public activities contributed to the further valorization of Syriac Christians as integral to the city by depicting them as part of the city's past and its daily life. On the other hand, because these new institutions played vital roles in urban restructuring, their invocation of a Syriac Christian presence entered into the restructuring process. Artuklu University, Mardin City Museum, and the Biennial art festival are examples of such institutions that were established in the second half of 2000s. They used decaying but occupied or abandoned historical buildings in the city that were made available to them through the city governorship or the central state. All contributed to the regeneration of those parts of the city in which they were located. And all three invoked Mardin's Syriac Christian population (past and present), their language, and their architectural and religious legacy as part of the revaluation of urban districts and structures.

The teaching staff of the newly founded Mardin's Artuklu University (2007) included both foreign- and Turkish-born faculty and North American —or European-educated staff as well as well-known scholars commuting from Istanbul or Ankara to Mardin. The transnational reach of the university faculty to the United States and Europe was remarkable. The old-town campus, located in historical buildings, became a particularly important factor in regenerating a very run-down city area. The campus offered attractive, restored buildings and restaurants and cafes catering to students, the faculty, and frequent visitors from different parts of Turkey and abroad. Former residents of this area were displaced.

The university was established with a global vision. In the words of a City Council member, "We had an idea of a university in which the language of instruction would be Arabic, Kurdish, Turkish, Assyrian, and the Chaldean language. There are many examples of such universities in Tokyo or London. With this project, we were planning to promote Mardin to the world" (interview M., December 2014). Indeed, with the initiation of the Institute of Living Languages in Mardin, Kurdish, Arabic, Aramaic, and Chaldean were taught at a university institute in Turkey for the first time. Mardin's very first Syriac Christian co-mayor, elected in 2014, was a graduate of this institute.

Mardin City Museum, which opened its doors to visitors in 2009 with the support of an influential private holding company, was located in a renovated historical building facing Artuklu University's newly refurbished Department of Architecture. The structure that housed the museum had previously been a decaying building owned by the Ministry of Tourism and Culture but had since been transferred to an Istanbul-based private foundation. The governor at that time expected a regenerational synergy from the comprehensive renovation of abandoned and decaying historical buildings in the area such as the one housing the museum.[21] According to him, the museum would transform its immediate vicinity "[in]to a square like those in European cities" (Yavuz 2012, 54–55). The director of Mardin City Museum in 2015 was well aware of the museum's regenerative impact.

He saw "the opening of the Museum as a milestone of urban restructuring in that part of the old town in Mardin":

> Before the opening of the Museum, on that road one could not even walk because of the mud. . . . There was not even a road. . . . The facades of these houses were also restored afterwards. Then, the tide in this part completely changed. . . . This street found life, became rejuvenated, Mardin became rejuvenated. The number of tourists increased ten times. . . . The activities in the museum, the exhibitions and the symposiums all changed the social texture and the social and cultural life in Mardin (interview E., February 22, 2015).

According to Mardin's governor, the museum was expected to develop a sense of urban history (Yavuz 2012, 54–55). Indeed, its permanent exhibition on Mardin's history and everyday life and culture contributed to the popularization and valorization of the city's minorities (especially its Christian minority) and the multifaith character of city life. Starting in 2010, the three Mardin Biennials (2010, 2012, 2015) utilized historical sites in Mardin, with the aims of "transforming Mardin into a center of contemporary art" and making the city "a part of the cultural and artistic map of the world" (Mardin Biennial 2015). They utilized historical religious sites and places of daily life for exhibitions and installations. Curators of the first and second Biennials had internationally acknowledged track records with other international celebrations in Thessaloniki and Istanbul and exhibitions in art institutions in Rome, Italy; Manchester, United Kingdom; and the Dallas Museum of Art in the United States (Mardin Biennial 2012). Enjoying support from a broad spectrum of public, private, and civil society actors ranging from the British Council and the French and Spanish Cultural Institutes to the Catholic Syriac Foundation and the Chaldean and Mor Benham (Syriac) Church, selected Biennial sites often highlighted Mardin's built environment, which was portrayed as representing the city's Christian (Orthodox and Catholic) and Muslim heritage. However, the broad resonance these Biennials found in Turkish and international media and their remarkable multiscalar reach stood in contrast to their presence in local inhabitants' everyday life.

While attending the third Biennial, Ayşe and Seda experienced the contrast between, on the one hand, the degree to which Christian minorities and the festival were absent in the everyday life of most of the city's residents and, on the other, the remarkable multiscalar reach of Mardin's Biennial. Excited by an invitation announcing that local Mardin residents, rather than professionals, would curate exhibits, Ayşe started asking directions to the monastery where the Biennial's opening would take place. First, she inquired at a renovated historic inn, turned hotel, the Artuklu Caravan Palace. While waiting for someone to assist her, Ayşe examined pictures on the walls of the empty guest corridor. They documented visits of political and business celebrities—from Prince Charles to well-known businesspeople in Turkey—to Mardin and to the hotel.

Surprised to learn that no one at the hotel knew anything about the Biennial, Ayşe sought information from people on the old town's newly renovated 1st Avenue, replete with shops displaying specialties from Mardin, such as soaps, spiced almonds and tea, Syriac wine, and jewelry. She was certain that someone would know the way. But the shopkeeper's customers and the pedestrians had not heard of the Biennial or did not know where the monastery was located. Finally, by chance, she ran into a Syriac shopkeeper whom she knew was involved in the Biennial. He was on his way to the opening and told Ayşe he would escort her. When they arrived at the Catholic Monastery, which had stood abandoned and decaying for more than eighty years, Ayşe once again was surprised. The courtyard of the monastery Ayşe had so much difficulty finding was filled with Turkish and international artists and journalists, city leaders and representatives of several NGOs and international organizations, as well as a group of locals who were closely involved with the Biennial. The opening was held in Turkish with English translation (field notes, May 2015).

The project to make Mardin a global city renowned for its unique, centuries-old, multireligious heritage included attempts by city leaders and developers to ensure that certain religious sites were included on the UNESCO World Heritage list of historical sites. Inclusion became important in the city leadership's agenda for re-empowerment. As the governor of Mardin said at the completion of an IPA-funded project, "Mardin needs to be renewed to become a value and Mardin needs to become part of UNESCO." However, since the city withdrew its first application in 2002, when it seemed destined to fail, it has not officially submitted other applications.

There was a renewed attempt in 2013 to submit an application to UNESCO. This effort was a good example of not only the importance of historical conjuncture in the positioning of Syriac Christians in city narratives and urban regeneration projects but also of the positioning of Syriac Christian returnees and minorities within city politics. The dynamics around this attempt were an early indicator that power constellations in the region were once again changing as a result of the shifting priorities of the Turkish state and the positioning of Syriac Christians within them. At the same time, this application process highlighted the emerging agendas and trajectories of the returnees themselves.

In this new UNESCO application attempt, international and local actors involved in Mardin's large-scale sustainable tourism project brought in "a top consultant, a retired UNESCO expert." The consultant's report stated, "The best chance that Mardin has got for UNESCO nomination is to concentrate on the Syriac Christian population." Furthermore, the expert clearly recommended the "promotion of the Syriac culture, Syriac churches and monasteries, especially Deyrulzafaran" (interview P., February 2015). According to the president of the Association of Syriac Unity, "UNESCO officials noticed not only the exclusion of (Syriac) Deyrulzeferan Monastery in the [former] application, but they noticed the official mentality of this country, negating this people [the Syriacs].... UNESCO saw this." He proudly added that UNESCO's realization of the Turkish State's hostile and exclusionary attitude was the result of the "coordinated work [of Mardin's returnees and Syriac minorities] with the Syriacs abroad" (interview G., December 2014).

However, by 2015, the political climate in Turkey changed. Especially after the escalation and expansion of the Syrian Civil War, Turkey changed its regional priorities and aspirations, and moved away from the EU. In these new conditions, the Mardinate governorate (under control of the central government) rejected the consultant's advice because of the primacy of Syriac Christians and their heritage in his report. The application process stopped.

Turkey's EU Accession, Minority Rights, and the Christian Presence in Mardin

By 2015, the Syriac Christian inhabitants of Mardin and the city's multifaith heritage acquired value in the city's public, social, economic, and cultural life as Syriac Christians became part of city leaderships' efforts to reposition Mardin in relation to global and supranational fields of power. However, despite the prominence of religious diversity and the heritage industry in these efforts and hopes, the valorization of Mardin's Syriac minority and its success in reaching out to powerful regional, supranational, and global actors were not simply an issue of religious and cultural diversity. It would be misleading to simply frame Mardin's repositioning dynamics as culture-led urban restructuring fueled by cultural diversity and cultural industries.

The EU, as an institution and as a political body, had been present in regeneration processes, discourses, and imaginaries in Mardin in multiple ways. The EU was present in Mardin in terms of funding mechanisms and schemes but also as part of cultural and religious rights discourses. EU funding schemes and policies and its mechanisms for monitoring and supervising improvements in Turkey's democratization (in line with the EU mission) were very much entangled with each other. The financial assistance through the IPA schemes we referred to and the EU mission of fostering respect for democracy, the rule of law, and human rights were closely connected. Turkey's accession status implied that the EU assistance would "be used to support a stable, modern, democratic, multi ethnic and open society based on the rule of law . . . where promoting respect for human rights is often linked to promoting cultural and religious rights . . . and above all tolerance and religious freedom to religious minorities" (Bodirsky 2012, 15). Monitoring Turkey's governance of its minorities, especially Christians, has been crucial to the EU's "regime of supervision" (Cowan 2007b).

Since its acceptance of the Lisbon Strategy in 2001 and its further neoliberalization, EU funding policies increasingly connected the endorsement of diversity to the generation of wealth. Thus, the utility of culture for making places conducive to capital, especially by creating business- and investment-friendly climates, came increasingly to the forefront in EU funding schemes. Since adopting laws of harmonization in 2001, debates on Turkey's suitability for EU membership were marked by Turkey's record of violations of minority cultural and/or religious rights and the potential value of religious diversity and rights for economic competitiveness (Arıkan 2003, 25, quoted in Bodirsky 2012).

With the start of accession negotiations in 2005, the rights of religious minorities increasingly occupied an important place in EU narratives. In all EU funding provided to Mardin, the need to embrace and strengthen minority rights and religious freedom and the urgency to strengthen local and civil society institutions and governance to attract business to the region were strikingly present. Driven by the contestations surrounding Turkey's accession to the EU within Europe and by the importance of religious and linguistic diversity and freedom within EU criteria, the physical presence and well-being of religious minorities like Syriac Christians in their ancestral land became an index of Turkey's observance of minority rights, religious freedom and tolerance, and the rule of law.

It is important to note that Mardin's multilingual and Christian heritage, personified by Syriac Christians, acquired importance in city-making processes once they became assets for city leaders reaching out to supranational and global institutions and once their presence was taken as an indicator that the city was a safe place for capital investment. They became a valorized political asset because of a constellation of global, political, and regional dynamics, aspirations, and policies that acquired salience in Mardin at the historical conjuncture we have outlined.

The actual return of persecuted and displaced Syriac Christians to Mardin acquired a crucial importance in all public discourses about the EU and Turkey's EU accession. Turkey's desire to join the European Union, and EU pressures on the Turkish state to secure and protect its religious minorities, particularly in light of past failures to do so, played an important role in the prime minister's address in 2001 concerning displaced Syriac Christians from Mardin then living in Europe:

> It has been alleged that citizens of Syriac origin who left the country due to the PKK terror or other reasons have been confronted with certain problems when returning to their villages. . . . *It is thought that these allegations could become the subject of new human rights violations complaints against Turkey by international circles. In order to prevent this turning into a campaign against Turkey,* the Ministry of the Interior will carry out the necessary measures to permit those citizens of Syriac origin who have sought asylum or settled in European countries to return to their villages if they so wish (quoted in Güsten 2016, 11, our emphasis).

Immediately after this address by the prime minister to displaced Christians from Mardin in Europe, restoration began on many of the abandoned convents and monasteries of Christian minorities in southeastern Turkey.[22]

Concomitantly, the EU assessment about whether Christian rights would be respected was reflected in Syriac Christians' discourse about the return to Mardin. The Archbishop of Mor Gebreil believed that the continuity of the positive developments regarding Mardin's Syriac population depended on EU surveillance. The Archbishop of the Deyrulzfaran Monastery saw a direct connection between protection of Christian minority rights and Turkey–EU relations: "We would like to see Turkey in the EU to live better and practice our culture better. We, as Christian minorities, have a great task in establishing ties between Turkey and the European Union" (Çulpan 2004). It is noteworthy that the minister responsible for human rights in the Turkish parliament was part of the group visiting Mardin and its villages in June 2006 to assess the Syriac migrants' return (Midyat Habur 2006). Officials from the European Parliament also took part in Mardin's many festivities celebrating the resettlement of Syriac Christians. Symbolically, a EU flag waved on the Syriac Cultural Center in Midyat.

In short, the return of the displaced Christians and their continued presence in Mardin was understood as an indicator both of an improvement in Turkey's human rights record of securing Christians' property and religious rights and of the restoration of political stability and the success of the peace process in the region. The return of Mardin's persecuted Syriac Christian minority became an enactment of its safe environment. Providing a safe, business-friendly environment was crucial in reaching out to powerful institutions and attracting much-desired business and investment to the city. Public enactments of religious diversity, human rights, and the rule of law with a prominent role accorded to Christians were crucial for Mardin's hopes of regeneration and re-empowerment.

When the Archbishop of Tur Abdin said that "the church, the government and the Muslim population all hope that the returnees will develop the region" (Trauthig 2003), he was indeed expressing hopes integrally linked to global players including investors. For this reason, not only the Syriac Christian heritage in the city but also the actual return of Syriac Christians, despite their small numbers, were highlighted on every occasion. Their continued presence in the city was repeatedly and publicly performed as contributing to Mardin's cultural, economic, and *political* capital. They also became a political asset in Turkey–EU relations.[23]

Thus, for Mardin's leaders, performances of tolerance and religious diversity became part of providing a "good business climate" for attracting capital. Given the conflict-ridden, war-torn image of Mardin from the 1990s to 2000, public enactments of safety and tolerance by returnees in the second half of the 2000s became important for attracting any business to the city. This is what the governor of Mardin highlighted when he hailed Mardin's progress, in "becoming an important world brand." Referring to the peace process, he added, "People are now thinking that the city is safer than it used to be, and they are coming to our city to see its historical and cultural richness. And many businessmen have also been investing in the city" (World Bulletin 2013).

To improve Mardin's image by diminishing its associations with war and violence, Mardiniate businessmen invited powerful businessmen from Istanbul and Ankara to Mardin, including the president of the Turkish Industrialists' and Businessmen's Association (TÜSIAD), the most powerful business association in Turkey. They organized important annual meetings of business federations and associations in Mardin and hosted the leaders of major holdings in Turkey. At these meetings, the Mardiniate businessmen promoted Mardin's safe and investment-conducive environment (interview F.,

March 3, 2015). Their hopes for repositioning Mardin were shaped by the reconfiguring of forces and emerging markets in the Middle East, especially after the 2008 crisis, the Turkish state's regional and global aspirations, and Turkey–EU relations.

As a result, as we show in chapter 1, domestic as well as foreign investments increased along with Mardin's export volume. Between 2002 and 2012, the city's share in Turkey's exports increased tenfold, and between 2009 and 2012 it increased by 120 percent. However, as we also detail in chapter 1, the increased investments, impressive exports, and acquisition of funds and subsidies from the Turkish state, the EU, the World Bank, and UNDP did not increase income levels in Mardin. Increasing exports of low value-added products failed to translate into higher income levels. The use of public monies and resources, especially by TOKİ, for urban regeneration drained public coffers while contributing to private corporate profits. In terms of its life quality according to the Human Capital index, Mardin dropped from seventy-sixth to eightieth in Turkey from 2009 to 2010 (Urak 2011, quoted in Ekinci 2015).

Presence but Not Entitlement

"We were promised several things for both sides [EU and Turkish state] and were disappointed by both sides." So one returnee summarized the lessons that he and others who sought emplacement in Mardin had learned. According to him, both the EU and the Turkish state did not live up to their promises. Land entitlements continue to be a problem. Neither the five thousand euro from a Swiss church organization to restore Kafro's church nor the water pump donated by the German ambassador was enough to sustain returnees' hopes. Construction by the Turkish state of Internet infrastructure accompanied by donated computers was also an insufficient encouragement for people eagerly returning to lands from which they had been violently displaced (field notes, May 2015).

The road to Kafro was in very bad condition, and repeated complaints to the Mardin metropolitan municipality remained unheeded until 2014, when Kurdish and Syriac co-mayors were elected. One returnee, who was also a member of the Kafro HTA, expressed very clearly that "if we [Syriacs] *accept* returning and being here, then conditions for us here should be very good, this is very clear" (interview A., May 14, 2015, our emphasis). As he complained of the lack of follow-up projects, Ayşe asked what would be his dream project. Without hesitation, he answered, "The settlement of 2,000–

3,000 Syriac families from Europe through a collaborative project between the Turkish state and the EU."

Many returnees underlined the need for a broader project with sustainable support, possibly from European and international institutions. However, they were all quick to add, "for that, one needs the necessary know-how and the local contacts and power," which, according to them, they lacked. Complaints about the lack of daily political power at the local level contrasts with the striking presence of Mardin's Syriacs in the agendas of the aforementioned powerful institutions and actors, in all imaginaries about Mardin in media, in cultural and tourist industries centered on Mardin, in development projects and reports, in cultural and art events in and about Mardin, and above all in narratives of city leaders since the millennium. Without exception, Syriac Christians and their resettlement in Mardin were central to reports about the city and to promotional features in numerous magazines and newspapers between 2000 and 2015.[24]

While city leaders and businessmen positioned Syriac Christian returnees as a cultural, economic, and political asset for the heritage industry and highlighted their presence in efforts to reassure potential investors about the city's safety as well as to demonstrate Turkey's improvement in respecting minority rights and religious freedom, they failed to acknowledge the multiplicity of Christian Syriacs returnees' involvement, together with other Mardinates, in other forms of city-making. After their return, Syriac Christians continued to be strongly embedded within a multiscalar social field connecting them and their HTAS not only throughout the region[25] but also throughout Europe via multiple institutionalized, interconnecting networks and umbrella Syriac associations (such as European Syriac Unity and Federation of Syriac Associations).

Once we adopted a multiscalar perspective, we were able to trace the simultaneity and multiplicity of Mardin's residents' interconnected network relationships. Though overlapping, these networks were never isomorphic. However, through mutual relationships, minorities, migrants, returnees, and non-migrants mutually constituted networks of multiple scales, although these interconnections never encompassed all Mardin's residents or all those displaced from Mardin. Nor were these relationships fixed; they were ever changing within contingent conjunctural forces.

For example, by following the daily activities of Mahmut, a shopkeeper, we could trace a multiscalar field encompassing not only Syriac Christians abroad and the residents of the city, including Mardinite returnees, but also political, religious, and economic local, national, supranational, and global institutional networks. Mahmut had an artisan jewelry shop on the reno-vated 1st Avenue of the old town. Neither a migrant nor a returnee, Mahmut was a Syriac Christian Mardinate who had never left Mardin. As a shop-keeper, he became part of the regeneration processes at the "heart" of the old town. Producing and exhibiting jewelry inspired by traditional Syriac de-signs, which he developed as an art form, Mahmut sought international and domestic tourists as his customer base.

However, his shop, situated centrally on the main street of the old town, connected his small business to the powerful multiscalar actors seeking to rebuild and reposition the city. These included the heritage-based tourism industry and the infrastructure renewal projects, as we highlight in chap-ter 1, funded by global actors such as the EU, UNDP, and powerful domestic and international institutions. At the same time, Mahmut's family and so-cial networks connected him closely to city narratives of Mardin's multifaith legacy, which had been circulating widely in domestic and international me-dia since 2000. These branding narratives and their transnational reach were facilitated by international consulting agencies, with funding and publicity coming in part from pre-accession EU funds. One of Mahmut's relatives' em-broidery and printed textiles depicting Syriac Christian figures and themes became part of the multifaith heritage display in the Mardin City Museum, which contributed to the regeneration of a dilapidated part of the old town.

Mahmut simultaneously participated in broader networks of cultural and art institutions with a clear transnational and multiscalar reach. He became part of the team of city resident curators for the third Biennial, which was tightly integrated into, and benefited from, funding and support from Brit-ish, French, and Spanish cultural institutes as well as from global religious foundations, numerous religious institutions, and churches. The opening of the third Biennial at an abandoned and decaying Syriac Catholic Monastery (Mor Ephraim) occupied by squatters connected Mahmut to the ongoing contestations to raise the visibility of and to reclaim abandoned and/or ap-propriated Syriac Christian and church properties.

However, Mahmut's most contentious political activity was his simultane-ous involvement in political struggles for international and state recognition of the Syriac genocide, Seyfo, as part of the genocide of Armenians by the Ottoman military forces. This political engagement connected him to a mul-tiscalar political field with very powerful global religious and political actors, including Syriac Christian diasporic organizations such as the Swedish As-syrian Federation and an array of religious and political associations that ex-tended beyond Syriac Christians. These networked organizations contested the official narratives of the Turkish state. Within this multiscalar social field, at the intersection of the conjunctural forces that were facilitating their presence and prominence in Mardin, Syriac Christian returnees developed their own agendas and forms of participation in city-making.

Returnees acquired a significant presence in the public sphere and in social justice claims in the city. They increasingly participated in the political life and public sphere of the city. One Syriac returnee who had fled Mardin in 1989 and lived and worked in Sweden, Germany, the Netherlands, Austria, and Belgium before returning to Mardin from Switzerland in 2010 became head of the Federation of Syriac Associations established in Midyat, Mardin, in 2012. He was also a member of the Brussels-based European Syriac Unity. These associations in Mardin as well as the numerous Syriac Christian associations in Europe (including the Syriac Christian HTAs) became important stakeholders in the 2014 local elections, especially in the contested race of a Syriac Christian running to become co-mayor.

Another Syriac returnee, who had spent twenty-five years in Europe, started publishing a monthly, Midyat-based newspaper, *Sabro*,[26] with offices in Istanbul, Switzerland, and the United States. Published in Aramaic and Turkish, *Sabro* became the first Syriac newspaper printed during the Turkish Republic since the closing of the last Syriac newspaper in the aftermath of the Armenian and Syriac genocides under the Ottomans.

Global Christian Networks and Mardin

Global Christian networks were another aspect of the multiscalar social field within which Syriac Christians' emplacement in Mardin was embedded. Historically, Mardin as a city-region had been very important for both Orthodox and Catholic Christians. With its numerous churches, monasteries, mosques, and madrasas, Mardin was a centuries-old center for religion, education, and art long before its peripheralization and disempowerment. Monasteries and churches in Mardin province were especially important in the history of Eastern Christianity. Deyrulzafaran Monastery was the seat of the Orthodox Syriac Patriarch from the thirteenth century until the early 1930s. Mor Behram Church was an important center of worship for Orthodox Syriacs and the summer seat of the Patriarch. Mor Ephraim Monastery, where in 2015 the opening of the third Biennial took place, was very important for Syriac Catholics. Thus, both Catholic and Orthodox hierarchies felt it was imperative to keep a Christian presence in the Syriacs' ancestral home as a holy land for Eastern Christianity.

Maintaining Christian populations, their religious freedom, and the possibility of Christian education as well as restoring Christian religious sites in Mardin and around the Middle East have been major concerns not only for Christian clergy and religious leaders but also for numerous European and American officials (including chairmen of the secretary of state's Advisory Committee on Religious Freedom abroad). With the reconfiguration of the Middle East through wars, this became an even stronger concern. In the face of increasing violence toward Christian populations in Syria and Iraq, religious leaders of Christian churches, including the pope, repeatedly underlined the importance of keeping Christians in the "Orient" (interview U., December 7, 2015).

Representatives of different European Syriac churches, organizations for the protection of Christian rights—particularly in the Orient, and representatives of diverse Syriac and Aramaic associations and federations from different parts of Europe all came together at several events and celebrations that took place within the framework of Syriac migrants' return to Mardin from Europe. Encouraging Syriac Christians' return to Mardin had been important to the agenda of many of these organizations (Wikileaks 2006). For example, a five-year project aimed at securing Christian migrants' return to Mardin (particularly to Tur Abdin) was the result of such organizations' concern. This project was initiated and led by a Catholic priest, but the Evangelical Church in Bayern and Baden Wüttenburg and the Austrian organization Christian Orient–Friends of Tur Abdin were also patrons. Keeping a Christian population in the area became an urgent concern for global Christian networks. It is no coincidence that following Pope Francis's visit to Turkey in 2014, returnees expected the "Vatican to act" to secure the rights of Christians in eastern Turkey to live on their own lands and to teach in their own mother tongue. They hoped that ultimately the Turkish government would publicly acknowledge the Syriac genocide and allow Syriac Christians to control and administer churches and monasteries.

The presence of Syriacs in Mardin on their historical lands and issues of religious freedom, particularly for Christian minorities, were also ongoing concerns of the US government. As Wikileaks documents and a report by the Archbishop of Canterbury's Apocrisiarius in Syria and Lebanon indicate, US State Department officials closely monitored Turkey's record vis-à-vis religious minorities. According to the chairman of the US State Department's Advisory Committee on Religious Freedom Abroad, part of their concern about this NATO ally's observance of human rights focused on religious freedom. These documents indicate that US officials were regularly in touch with numerous Orthodox and Catholic religious networks to monitor the local conditions of Christians. The US secretary of state made at least two official visits (in 1994 and 1998) to Mardin and wrote reports on these visits. Through visits to the monasteries and talks with priests, archbishops, and representatives of Syriac churches in the region, the United States was able to probe the state of religious freedom and violations of human rights.

In Turkey–US relations, however, human rights and religious freedom were also closely entangled with global warring and the delivery of military equipment to Turkey.[27] There also had been a NATO Combined Air Operations Center in Mardin since 1960. The historical castle area in Mardin had been allocated to NATO for air defense early-warning radar. To the surprise of local cultural officials, the castle, located within the Mardin old town area that they had officially designated as a heritage zone, belonged to NATO, and this southeastern NATO radar post remained a forbidden military compound.[28]

Conclusion

A multiscalar analysis of the emplacement of Syriac Christians from Europe in Mardin shows that Syriac Christians' "project of return" and HTAS were embedded within a field constituted and shaped by several regional, supranational, and global institutions and actors. Unfortunately, many transnational migration scholars fail to see the significance of temporality in the emplacement of minorities and returnees and the role of the historical conjuncture in configuring institutionalized power. This scholarship, when it addresses migrants' HTAS and their institutional connections, often focuses on remittance markets and development agencies without assessing the potency of these institutions in relationship to multiscalar transformations of places over time. Migrants from Mardin forged hometown ties and established HTAS only when they could situate themselves as social and political actors vis-à-vis an array of global, regional, and European institutions in the context of reconfiguring power relations in Mardin and in the Middle East at a given conjuncture. The Syriac minority and the previously dispossessed and displaced Syriac returnees were emplaced in Mardin as part of an array of social and political forces of city-making. Thus, the salience they acquired was temporarily contingent.

Valorization of the Syriac Christian minority and their built environment in Mardin and the emplacement of previously displaced returnees were closely entangled with efforts to strengthen place-specific assets of the disempowered city of Mardin and thereby make it attractive to capital and investments, allow it to generate wealth, and reposition the city regionally and globally. Syriac Christians' return and their resultant HTAs were emplaced in Mardin as part of the process of capital accumulation by dispossession. The practices and subjectivities of Syriac minorities and Syriac returnees were constituted within this multiscalar field.

Yet, although culture and religious and architectural heritage were at the forefront of these projects, policies, funding schemes, and narratives centered on restructuring Mardin, as we have argued the valorization of Syriac Christians' heritage and the emplacement of returnees cannot be attributed merely to the dynamics of culture-led urban restructuring. Of course, EU funding schemes were geared toward enhancing and encouraging heritage and cultural industries and toward attracting "creative classes" (Florida 2003), but far more than cultural regeneration was at stake. Cultural, religious, and architectural heritage acquired salience primarily because of the conjunctural intersection of Turkey's EU accession, its emerging markets, and the shifting alliances of global warring in the Middle East in the 2000s. The emplacement of Syriac Christian returnees described in this chapter was part of this temporal dimension of Mardin's intersecting networks of power.

As we have also shown in this chapter, because the revaluation of the legacy of Mardin's minorities was also related to the Turkish government's aspirations, priorities, and policies, changes in these goals affected the positioning of these minorities. As Turkish officials repositioned Turkey within a multiscalar field of regional and global political power hierarchies, especially vis-à-vis the EU and the United States, the institutional reach and resources of Syriac Christians with respect to the Turkish state, especially after 2012, also changed.

Global networks of Christianity (especially of Eastern Christianity) acquired salience in the emplacement of Syriac Christians within the context of the wars in the Middle East beginning in the 1990s. This warring unleashed radical Islamic forces and violence that threatened Christian populations in Eastern Christianity's historic homeland.

Without the concept of historical conjuncture developed in chapter 1, it would have been difficult to analyze the emplacement of the Syriac minority in Mardin's city-making processes. As we show in this chapter, Syriac Christian returnees' institutional emplacement extended not only to these powerful religious networks but also to EU- and US-centered supranational hierarchies of power and were conjunctural in that they depended upon the broader global agendas and interests in the region of powerful, globe-spanning institutions and states. While these institutions supported and facilitated the return and continued presence of Syriac Christians in Mardin, they did not intend to grant these Syriacs political power within a project of sociopolitical transformation. Moreover, the guarantee of Syriac Christian minority rights within these global institutions' general "anti-political politics of human rights" (Ranciere 2004; Zizek 2005) remained rather shallow, limited, and depoliticizing. Largely, global institutions' regional and global politico-economic and military interests motivated the promise of rights. Consequently, Christian Syriacs becoming emplaced as cultural, symbolic, and political actors within the processes of city-making was painfully ephemeral.

Since June 2015, the peace processes between the PKK and the Turkish state, on the one hand, and multifaith heritage valorizations and diversity narratives, on the other, have disappeared almost without a trace. The Turkish state again wages war against the PKK. Combined with the escalating wars in Syria and Iraq and the increasing authoritarianism of the regime in Turkey—with a clear turn away from securing any kind of rights, including minority rights—Mardin once more became a conflict-ridden, violent area marked by bombings, shootings, and armed attacks followed by massive displacements and dispossessions. Tourism and the business sectors suffered drastic losses, and most hotels stood either empty or closed. The contracts of many international academics at Artuklu University were terminated, and many of them left the city. Many places in the region and several districts in the Mardin city-region, including Midyat, experienced military siege with long periods of curfew and suppressive violence. The central government changed Midyat's administrative status from a district of Mardin to a city so that it would no longer fall under the governance of the elected Kurdish and Syriac co-mayors of Mardin, who at any rate were removed from office in 2016. Kafro and Syriac Christians were caught up in the escalating violence. Within the changed historical conjuncture, the revaluing of Syriac Christians within city narratives, as part of efforts to restructure Mardin and generate wealth, came to a halt. "We are being pulverized between the fronts again just like in the 90s," said a returnee who came back to Kafro from Switzerland (Güsten 2016). By 2016, many returnees were again on their way to Europe, seeking safety.

Time, Space, and Agency

Most current discussions of social inequality, downward social mobility, and injustice fail to account for the systemic nature of the multiple massive dispossessions taking place around the globe as a new conjunctural alignment emerges (Johnston 2014; Sandbrook et al. 2007). Data gathered by the International Monetary Fund (IMF) document substantial contractions in public expenditure as structural adjustment measures exacerbate the multiple dispossessive processes that erode livelihoods (Oritz and Cummins 2013). Using the concept of "expulsions," Saskia Sassen (2014) has begun to analyze current transformations of the global economy and the new complexities, curtailments, and forms of brutality these transformations are producing.

Increased migration and desperate searches for a haven are part of the processes of displacement that accompany war and capital destruction and accumulation by dispossession. These displacements are facilitated by new, complex legal and financial structures; different forms of truth claims and knowledge production; and a migration industrial complex built on accumulating profit by detaining and storing living bodies (Sørensen 2013). The resurgence of xenophobic, antimigrant nationalism in the midst of intensive global interconnections is a potent manifestation of the emerging contradictions and disparities.

Migrants and City-Making speaks to these contradictions by offering a perspective on the question of dispossession and displacement that differs from those common in debates about mobility, cities, urban restructuring, and struggles for rights to the city. In so doing, we have challenged the concept that a metropolitan revolution offers a spatial fix for contemporary crises and economic stagnation and disparities (Katz and Bradley 2013). Our comparative analysis has tracked the spiraling trajectories of debt and displacement produced by policies that have promised "economic recovery" through celebrations of tourism, neoliberal public–private governance, urban rebranding, the creation of business- and investment-friendly environments, and the fostering of "ethnic" entrepreneurs.

We have developed an analytical vocabulary and framework that explicates how city residents participate in the processes and struggles that remake their cities and our world. We approached all residents of cities— migrants, minorities, and non-migrants alike—as city-makers operating within unequal networks of multiscalar power. We traced dispossession back to reconstituted forms of obtaining capital through the direct seizure of land, resources, and bodies. Then we showed how these economic processes relate to cultural processes of the racialization, stigmatization, and delegitimization of claims to humanity and the rights associated with such claims. We highlighted how all residents of a place were imbricated in the processes that displaced them. Yet, tracing the entanglements of dispossessive forces does not lead us to conclude that there is no exit. Rather, our analysis not only critiques categories often deployed in discussions of the relationships between migrants and cities but also serves as an approach to city-making processes and migrant agency that can strengthen social movements.

To formulate this approach, we questioned the penchant for theorizing from research on urban restructuring and migrant settlement in world centers of political and economic power. *Migrants and City-Making* provides comparative studies of the multiscalar networks of power within which residents of disempowered cities, migrant and non-migrant alike, build their lives. We have argued that research in disempowered cities can provide new insights into established analytical categories and organizing mantras, including "local actors," "global cities," "diversity," "difference," "multi-sited ethnography," "social citizenship," "new mobilities," and the "right to the city."

Our argument in *Migrants and City-Making* for the usefulness of theorizing from disempowered cities and our elucidation of the displacements and emplacements integral to city-making in three such cities—Halle/Saale, Germany; Manchester, New Hampshire, in the United States; and Mardin, Turkey—contributes to our broader agenda of speaking to the nature of struggles for social justice in our times. Our comparative analytical framework calls for an examination of relationships that all of us, everywhere, have to the dispossessive and reconstitutive powers of contemporary capitalism. Our analysis allows us to raise questions of general interest: we ask who benefits from dispossession and displacement, and we ask how these processes engender struggles for dignity, respect, and life with meaning. It is our hope that such an analysis contributes to global movements that aspire to social and economic justice (Narotzky 2016).

In this concluding chapter, we emphasize how our comparative analytical framework highlights three insights that are crucial for further research on relationships between migrants and city-making. First, our work demonstrates the necessity of situating social analysis and action within a shared temporality of all a city's inhabitants as the city transforms within changing historical conjunctures. As we note in the introduction, we built on John Clarke's approach to conjunctural analysis not as a theory but as an orientation from which to assess "the forces, tendencies, forms of power, and relations of domination" that at any moment in history can lead to different yet interdependent regional and local political, economic, and social arrangements (Clarke 2014, 115).

Second, we have argued that analyses of city-making processes must be multiscalar because conjunctural forces always involve multiple globe-spanning actors within intersecting social fields of power. Moreover, the constellation of forces at a given historical conjuncture—their mix and relative potency, so to speak—is an integral component of place making. When economic "bubbles" burst, when politics in a place, state, or region turn anti-immigrant, when demagogues seize the moment, when new communication technologies transform information flows, and when religious, social, or political movements rise or fall, peoples' lives are affected not only in specific places but also in ways that intersect and interact within interconnected networks. All these forces, coming together in what Doreen Massey (2012) termed a "power geometry," were apparent in the data we collected and in our analyses of conditions in Mardin, Halle, and Manchester. Each city's disempowered positioning and its leaders' repositioning efforts were part and parcel of its distinct constitution of these forces.

Finally, our analytical framework makes clear that it is essential to move beyond concepts of urban citizenship and the right to the city when addressing the complex terrain of rights, legality, and social justice claims. To seek the transformative change necessary for social justice and for the empowerment of the dispossessed, researchers and activists must directly address multiscalar globe-spanning relationships of power, including the changing and increasingly fraught processes of capital accumulation.

1) The Importance of Thinking about Shared Temporality
within Changing Historical Conjunctures
TEMPORALITY

Research on the relationship between cities and migrants serves as a potent critique of the ethnographic present. As we conducted the research that led to this book, it became clear that even the relatively brief fifteen-year period in which we analyzed the history of these city-making processes contained drastic fluctuations and variations that our analytical framework had to address.

By focusing our analysis of migrants and city-making in three disempowered cities on the shifting historical conjuncture and conditions of urban restructuring, we sought to move debates beyond the static temporal focus of much urban restructuring literature, namely, the focus on the neoliberal moment that began in the 1970s. Such formulations in migration and urban studies have paid too little attention to the trends that so clearly emerged from our comparison of the three disempowered cities: the recent transformations in processes of capital accumulation that reconfigured processes and structures of accumulation; the heightened intensity and prevalence of nationalism, racism, and anti-immigrant, antiminority discourses; and the significance of war. Wars shaped by and constitutive of new fields of power led to untold death, destruction, and desperate movements of refugees in one location and to opportunities for employment and the growth of new industrial sectors elsewhere. Mardin, Halle, and Manchester, seemingly so disparate, proved to be interconnected not only because their leaders deployed similar restructuring strategies but also because of their relationships to the death and destruction wrought by war.

To highlight the synergies among all actors within a process of city-making as part of the power geometry at a historical conjuncture—namely, at a meeting of intersecting forces within a place and a time—the concept of temporality proved useful. The importance of time became clear when we analyzed the social relationships that various actors forged within the realignment of conjunctural forces. In much of the migration literature, those captured by the terms "migrants/minorities" and "non-migrants" are approached within different temporal frames, producing what Fabian (1983, 2006) has called the denial of coevalness, that is, the denial of contemporaneity. The ethnic lens deployed by many mainstream migration scholars is based on and reproduces just such a denial of shared temporality (Çağlar 2013). Scholars analyze migrants within the "categorical time" of culture, of elsewhere, and outside of contemporary time while analyzing non-migrants as actors within historical time and subject to the conjunctural forces of the political economy. By denying coevalness, migration scholars disregard the experiences, values, and practices that migrants and non-migrants share as they become embedded in common contemporary social, economic, and political processes (Çağlar 2016b).

A disregard for shared temporality within changing historical conjunctures underlies the various literatures critiqued in our ethnographic chapters including those based in the concept of ethnic entrepreneurs, the study of urban life as if it was lived within discrete neighborhoods, claim making as an avenue to social citizenship, and hometown ties as a natural outcome of a transnational ethnic community. In our ethnographic chapters, we took the shared temporality of all actors as our analytical entry point in assessing the significance of their differential access to multiscalar institutions, differential engagements in processes of capital accumulation and dispossession, and differential racializations.

By deploying this perspective on temporality in chapter 2, we demonstrated that migrant small businesses in Halle were subject to the sectorial and dispossessive dynamics of urban regeneration in that city. In confronting these forces, our starting point for analysis was the constraints and opportunities confronting small businesspeople within a disempowered city. We could not have made this analysis without insisting on the contemporaneity of all actors and discarding the tendency of scholars to assume that migrant businesspeople were constrained by differential logics deriving from their ethnic and cultural backgrounds. In the growth and demise of their businesses, and in their displacements from the city center, migrant small businesses were coeval to non-migrant small businesses in Halle.

Because we considered migrants and non-migrants to be sharing the same temporal frame—contemporaneous and operating within the same conjunctural configuration—we were able in chapter 3 to theorize and make visible domains of commonality that emerged in Manchester and Halle. By highlighting the conditions within which "domains of commonality" emerge, we could distinguish our approach from the scholarship of multiculturalism, diversity, superdiversity, and tolerance for difference. As migrants and non-migrants confronted the range of dispossessive multiscalar forces constituting their lives, sought ways of living within them, and struggled to reshape these conditions, they built sociabilities of emplacement.

Our studies of relationality in chapters 3 and 4 moved beyond methodological individualism to situate emergent sociabilities of emplacement within time and place. In chapter 3 we drew on data from Manchester to explore various locations and situations in which migrants and non-migrants forged domains of commonality based on a common sense of their humanity. We could have presented similar data from Halle, but to expand on the concept of sociabilities of emplacement, we instead drew from our studies of born-again Christians in both cities.

In chapter 4, our temporal frame made clear the commonalities within shared conjunctural forces that brought together born-again Christians in Halle and Manchester. We noted the relationships between believers' critique of governmental power and the dispossession they experienced. We documented their efforts to respond to their displacement and disempowerment by participating in powerful globe-spanning Christian networks that put aside narratives of national or cultural difference. We suggested that, to address their experiences within changing conjunctural conditions, people in different locations around the world situated themselves within their shared biblical understanding of God's prophecy and power.

In chapter 5, we noted that the frames and references of action for Syriac Christians returning to Mardin were anchored in the same sense of time in which other city residents operated. All individual, organizational, and institutional actors were shaped by the urban restructuring unfolding in Mardin, although their experience in the city was shaped by their unequal access to the networks of power that differentiated city residents. Taking as our analytical entry point the shared conjunctural forces that were reconfiguring geopolitics in the region and the location of the Turkish state in these changing relations, we explored how all residents sought to respond to the opportunities and constraints at the turn of the millennium. In this way, we were able to see that in some cases these shared conditions led to heightened tensions between local actors. We situated the return and emplacement of Syriac Christians in Mardin's city-making within the new, contentious dynamics unleashed by the minority rights and geopolitical agendas of global and religious networks of power. We also noted that, as the historical conjuncture changed with the expansion of the Syrian Civil War, the changing power geometry in the region, within Europe and the EU ultimately marginalized minority rights and peace process agendas. Syriac Christians as well as other minority groups increasingly lost their value to more powerful actors, and their emplacement in city-making altered drastically.

Throughout this book, we sought not only to challenge concepts that have shaped migration studies and approaches to urban restructuring but also to set the stage for further work on the relationship between historical conjuncture and theory production. As we examined the contemporary literature on migration and urban restructuring, the implications of the fact that migration scholars often live at a different conjunctural moment than that in which their key concepts were constituted became clear (Glick Schiller 2015b; Wimmer and Glick Schiller 2002). Many scholars write as if conceptual tools forged under one set of conditions can be used to speak to a very different world.

For example, the concept of assimilation reflected the developing US economy in the twentieth century. The concept reflected and enabled the growth of an imperial American economy within the context of twentieth-century war, revolution, and Cold War competition between the United States and the Soviet Union (Piketty 2014). In that context, assimilation was assumed to entail upward social mobility. Theories of assimilationism past and present (and their multiple derivatives), including those acknowledging a period in which migrants maintain their transnational homeland connections (Waldinger 2015), disregard the configuration of conjunctural forces that made possible the post–World War II settlement of immigrants and their social mobility. Such theories discount how radically different the world is now.

Disregarding the historical conjuncture in which theories and concepts were constructed, migration scholars generalized and universalized US post–World War II patterns of immigrant settlement into a universal and timeless assimilation theory of migrant emplacement. However, conditions faced by migrants and as well as by non-migrants are qualitatively different today because of transformations in the processes of capital accumulation and dispossession and the austerity narratives and reductions in public services that have accompanied and legitimated these changes. Yet, in Europe, integration scholars, political pundits, and policy makers have repeatedly declared that if refugees would only assimilate by learning the language and culture of the country of settlement, then they would be able to enter the mainstream, as generations of immigrants previously did in the United States (Heckmann 2015). Such assumptions about migration processes are provincial (Chakrabarty 2000), lacking a sense of space as well as time.

Migration theorists' failure to reflect on the empirical bases and historical conjuncture that shape specific theories resembles studies of modernity that universalize a particular reading of the specific European experience as a valid theory for everywhere and any time (Therborn 2003; Beck and Grande 2010). In both cases, analysts fail to reflect on the conditions that shape their theory and fail to theorize the temporal-spatial dimensions of their core concepts.

2) Multiscalar as Method/Theory/Analysis

The multiple intersecting trajectories of forces that a conjunctural analysis brings into view are always multiscalar. Throughout the book, we repeatedly used the term "multiscalar" not as a metaphor of complexity or connectedness but as an essential form of methodology, theory, and analysis. Building on our argument that theory, method, and analysis are ongoing processes of engagement with the world (Xiang 2016; Hertz 2016; Harrison 2016), we explored the multiple disparate but interconnected ways in which the daily lives of residents in the three cities were situated within networks that made them actors within simultaneous, interconnected local, regional, national, supranational, and global relations of power.

Our observations, interviews, and data collected from multiple sources made it clear that, had we approached various city leaders and residents, both migrant and non-migrant, as "local actors," our analysis would have been distorted. Whether or not they were "mobile people," they entered into and refashioned multiple intersecting networks of social, economic, political, and religious relationships across space and time. In many cases, it was by scrutinizing collected documents and websites and, toward the end of the research, Facebook (when many organizational websites changed their media interfaces) that we became fully aware of the scope of the multiscalar networks, whose substantiation had been unfolding before our eyes. Thus, we more fully comprehended the extent to which social relations were indeed multiscalar, enacted by individual people as they lived their daily lives.

The multiscalar analysis of this book reframes and deepens the critique of methodological nationalism that we and a growing number of authors have put forth (Beck 2002; Wimmer and Glick Schiller 2002; Amelina et al. 2012; Çağlar and Glick Schiller 2011; Glick Schiller 2005b, 2010, 2015b; Glick Schiller and Çağlar 2011a, 2011b; Nowicka and Cieslik 2013; Clarke et al. 2015). We demonstrated that we need to do more than critique the conflation of national and societal boundaries. *Migrants and City-Making* traced the globespanning institutional, corporate, financial, and cultural configurations of power that connect actors, places, resources, and forms of coercion, dispossession, and persuasion.

We demonstrated that to reposition their city, the leaders of Halle, Manchester, and Mardin sought ways of reconstituting their connections to power hierarchies. We delineated their strategies of urban reempowerment: reinvigorating local histories and creating new, welcoming city narratives; working to attract new investment; changing tax policies or property assessments; negotiating loans on the basis of public credit; and redrawing institutional lines of authority. In each case, our exploration of these repositioning efforts made it clear that not only city leaders but also city residents became actors within broader configurations of regional, national, and global power. Our explorations of urban regeneration projects and the actors involved in their development—small entrepreneurs and consumers, apartment dwellers and homeowners, employees of urban institutions, individual newcomers seeking social ties, born-again Christian organizations and formerly persecuted returnees, migrants seeking their rights and place in their city's political, economic, and social life and citizens aspiring to political office—made clear that the local was not a level of analysis or a discrete domain but an arena of multiple institutional actors within the power geometry of a specific conjuncture.

Disempowering processes that shaped cityscapes in each region—including unmet promises of new economy jobs, the replacement of public services with public debt, and new inequalities built into transformed housing stocks and neighborhoods—provided the terrain on which daily life played out and social relations were constituted for all city residents.

At first glance, the social relations we traced between newcomers and non-migrants, who met variously in city shops and on city streets, in places of worship and of education, and even at local political meetings, would not seem to require a multiscalar analysis. However, as we tried to make sense of the welcoming narratives of each city, we found they were very much embedded within efforts to regenerate the city, which required challenging negative images of that city: terror and poverty in Mardin, racism in Halle, disreputable abandonment in Manchester. Through a comparative analysis of regeneration, we were able to understand each city's residents' experiences of displacement, their daily practices, and their politics, including their sociabilities. And in each city, these daily sociabilities situated residents within multiscalar social fields.

The data in our ethnographic chapters extended our discussion, begun in the introduction, of the inadequacies of the current penchant to celebrate ethnographies of daily life. While multisited research is necessary for the study of specific topics—for example, commodity chains or human mobility—we have argued that multiscalar research must be a component of all ethnography (Gardiner and Lem 2012a; Miraftab 2014). By examining city-making processes in three disempowered cities, we have demonstrated that working in a single site is not synonymous with a bounded ethnography of the local. *Migrants and City-Making* documents the multiple ways in which all sites are interconnected through time within hierarchies of differential power.

Because each ethnographic chapter emphasizes a different aspect of the processes of displacement and emplacement, the fact that migrants and nonmigrants engage in simultaneous forms of city-making may not be obvious. However, it is important to take note of the simultaneity of their engagements. We mean by simultaneity that individuals may be entangled at the same time in multiple networks organized around different spheres of life, each of which is multiscalar. By tracing city-making processes as the simultaneous relational constitution of scales, we have demonstrated that, whether we as individuals build personal transnational networks or maintain that we live within the confines of a single neighborhood or locality, we are all actors within multiple simultaneous processes that make and remake the mutually constituting scales of locality, region, nation-state, the supranational, and the global. This simultaneity and multiplicity allows individuals multiple forms of belonging, multiple possibilities for finding domains of sociability, and multiple possibilities of becoming politically active within a range of social movements.

There are many ways to document the simultaneity and multiplicity of multiscalar interconnections. They pervade our data and run through our chapters. Throughout the various chapters, we provided examples for each city of how the networks of individuals were both multidimensional and inserted into multiple different social fields. In each case, these individuals participated simultaneously in personal, economic, political, and religious networks that connected them, directly or indirectly, to multiple elsewheres.

Much of the literature on migrants' daily lives in cities misses migrants' multiple simultaneous forms of relationality and participation in economic, political, religious, social, and cultural city-making processes. This is because, as our review of the literatures on migrant businesspeople, social citizenship, and hometown associations in chapters 2 through 5 demonstrates, scholars tend to study single domains of migrant life or focus on neighborhoods. It was only through tracing the multiscalar networks of various migrants as they entered into a range of different relations of emplacement and by finding that they appeared as actors in many different domains—sometimes as main players and sometimes in walk-in roles—that we fully appreciated the importance of theorizing simultaneous multiscalar networks of emplacement. However, we emphasize that scholars must always be cognizant of the very different power of institutions and of individual actors in these networks.

MULTISCALAR FIELDS AS TRANSFORMING
AND TRANSFORMATIVE

Multiscalar analysis must always be carried out with an eye to changing conjunctural conditions. Multiscalar social fields are never fixed. The power geometry of changing conjunctures means that political climates can alter dramatically across city, state, nation, and region. Recent transformations have altered the possibilities for and barriers to emplacement of migrants and non-migrants. As our research ended, we began to witness new spirals of capital accumulation, dispossession, and displacements as new opportunity structures and barriers to emplacement and sociability emerged, affecting—differentially—the residents of the three cities.

Our research began in one conjectural moment and extended into transformations accompanying the emergence of a new historical conjuncture. Therefore, throughout the book, our challenge has been not only to assess the intertwined multiscalar forces at play within each city's re-empowerment efforts and to analyze the relationship between the city and its migrants within these dynamics but also to pay close attention to conjunctural transformations. Our discussion of urban regeneration in Mardin, with outcomes configured by dramatically shifting geopolitical terrains, provides a clear example of the importance of noting transformations from one alignment of globe-spanning forces to another within an emergent historical conjuncture.

As Mardin's relationships to military battlefields and Turkey's relationship to the EU and to the Middle East changed, its urban restructuring and narratives of multifaith harmony also dramatically changed. Almost overnight, the emplacement of the Syriac Christian minority and returnees within EU institutions, the Turkish state, and global Christian networks that we had been documenting and their potential roles in city-making were rapidly transformed. By the summer of 2016, even various newspaper archives and websites we had used to document urban regeneration in Mardin had been taken down from the Internet. As repression increased, many of these media were banned.

Attention to changing historical conjunctures was also necessary for assessing the relationship between migrants and Halle's regeneration efforts. Our story began at the moment that residents and newcomers were beginning to come to terms with the demise of socialist governance and to assess the emergent and ongoing transformations in neoliberal governance in which they were enmeshed. By the end of our research, relations between migrants and their cities were being altered by a different concomitance of political, economic, religious, and cultural forces and actors. Conditions seemingly distant and disconnected—continuing warring in the Middle East centered on heightened war making in Syria, terrorist attacks in Afghanistan and Pakistan, intensified accumulation by dispossession in the form of vast land privatization by Chinese, European, and US corporate interests in Africa, together with land clearance via militia activity—brought a new wave of migrants to Halle. They arrived in the city and region when costly urban regeneration had intensified income equalities, increased residential segregation, failed to eliminate high unemployment, and strained public coffers.

Consequently, the arrival of refugees was met with growing contestation. On the one hand, the new nationalist, anti-immigrant populist party, the Alternative for Germany (AfD), was growing in strength. This political party spoke to non-migrants' frustrations at the failure of neoliberal urban regeneration to alter their various ongoing dispossessions: job insecurities, increasingly privatized services, and shrinking proportions of the national wealth and of prospects for social mobility. Frustration took the form of attacks on or threats to buildings sheltering refugees and random acts of violence against refugees on the street.

At the same time, Halle and surrounding villages witnessed an upsurge in support for refugees as volunteers came forward offering food, clothing, and services. Old multiscalar networks of support were reinforced and new ones built joining non-migrants and migrants who had become emplaced in the city. City leaders worked with an array of civic and religious organizations. New funding arrived from the EU, the German state, and Saxony-Anhalt to coordinate volunteer services. Local nuns offered sanctuary for failed asylum seekers. Migrants in the city found the streets both more welcoming and more dangerous. Some new migrants joined the Miracle Healing Church, which continued within its multiscalar networks. But in the changing conjunctural moment, nationalist rhetoric in the United States and Europe began to reduce the saliency of born-again Christians' global anti-racist stance.

Conjunctural analysis was also essential to disentangling the dynamics of urban restructuring in Manchester, New Hampshire. On the surface, Manchester might seem remote from the dramatic changes transforming the other two cities. However, Manchester's possibilities and constraints were also linked to the broader dynamics of finance capital and subprime markets as well as to the US and global military industrial complex's changing modes of war making, war funding, and production chains. Unemployment rates dropped as weapons production increased in relation to enlarged US war efforts in Syria and Iraq.

Meanwhile, growing public anger across much of the country, which was fueled by vast new inequalities produced not only by urban regeneration but also by new waves of dispossessive accumulation, was evident also in Manchester. These dispossessions in Manchester and elsewhere took multiple forms. Banks and finance corporations developed new loan instruments to sell automobiles and housing to the poor. Local governments increasingly used a structure of fines and penalties to fill public coffers that were no longer supplemented by state and federal subsidies. Politicians, particularly those in the Republican Party and centered in the Trump political movement, gave vent to public angers by targeting immigrants, people of color, Muslims, and government regulation. Meanwhile the US refugee resettlement program continued to settle newcomers across the country. After a pause fueled by the protests of some local Republican leaders, in 2016 Manchester was once again a city of refugee resettlement. As in Halle, newcomers were met by both public and private welcome and local acts of individual hostility. In Manchester, the anti-immigrant political narrative was by 2016 orchestrated by the national and state Republican Party.

When we began our research, the Republican Party had welcomed immigrants on national and state levels as well as within Manchester city politics. Heightened tensions and a political realignment that positioned the Republican Party as militantly anti-immigrant altered the multiscalar connections and possibilities in Manchester but certainly did not end the development of sociabilities of emplacement. The types of Republican networks that we described in chapter 1, which allowed Carlos Gonzalez or Saggy Tahir to become, first, party activists and, then, elected officials and made Tahir the first Muslim elected to a US state legislature, were no longer possible. After 2009, in the aftermath of the subprime mortgage crisis, Godsword abandoned his efforts to become a Christian political activist in Manchester and recentered his Resurrection Crusade in Nigeria. Although the development of the local health-care industry in the city center continued with a public funding for redevelopment, Manchester's political leadership had generally abandoned their high-profile efforts to reposition and re-empower the city amid public debt and reduced funding streams.

However, new, more politicized organizations and networks uniting migrants and non-migrants developed in response to the inequalities, growing racism, and demands for social justice. Activities ranged from actions within the local, state, and national Democratic Party to demonstrations in support of the Black Lives Matter movement. In the summer of 2016, Black Lives Matter demonstrators, including people of migrant and non-migrant backgrounds, marched through the regenerated city center to the same park where Godsword celebrated the National Day of Prayer in 2004 (Galioto 2016; WMUR 2016). They were followed by small bands of counter demonstrators carrying guns. Several children of the migrants, whose emplacement through domains of sociability we traced in this book, emerged as activists in Manchester's emerging social justice movements. They built their own domains of sociability and political solidarities in the changed conjunctural conditions they confronted.

By addressing the dynamics and processes of conjunctural multiscalar restructuring in Manchester, Halle, and Mardin, we went beyond a structural reading of these convergences. We explored how the historical and discursive legacies of each disempowered city contribute to the terms and imaginaries within which migrants are situated and mobilized as part of urban redevelopment processes. In these cities, as in many others, city leaders and developers projected a version of cosmopolitan urbanism and culture-led or knowledge-led regeneration that often has ignored the contributions of migrants or addressed their presence primarily through narratives that rebrand a city as open and diverse.

As we have seen, on occasions, migrants, together with other urban residents, advocated and strengthened neoliberal discourses that legitimated growing social and economic inequalities. On the other hand, as they confronted the inequalities, displacements, and insecurities that accompanied social and economic inequalities, migrants and non-migrants joined together in movements for justice and against various forms of structural adjustment. However, the configuration of and possibilities for the emergence of such social movements vary with changing conjunctures.

3) Beyond Urban Citizenship and Toward Social Movements of the Dispossessed

As our review in chapter 4 of the social citizenship literature made clear, many contemporary scholars have sought to move beyond the state-centered liberal model of citizenship by arguing that, in the context of globalization, cities rather than nation-states are the axis and locus for political belonging and membership. They have argued that, rather than legal status, residence and participation are pivotal for rights and entitlements (Sassen 2001; Bauböck 1994, 2003; Benhabib 2007; Varsayni 2006; Lazar and Nuijten 2013; Lazar 2013). Those who look to cities and struggle for the right to the city as the new terrain for struggles for social justice point to the deprecations of state authority that result from neoliberal governance. Commenting on the contemporary situation in which the state shares its powers of control and discipline with other actors and agencies, Rose and Osborne (2000, 108) have noted that "citizenship is no longer primarily realized in relation with the state" but instead through "a set of dispersed and non-totalized practices."

While recognizing the significance of claim making through acts of social citizenship performed by asylum seekers, migrants without papers, and those whose rights within the state are devalued, *Migrants and City-Making* critiques the celebration of "urban citizenship" as an alternative site for rights and entitlements. Although cities are crucial units of governance and strategic sites for generating wealth and amassing power, their powers and their citizens' struggles for rights and justice take place within global hierarchical networks of power and concomitant processes of capital accumulation. Both cities and neoliberal states do indeed, as Rose and Osborne remind us, share the powers of control and discipline with other actors and agencies. Our analysis of the intersecting multiscalar networks of power and their changing conjunctural configurations makes this clear.

Moreover, in our assessments of the potentiality and limitations of social movements organized to claim "the right to the city," we cannot ignore the continuing role of nation-states as identity makers, definers of membership, and enforcers of difference. In the last few years we have seen a resurgence of political leaders, demagogues, and intellectuals organizing what Rose and Osborne (2000) have labeled "citizenship games." These games refer to those practices, such as drawing lines of difference based on racism or tolerance, by which persons with citizenship in nation-states seek to constitute themselves as players. Constituting themselves in this way, citizens become part of the games that govern them as they play their own parts. As they seek belonging, the dispossessed who identify themselves as natives join mobilizations and political movements against those who face even greater degrees of precarity. In these processes, scholars and policy makers play a role. Much contemporary scholarship in migration and urban studies contributes to institutionalizing categories of difference in public discourse and, most importantly, in migration and urban policies. These distinctions and semantics are central to the "policy worlds" and often to the governmentality of populations (Shore, Wright, and Però 2011).

The lessons from the transformations wrought from the new conjuncture of intensified nationalism built on categories of difference should be clear, but often they have been lost underneath the slogan of "rights to the city." Even if formally granted by urban authorities, urban-based rights can never be secured. Those able to practice urban social citizenship are particularly vulnerable to changing local and national power geometries within new institutional, local, or state-level political configurations (Varsayni 2006). Even people with formal citizenship rights granted by the state are finding their urban citizenship entitlements negated within such transformations.

The example of Mardin makes this clear. Formal citizenship neither guaranteed the rights of Syriac Christians and Kurds who entered local citymaking as legal citizens nor protected them from persecution. Despite the multiple governing bodies involved in securing and monitoring the rights of minorities, including the EU, Turkish state power was crucial for the enactment of Syriac Christians' and Kurds' citizenship in Mardin, including office holding, and state power could take these rights away. In 2015, when the global and regional positioning of Turkish state power changed, the same Turkish state that had urged Syriac Christians in Europe to return in 2001 and promised to protect their rights as citizens did not hesitate to violently deprive these Syriac Christians and Kurdish citizens of Mardin of their citizenship rights. Many local Kurdish office holders, including the Kurdish co-mayor of Mardin, were persecuted and some of them were imprisoned. Thus, any analysis of formal, as well as social and urban, citizenship must account for the historical conjuncture within which relations between state power and multiple governance structures are shaped. Beginning in 2017, the US federal government began to abrogate long-held rights of even legal immigrants and naturalized citizens of migrant background.

In *Rebel Cities*, Harvey (2012) questioned the potency of rights to the city movements, which limit their terrain of struggle and organizing power to demands for access to local resources and spaces. He calls on people to organize social movements around their experiences of struggling against dispossession. If demands for the right to the city are to yield social justice movements with staying power, they must recover the original understanding of the phrase "right to the city," which arose from anticapitalist struggles (Lefebvre 1996; Harvey 2003, 2008). That is to say, struggles for urban citizenship and the right to the city cannot be separated from anticapitalist struggles that confront the global power of capital. Harvey argues that urban contestations must be waged as multiscalar struggles, and we agree. As we have shown by tracing the ongoing disempowerment of Halle, Manchester, and Mardin, cities cannot be taken as units of analysis. And of course, city limits also should not become the horizons of political struggles.

In each city, we identified diverse forms of precarity that are shaped by the many forms of dispossession and displacement that residents of these disempowered cities experienced daily. Those facing precarious lives and the loss of prospects range from the urban poor to larger sectors of people who considered themselves middle class. Our analytical framework makes it possible to join older questions of class struggle against those who control the means of production with the emergence of contemporary struggles of the dispossessed.

How to construct solidarities among city residents of diverse social, political, and economic backgrounds and legal statuses has been a major challenge for those aspiring to alternative visions of society and urban life (Harvey 2012; Mayer and Boudreau 2012; Mayer 2017). All agree on the importance of building solidarities beyond institutionalized lines of race, class, ethnicity, and migrancy and on the importance of building on bonds that occur between people and places (Lazar 2013; Harvey 2012). However, rather than glossing over forms of social relations that are crucial to social movements by speaking of "forces of culture," "cultural solidarities," a "collective sense of the self," and "collective memories" (Harvey 2012, 148, 151), we focus on the sociabilities of the displaced. We argue that these sociabilities, which we have situated within "domains of commonality" rather than tolerance of difference, are built by city dwellers, migrant and non-migrant alike, upon shared affect, mutual respect, and aspirations.

Ironically, unlike much of the research that has emerged from more powerful cities, our research in the disempowered cities of Halle, Manchester, and Mardin made visible sociabilities that may prove crucial to building movements for social and economic justice. Because of their initial relative disempowerment and their leaders' regeneration strategies, these cities could not increase revenues or provide many public services. Confronted by increasing dispossessive processes of capital accumulation and the drain on public resources for the provision of public services to city residents, these cities could not institutionalize difference based on religion, ethnicity, or race. Under these conditions, domains of commonality established despite differences became more visible and may well be more significant for the displaced and the dispossessed than in more powerful, well-resourced cities.

However, the importance of conjunctural forces in building sociabilities of displacement was also very clear in all three cities. Among the results of the changing conjuncture of global and regional power hierarchies, manifested and escalated by global warring in Syria and Iraq, were the massive dispossessions and violent displacements of fleeing refugees. These changes altered the formation of the sociabilities, out of which the solidarities of social movements emerge. In Mardin, social movements were violently destroyed, in Halle and in Manchester they were polarized and politicized.

At the current moment, antiglobalization movements that critique political and economic projects actuated by neoliberal flexible accumulation seem to have morphed into a resurgent nationalist fervor and repressive surveillance of difference, reinforced by racist and antimigrant rhetoric and policy. Mobilized by leading politicians, in most places these sentiments voice the angers of a militant, albeit frightening, minority whose path to power is to mobilize the nationalism of the dispossessed "natives." However, some movements that seem right wing in essence encompass many people who can find no other political outlet for their rage (wNYC and Nation 2016; Hochschild 2016). Through the lens of disempowered cities, we have sought to understand the nature of dispossessive globe-spanning processes that generate and legitimate rhetorics of rage against difference and to theorize how dispossessive capitalism situates those categorized as migrants and those categorized as natives within the same processes of displacement and search for emplacement.

Migrants and City-Making has placed both people categorized as migrants and people categorized as non-migrants under a common analytical lens that can recognize domains of commonality while speaking to the divisive powers of racialization, criminalization, Islamophobia, and multiple disempowering forms of otherizing. Therefore, our analysis calls for rethinking discussions of governance, the universe of policies and scholarship on migrants and city-making processes, and the historiography of cities. In this sense, we see this book as a political act.

NOTES

Introduction

Some of the arguments in this chapter draw on Nina Glick Schiller, Ayşe Çağlar, and Thaddeus Guldbrandsen (2006), "Beyond the Ethnic Lens: Locality, Globality, and Born-Again Incorporation." *American Ethnologist* 33, no. 4: 612–33; Ayşe Çağlar (2016b), "Still 'Migrants' after All Those Years: Foundational Mobilities, Temporal Frames and Emplacement of Migrants," *Journal of Ethnic and Migration Studies* 42, no. 6: 952–69; Nina Glick Schiller and Ayşe Çağlar (2009), "Towards a Comparative Theory of Locality in Migration Studies: Migrant Incorporation and City Scale," *Journal of Ethnic and Migration Studies* 35, no. 2: 177–202; Ayşe Çağlar and Nina Glick Schiller (2011), "Introduction: Migrants and Cities," in *Locating Migration: Rescaling Cities and Migrants*, edited by Nina Glick Schiller and Ayşe Çağlar, 1–22 (Ithaca, NY: Cornell University Press).

1. The conventions of publishing make it difficult to indicate that this book is a product of ongoing coauthorship. It could not have happened without our equal collaboration in developing and refining our theoretical and methodological framework and our ability to draw from our different linguistic skills.

2. As in most cities in Turkey, in Mardin the name of the city and the province are identical. Thus, Mardin refers to both the city and the province. The city is the district where the provincial administrative seat is located. The province is composed of several districts, with their own municipalities and villages. In Turkey's administrative structure, provinces are different from territorial divisions designated as provinces in other countries, such as Canada. While Canadian provinces contain more than one city, in Turkey, there is only one city in each province. Each province therefore is a city-region.

3. The terms "minority" and "migrant" or "migrant background" are defined differently in different countries, regions, and periods. "Minority" is a particularly contested and contextually defined term (Council of Europe 1995). In this book, we focus on people residing in cities who migrated across international borders, but we do not situate cross-border and internal migrants within different analytical frameworks, as do methodological nationalists. In two of the cities we studied, Halle/Saale, Germany, and Manchester, New Hampshire in the United States,

people with a cross-border migration history are generally assigned to a migration category (refugee, legal immigrant, failed asylum seeker, international student, etc.). Historically, in Mardin, besides categories of migrants, various populations such as Armenian and Syriac Christians have been seen as minorities. When Syriac Christian émigrés returned from Europe to Mardin, they were generally positioned in regeneration narratives as a "minority," rather than as migrants. In Mardin, we identify internally displaced people in our analysis to highlight the violent displacement and dispossession dynamics that they experienced and that played a role in their emplacement processes.

4. In other writing, we have developed this concept further, using the term "methodological ethnicity" (Glick Schiller and Çağlar 2008). With the rise of diaspora studies, long-standing minorities, such as the Chinese in regions of Asia, were increasingly approached as diasporic populations. Although scholars of these populations rightly emphasized their diversity of class and history and the role of these populations within state and class formation, many of these scholars continued to operate within an ethnic category and/or ended up contributing to the reproduction of an ethnic category, such as Chinese (Nonini 2015; Hearn 2016).

5. In Europe the terms "undocumented" or *sans papier* are used by political activists and scholars to defy the aspiration of "illegality." In the United States, the term "undocumented" has increasingly been used as a pejorative, casting these migrants as illegal and criminal, although border crossing is not a criminal act. Some scholars in the United States refer to this status as "unauthorized," but since this term is not widely known, we use the term "undocumented" but reject the binary between legality and illegality established on the basis of documents.

6. Citing further examples in the United States, the *Atlantic* magazine ran an article under the headline, "Why American Cities Are Fighting to Attract Immigrants" (Hesson 2015b). The article notes that "many metro areas with large foreign-born populations have thriving local economies. And now local governments all over the U.S. are trying to replicate their successes." James Brasuell (2015) argues that "new immigrants revitalized Main Street" in Nashville, Philadelphia, and Minneapolis–Saint Paul.

7. Urban anthropologists and sociologists previously called attention to the stigmatization processes that accompanied the dispossession of the urban poor in urban renewal programs in the post–World War II era (Safa 1974; Gans 1962; see also Harvey 2012).

8. In earlier writings, we have used the term "incorporation" in an effort to theorize settlement outside the expectations of assimilation and the political values embedded in integration discourses. We find the term "emplacement" more useful because it emphasizes the ongoing processes of establishing social relationships within space and time and situates both migrants and non-migrants within these processes.

9. For a different conceptualization, see Kalb's exploration of critical junctions (2005).

10. In keeping with the Institutional Review Board protocols of the University of New Hampshire, in the United States, and the University of Manchester, in the United Kingdom, we have anonymized all interviews with migrants and with all actors other than public officials, with the exception of those migrants who became public figures in the course of our research and who gave us permission to use their

names. In Halle, Nina Glick Schiller initially worked with Julia Wenzel, Marcus Rau, Martin Sieber, and a handful of student volunteers. Between 2003 and 2005, Halle's ethnographic team of student researchers was managed by Evangelos Karagiannis and co-led by Nina Glick Schiller and Ayşe Çağlar. Julia Wenger contributed to updating research material and additional interviews beginning in 2013. Ronn Müller also provided data and advice. From 2003 to 2005, another ethnographic team, led by Nina Glick Schiller and Thaddeus Guldbrandsen, included Peter Buchannan and built on the previous and continuing work of numerous student assistants. Further assistance was provided by Molly Messinger and Geraldine Boggs, who focused on the study of refugee resettlement in New Hampshire. In Manchester, Hubert Weterwami, Helene Simerwayi, and Faten al Hassun contributed additional interviews, updated research material, and provided analytical perspectives. In Mardin, the research team was composed of Ayşe Seda Yüksel and Ayşe Çağlar.

11. Our approach resonates with the work of scholars who have examined postsocialist transformations as part of global neoliberal restructuring of capital. Our framework also speaks to the recent Marxist critique of new social movements. However, our focus in this book is on migration and urban studies.

Chapter 1

1. Apparently, all these wonders have been located by archeologists, except for the Hanging Gardens of Babylon, which are now thought to have existed in the capital of its rival Assyrian empire, Nineveh (Dalley 2013).

2. Hillsborough County also contains the smaller city of Nashua, with a population of 86,788 in 2000 (NH Employment Security 2017). In contrast, Boston was a city of 667,137 in 2016 (US Census 2017a).

3. The funds came in large part from the Manchester Housing and Redevelopment Authority (MHRA), which sold 50 million dollars' worth of bonds to finance the arena and then leased the arena to the city. As redevelopment continued, this public housing authority channeled public funds into private investment projects while serving as a conduit for massive amounts of federal money from the US Department of Housing and Urban Development (HUD). This money also supported private real estate development and construction, although applications to HUD for public funding claimed that funded programs provided housing and services for the impoverished local population and for refugees who had been concentrated in the downtown and surrounding neighborhoods.

4. The volatility of defense industry funding is apparent in the contracts awarded each year. In 2003, the percent of contracts awarded increased 50.3 percent from the previous year. Between 2004 and 2006, there were annual increases (2004: 7.5 percent; 2005: 24.5 percent; 2006: 11.1 percent.) Then 2007 and 2008 were years of declining contracts (2007: –3.5 percent; 2008: –33.8 percent). The years since the 2008 recession were marked by both sharp growth (2010: 32.3 percent) and decline (2011: –6.6 percent) (Donahue Institute 2015). In 2011, there were 560 "New Hampshire firms and institutions tied to DOD and DHS [Department of Defense and Department of Homeland Security] contracts" (Anderson 2012), while in 2013 there were only 470 such contractors (Donahue Institute 2015).

5. MEDO was a city agency which described itself during its tenure as the "face of economic activity of the City" and "responsible for marketing the city" (Office of the Independent City Auditor 2013, 4, 6).

6. After the attacks on the World Trade Center and the Pentagon on September 11, 2001, the United States Congress and President George W. Bush passed the USA PATRIOT Act. It initially "significantly expanded the search and surveillance powers of federal law-enforcement and intelligence agencies" and, when amended and reauthorized in 2003, extended surveillance into "the privacy of telephone and electronic communications, the operation of the Foreign Intelligence Surveillance Court, money laundering, immigration, and other areas." (Duignan 2017)

7. It is important to remember that, nationally as well as locally, there were leading Republican and Democratic politicians who saw new immigrants as part of their constituencies. These were the years when, nationally, George W. Bush, a Republican president, proposed immigration reform that would have given "legal status to millions of Americans," a strategy that the New York Times argued was designed to appeal to Hispanics groups (Bumiller 2004).

8. Official numbers included long-term residents and naturalized citizens as well as newly arrived legal refugees and immigrants. These statistics did not count those without legal residence papers, nor did they include migrants from Puerto Rico who came as US citizens but whose numbers were added to the growing Hispanic population in official demographic statistics.

9. There were a considerable number of poor in Manchester, but they were working poor. The percentage of individuals living in poverty according to official definitions was 9.8 percent in 1990 and even higher, 10.6 percent, in 2000 (City Data 2009).

10. After closure by Napoleon, the University of Wittenberg was merged with the University of Halle in 1817 and today is the Martin Luther University of Halle-Wittenberg, primarily located in Halle.

11. The term "ethnic Germans" (classified as Volksduetche, Aussiedler, and Spätaussiedler) is used to designate people whose ancestors are classified as of German origin. These people either lived outside of Germany after various wars led to a redrawing of the state's borders or were the descendants of people who migrated as part of the expansionist projects of various German rulers.

12. In 2013, the number of such attacks doubled from the previous year, and in 2014, 150 such racist attacks were registered in Germany (Abdi-Herle 2015).

13. It included funding for the replacement of demolished buildings with green spaces. Beginning in 2010, the emphasis was on renovating buildings constructed before 1948. This implied revaluing the land and properties of the inner city (Baum, Vondroušová, and Tichá 2014, 22–23).

14. While this was the case throughout the eurozone, the mandated lower wages in eastern Germany aggravated structural impoverishment for most city residents.

15. "Quartier management" refers to a form of district management in urban planning and governance in Germany.

16. Major German Christian organizations initiated the intercultural week in 1975 as a Day of Foreign Co-Citizens. Celebrated in Halle since 1992, in 2001 activities of the Intercultural Week / Day of Foreign Citizens were launched by a speech from

the mayor and hosted by a broad range of organizations. The day continued to be celebrated in 2015 within the nationwide theme of diversity. The opening ceremony in the central marketplace emphasized migration (Jugendwerkstatt 2015). African Week in Halle was celebrated in the city center for a number of years with a public ceremony and speeches by public officials, such as the vice mayor. It then moved to Halle-Neustadt.

17. One of the oldest monasteries in the world, the Syriac Orthodox Saffron Monastery (Dayriu'z Zaffaran Monastery) is in Mardin.

18. The Patriarchate is the office of jurisdiction of an ecclesiastical patriarch.

19. The population of Mardin was 564,967 in 1980, reached to 652,069 in 1985, and then dropped drastically to 557,727 in 1990 (Mardin Valiliği 2013).

20. There was also unrestricted military and police control, with regular curfews, road-blocks, identity checks, and the suspension of human rights between 1925 and 1927, 1978 and 1980, and 1980 and 1987. After the OHAL governorship was lifted, Mardin continued to have a special legal status until 2002.

21. The rate of net migration was 70.2 percent between 1985 and 1990 and 67.6 percent between 1995 and 2000 (Results of General Population Census 1980–2000).

22. In Turkey, governors are appointed by the national government (president) and are responsible for the implementation of national legislation and government decisions in the province to which they are appointed. Governorship refers to the local bureaucratic apparatus of the governor.

23. See also the website of Mardin OIZ (http://www.mardinosb.org.tr/Sayfalar/7/0/14/mardin-osb.aspx).

24. In addition to numerous articles on Mardin in Turkish and international newspapers, such as the *Guardian* and the *New York Times*, articles about Mardin's uniqueness and aura, appeared in Turkish Airlines and affiliated airline company magazines (such as *Skylife* and *AnadoluJet*).

25. As Biner (2007) correctly underlines, the distinction city leaders make between restoration and rehabilitation (using the concept of *iade-i itibar*) is significant. This distinction highlights what we have addressed, namely, the consciousness of the glorious past in the face of Mardin's current disempowerment.

26. This housing administration was initially established as a social housing institution in 1984, but since 2002, its bureaucratic status, financial structure, and scope of activities have significantly changed.

27. According to the governor at that time, land prices exceeded prices in New York (*Haberler* 2012).

28. It is important to note that, in debates about Christian minorities in Mardin at the turn of the millennium, Armenians from Mardin who were subject to genocide in 1915 were absent. The statuses of Armenians and Syriacs in terms of their rights and recognition within the Republic was very different. Furthermore, the global disputes and conflicts about the Armenian past in Turkey in general and in the region in particular have been different from those surrounding Syriac Christians, although both groups were subject to systematic state violence in 1915.

29. This was the title of a very well received exhibition about Mardin that was first displayed in that city and later in Istanbul. It was appropriated as a slogan to promote the city (Biner 2007, 35).

30. See the official website of the Mardin Biennial: http://www.mardinbienali.org/2011/english.asp accessed June 10, 2015.
31. The Syriacs were the only non-Muslim minority who were not granted official minority rights in the Lausanne Treaty (1923), which defined and secured the borders of the Turkish Republic. In contrast to the other non-Muslim minorities, such as Armenians, Greeks, and Jews, Syriac Christians were not granted linguistic and religious rights.
32. The city was able to pay only $590 of this debt in 2009.
33. Invest in Mardin is itself part of the Invest in Turkey campaign fostered by the Republic of Turkey Prime Ministry Investment Support and Promotion Agency. DİKA functions as an entrepreneurial hub for attracting and assisting potential investors.
34. Mor Gabriel is one of the oldest active monasteries in the world. It serves as the seat of the Bishop of Tur Abdin.
35. Syriacs are thought to be among the first populations in the world to adopt Christianity. A close association between Syriacs and Christianity is very prominent in the Syriac Christians' and Eastern Christian Churches' narratives about their history and their importance for world civilization and Christianity.
36. However, her candidacy from the BDP caused some controversies in Mardin. Several Syriac associations (in Mardin and in Europe) suggested another Syriac candidate for the 2014 elections.
37. The Peoples Democratic Party is often referred to by its Turkish initials, HDP.
38. For the differences, dynamics, and conflicts between organizations focusing on culture and those concerned with human rights and discrimination in Mardin, see Biner 2007.

Chapter 2

Some of the arguments and data in this chapter draw from Nina Glick Schiller and Ayşe Çağlar (2013), "Locating Migrant Pathways of Economic Emplacement: Thinking Beyond the Ethnic Lens," *Ethnicities* 13: 494–514.
1. This interview was conducted by Nina Glick Schiller with assistance from Dr. Minh Nguen, who kindly provided the translation from Vietnamese to English and shared her ethnographic insights.
2. The public transport company HVG said that funding came from the STADTBAHN Halle program. Money for upgrading the tramline came in part from the federal government's Municipal Transport Financing Act, which provided 18 million euro, with both Saxony-Anhalt and Halle contributing some funding (*Halle Spektrum* 2013). The plan to obtain light-rail development money as a means of repairing key intersections was also described by the local online press. "The streets in Halle (Saale) must be rehabilitated. But the city lacks the money. Therefore, Halle now wants to participate in the 'rail program 2025.' The great advantage of this is that at the same time funds for road development can flow through the expansion of the tram network. And most of it is intended to come from grants, a whopping 305 million euros over the next 15 years. Halle must provide only 12.5 million Euros" (Seppelt 2011).
3. Light (1972) subsequently developed and clarified his position, stressing the signifi-

cance of class resources, which, as Light and Gold noted, included financial, social, human, and cultural forms of capital (Light and Gold 2000).

4. When migrants are seen in social movements, researchers generally focus on struggles for economic or immigrants rights rather than on broader movements for social justice. See, for example, Theodore and Martin (2007). It is important to note that scholars examining spatialized claim making and land rights within urban restructuring and gentrification in Asian cities have highlighted complex "cultural politics of place" among minority and migrant populations (Yeoh 2005, 954).

5. There were claims that, according to "the official price index as a whole, . . . the changeover from D-Mark to euro did not play a major role in pushing up prices" (Deutsche Bundesbank 2002). Our daily experience in Halle at the time and that of our respondents, including shopkeepers buying from wholesale sources, was that the prices of many goods doubled.

Chapter 3

Some of the arguments and data in this chapter are drawn from Nina Glick Schiller and Ayşe Çağlar (2016), "Displacement, Emplacement and Migrant Newcomers: Rethinking Urban Sociabilities within Multiscalar Power," *Identities* 23, no. 1: 17–34.

1. The "diversity visa lottery," often referred to as the "green card lottery," is a US system of immigrant visas issued by the luck of the draw. It extends legal entry with a permanent resident visa to people from countries that the US government deems historically underrepresented in terms of settlement in the United States (US Department of State 2016).

2. In many ways, the refugee support networks in European cities resembled the network of sanctuary cities in the US, where citizens voted to make their cities sanctuaries for undocumented migrants (Mount 2015). In the face of President Trump's intensification of deportations, many US mayors and public officials promised to protect the undocumented migrants settled in their city.

3. Those who popularized his research concluded that too many "foreigners" were a threat to the national social fabric. A robust debate has since taken place about whether Putnam's findings and construction of a trust variable could be substantiated in the United States and were as globally applicable as he claimed. His work has generated numerous critiques and debates (Li, Pickles, and Savage 2005; Gijsberts, van der Meer, and Dagevos 2012).

4. Openness to commonality can be called "situated cosmopolitanism," a topic explored elsewhere (see Glick Schiller 2015a, 2012b; Frykman 2016; Nashashibi 2013). While some of our respondents used the term "friend" to designate those with whom they formed domains of commonality, we must note several caveats. On other occasions, some of these same people might contrast those relationships with true friends left behind "back home." We don't always know whether the local person also used the term "friend" in describing these relationships. We are also aware of the ambivalences imbricated in the concept of "friend." However, our concern here is neither to designate who is or is not a true friend nor to disentangle a friendship from other forms of interpersonal relationships marked by positive affect (Eisenstadt and Roniger 1984).

5. City planning documents spoke of neighborhoods, but the planning process in most

cases neither reflected nor created a contemporary sense of neighborhood identity (City of Manchester 2009; City of Manchester 2010a). With differing degrees of success, elementary schools worked to build a localized identity among parents whose children attended them. See Young (2015) and Rogers and Garner (2015).

6. The global financial crisis of 2008, rising unemployment, and the subprime mortgage crisis, which further displaced many city residents, including migrants, in some respects made Manchester less welcoming, but over the years, there was polarization rather than rejection. The Obama administration's mass deportations that "removed" 2.5 million people (more than the total deported by all nineteen US presidents from 1892 to 2000) affected the daily sociabilities and levels of trust that were possible for both authorized and unauthorized migrants. Subsequently, after the election of Donald Trump, both antimigrant politics and a politics of open support for migrants, including those without papers, increased in a range of cities around the United States, including Manchester.

7. According to a 2009 city planning document, the vacancy rate of 0.8 percent in 2000 fell to 0.5 percent the following year, indicating a very tight rental market with escalating costs and poor affordability (City of Manchester 2009).

8. Often the terms "institution" and "organization" are conflated or used in overlapping ways. Here, we use the term "institution" to refer to established, normatively endorsed, long-standing "social structures" that may be public, private, or nonprofit foundations, charities, political parties, hospitals, established religious bodies, schools, and media all count as "institutions." In contrast, we use the term "organization" as it is used in the migration literature, that is, to refer to more short-lived social groups that are reliant on voluntary activity but tend toward professionalization and may receive public funding to deliver certain services. Storefront-type churches would be organizations in this categorization. Of course, these are ideal types, and in English the two words are often used interchangeably.

9. There were some exceptions. For example, Korean migrant store owners referenced Korean Protestant congregations, and a student researcher visited one such church. These churches may have provided means of emplacement. Language-based masses in Catholic parishes provided social and religious activities for participants. Our research within these parishes revealed a tendency on the part of church leadership to homogenize migrants in terms of "communities," organizing Vietnamese language and Hispanic language masses.

10. *Der Spiegel*, an influential German news magazine, reported that "in the train stations of major cities, . . . Germans wearing bright yellow vests kneeled next to the foreigners to serve them tea and sandwiches. . . . Wherever they arrived, it was to the applause of local residents, and even mayors, standing along the platform. . . . Citizens' initiatives were formed in cities and villages—not in opposition to, but in support of these new neighbors" (Kermani 2015). With the support of local public opinion behind them, mayors across Europe welcomed refugees. The City of Sanctuary network stretched across Europe and to forty cities in the United Kingdom (Mount 2015): "Twenty-four hours after Barcelona's city hall published an email address for citizens who want to help, . . . it received 1,200 offers of everything from housing to language lessons. . . . People in both France and Germany have set up housing sites known as 'Airbnb for refugees' whereby private citizens can offer bed-

rooms or complete apartments and crowdfund rent for the migrants they take in" (Mount 2015).

Chapter 4

Some of the arguments and data in this chapter draw on Ayşe Çağlar (2015), "Anthropology of Citizenship," in *The International Encyclopedia of the Social & Behavioral Sciences*, 2nd ed., vol. 3, edited by J. D. Wright, 637–42 (Oxford, UK: Elsevier); Nina Glick Schiller (2005), "Transborder Citizenship: Legal Pluralism within a Transnational Social Field," in *Mobile People, Mobile Law: Expanding Legal Relations in a Contracting World*, edited by F. von Benda-Beckmann, K. von Benda-Beckmann, and A. Griffiths, 27–50 (London: Ashgate); Nina Glick Schiller (2005), "Transnational Social Fields and Imperialism: Bringing a Theory of Power to Transnational Studies," *Anthropological Theory* 5, no. 4: 439–61; Nina Glick Schiller (2009), "'There Is No Power Except for God': Locality, Global Christianity, and Immigrant Transnational Incorporation," in *Permutations of Order*, edited by B. Turner and T. Kirsch, 125–47 (Farnham, UK: Ashgate); Nina Glick Schiller and Ayşe Çağlar (2008), "'And Ye Shall Possess It, and Dwell Therein': Social Citizenship, Global Christianity, and Non-Ethnic Immigrant Incorporation," in *Immigration and Citizenship in Europe and the United States: Anthropological Perspectives*, edited by D. Reed-Danahay and C. Brettell, 201–55 (New Brunswick, NJ: Rutgers University Press).

1. The names of the pastors and the migrant-initiated churches or religious organizations have been changed in keeping with University of Manchester and University of New Hampshire Institutional Review Board interview protocols.

2. During our research, the Miracle Healing Church and the Resurrection Crusade identified themselves predominantly as born-again rather than Pentecostal. In subsequent years, they spoke more directly of links to Pentecostal churches and networks. Pastor Mpenza had led a Pentecostal congregation before coming to Europe but claimed that his church was "independent." For a fuller exposition of the belief system of the congregations in which we worked, see Glick Schiller and Çağlar (2008).

3. The celebration dates to GDR times. African students initiated African week in Halle in 1988. However, in 2002, the week became a prominent public celebration organized by the Heinrich-Böll-Stiftung, the Green Party Foundation. The lord mayor endorsed the week, the deputy mayor spoke at one of the events, and official sponsorship also came from Saxony-Anhalt, Martin Luther University, the Max Planck Institute for Social Anthropology, and a number of NGOs, civil and religious (field notes 2002). The weeks' festivities included "Oriental" dancing from North Africa, a workshop on African cooking, and African music and dancing.

4. In Germany, the term "Evangelical" refers to a mainstream organization that links Lutheran, Reformed, and United regional churches (Landeskirchen), which together form the Evangelical Church in Germany (Evangelische Kirche in Deutschland, EKD) (Evangelischen Kirche in Deutschland 2016). The EKD is allocated tax revenues paid by citizens who are official members of these denominations. The Evangelical Church does not include members of independent Pentecostal con-

gregations. Pentecostal congregations are accorded official recognition through a separate organization, the Organization of Free Churches (Bund freikirchlicher Pfingstgemeinden). Member churches received no tax revenues and were supported by donations from their congregants.

5. This interview was conducted by Evangelis Karagiannis.

6. This interview was conducted by Evangelis Karagiannis.

7. The Christian Coalition was founded in 1989 by preacher Pat Robinson with the goal of "defending America's Godly heritage by getting Christians involved in their government again" (Christian Coalition 2005).

8. When Donald Trump came to power in 2017, right-wing Christian activists gained influential positions in the US administration, including Vice President Mike Pence, Secretary of Education Betsy Devos, and presidential advisor and member of the National Security Council Steve Bannon. Foundations linked to Devos and her family donated large sums to the Family Research Council (FRC) and to Focus on the Family. These organizations have been interlinked at various points of time but publicly differentiate their missions, with the FRC working on public policy and Focus on the Family functioning as a ministry (Rizga 2017; Family Research Council 2017).

Chapter 5

Some of the arguments in this chapter draw on Ayşe Çağlar (2006), "Hometown Associations, the Rescaling of State Spatiality and Migrant Grassroots Transnationalism," *Global Networks* 6: 1–22; and Ayşe Çağlar (2013), "Locating Migrant Hometown Ties in Time and Space: Locality as a Blind Spot of Migration Scholarship," *Historische Anthropologie* 21, no. 1: 26–42.

1. A mukhtar is the elected head of a village or a neighborhood in Turkey.

2. In 2016, only 1,765 Syriacs were living in Tur Abdin, the area referred to as the ancestral homeland of Syriac Christians (Güsten 2016, 9).

3. Between 2002 and 2004, 120,000 internally displaced people returned within the RVRP framework (Ayata and Yükseker 2005).

4. Not all the inhabitants of some of these other villages were Syriac, and in these cases the returnees faced more difficulties than the case of Kafro would suggest (field notes, May 2015).

5. About 182 Syriac families from Kafro had been living in different European countries.

6. Tur Abdin refers to an area bordered by the Tigris, by the mountain ranges of southeastern Anatolia to the north and the east, and by the Syrian plains to the south.

7. At the turn of the century, Syriacs numbered around two hundred thousand in the region. According to some sources, half of them were killed during the massacres in 1915 (Gaunt 2006).

8. For an excellent and elaborate analysis of intercommunity relations in Mardin and abroad, see Biner and Biner (2007; 2011).

9. Around forty thousand Syriacs are estimated to have emigrated from Turkey since the 1980s.

10. The numbers of internally displaced people are reported differently by various

agencies. According to reports by the United Nations High Commissioner for Refugees (UNHCR), 2 million people were forced to leave their villages. Reports by the UN Helsinki Commission and Turkish Grand National Assembly state that the number of people forced to leave their villages was 1 to 3 million, and 400,000, respectively (Kurban et al. 2008).

11. Before 2000, Mardin came under martial law three times (1925–27, 1978–80, and 1980–87). This took the form of unrestricted military and police control, with regular curfews, roadblocks, identity checks, and the suspension of human rights. Between 1987 and 1996, the city operated under State of Emergency Governorship (OHAL Governorship), and until 2002, it had a special legal status with a series of restrictive regulations.

12. Between 1985 and 1995, at least fifty-two Syriacs were killed in Mardin (interview L., May 19, 2015).

13. For an excellent account of this complex landscape, see Biner (2011).

14. Although seasonal returns of Syriac Christians from Europe to the Mardin city-region reached the thousands, permanent returns never exceeded one thousand people (Güsten 2016).

15. According to the president of the World Council of Arameans (Syriacs), twenty-five thousand Syriacs in the diaspora are affected by expropriations in Tur Abdin (Güsten 2015).

16. MAREV was initially established primarily (but not only) by Syriac Christian businessmen from Mardin. We are thankful to the members of MAREV for the support they have provided to our research.

17. "Turkey's Mardin Prepares to Become a Brand City," in *Hürriyet Daily News*, June 14, 2013.

18. Funding schemes of EU projects for the second term IPA were 85 percent EU funds and 15 percent public (national) funds: 7,819,815 euro of the 9,199,782-euro project came from the EU, with the remaining 1,379,976 euro contributed by the national government.

19. Development agencies were public institutions, and they had no direct link to the EU. Although they served as entrepreneurial hubs for attracting EU funds, their main financial supporter was the Turkish government. As stated in the law 26303, the budget of development agencies consisted of (1) funds from the central government, (2) funds from the local governorship, (3) funds from the municipalities, and (4) funds from local chambers of commerce (*Resmi Gazete* 2006). EU funds were attracted through local development projects and were channeled directly to project-specific aims.

20. The number of people working in certified tourist facilities in 2013 was 1,564 (Mardin Strategic Tourism Plan 2014).

21. Allocation of the building to the Sabanci Foundation and negotiations with the governorate, treasury, and municipality had been a complicated process, with some conflicts and changes in the terms of ownership and the directorship of the museum (interview E., March 23, 2015).

22. It is noteworthy that not all displaced Christians from Turkey (such as displaced Greeks or Armenians from different parts of Turkey) were addressed by this call, al-

though the question of religious freedom affected all Christian minorities in terms of religious and theological education and the situation of their monasteries (see Griffith 1999).

23. The EU's insistence on securing and facilitating Syriac migrants' return was also partly related to the desire of some EU member states to see refugees in Europe return to Mardin on the premise that they were no longer in danger as a religious minority in Turkey (Wikileaks no. 06Ankara5835_a, field notes May 16, 2015).

24. Between 2000 and 2015, at least fifteen articles about Mardin appeared in Turkish airline magazines as well as in newspapers such as the *New York Times* and the *Guardian*. See Uslu (2013); Kaya (2011, 2012, 2013); Eckhard (2010); and Gould (2008).

25. Some of these HTAS were Nusaybin Süryani Kültür ve Dayanışma Derneği, in Midyat; Öğündük (Midin) Köyü Kalkındırma ve Kültür Derneği, in İdil; Gülgöze (İvardo) Süryani Kültürü, Dayanışma ve Kalkındırma Derneği, in Midyat; and Yemişli (Enhil) Köyü Kalkındırma ve Uzlaştırma ve Kiliselerini Koruma Derneği, in Yemişli.

26. *Sabro* means "hope." It was printed in Istanbul, but its main office was in Midyat.

27. In the United States, the negative report of the visit in 1994 stopped the delivery of some military arms to the Turkish army (Milliyet 1998). According to the chairman of the secretary of state's Advisory Committee on Religious Freedom Abroad, who paid a second visit in 1998 and reported on it, this visit to Mardin was initiated by the Turkish military in relation to the delivery of military equipment (i.e., Cobra helicopters) (personal communication, March 2016). These visits and reports continued after 1998 until 2003, despite a change in chairmen of the Advisory Committee on Religious Freedom Abroad.

28. The silent presence of NATO in Mardin became a topic of public debate once plans to convert the castle into a public park were put on hold due to NATO's presence there. In 2012, the difficulty of transferring control of this landmark from the Turkish Defense Ministry to the Ministry of Culture because of NATO's presence became apparent (*Gazete Vatan* 2012).

REFERENCES

Abdi-Herrle, Sasan. 2015. "Tröglitz ist kein Einzelfall." *Zeit* online. April 4, 2015.
Accessed July 13, 2016, at: http://www.zeit.de/gesellschaft/zeitgeschehen/2015-04/
troeglitz-anschlag-kein-einzelfall-uebersicht.

Akers, Joshua M. 2013. "Making Markets: Think Tank Legislation and Private Property
in Detroit." *Urban Geography* 34, no. 8: 1070–95.

Altuğ, Seda. 2011. "Sectarianism in the Syrian Jazira: Community, Land and Violence
in the Memories of World War I and the French Mandate (1915–1939)." Unpublished
PhD manuscript, submitted to Utrecht University.

Amazon. "Dr. James Dobson." Accessed October 20, 2016, at: https://www.amazon
.com/Dr-James-Dobson/e/B000APW66Q/ref=ntt_dp_epwbk_0.

Amelina, Anna, Thomas Faist, Nina Glick Schiller, and Devirmsel D. Nergiz. 2012.
"Methodological Predicaments of Cross-Border Studies." In *Beyond Methodological
Nationalism: Research Methodologies for Cross-Border Studies*, edited by A. Amelina,
D. Nergiz, T. Faist, and N. Glick Schiller, 1–22. New York: Routledge.

Amelina, Anna, Devirmsel Nergiz, Thomas Faist, and Nina Glick Schiller, eds. 2012.
*Beyond Methodological Nationalism: Research Methodologies for Cross-Border Stud-
ies.* New York: Routledge.

Amin, Ash, ed. 1994. *Post-Fordism: A Reader.* Malden, MA: Blackwell.

Amin, Ash. 2012. *Land of Strangers.* Cambridge, UK: Polity.

Ana-Mardelli. 2011. Accessed May 5, 2015, at: http://ana-mardelli.ahlamontada.com/
t2072-topic.

Anderson, Christopher. 2012. *The New England Defense Industry: Current Profile and
Economic Significance.* Hadley, MA: University of Massachusetts, Defense Technology Initiative. Accessed April 6, 2016, at: http://www.donahue.umassp.edu/
documents/New_England_Defense_Industry_2012.pdf.

Angelou. 2005. *Global Economic Development Strategy Report 1: Community Assessment.* Presented to Manchester, NH, Austin, TX: AngelouEconomics.

Aparicio, Ana. 2006. *Dominican-Americans and the Politics of Empowerment.* Gaines-
ville: University Press of Florida.

Applied Economic Research. 2010. *Economic Impact Analysis: Elliot Hospital's River's
Edge Manchester.* Accessed April 5, 2015, at: http://www.library.unh.edu/find/digital/
object/mrg:0109.

Arapoglou, V. 2012. "Diversity, Inequality and Urban Change." *European Urban and Regional Studies* 19, no. 3: 223–37.

Arıkan, Harun. 2003. *Turkey and the EU: An Awkward Candidate for EU Membership?* Aldershot: Ashgate.

Avuka, Adnan. 2015. "Dünya Bankası Türkiye Ülke Direktörü Martin Raiser Mardin'de." *Hürses,* March 12, 2015. Accessed July 15, 2015, at: http://www.hurses.com.tr/goster.php?id=3129&tur=3.

Ayata, Bilgin, and Deniz Yükseker. 2005. "A Belated Awakening: National and International Responses to the Internal Displacement of Kurds in Turkey." *New Perspectives on Turkey* 32: 5–42.

Aydın, Suavi, Kudret Emiroğlu, Oktay Özel, and Süha Ünsal. 2000. *Mardin: Aşiret-Cemaat-Devlet.* İstanbul: Tarih Vakfı.

Aytar, Volkan, and Jan Rath, eds. 2012. *Selling Ethnic Neighborhoods: The Rise of Neighborhoods as Places of Leisure and Consumption.* London: Routledge.

Back, Les. 1996. *New Ethnicities and Urban Culture: Racisms and Multiculture in Young Lives.* London: University College London Press.

Bada, Xóchitl, Jonathan Fox, and Andrew Selee. 2006. *Invisible No More: Mexican Migrant Civic Participation in the United States.* Washington, DC: Mexico Institute. Accessed October 30, 2016, at: https://escholarship.org/uc/item/7624m65m.

Baines, Robert A. 2002. "Inaugural Address." Manchester, NH: City Clerk's Office, Board of Mayor and Alderman Inaugural Ceremonies. Accessed April 23, 2013, at: http://www.manchesternh.gov/portals/2/departments/city_clerk/agendas_and_minutes/BMA/2002-01-01-Inauguration.pdf.

Baines, Robert A. 2004. "Letter to Prayer Conference." Copy in files of N. Glick Schiller.

Balibar, Étienne. 2003. *We, the People of Europe? Reflections on Transnational Citizenship.* Translated by James Swenson. Princeton, NJ: Princeton University Press.

Ballotpedia. 2017. *Carlos Gonzalez (New Hampshire).* Accessed January 5, 2015, at: https://ballotpedia.org/Carlos_Gonzalez_(New_Hampshire).

Banerjee-Guha, Swapna. 2010. "Revisiting Accumulation by Dispossession: Neoliberalising Mumbai." In *Accumulation by Dispossession: Transformative Cities in the New Global Order,* edited by S. Banerjee-Guha, 198–226. New Delhi: Sage.

Barabantseva, Elena. 2016. "Seeing beyond an 'Ethnic Enclave': The Time/Space of Manchester Chinatown." *Identities: Global Perspectives on Culture and Power* 23, no. 1: 99–115.

Barth, Frederik. 1969. *Ethnic Groups and Boundaries: The Social Organization of Cultural Difference.* Boston: Little, Brown.

Bauböck, Rainer. 1994. *Transnational Citizenship: Membership and Rights in International Migration.* Cheltenham and Camberley, UK: Edward Elgar.

Bauböck, Rainer. 2003. "Reinventing Urban Citizenship." *Citizenship Studies* 7, no. 2: 139–60.

Baum, Detleft, Kamila Vondroušová, and Iva Tichá. 2014. *Characteristics of Socio-Spatial Segregation in Comparison of Two Cities (Halle–Ostrava).* Ostrava, CZ: University of Ostrava. Accessed May 13, 2015, at: http://projekty.osu.cz/vedtym/dok/publikace/baum_mesta.pdf.

Baumann, Gerd. 1996. *Contesting Culture: Discourses of Identity in Multi-Ethnic London*. Cambridge, UK: Cambridge University Press.

Beck, Ulrich. 2002. "The Cosmopolitan Society and Its Enemies." *Theory, Culture, and Society* 19, nos. 1-2: 17–44.

Beck, Ulrich, and Edgar Grande. 2010. "Varieties of Second Modernity: Extra-European and European Experiences and Perspectives." *British Journal of Sociology* 61, no. 3: 409–43.

Bendick, Kathleen, and Michael Tempel. 2014. "Neues Call-Center in Halle. Geringe Löhne, Großes Personalangebot." *Mitteldeutsche Zeitung*, March 17, 2014.

Benhabib, Seyla. 2007. "Twilight of Sovereignty or the Emergence of Cosmopolitan Norms? Rethinking Citizenship in Volatile Times." *Citizenship Studies* 11, no. 1: 19–36.

Benton-Short, Lisa, and Marie Price. 2008. "Migrants to the Metropolis: The Rise of Gateway Cities." In *Migrants to the Metropolis: The Rise of Immigrant Gateway Cities*, edited by M. Price and L. Benton-Short, 1–22. Syracuse, NY: Syracuse University.

Berg, Mette Louise, and Nando Sigona. 2013. "Ethnography, Diversity and Urban Space." *Identities: Global Studies in Culture and Power* 20, no. 4: 347–60.

Berger, John. 1972. *Ways of Seeing*. London: Penguin.

Berking, Helmuth. 2008. "'Städte lassen sich an ihrem Gang erkennen wie Menschen': Skizzen zur Erforschung der Stadt und der Städte." In *Die Eigenlogik der Städte: Neue Wege für die Stadtforschung*, edited by H. Berking and M. Löw, 15–31. Frankfurt am Main: Campus Verlag.

Biner, Zerrin Özlem. 2007. "Retrieving the Dignity of a Cosmopolitan City: Contested Perspectives on Rights, Culture and Ethnicity in Mardin." *New Perspectives on Turkey* 37: 31–58.

Biner, Zerrin Özlem. 2010. "Acts of Defacement, Memory of Loss: Ghostly Effects of the 'Armenian Crisis' in Mardin, Southeastern Turkey." *History and Memory* 22, no. 2: 68–94.

Biner, Zerrin Özlem. 2011. "Multiple Imaginations of the State: Understanding a Mobile Conflict on Justice and Accountability from the Perspective of Assyrian-Syriac Communities." *Citizenship Studies* 15, nos. 3–4: 367–79.

Birch, Douglas. 2003. "Presence of U.S. Troops Alarms Town in Turkey." *Baltimore Sun*, March 13, 2003. Accessed May 30, 2015, at: http://articles.baltimoresun.com/2003-03-13/news/0303130149_1_turkey-mardin-kurds.

Blood, Grace Everlina Holbrook. 1975. *Manchester on the Merrimac: The Story of a City*. Manchester, NH: Manchester Historic Association.

Bodirsky, Katharina. 2012. "The Value of Diversity: Culture, Cohesion, and Competitiveness in the Making of EU-Europe." Unpublished PhD manuscript, submitted to City University of New York.

Bodnár, Judit. 2014. "Comparisons and Gentrification as a Global Strategy." Paper presented at the American Sociological Association Annual Meeting, Hilton San Francisco, San Francisco, CA, July 5, 2014.

Bonacich, Edna, and John Modell. 1980. *The Economic Basis of Ethnic Solidarity: Small Business in the Japanese American Community*. Berkeley: University of California Press.

Brasuell, James. 2015. "Three Cities Where New Immigrants Revitalized Main Street."
Planetizen, January 14, 2015. Accessed February 5, 2016, at: http://www.planetizen
.com/node/73273.

Braudel, Fernand. 1974. *Capitalism and Material Life, 1400–1800*. New York: Harper
Torchbooks.

Brenner, Neil. 1999. "Beyond State-Centrism? Space, Territoriality and Geographical
Scale in Globalization Studies." *Theory and Society* 28: 39–78.

Brenner, Neil. 2001. "The Limits to Scale? Methodological Reflections on Scalar Structuration." *Progress in Human Geography* 25: 591–614.

Brenner, Neil. 2004. "Urban Governance and the Production of New State Spaces in
Western Europe, 1960–2000." *Review of International Political Economy* 11, no. 3:
447–88.

Brenner, Neil. 2009. "A Thousand Leaves: Notes on the Geographies of Uneven Spatial
Development." In *Leviathan Undone? Towards a Political Economy of Scale*, edited
by R. Keil and R. Mahon, 27–50. Vancouver: University of British Columbia Press.

Brenner, Neil. 2011. "The Urban Question and the Scale Question: Some Conceptual
Clarifications." In *Locating Migration: Rescaling Cities and Migrants*, edited by
N. Glick Schiller and A. Çaglar, 23–41. Ithaca, NY: Cornell University Press.

Brenner, Neil, Peter Marcuse, and Margit Mayer. 2009. "Cities for People, Not for
Profit." *City: Analysis of Urban Trends, Culture, Theory, Policy, Action* 13, nos. 2–3:
176–84.

Brenner, Neil, and Nik Theodore, eds. 2002. *Spaces of Neoliberalism: Urban Restructuring in North America and Western Europe*. Oxford, UK: Wiley-Blackwell.

Brettell, Caroline. 2003. "Bringing the City Back In: Cities as Contexts for Immigrant
Incorporation." In *American Arrivals: Anthropology Engages the New Immigration*,
edited by N. Foner, 163–95. Santa Fe, NM: School of American Research Press.

Brodie, Janine. 2008. "The Social in Social Citizenship." In *Recasting Social Citizenship*,
edited by E. F. Isin, 20–43. Toronto, Canada: University of Toronto Press.

Broussard, Rick. 2015. "Celebrating 100 Years at the Palace Theatre: The Crown Jewel of
the 'Queen City' Shines Brighter than Ever at Age 100. Here's Why." *nhmagazine
.com*. Accessed October 30, 2016, at: http://www.nhmagazine.com/March-2015/
Celebrating-100-Years-at-the-Palace-Theatre/.

Buchannan, Peter. 2002. "Interviews for 'Can You Buy a House with Social Capital?
The Role of Social Capital in Immigrant Homeownership.'" Manchester interviews
at the University of New Hampshire. In the files of N. Glick Schiller.

Bumiller, Elisabeth. 2004. "Bush Would Give Illegal Workers Broad New Rights." *New
York Times*, January 7, 2004. Accessed April 18, 2016 at: https://www.nytimes.com/
2004/01/07/us/bush-would-give-illegal-workers-broad-new-rights.html.

Bundesinstitut für Bau-, Stadt- und Raumforschung. 2015. "Stadtumbau Ost."
Bundesamt für Bauwesen und Raumordnung. Accessed July 1, 2015, at: http://
www.staedtebaufoerderung.info/StBauF/DE/Programm/StadtumbauOst/Praxis/
Massnahmen/Halle/Halle_node.html.

Business and Science Support Centre (Halle). 2015. *Business: Halle (Saale) Numbers, Facts and Contacts*. Halle: np. Accessed July 12, 2015, at: http://www.halle.de/
VeroeffentlichungenBinaries/323/882/wirtschaftsstandort_halle_2015_en.pdf.

Butler, Judit. 2009. *Frames of War: When Is Life Grievable?* London: Verso.

Cadge, Wendy, Sara Curran, Nadya Jaworsky, and Peggy Levitt. 2010. "The City as Context: Culture and Scale in New Immigrant Destinations." *Amérique Latine Histoire et Mémoire*. Les Cahiers ALHIM 20. Accessed October 30, 2016, at: http://alhim .revues.org/3640.

Çağlar, Ayşe. 2004. "'Citizenship Light': Transnational Ties, Multiple Rules of Membership, and 'The Pink Card.'" In *Worlds on the Move: Globalization, Migration, and Cultural Security*, edited by J. Friedmann and S. Randeria. London/New York: I. B. Tauris.

Çağlar, Ayşe. 2006. "Hometown Associations, the Rescaling of State Spatiality and Migrant Grassroots Transnationalism." *Global Networks* 6: 1–22.

Çağlar, Ayşe. 2013. "Locating Migrant Hometown Ties in Time and Space: Locality as a Blind Spot of Migration Scholarship." *Historische Anthropologie* 21, no. 1: 26–42.

Çağlar, Ayşe. 2015. "Anthropology of Citizenship." In the *International Encyclopedia of the Social & Behavioral Sciences*, 2nd ed., vol. 3, edited by J. D. Wright, 637–42. Oxford: Elsevier.

Çağlar, Ayşe. 2016a. "Displacement of European Citizen Roma in Berlin: Acts of Citizenship and Sites of Contentious Politics." *Citizenship Studies* 20, no. 5: 647–63.

Çağlar, Ayşe. 2016b. "Still 'Migrants' after All Those Years: Foundational Mobilities, Temporal Frames and Emplacement of Migrants." *Journal of Ethnic and Migration Studies* 42, no. 6: 952–69.

Çağlar, Ayşe, and Nina Glick Schiller. 2011. "Introduction: Migrants and Cities." In *Locating Migration: Rescaling Cities and Migrants*, edited by N. Glick Schiller and A. Çağlar, 1–22. Ithaca, NY: Cornell University Press.

Çağlar, Ayşe, and Sebastian Mehling. 2012. "Sites and the Scales of the Law: Third Country Nationals and EU Roma Citizens." In *Enacting European Citizenship*, edited by E. F. Isin and M. Saward, 155–77. Cambridge: Cambridge University Press.

Call-Center-Agent. 2015. *Gehalt Bundesweit*. Accessed July 12, 2015, at: http://www .gehaltsvergleich.com/gehalt/call-center-agent-Call-Center-Agentin.

Castells, Manuel. 1977. "Towards a Political Urban Sociology." In *Captive Cities: Studies in the Political Economy of Cities*, edited by M. Herloe, 61–78. London: Wiley and Sons.

Center for World-Class Universities. 2015. "University of Halle-Wittenberg." In *Academic Ranking of World Universities*. Accessed June 5, 2016, at: http://www .shanghairanking.com/World-University-Rankings/University-of-Halle-Wittenberg.html.

Cerullo, Morris. 2002. "Welcome to Morris Cerullo World Evangelism!" Accessed July 2002 at: http://www.mcwe.com/html.

Cerullo, Morris. 2016. *Morris Cerullo World Evangelism*. Accessed April 4, 2016, at: https://mcwe.com/about-morris-cerullo/.

Chen, Xiangmeng, and Ahmed Kanna. 2012. *Rethinking Global Urbanism: Comparative Insights from Secondary Cities*, vol. 7. New York: Routledge.

Chakrabarty, Dipesh. 2000. *Provincializing Europe: Postcolonial Thought and Historical Difference*. Princeton, NJ: Princeton University Press.

Christian Coalition. 2005. "Roberta Combs: A Message from Our President." Accessed August 5, 2005, at: http://www.cc.org/about.cfm.

Cifuentes, Camilo, and Nicolas Tixier. 2012. "An Inside Look at Bogotá's Urban Renewal from Broad Urban Stories to Everyday Tales." In 6th Conference of the International Forum on Urbanism, IFoU TOURBANISM, Barcelona, January 25–27. Accessed February 7, 2017, at: https://upcommons.upc.edu/handle/2099/12138.

City Data.com. 2009. "Manchester, New Hampshire." Accessed July 23, 2015, at: http://www.city-data.com/city/Manchester-New-Hampshire.html#b.

City Data.com. 2015 "[City of Manchester] Unemployment." Accessed July 23, 2015, at: http://www.city-data.com/city/Manchester-New-Hampshire.html.

City Data.com. 2018. "Manchester, New Hampshire Poverty Rate Data." Accessed January 10, 2018, at: http://www.city-data.com/poverty/poverty-Manchester-New-Hampshire.html#ixzz53cFQUdx1.

City of Halle. 2004. *Das Riebeckviertel*. Halle, Germany: Stadtsanierung Riebeckviertel. Brochure in files of Nina Glick Schiller.

City of Halle. 2011. *Stadtplanungsamt*. Wohnungsmarktbericht 2010. Accessed July 25, 2015, at: http://www.halle.de/VeroeffentlichungenBinaries/529/565/Wohnungsmarkt bericht_2010.pdf.

City of Halle. 2013. *Statistisches Jahrbuch*. Stadt Halle. Accessed October 30, 2016, at: http://www.halle.de/de/Verwaltung/Online-Angebote/Veroeffentlichungen/ ?recID=652.

City of Halle. 2015. *Statistisches Jahrbuch*. Stadt Halle. Accessed September 23, 2016, at: http://www.halle.de/VeroeffentlichungenBinaries/719/1029/statistisches_jahr-buch_2015.pdf.

City of Halle. 2016. "Bevölkerung." Accessed October 30, 2016, at: http://www.halle.de/ de/Verwaltung/Statistik/Bevoelkerung/Einwohner-mit-Hauptw-06101/.

City of Halle. "Bevölkerung." Accessed July 12, 2014, at: http://www.halle.de/de/ Rathaus-Stadtrat/Statistik/Bevoelkerung/Bevoelkerungsentwick-06050/.

City of Halle. *Door-Opener*. Accessed July 7, 2015, at: http://tueroeffner-halle.de/ Englisch/information.htm.

City of Manchester. 2004. "Relocating in Manchester." Accessed January 8, 2007, at: https://www.yourmanchesternh.com/Business/Relocation.

City of Manchester. 2006. "Downtown Strategic Plan, Section 2: Exiting Conditions." Accessed March 5, 2010, at: https://www.manchesternh.gov/pcd/cip/Downtown StrategicPlanSection2.pdf.

City of Manchester. 2009. *Comprehensive Economic Development Strategy*. Accessed October 30, 2016, at: http://www.manchesternh.gov/portals/2/departments/econ_dev/Manchester_NH_CEDS_Final.pdf.

City of Manchester. 2010a. "Neighborhood Revitalization Strategic Area Application to HUD." Accessed July 13, 2015, at: https://www.manchesternh.gov/pcd/cip/ NeighborhoodRevitalizationStrategyArea.pdf.

City of Manchester. 2010b. "Quick Facts: Population." Accessed March 11, 2010, at: http://www.yourmanchesternh.com/quick-facts.aspx.

City of Manchester. 2012. *Comprehensive Annual Financial Report for the Fiscal Year Ended June 30, 2003*. Accessed March 15, 2016, at: http://www.manchesternh.gov/ finance/2003%20CAFR.pdf.

City of Manchester. 2014. "Relocation Assistance." Accessed April 18, 2014, at: http:// www.yourmanchesternh.com/Grow-Your-Business/Relocation-Assistance.

City of Manchester Health Department. 2011. *City of Manchester Blueprint for Vio-*

lence Prevention. Accessed February 28, 2013, at: http://www.manchesternh.gov/health/2011WNSManchesterBlueprintforViolencePrevention.pdf.

City of Manchester Planning and Community Development Department. 2014. "Annual Action Plan." Accessed March 27, 2017, at: http://www.manchesternh.gov/pcd/cip/ActionPlan2014Draft.pdf.

Clarke, John. 2010. "Crises and Conjunctures: Looking for the Here and Now." Birkbeck Institute for Social Research, Academic Podcasts. Accessed July 20, 2016, at: http://backdoorbroadcasting.net/2010/03/john-clarke-crises-and-conjunctures-looking-for-the-here-and-now/.

Clarke, John. 2014. "Conjunctures, Crises, and Cultures: Valuing Stuart Hall." *Focaal: Journal of Global and Historical Anthropology* 70: 113–22.

Clarke, John, Dave Bainton, Noemi Lendvai, and Paul Stubbs. 2015. *Making Policy Move: Towards a Politics of Translation and Assemblage.* Bristol, UK: Policy Press.

Clarke, John, Kathleen Coll, Evelina Dagnino, and Catherine Neveu. 2014. "Conclusion: Disputing Citizenship." In *Disputing Citizenship,* edited by J. Clarke, K. Coll, E. Dagnino, and C. Neveu, 169–77. Bristol, UK: Policy.

Clarke, Susan E., and Gary L. Gaile. 1998. *The Work of Cities,* vol. 1. Minneapolis: University of Minnesota Press.

CLIP [Cities for Local Integration Policy] network. 2010. "Ethnic Entrepreneurship: Case Study: Frankfurt am Main Germany." Accessed July 27, 2012, at: http//www.europa.eu/pubdocs/2011/ 211/en/EF11211EN.pdf.

Cohen, Robin. 1997. *Global Diasporas.* Seattle: University of Washington Press.

Coleman, Simon, and Pauline von Hellermann. 2011. *Multi-Sited Ethnography: Problems and Possibilities in the Translocation of Research Methods.* New York: Routledge.

Collins, Catherine. 2003. "Prospect of War Worries 'Risky Region.'" *Chicago Tribune,* March 19, 2003. Accessed July 14, 2014, at: http://articles.chicagotribune.com/2003-03-19/news/0303190153_1_oil-industry-turkish-iraqi-border-industrial-zone.

Constant Amelie, Yochanan Shachmurove, and Klaus Zimmermann. 2007. "What Makes an Entrepreneur and Does It Pay? Native Men, Turks, and Other Migrants in Germany." *International Migration* 45, no. 4: 71–100.

Cottrell, Chris. 2013. "German from Senegal Vies to Break Bundestag Barrier," *New York Times,* May 31, 2013. Accessed June 20, 2015, at: http://www.nytimes.com/2013/06/01/world/europe/german-from-senegal-vies-for-bundestag-and-a-first.html?_r=0.

Council of Europe. 1995. *Framework Convention for the Protection of National Minorities and Explanatory Report.* Strasbourg, France: Ad Hoc Committee for the Protection of National Minorities (CAHMIN). Accessed October 30, 2016, at: https://rm.coe.int/CoERMPublicCommonSearchServices/DisplayDCTMContent?documentId=09000016800c10cf.

Coughlin, Adam. 2010. "Building Tomorrow's Military: NH's Surprising Role in the Defense Industry." *HippoPress,* September 16, 2010. Accessed July 28, 2015, at: http://archives.hippopress.com/100916/CVR.html.

Cousineau, Michael. 2015. "It's the Good and Bad of NH's Defense Contract Dilemma." *New Hampshire Union Leader,* June 6, 2015. Accessed July 8, 2015, at: http://www.unionleader.com/article/20150607/NEWS02/150609367.

Cowan, Jane. 2007a. "The Success of Failure? Minority Supervision at the League of Nations." In *Paths to International Justice: Social and Legal Perspectives*, edited by M. Dembour and T. Kelly, 29–56. Cambridge, UK: Cambridge University Press.

Cowan, Jane. 2007b. "The Supervised State." *Identities: Global Studies in Culture and Power* 14, no. 5: 545–78.

Cross, Malcolm, and Robert Moore. 2002. *Globalization and the New City: Migrants, Minorities, and Urban Transformations in Comparative Perspective*. New York: Palgrave Macmillan.

Çulpan, Hande. 2004. "Turkey's Ancient Christians Seek to Resettle Villages." *Daily Star*, June 2, 2004.

Dabringer, Maria, and Alexander Trupp, eds. 2011. *Wirtschaften mit Migrationshintergrund: Zur soziokulturellen Bedeutung ethnischer Ökonomien in urbanen Räumen*. Wien: StudienVerlag.

Dalley, Stephanie. 2013. *The Mystery of the Hanging Garden of Babylon*. Oxford: Oxford University Press.

De Genova, Nicholas. 2013. "Spectacles of Migrant 'Illegality': The Scene of Exclusion, the Obscene of Inclusion." *Ethnic and Racial Studies* 36, no. 7: 1180–98.

de Haas, Hein. 2012. "The Migration and Development Pendulum: A Critical View on Research and Policy." *International Migration* 50: 8–25.

Deakins, David, David Smallbone, Mohammed Ishaq, Geoff Whittam, and Janette Wyper. 2009. "Minority Ethnic Enterprise in Scotland." *Journal of Ethnic and Migration Studies* 35, no. 2: 309–30.

Dear, Michael. 2005. "Comparative Urbanism." *Urban Geography* 26, no. 3: 247–51.

Delay, Dennis. 2014. "New Hampshire Economic Outlook." Concord: New Hampshire Center for Public Policy Studies. Accessed July 8, 2015, at: http://www.nhpolicy.org/UploadedFiles/Resources/New_Hampshire_Economic_Outlook1014v2.pdf.

Deleuze, Gilles, and Félix Guattari. 1988. *A Thousand Plateaus*. Minneapolis: University of Minnesota Press.

Denning, Michael. 1996. *The Cultural Front: The Laboring of American Culture in the Twentieth Century*. Brooklyn, NY: Verso.

Der Spiegel Online. 2015. "'A Disgrace for Tröglitz': Refugee-Home Fire Spurs Xenophobia Fears." April 7, 2015. Accessed July 12, 2015, at: http://www.spiegel.de/international/germany/a-refugee-attack-and-the-specter-of-xenophobia-in-germany-a-1027345.html.

Deutsche Bundesbank. 2002. "Monthly Report July 2002." Accessed on October 31, 2016, at: https://www.bundesbank.de/Redaktion/EN/Downloads/Publications/Monthly_Report_Articles/2002/2002_07_consumer_price.pdf?_blob=publicationFile.

Dhaliwal, Spinder. 2008. "Business Support and Minority Ethnic Businesses in England." *Journal of Immigrant & Refugee Studies* 6, no. 2: 230–46.

DİKA. 2010a. *Sanayi Sektörü Mevcut Durum Raporu*. Mardin: Dicle Kalkınma Ajansi.

DİKA. 2010b. *Ön Bölgesel Gelişme Planı*. Mardin: Dicle Kalkınma Ajansi.

DİKA. 2010c. *Dicle Bölgesi Stratejik Gelisme Raporu*. Mardin: Dicle Kalkınma Ajansi. Accessed October 31, 2010, at: http://www.DİKA.org.tr/photos/files/DicleStratejik GelişmeRaporu.pdf.

DİKA. 2010d. *Ticaret Raporu.* Accessed October 30, 2010, at: http://www.kiziltepetb
.org.tr/site/bilgi/dosyalar/ticaret_raporu.pdf.

DİKA. 2010e. *Bölge Planı, 2011–2013.* Mardin: Dicle Kalkinma Ajansi.

DİKA. 2011. *Rakamlarla Mardin.* Mardin: Dicle Kalkinma Ajansi.

DİKA. 2013. *Bölgesel Gelişme Planı, 2014–2023.* Mardin: Dicle Kalkinma Ajansi.

DİKA. Mardin Destek Ofisi. 2010. *Mardin'de Yatirim Ortami.* Mardin: Dicle kalkinma
Ajansi.

DİKA. Mardin Yatirim Destek Ofisi. 2014. *Mardin: Bereketli Hilal'in Zirvesi.* Mardin:
Dicle Kalkinma Ajansi.

Donahue Institute. 2015. *The New England Defense Industry: Current Profile and Economic Significance.* Donahue Institute, Economic and Public Policy. Hadley: University of Massachusetts. Accessed April 6, 2016, at: https://www.massdevelopment
.com/assets/pdfs/annual-reports/NEDIS_122015.pdf.

Dora, Erol. 2011. *Türkiye nin İlk Süryani Milletvekili Seçilen Dora: "AB ye En Güzel
Örnek Benim."* Accessed on October 31, 2016, at: http://www.suryaniler.com/forum
.asp?fislem=cevaplar&kategoriid=4&ustid=5083.

Duigan, Brian 2017. "USA PATRIOT Act" *Encyclopedia Britannica.* Accessed February 03, 2018, at: https://www.britannica.com/topic/USA-PATRIOT-Act.

Dutt, Ela. 2006. "Saghir Tahir Retains Seat in New Hampshire": Indian American Center for Political Awareness. Accessed September 8, 2016, at: https://en.wikipedia
.org/wiki/Saggy_Tahir.

Durand, Cedric. 2017. *Fictitious Capital: How Finance Is Appropriating Our Future.*
London: Verso.

Eaton, Aurore. 2015. *The Amoskeag Manufacturing Company: A History of Enterprise
on the Merrimack River.* Charleston, SC: History.

Echikson, William. 2000. "Unsung Heroes: Europe's Immigrant Entrepreneurs Are
Creating Thriving Businesses and Thousands of Jobs." *Bloomberg Business Week,*
February 28, 2000. Accessed July 27, 2012, at: http://www.businessweek.com/
stories/2000-02-27/unsung-heroes-intl-edition.

Eckert, Julia. 2016. "Beyond Agatha Christie: Relationality and Critique in Anthropological Theory." *Anthropological Theory* 16, nos. 2–3: 241–48.

Eckhardt, Robyn. 2010. "An Ancient City in Turkey Finds New Life in Modern Art."
New York Times. Accessed August 19, 2010, at: http://www.nytimes.com/2010/08/22/
travel/22nextstop.html?_r=0.

Eckstein, Susan, and Thanh-Nghi Nguyen. 2011. "The Making and Transnationaliza-
tion of an Ethnic Niche: Vietnamese Manicurists." *International Migration Review*
45, no. 3: 639–74.

Edis, S. 2012. "Mardin to Regain Historic Look in New Project." Accessed July 8, 2014,
at: https://www.thefreelibrary.com/Mardin+to+regain+historic+look+in+new+
project.-a0310111476.

Eger, Christian. 2016. "Unesco Welterbe-Bewerbung der Franckesche Stiftungen
Rückzug soll Schaden abwenden." *Mitteldeutsche Zeitung,* January 7, 2016. Accessed
October 31, 2016, at: http://www.mz-web.de/kultur/unesco-welterbe-bewerbung-
der-franckesche-stiftungen-rueckzug-soll-schaden-abwenden-23435380.

Egresi, Istvan, Fatih Kara, and Büşra Bayram. 2012. "Economic Impact of Religious

Tourism in Mardin, Turkey." *Journal of Economic and Business Research* 18, no. 2: 7–22.

Eisenstadt, Shmuel N., and Luis Roniger. 1984. *Patrons, Clients and Friends: Interpersonal Relations and the Structure of Trust in Society.* Cambridge: Cambridge University Press.

Ekinci, Behzat Mehmet. 2015. *Mardin'in Ekonomik Panoraması: Şehrin Sektörel, Kurumsal, Rekabetçilik ve Müteşebbislik Yapısına Dair Tahliller.* Accessed July 14, 2016, at: http://nusaybintso.org.tr/site/dosyalar/2014_merdin_econ_tepav.pdf.

Endres, Alexandra. 2010. "Halle, die schrumpfende Stadt." *Zeit Online,* November 9, 2010. Accessed October 31, 2016, at: http://www.zeit.de/wirtschaft/2010-11/halle-saale-stadtumbau.

Eriksen, Thomas Hylland. 2010. "Complexity in Social and Cultural Integration: Some Analytical Dimensions." In *Anthropology of Migration and Multiculturalism: New Directions,* edited by Steven Vertovec, 97–112. London: Routledge.

Erkeskin, Turgut. 2013. "Logistics Hubs and New Perspectives in Turkey." Paper presented at the 11th South East European Freight Forwarders and Logistics Operators Congress, Athens, May 16–17, 2013. Accessed July 17, 2015, at: http://slideplayer.com/slide/1479879/.

European Commission. 2008. *Supporting Entrepreneurial Diversity in Europe: Ethnic Minority Entrepreneurship/Migrant Entrepreneurship.* Conclusions and Recommendations of the European Commission's Network "Ethnic Minority Businesses." Brussels: European Commission, Enterprise, and Industry Directorate General.

Evangelische Kirche in Deutschland. Accessed on October 31, 2016, at: http://www.ekd.de/english/about_ekd.html.

Fabian, Johannes. 1983. *Time and the Other: How Anthropology Makes Its Object.* New York: Columbia University Press.

Fabian, Johannes. 2006. "The Other Revisited: Critical Afterthoughts." *Anthropological Theory* 6, no. 2: 139–52.

Fabian, Jordan. 2012. "Q&A with N.H. State Rep. Carlos Gonzalez." January 8, 2012. Accessed August 14, 2015, at: http://thisisfusion.tumblr.com/post/15510334333/qa-with-nh-state-rep-carlos-gonzalez.

Fairlie, Robert. 2012. "Immigrant Entrepreneurs and Small Business Owners and Their Access to Financial Capital." US Small Business Administration, Office of Advocacy Document No. 396. Accessed April 20, 2015, at: https://www.sba.gov/content/immigrant-entrepreneurs-and-small-business-owners-and-their-access-financial-capital.

Faist, Thomas, Margit Fauser, and Peter Kivisto, eds. 2011. *The Migration-Development Nexus: Transnational Perspectives.* Basingstoke, UK: Palgrave Macmillian.

Falzon, Mark-Anthony, ed. 2009. *Multi-Sited Ethnography: Theory, Praxis and Locality in Contemporary Research.* Farnham, UK: Ashgate.

Family Research Council. 2017. Accessed December 16, 2017, at: http://www.frc.org/faqs.

Fassin, Didier. 2015. "Introduction: Governing Precariousness." In *At the Heart of the State: The Moral World of Institutions,* edited by D. Fassin et al., 1–12. Chicago: University of Chicago Press.

Federal Deposit Insurance Corporation. Nd. "Seven Banks in New Hampshire." Accessed September 17, 2016, at: https://www.fdic.gov/bank/historical/managing/history2-10.pdf.

Federal Ministry of Education and Research. 2015. "Halle." Accessed July 23, 2014, at: https://www.study-in.de/en/discover-germany/german-cities/halle_26972.php.

Feely, Paul. 2015. "Manchester Chief: Granite State May Host 500 Refugees, Some Syrian." *New Hampshire Union Leader*, November 17, 2015. Accessed April 23, 2016, at: http://www.unionleader.com/Chief-Granite-State-may-host-500-Syrian-refugees.

Feldman, Gregory. 2011. "If Ethnography Is More Than Participant-Observation, Then Relations Are More Than Connections: The Case for Nonlocal Ethnography in a World of Apparatuses." *Anthropological Theory* 11: 375–95.

Feldman-Bianco, Bela. n.d. "Anthropology and Ethnography: The Transnational Perspective on Migration and Beyond." *Etnográfica*. Forthcoming 2018.

Fitch. 2014. "Fitch Lowers Manchester's Bond Credit Rating: New Hampshire." Accessed November 20, 2015, at: https://nhpr.org/post/fitch-lowers-manchesters-bond-credit-rating.

Florida, Richard. 2002. *The Rise of the Creative Class: And How It's Transforming Work, Leisure, Community, and Everyday Life*. New York: Basic Books.

Fonseca, Juanita, and Camilo Pinilla. 2008. "Bogotá: The Proud Revival of a City." *Archined* (Amsterdam), September 1. Accessed February 7, 2017, at: https://www.archined.nl/2008/01/bogota-the-proud-revival-of-a-city.

Forrest, Ray, and Ade Kearns. 2001. "Social Cohesion, Social Capital and the Neighbourhood." *Urban Studies* 38: 2125–43.

Freeman, James. 2012. "Neoliberal Accumulation Strategies and the Visible Hand of Police Pacification in Rio de Janeiro." *Revista de Estudos Universitários* 38, no. 1: 95–126.

Friedman, Jonathan. 2004. "Globalization, Dis-Integration, Re-Organization: The Transformations of Violence." In *Globalization, the State, and Violence*, edited by J. Friedman, 1–34. Walnut Creek, CA: Altamira.

Frykman, Maja Povrzanovic. 2016. "Cosmopolitanism in Situ: Conjoining Local and Universal Concerns in a Malmö Neighbourhood." *Identities: Global Studies in Culture and Power* 23, no. 1: 35–50.

Galioto, Katie. 2016. "Black Lives Matter Rally in Manchester Seeks Justice, Peace." *Concord Monitor*, Sunday, July 17, 2016. Accessed September 3, at: http://www.concordmonitor.com/Black-Lives-Matter-march-in-Manchester-3485257.

Gans, Herbert J. 1962. *The Urban Villagers: Group and Class in the Life of Italian-American*. New York: Free Press of Glencoe.

Gardiner Barber, Pauline, and Winnie Lem. 2012a. "Migration, Political Economy and Beyond." In *Migration in the 21st Century: Political Economy and Ethnography*, edited by P. Gardiner Barber and Winnie Lem, 236–42. New York: Routledge.

Gardiner Barber, Pauline, and Winnie Lem. 2012b. "Migration, Political Economy and Ethnography." In *Migration in the 21st Century: Political Economy and Ethnography*, edited by P. Gardiner Barber and Winnie Lem, 1–16. New York: Routledge.

Gaunt, David. 2006. *Massacres, Resistance, Protectors: Muslim-Christian Relations in Eastern Anatolia during World War I*. Piscataway, NJ: Gorgias.

Gazete Vatan. 2012. "Mardin Kalesi'nin içinden NATO radarı çıktı restorasyon durdu."

Accessed June 21, 2014, at: http://www.gazetevatan.com/mardin-kalesi-nin-icinden-nato-radari-cikti-restorasyon-durdu-460628-gundem.

Geertz, Clifford. 1973. *Interpretation of Cultures: Selected Essays.* New York: Basic Books.

Ghertner, D. Asher. 2014. "India's Urban Revolution: Geographies of Displacement beyond Gentrification." *Environment and Planning A* 46: 1554–71.

Gibson, Chris, and Natascha Klocker. 2004. "Academic Publishing as a 'Creative' Industry: Some Critical Reflections." *Area* 36: 423–34.

Giddens, Anthony. 1984. *The Constitution of Society: Outline of the Theory of Structuration.* Berkeley: University of California Press.

Gittell, Ross. 2001. *Manufacturing: New Hampshire's Secret Strength; Building on Our Advantage.* Durham: New Hampshire Small Business Manufacturing Management Center.

Gijsberts, Merove, Tom van der Meer, and Jaco Dagevos. 2012. "'Hunkering Down' in Multi-Ethnic Neighbourhoods? The Effects of Ethnic Diversity on Dimensions of Social Cohesion." *European Sociological Review* 28, no. 4: 527–37.

Gill, Stephen. 1992. "Economic Globalization and the Internationalization of Authority: Limits and Contradictions." *Geoforum* 23, no. 3: 269–83.

Gilroy, Paul. 2004. *After Empire: Melancholia or Convivial Culture?* London: Routledge.

Glassman, Jim. 2006. "Primitive Accumulation, Accumulation by Dispossession, Accumulation by 'Extra-Economic' Means." *Progress in Human Geography* 30, no. 5: 608–25.

Glick Schiller, Nina. 1977. "Ethnic Groups Are Made Not Born." In *Ethnic Encounters: Identities and Contexts*, edited by G. Hicks and P. Leis, 23–35. North Scituate, MA: Duxbury.

Glick Schiller, Nina. 1999. "Transmigrants and Nation-States: Something Old and Something New in the US Immigrant Experience." In *The Hand-book of International Migration: The American Experience*, edited by C. Hirshman, P. Kasinitz, and J. DeWind, 94–119. New York: Russell Sage Foundation.

Glick Schiller, Nina. 2003. "The Centrality of Ethnography in the Study of Transnational Migration: Seeing the Wetland Instead of the Swamp." In *American Arrivals*, edited by N. Foner, 99–128. Santa Fe, NM: School of American Research.

Glick Schiller, Nina. 2005a. "Transborder Citizenship: Legal Pluralism within a Transnational Social Field." In *Mobile People, Mobile Law: Expanding Legal Relations in a Contracting World*, edited by F. von Benda-Beckmann, K. von Benda-Beckmann, and A. Griffiths, 27–50. London: Ashgate.

Glick Schiller, Nina. 2005b. "Transnational Social Fields and Imperialism: Bringing a Theory of Power to Transnational Studies." *Anthropological Theory* 5, no. 4: 439–61.

Glick Schiller, Nina. 2009. "A Global Perspective on Migration and Development." *Social Analysis* 53, no. 3: 14–37.

Glick Schiller, Nina. 2010. "A Global Perspective on Transnational Migration: Theorizing Migration without Methodological Nationalism." In *Diaspora and Transnationalism: Concepts, Theories and Methods,* edited by R. Bauböck and T. Faist, 109–30. Amsterdam: Amsterdam University Press and IMISCOE.

Glick Schiller, Nina. 2011. "Localized Neoliberalism, Multiculturalism and Global Religion: Exploring the Agency of Migrants and City Boosters." *Economy and Society* 40: 211–38.

Glick Schiller, Nina. 2012a. "A Comparative Relative Perspective on the Relationships between Migrants and Cities." *Urban Geography* 33, no. 6: 879–903.

Glick Schiller, Nina. 2012b. "Situating Identities: Towards an Identities Studies without Binaries of Difference." *Identities: Global Studies in Culture and Power* 19, no. 4: 520–32.

Glick Schiller, Nina. 2015a. "Diasporic Cosmopolitanism: Migrants, Sociabilities and City-Making." In *Whose Cosmpolitanism: Critical Perspectives, Relationalities, and Discontents*, edited by N. Glick Schiller and A. Irving, 103–20. New York: Berghahn.

Glick Schiller, Nina. 2015b. "Explanatory Frameworks in Transnational Migration Studies: The Missing Multi-Scalar Global Perspective." *Ethnic and Racial Studies* 8, no. 13: 2275–82.

Glick Schiller, Nina. 2016. "The Question of Solidarity and Society: Comment on Will Kymlicka's Article 'Solidarity in Diverse Societies.'" *Comparative Migration Studies* 4, no. 6: 1–9.

Glick Schiller, Nina, and Ayşe Çağlar. 2008. "'And Ye Shall Possess It, and Dwell Therein': Social Citizenship, Global Christianity, and Non-Ethnic Immigrant Incorporation." In *Immigration and Citizenship in Europe and the United States: Anthropological Perspectives*, edited by D. Reed-Danahay and C. Brettell, 201–55. New Brunswick, NJ: Rutgers University Press.

Glick Schiller, Nina, and Ayşe Çağlar. 2009. "Towards a Comparative Theory of Locality in Migration Studies: Migrant Incorporation and City Scale." *Journal of Ethnic and Migration Studies* 35, no. 2: 177–202.

Glick Schiller, Nina, and Ayşe Çağlar. 2011a. "Locality and Globality: Building a Comparative Analytical Framework in Migration and Urban Studies." In *Locating Migration: Rescaling Cities and Migrants*, edited by N. Glick Schiller and A. Çaglar, 60–84. Ithaca, NY: Cornell University Press.

Glick Schiller, Nina, and Ayşe Çağlar. 2011b. "Rejecting Autonomy: A Global Perspective on Migrant Agency." *Zeitschrift für Kulturwissenschaften* 2: 147–50.

Glick Schiller, Nina, Ayşe Çağlar, and Thaddeus C. Guldbrandsen. 2006. "Beyond the Ethnic Lens: Locality, Globality, and Born-Again Incorporation." *American Ethnologist* 33, no. 4: 612–33.

Glick Schiller, Nina, Tsypylma Darieva, and Sandra Gruner-Domic. 2011. "Defining Cosmopolitan Sociability in a Transnational Age: An Introduction." *Ethnic and Racial Studies* 34, no. 3: 399–418.

Glick Schiller, Nina, and Andrew Irving. 2015. "What's in a Word? What's in a Question? Introduction." In *Whose Cosmopolitanism: Critical Perspectives, Relationalities and Discontents*, edited by N. Glick Schiller and A. Irving, 1–22. New York: Berghahn.

Gluckman, Max. 1940. "Analysis of a Social Situation in Modern Zululand." *Bantu Studies* 14, no. 1: 1–30.

Goldring, Luin. 1998. "The Power of Status in Transnational Social Fields." In *Transnationalism from Below*, edited by M. P. Smith and L. E. Guernizo, 165–95. New Brunswick, NJ: Rutgers University Press.

González, Sara. 2006. "Scalar Narratives in Bilbao: A Cultural Politics of Scales Approach to the Study of Urban Policy." In *International Journal of Urban and Regional Research* 30, no. 4: 836–57.

GOPA Worldwide Consultants. 2012. "Technical Assistance for Sustainable Tourism Development in Mardin." Accessed June 10, 2015, at: http://www.gopa.de/en/projects/technical-assistance-sustainable-tourism-development-mardin.

Gould, Kevin. 2008. "Double History." *Guardian*, August 16, 2008. Accessed July 14, 2014, at: http://www.theguardian.com/travel/2008/aug/16/turkey.heritage.

Greater Manchester Chamber of Commerce. 2009. *About Manchester and NH*. Accessed February 8, 2009, at: http://www. manchesterareacolleges.com/manchester-area/about-manchester-and-nh.asp.

Griffith, Stephen. 1999. "The Situation among Christians in Tur Abdin: A Summary of Visits to South-eastern Turkey, 1997–99." *Syriac Orthodox Sources*. Accessed July 15, 2015, at: http://sor.cua.edu/Pub/StephenGriffith/VisitSETurkeySum1999.html.

Griffith, Stephen. 2000. "The Situation in Tur Abdin: Report on Visit to South-eastern Turkey, 2000." *Syriac Othodox Sources*. Accessed July 19, 2014, at: http://sor.cua.edu/Pub/StephenGriffith/VisitSETurkeySum1999.html.

Griffith, Stephen. 2001. "The Situation in Tur Abdin: Report on Visit to South-eastern Turkey, 2001." *Syriac Orthodox Sources*. Accessed July 19, 2014, at: http://sor.cua.edu/Pub/StephenGriffith/VisitSETurkeySum1999.html.

Grillo, Ralph. 2005. "Backlash against Diversity? Identity and Cultural Politics in European Cities." Working Paper no. 14. Centre on Migration, Policy and Society: University of Oxford.

Guilmet, April. 2014. "FedEx to Hire 500 at Londonderry Center." *New Hampshire Union Leader*, May 16, 2014. Accessed July 8, 2015, at: http://www.unionleader.com/apps/pbcs.dll/article?AID=/20140516/NEWS02/14051927.

Guinta, Frank. 2009. *Community Improvement Program, Fiscal Year 2009*. City of Manchester, NH: Office of the Mayor.

Güsten, Susanne. 2015. *The Syriac Property Issue in Tur Abdin*. Istanbul: Istanbul Policy Center, A Mercator Project.

Güsten, Susanne. 2016. *A Farewell to Tur Abdin*. Istanbul: Istanbul Policy Center, a Mercator Project.

Gutiérrez-Rodríguez, Encarnación. 2010. *Migration, Domestic Work and Affect: A Decolonial Approach on Value and the Feminization of Labor*. New York: Routledge.

Haberler. 2012. "Mardin'de Tarihi Ev ve Arsa Fiyatları Milyon Dolarları Aştı." December 10, 2012. Accessed July 17, 2014, at: http://www.haberler.com/mardin-de-tarihi-ev-ve-arsa-fiyatlari-milyon-4158756-haberi/.

Haberlermardinimiz. 2010. "Mardinspor Borcu Dudak Uçuklatıyor!" Accessed November 1, 2016, at: http://haberler.mardinimiz.com/popup/haber-yazdir.asp?haber=1119.

Hackworth, Jason, and Josephine Rekers. 2005. "Ethnic Packaging and Gentrification: The Case of Four Neighborhoods in Toronto." *Urban Affairs Review* 41, no. 2: 211–36.

Hage, Ghassan. 2014. "Continuity and Change in Australian Racism." *Journal of Intercultural Studies* 35, no. 3: 232–37.

Hall, Stuart, Chas Critcher, Tony Jefferson, John Clarke, and Brian Roberts. 1978. *Policing the Crisis: Mugging, the State, and Law and Order*. London: Macmillan.

Hall, Tim, and Phil Hubbard. 1998. *The Entrepreneurial City: Geographies of Politics, Regime, and Representation*. Hoboken, NJ: John Wiley and Sons.

HalleSaale Investvision Entwicklungs- und Verwaltungsgesellschaft Halle-Saalkreis GmbH. 2015. *Die Bühne für Ihren Erfolg. Zahlen, Fakten und Kontakte. Halle/ Saale Ha.* Accessed March 23, 2017, at: http://www.halle-investvision.de/wp-content/uploads/2016/09/Halle-Saale-Investvision-Broschüre-Deutsch.pdf.

Halle Spektrum. 2013. "Stadtbahnprogramm: Bundesregierung macht für Halle 18 Millionen Euro locker." October 15, 2013. Accessed May 3, 2014, at: http://hallespektrum .de/nachrichten/umwelt-verkehr/stadtbahnprogramm-bundesregierung-macht-fuer-halle-18-millionen-euro-locker/71066/.

Halle Spektrum. 2014. "Wandern–Siedeln–Gestalten: Halles Migrationsgeschichte." Accessed March 12, 2015, at: http://hallespektrum.de/nachrichten/vermischtes/wandern-siedeln-gestalten-halles-migrationsgeschichte/91628/.

Hamidi, Camille. 2003. "Voluntary Associations of Migrants and Politics: The Case of North African Immigrants in France." *Immigrants & Minorities: Historical Studies in Ethnicity, Migration and Diaspora* 22, nos. 2–3: 317–32.

Hamilton, Dona Cooper, and Charles V. Hamilton. 1997. *The Dual Agenda: The African-American Struggle for Civil and Economic Equality.* New York: Columbia University Press.

Haney López, Ian. 1998. *White by Law: The Legal Construction of Race.* New York: New York University Press.

Hannerz, Ulf. 1990. "Cosmopolitans and Locals in World Culture." *Theory, Culture and Society* 7: 237–51.

Hannerz, Ulf. 2003. "Being There . . . and There . . . and There! Reflections on Multi-Sited Ethnography." *Ethnography* 4, no. 2: 201–16.

Hareven, Tamara, and Randolph Langenbach. 1978. *Amoskeag: Life and Work in an American Factory-City.* New York: Pantheon Books.

Harrison, Faye. 2016. "Theorizing in Ex-Centric Sites." *Anthropological Theory* 16: 160–76.

Hart, Gillian. 2006. "Denaturalizing Dispossession: Critical Ethnography in the Age of Resurgent Imperialism." *Antipode* 38, no. 5: 977–1004.

Hart, Keith. 2001. "Money in an Unequal World." *Anthropological Theory* 1, no. 3: 307–30.

Harvey, David. 2003. *The New Imperialism.* Oxford: Oxford University Press.

Harvey, David. 2004. "The 'New' Imperialism: Accumulation through Dispossession." *Socialist Register* 40: 63–87.

Harvey, David. 2005. *Brief History of Neoliberalism.* New York: Oxford University Press.

Harvey, David. 2006. *Spaces of Global Capitalism: Towards a Theory of Uneven Geographical Development.* London: Verso.

Harvey, David. 2008. "The Right to the City." *New Left Review* 53: 23–40.

Harvey, David. 2012. *Rebel Cities: From the Right of the City to Urban Revolution.* New York: Verso.

Häußermann, Harmut, Andrej Holm, and Daniela Zunzer. 2002. "Stadterneuerung in der Berliner Republik: Modernisierung in Berlin-Prenzlauer Berg." Opladen: Leske und Budrich.

Hayward, Mark. 2015. "NH's Role in Primary History Subject of MHA Exhibit." *Manchester Union Leader*, December 14, 2015. Accessed May 14, 2015, at: http://www

.unionleader.com/NHs-role-in-primary-history-subject-of-MHA-exhibit#sthash
.gbFJ10En.dpuf.

Hearn, Adrian H. 2016. *Diaspora and Trust: Cuba, Mexico, and the Rise of China.* Durham, NC: Duke University Press.

Heckmann, Friedrich. 1998. "Ethnische Kolonien: Schonraum für Integration oder Verstärker der Ausgrenzung?" In *Ghettos oder ethnische Kolonien? Entwicklungschancen von Stadtteilen mit hohem Zuwandereranteil,* edited by Forschungsinstitut der Friedrich-Ebert-Stiftung, Abt. Arbeit und Sozialpolitik, 29–42. Bonn: n.p.

Heckmann, Friedrich. 2015. *Integration von Migranten.* Wiesbaden: Springer Fachmedien.

Hengst, Björn. 2011. "Herr Diaby bekommt Morddrohungen." *Der Spiegel Online,* August 5, 2011. Accessed June 8, 2015, at: http://www.spiegel.de/politik/deutschland/rechtsextremismus-hochburg-sachsen-anhalt-herr-diaby-bekommt-morddro hungen-a-778461.html.

Hertz, Ellen. 2016. "Pimp My Fluff: A Thousand Plateaus and Other Theoretical Extravaganzas." *Anthropological Theory* 16: 146–59.

Hesson, Ted. 2015a. "3 Cities Where Immigrants Helped Save Main Street." *Fusion News,* January 14, 2015. Accessed April 23, 2015, at: http://fusion.net/story/38313/3-cities-where-immigrants-helped-save-main-street/.

Hesson, Ted. 2015b. "Why American Cities Are Fighting to Attract Immigrants." *The Atlantic,* July 21, 2015. Accessed April 23, 2015, at: http://www.theatlantic.com/business/archive/2015/07/us-cities-immigrants-economy/398987/.

Hill, Jenny. 2016. "Migrant Attacks Reveal Dark Side of Germany." *BBC,* February 22, 2016. Accessed August 28, 2016, at: http://www.bbc.com/news/world-europe-35633318.

Hillier Architecture. 2006. *Downtown Strategic Development Plan.* Accessed April 12, 2018, at: https://www.manchesternh.gov/Departments/Planning-and-Comm-Dev/Long-Range-Planning/Strategic-Development-Plan.

Hochschild, Arlie. 2016. *Strangers in Their Own Land: Anger and Mourning on the American Right.* New York: New Press.

Hoefle, Scott William. 2006. "Eliminating Scale and Killing the Goose That Laid the Golden Egg?" *Transactions of the Institute of British Geographers* 31: 238–43.

Holm, Andrej. 2006. *Die Restrukturierung des Raumes: Machtverhältnisse in der Stadterneuerung der 90er Jahre in Ostberlin.* Bielefeld: transcript Verlag.

Holm, Andrej. 2010. "Gentrification und Kultur: Zur Logik kulturell vermittelter Aufwertungsprozesse." In *Jahrbuch Stadtregion 2009/10,* ed. Christine Hannemann et al., 64–82.

Holston, James. 2008. *Insurgent Citizenship: Disjunctions of Democracy and Modernity in Brazil.* Princeton, NJ: Princeton University Press.

Holston, James, and Arjun Appadurai. 1999. "Introduction." In *Cities and Citizenship,* edited by J. Holston, 1–18. Durham, NC: Duke University Press.

Hsing, You-tien. 1998. *Making Capitalism in China: The Taiwan Connection.* Oxford: Oxford University Press.

Huntington, Samuel. 1996. *The Clash of Civilizations and the Remaking of World Order.* New York: Simon and Schuster.

Hürriyet Daily News. 2010. "Syriacks Back in Mardin as Investors." June 6, 2010.

Accessed October 21, 2016, at: http://www.hurriyetdailynews.com/default.aspx?pageid=438&n=assyrians-back-in-mardin-as-investors-2010-06-29.

IBA. 2010. "Balancing Act: Dual City." *International Building Exhibition Urban Redevelopment Saxony-Anhalt*. Ministry for Regional Development and Transport Saxony, Anhalt. Accessed July 24, 2012, at: http://www.fad.cat/citytocity/2/cat/wp-content/uploads/guanyadora/booklet_halle.pdf.

İlhan, Salim. 2011. "OSB ye 6 Milyonluk Yatirim." Accessed June 10, 2014, at: http://www.marova.com.tr/marovaun/haberdetay.asp?id=137&kategori=Duyurular.

Intown Manchester. 2005. *Benchmarking Downtown Manchester's Economic Development*. Accessed July 4, 2016, at: http://www.manchesternh.gov/portals/2/departments/city_clerk/agendas_and_minutes/BMA/2000-01-04-Inaugural_Ceremonies.pdf.

Isin, Engin F. 2002. *Being Political: Genealogies of Citizenship*. Minneapolis: University of Minnesota Press.

Isin, Engin F. 2008. "Conclusion: The Socius of Citizenship." In *Recasting the Social in Citizenship*, edited by E. Isin, 281–86. Toronto: University of Toronto Press.

Isin, Engin F., Janine Brodie, Danielle Juteau, and Daiva Stasiulis. 2008. "Recasting the Social in Citizenship." In *Recasting the Social in Citizenship*, edited by E. Isin, 3–19. Toronto: University of Toronto Press.

Isin, Engin F., and Greg M. Nielsen, eds. 2008. *Acts of Citizenship*. London: Zed Books.

Iskander, Natasha. 2011. "Comparing Migration and Development Policy in Morocco and Mexico," Essay No. 1350. Princeton, NJ: Princeton University Center for Migration and Development, Working Papers. Accessed on October 12, 2012, at: https://www.researchgate.net/publication/254444309.

İŞKUR. 2011. "Labor Force Research Mardin." Accessed July 16, 2015, at: http://www.iskur.gov.tr/kurumsalbilgi/istatistikler.aspx#dltop.

İŞKUR. 2014. "İşgücü Piyasası Talep Araştırması. Mardin." Accessed July 3, 2015, at: http://www.iskur.gov.tr/kurumsalbilgi/raporlar.aspx#dltop.

Ismi, Asad. 2014. "The Congo Still Ravaged by U.S.-Funded Conflict and Plunder." *Global Research: Center for Research On Globalization*. Accessed June 24, 2015, at: https://www.globalresearch.ca/the-congo-still-ravaged-by-u-s-funded-conflict-and-plunder/5375098.

Jessop, Bob, Neil Brenner, and Martin Jones. 2008. "Theorizing Sociospatial Relations." *Environment and Planning D: Society and Space* 26, no. 3: 389–401.

Johnston, David Clay, ed. 2014. *Divided: The Perils of Our Growing Inequality*. New York: New Press.

Johnston, Ron, Michael Poulsen, and James Forrest. 2010. "Moving on from Indices, Refocusing on Mix: On Measuring and Understanding Ethnic Patterns of Residential Segregation." *Journal of Ethnic and Migration Studies* 36, no. 4: 697–706.

Jones, Richard C. 2008. *Immigrants Outside Megalopolis: Ethnic Transformation in the Heartland*. Lanham, MD: Lexington Books.

Jones, Jeffrey M. 2016. "More Republicans Favor Path to Citizenship Than Wall." *Gallup*, July 20, 2016. Accessed September 3, 2016, at: http://www.gallup.com/poll/193817/republicans-favor-path-citizenship-wall.aspx.

Jones, Martin, Rhys Jones, and Michael Woods, eds. 2004. *An Introduction to Political Geography: Space, Place, and Politics*. London: Routledge.

Jugendwerkstatt. 2015. "Frohe Zukunft." Accessed June 2016 at: http://jw-frohe-zukunft
.de/begegnungszentrum/interkulturelle-woche.

Kalandides, Ares, and Dina Vaiou. 2012. "'Ethnic' Neighbourhoods? Practices of Belonging and Claims to the City." *European Urban and Regional Studies* 19, no. 3:
254–66.

Kalb, Don. 2013. "Regimes of Value and Worthlessness." Working paper no. 147. Halle:
Max Planck Institute for Social Anthropology.

Kalb, Don, and Herman Tak. 2005. "Introduction: Critical Junctions; Recapturing Anthropology and History." In *Critical Junctions: Anthropology and History beyond the
Cultural Turn*, edited by D. Kalb and H. Tak, 1–28. New York: Berghahn.

Kale. 2013. "Kale Grubu'ndan Mardin'e 5 milyon TL'lik yatırım Kalekim Mardin Fabri-
kası hizmete açıldı." Press Release, September 21, 2013. Accessed June 10, 2014, at:
https://seenews.com/news/turkeys-kale-group-inaugurates-20-mln-euro-factory-in-
mardin-379400.

Kallick, David Dyssegaard. 2015. *Bringing Vitality to Main Street: How Immigrant
Small Businesses Help Local Economies Grow*. Americas Society/Council of the
Americas and the Fiscal Policy Institute. Accessed August 6, 2016, at: http://www
.ascoa.org/sites/default/files/ImmigrantBusinessReport.pdf.

Kapferer, Bruce. 1972. *Strategy and Transaction in an African Factory*. Manchester, UK:
Manchester University Press.

Kaplan, David H., and Li Wei, eds. 2006. *Landscapes of the Ethnic Economy*. Lanham,
MD: Rowman & Littlefield.

Kasmir, Sharryn, and August Carbonella. 2008. "Dispossession and the Anthropology
of Labor." *Critique of Anthropology* 28, no. 1: 5–25.

Katz, Bruce, and Jennifer Bradley. 2013. *The Metropolitan Revolution: How Cities
and Metros Are Fixing Our Broken Politics and Fragile Economy*. Washington, DC:
Brookings Institution.

Kaya, Hasan Mert. 2011. "Mardin'de Parlayan Yıldız." *Anadolujet Magazin*. Accessed
July 4, 2014, at: http://www.anadolujet.com/aj-tr/anadolujet-magazin/2011/kasim/
makaleler/mardinde-parlayan-yildiz.aspx.

Kaya, Hasan Mert. 2012. "Kendine Âşık Ettiren Şehir: Mardin." Accessed April 7, 2014,
at: http://www.anadolujet.com/aj-tr/anadolujet-magazin/2012/mayis/makaleler/
kendine-asik-ettiren-sehir-mardin.aspx.

Kaya, Hasan Mert. 2013. "Mardin'de Müze İçinde Müze." Accessed April 7, 2014, at:
http://www.anadolujet.com/aj-tr/anadolujet-magazin/2013/haziran/makaleler/
mardinde-muze-icinde-muze.aspx.

Kayser, Peter. 2008. *Ethnische Ökonomie als Chance der Standortentwicklung: Untersuchung zu den regionalen Potenzialen der ethnischen Ökonomie im Bezirk Mitte von
Berlin*. Berlin: Berlin Steinbeis-Transferzentrum für Techn. Beratung und Tech-
nologiemarketing, FHTW. Accessed August 20, 2014, at: http://www.worldcat.org/
search?q=au%3AKayser%2C+Peter&qt=hot_author.

Kearns, Ade, and Ray Forrest. 2000. "Social Cohesion and Multilevel Urban Governance." *Urban Studies* 37, no. 5-6: 995–1017.

Kearney, Michael. 1995. "The Local and the Global: The Anthropology of Globalization
and Transnationalism." *Annual Review of Anthropology* 24: 547–65.

Keil, Roger, and Neil Brenner. 2006. *The Global Cities Reader*. New York: Routledge.

Kermani, Navid. 2015. "Awakening to the Reality of War: A Journey along the Refugee Trail." *Der Spiegel Online*, November 11, 2015. Accessed December 28, 2015, at: http://www.spiegel.de/international/europe/navid-kermani-on-the-odyssey-of-refugees-in-europe-a-1057896.html.

King, Anthony D. 1996. "Introduction: Cities, Texts, and Paradigms." In *Re-Presenting the City: Ethnicity, Capital and Culture in the Twenty-First Century Metropolis*, edited by A. King, 1–19. New York: New York University Press.

Kingfisher, Catherine. 2013. *A Policy Travelogue: Tracing Welfare Reform in Aotearoa/ New Zealand and Canada*. New York: Berghahn.

Kitching, John, David Smallbone, and Rosemary Athayde. 2009. "Ethnic Diasporas and Business Competitiveness: Minority-Owned Enterprises in London." *Journal of Ethnic and Migration Studies* 35, no. 4: 689–705.

Klein, Naomi. 2007. *The Shock Doctrine: The Rise of Disaster Capitalism*. London: Penguin Books.

Kloosterman R. 2010. "Matching Opportunities with Resources: A Framework for Analysing (Migrant) Entrepreneurship from a Mixed Embeddedness Perspective." *Entrepreneurship & Regional Development* 22, no. 1: 25–45.

Kloosterman, Robert C., Johanne van der Leun, and Jan Rath. 1999. "Mixed Embeddedness, Migrant Entrepreneurship and Informal Economic Activities." *International Journal of Urban and Regional Research* 23, no. 2: 253–67.

Kokot, Waltraud, Mijal Gandelsman-Trier, Kathrin Wildner, and Astrid Wonneberger, eds. 2008. *Port Cities as Areas of Transition Ethnographic Perspectives*. Bielefeld: transcript Verlag.

Künkel, Jenny, and Margit Mayer. 2011. *Neoliberal Urbanism and Its Contestations*. London: Palgrave.

Kurban, Dilek, Deniz Yükseker, Ayşe Betül Çelik, Turgay Ünalan, and Tamer Aker. 2008. *Zorunlu Göç ile Yüzleşmek [Facing Forced Migration]*. Istanbul: TESEV Yayınları. Accessed June 16, 2015, at: http://tesev.org.tr/wp-content/uploads/2015/11/ Zorunlu_Goc_Ile_Yuzlesmek_Turkiyede_Yerinden_Edilme_Sonrasi_Vatandasligin _Insasi.pdf.

Kymlicka, Will. 1998. "Multicultural Citizenship." In *The Citizenship Debates: A Reader*, edited by G. Shafir, 167–88. Minneapolis: University of Minnesota.

Kymlicka, Will. 2015. "Solidarity in Diverse Societies: Beyond Neoliberal Multiculturalism and Welfare Chauvinism." *Comparative Migration Studies* 3, no. 17: 1–19.

Landolt, Patricia, Lilian Autler, and Sonia Baires. 1999. "From Hermano Lejano to Hermano Mayor: The Dialectics of Salvadorian Transnationalism." *Ethnic and Racial Studies* 22: 290–315.

Langenbach, Randolph. 1969. "Lost City on the Merrimack." *Boston Globe Sunday Magazine*, March 9, 1969. Accessed February 3, 2016, at: http://www.conservation tech.com/RL%27s%20resume&%20pub%27s/RL-publications/Milltowns/1969- AMOSKEAG%28Globe%29.htm.

Latour, Bruno. 2005. *Reassembling the Social: An Introduction to Actor-Network-Theory*. Oxford: Oxford University Press.

Laurence James. 2011. "The Effect of Ethnic Diversity and Community Disadvantage on Social Cohesion: A Multi-Level Analysis of Social Capital and Interethnic Relations in UK Communities." *European Sociological Review* 27, no. 1: 70–89.

Law, John. 2009. "Actor Network Theory and Material Semiotics." In *The New Blackwell Companion to Social Theory*, edited by B. Turner, 141–58. Malden, MA: Blackwell.

Lazar, Sian. 2013. "Citizenship, Political Agency and Technologies of the Self in Argentinean Trade Unions." *Critique of Anthropology* 33: 110–28.

Lazar, Sian, and Monique Nuijten. 2013. "Citizenship, the Self, and Political Agency." *Critique of Anthropology* 33, no. 1: 3–7.

Lee, Richard B. 1998. "Anthropology at the Crossroads: From the Age of Ethnography to the Age of World Systems." *Social Dynamics* 24, no. 1: 34–65.

Leeds, Anthony. 1980. "Towns and Villages in Society: Hierarchies of Order and Cause." In *Cities in a Larger Context*, edited by T. W. Collins, 6–33. Athens: University of Georgia Press.

Lees, Loretta, Hzun Bang Shin, and Ernesto Lopez Morales. 2015. *Global Gentrifications: Uneven Development and Displacement*. Chichester, UK: Policy Press.

Lefebvre, Henri. 1996. "The Right to the City." In *Writings on Cities*, edited by E. Kofman and E. Lebas, 147–60. Cambridge, MA: Wiley-Blackwell.

Leitner, Helga, Jamie Peck, and Eric S. Sheppard, eds. 2007. *Contesting Neoliberalism: Urban Futures*. New York: Guilford.

Levitt, Peggy. 1998. "Social Remittances: A Local-Level, Migration-Driven Form of Cultural Diffusion." *International Migration Review* 32: 926–49.

Levitt, Peggy. 2003. "'You Know, Abraham Was Really the First Immigrant': Religion and Transnational Migration." *International Migration Review* 37, no. 3: 847–73.

Levitt, Peggy, and Rafael de la Dehasa. 2003. "Transnational Migration and the Redefinition of the State: Variations and Explanations." In *Ethnic and Racial Studies*, 26, no. 4: 587–611.

Li, Yaojun, Andrew Pickles, and Mike Savage. 2005. "Social Capital and Social Trust in Britain." *European Sociological Review* 21, no. 2: 109–23.

Liebow, Elliott. 1968. *Tally's Corner: A Study of Negro Streetcorner Men*. Boston: Little, Brown.

Light, Ivan H. 1972. *Ethnic Enterprise in America*. Berkeley: University of California Press.

Light, Ivan, and Steven J. Gold. 2000. *Ethnic Economies*. San Diego, CA: Academic Press.

Lincoln NE City Government. 2008. "Feasibility Analysis of Proposed New Arena and Convention Center Development in Lincoln." Draft copy. Conventions, Sports & Leisure International. Accessed July 12, 2015, at: http://lincoln.ne.gov/City/mayor/arena/assets/CSL_FARv1.pdf.

Lister, Ruth. 1997. "Citizenship: Towards a Feminist Synthesis." *Feminist Review* 57: 28–48.

Löbner, Lars. 2013. *Stadtentwicklung Halle (Saale) im Kontext der Region Halle*. Leipzig: Fachbereichs Planen der Stadt Halle (Saale).

Lofland, Lyn H. 1985. *A World of Strangers: Order and Action in Urban Public Space*. New York: Waveland.

Low, Setha M. 1999. "Introduction: Theorizing the City." In *Theorizing the City: The New Urban Anthropology Reader*, edited by S. M. Low, 1–33. New Brunswick, NJ: Rutgers University Press.

Löw, Martina 2009. "Pre-Structured Urban Development Opportunities: The Theoretical Idea of an Intrinsic Logic of Cities and European Case Studies." *Studies in Urban Humanities* 1, no. 2: 135–53.

Löw, Martina 2012. "The Intrinsic Logic of Cities: Towards a New Theory on Urbanism." *Urban Research & Practice* 5, no. 3: 303–15.

Lüken-Klaßen, Doris, and Franziska Pohl. 2011. "Ethnic Entrepreneurship: Case Study; Frankfurt am Main Germany." Available online from CLIP [Cities for Local Integration Policy] network. Accessed July 27, 2012, at: https://www.eurofound.europa.eu/printpdf/publications/case-study/2011/germany/social-policies-business/ethnic-entrepreneurship-case-study-frankfurt-am-main-germany.

Luxemburg, Rosa. 1951. *The Accumulation of Capital*. New Haven, CT: Yale University Press.

Malkki, Liisa. 1995. "Refugees and Exile: From 'Refugee Studies' to the National Order of Things." *Annual Review of Anthropology* 24: 495–523.

Manchester Housing and Redevelopment Authority. 2016. "Redevelopment Activity." Copy in files of N. Glick Schiller.

Manchester Office of Economic Development. 2009. *Manchester Comprehensive Economic Development Strategy 2009*. Accessed July 21, 2015, at: http://www.manchesternh.gov/portals/2/departments/econ_dev/Manchester_NH_CEDS_Final.pdf.

Manchester Republican Committee Newsletter. 2003. "Saggy Tahir's Annual Manchester GOP Barbecue," July 26, 2003. In files of NGS.

Marcus, George E. 1986. "Contemporary Problems of Ethnography in the Modern World System." In *Writing Culture: The Poetics and Politics of Ethnography*, edited by J. Clifford and G. Marcus, 165–293. Berkeley: University of California Press.

Marcus, George E. 1995. "Ethnography in/of the World System: The Emergence of Multi-Sited Ethnography." *Annual Review of Anthropology* 24: 95–117.

Mardin Biennial. 2010. Accessed July 19, 2013, at http://www.mardinbienali.org.

Mardin Biennial. 2012. Accessed July 7, 2015, at: http://www.mardinbienal.com/www/2012/eng.asp.

Mardin Biennial. 2015. Accessed July 7, 2015, at: http://www.mardinbienali.org/2014/eng/bienal.asp

Mardin Tourism Strategic Plan. 2014. *Situation Analysis Report*, vol. 1. Draft report.

Mardin Valiliği. 2013. *Yılı İkametgâha Göre Nüfus, Yüzölçümü Ve Nüfus Yoğunluğu Bilgileri*. Accessed July 8, 2015, at: http://www.mardin.gov.tr/web/mardinvaliligi/detay.asp?id=127&kategori=MARD%DDN.

Mardin Yerelnet. 2016. Accessed April 18, 2016, at: http://mardin.yerelnet.org.tr.

Marshall, Ruth. 2014. "Christianity, Anthropology, Politics." *Current Anthropology* 55, no. S10: 344–56.

Marshall, Thomas H. 1964. *Class, Citizenship, and Social Class: Essays by T. H. Marshall*. Garden City, NJ: Doubleday.

Marston, Sallie A. 2000. "The Social Construction of Scale." *Progress in Human Geography* 24: 219–42.

Marston, Sallie A., John Paul Jones III, and Keith Woodward. 2005. "Human Geography without Scale." *Transactions of the Institute of British Geographers* 30: 416–32.

Marx, Karl. 1967. *Capital*, vol. 1. New York: International Publishers.

Masboungi, Ariella. 2001. "La nouvelle Mecque de l'urbanisme: La nueva Meca del urbanismo." *Projet Urbain* 23: 17–21.

Massey, Doreen B. 2005. *For Space*. London: Sage.

Massey, Doreen B. 2007. *World City*. Cambridge UK: Polity Press.

Massey, Doreen B. 2012. "Power-Geometry and a Progressive Sense of Place." In *Mapping the Futures: Local Cultures, Global Change*, edited by J. Bird, B. Curtis, T. Putnam, and L. Tickner, 60–70. London: Routledge.

Masurel, Enno, and Peter Nijkam. 2004. "Breeding Places for Ethnic Entrepreneurs: A Comparative Marketing Approach." *Entrepreneurship & Regional Development: An International Journal* 16, no. 1: 77–86.

Mayer, Margit. 2010. *Social Movements in the (Post-) Neoliberal City 7 (Civic City Cahier 1)*. London: Bedford.

Mayer, Margit. 2017. "The Ambiguity of Participating the Social City." *Journalment*, no. 1. Published online. Accessed March 29, 2017, at: http://journalment.org/author/margit-mayer.

Mayer, Margit, and Julie-Anne Boudreau. 2012. "Social Movements in Urban Politics: Trends in Research and Practice." In *The Oxford Handbook of Urban Politics*, edited by P. John, K. Mossberger, and S. E. Clarke, 273–91. Oxford, UK: Oxford University Press.

Mayer, Margit, and Jenny Künkel, eds. 2012. *Neoliberal Urbanism and Its Contestations Crossing Theoretical Boundaries*. London: Palgrave.

Mazzucato, Valentina, and Miryam Kabki. 2009. "Small Is beautiful: The Micro-Politics of Transnational Relationships between Ghanaian Hometown Associations and Communities Back Home." *Global Networks* 9, no. 2: 227–51.

McCann, Eugene, and Kevin Ward. 2011. *Mobile Urbanism: City Policymaking in the Global Age*. Minneapolis: University of Minnesota Press.

McEwan, Cheryl, Jane Pollard, and Nick Henry. 2008. "The 'Non-Global City' of Birmingham." In *Migrants to the Metropolis: The Rise of Immigrant Gateway Cities*, edited by M. Price and L. Benton-Short, 128–49. Syracuse, NY: Syracuse University Press.

McFarlane, Colin, and Jennifer Robinson. 2012. "Introduction: Experiments in Comparative Urbanism." *Comparative Urbanism*, special issue of *Urban Geography* 33, no. 6.

Memurlarnet. 2009. "ѕɢк'ya en borçlu belediye; Kocaeli." December 19, 2009. Accessed July 17, 2014, at: http://www.memurlar.net/haber/155927.

Merry, Sally Eagle. 2006. *Human Rights and Gender Violence: Translating International Law into Local Justice*. Chicago: University of Chicago Press.

Midyat Habur. 2006. "Kafro (Elbeğendi) Süryanileri köylerine dönüyor." September 21, 2006.

Migdalovitz, Carol. 2003. *Iraq: Turkey, the Deployment of U.S. Forces, and Related Issues*. Report for Congress Received through the CRS Web. Order Code RL31794. Accessed May 30, 2015, at: https://digital.library.unt.edu/ark:/67531/metacrs8186/m1/1/high_res_d/RL31794_2003May02.pdf.

Milanovic, Branko. 2016. *Global Inequality: A New Approach for the Age of Globalization*. Cambridge, MA: Harvard University Press.

Miles, Steven, and Ronan Paddison. 2005. "Introduction: The Rise and Rise of Culture-led Urban Regeneration." *Urban Studies* 42, nos. 5/6: 833–39.

Mill, John Stuart. 1882 [1843]. *System of Logic, Ratiocinative and Inductive*. 8th edition. New York: Harper & Brothers. Accessed April 12, 2018, at: https://www.gutenberg .org/files/27942/27942-h/27942-h.html.

Milliyet. 1998. "Özgür ifadeye direniş büyük." Accessed June 7, 2015, at: http://www .milliyet.com.tr/1998/02/24/entel/ent.html.

Millyard Museum. 2015. "Welcome to the Millyard Museum." Accessed May 20, 2014, at: http://www.manchesterhistoric.org/index.php/millyard-museum.

Min, Pyong Gap, and Mehdi Bozorgmehr. 2000. "Immigrant Entrepreneurship and Business Patterns: A Comparison of Koreans and Iranians in Los Angeles." *International Migration Review* 34, no. 4: 707–38.

Miner, Horace. 1952. "The Folk-Urban Continuum." *American Sociological Review* 17, no. 5: 529–37.

Miracle Healing Church. 2005. "God's Gospel Army." Flyer in files of N. Glick Schiller.

Miraftab, Faranak. 2014. "Displacement: Framing the Global Relationally." In *Framing the Global: Entry Points for the Search*, edited by H. Kahn, 37–50. Bloomington: Indiana University Press.

Mittelman, James H., ed. 1996. *Globalization: Critical Reflections*. Boulder, CO: Lynne Rienner.

Modood, Tariq. 1997. *Ethnic Minorities in Britain: Diversity and Disadvantage*. London: Policy Studies.

Moody's. 2015. "Manchester (City of) NH." Accessed April 13, 2018, at: https://www .moodys.com/credit-ratings/Manchester-City-of-NH-credit-rating-600025169.

Morell, Marc. 2015. "When Space Draws the Line on Class." In *Anthropologies of Class: Power, Practice, and Inequality*, edited by J. Carrier and D. Kalb, 102–17. Cambridge: Cambridge University Press.

Morokvasic, Mirjana. 1993. "Immigrants in Garment Production in Paris and in Berlin." In *Immigration and Entrepreneurship: Culture, Capital, and Ethnic Networks*, edited by I. H. Light and P. Bhachu, 75–97. New Brunswick, NJ: Transaction Publishers.

Mount, Ian. 2015. "In Spain, and All of Europe, Cities Open Doors to Refugees." *Fortune*, September 8, 2015. Accessed December 10, 2015, at: http://fortune.com/2015/ 09/08/europe-refugee-crisis-spain/.

Müller, Alain. 2016. "Beyond Ethnographic Scriptocentrism: Modelling Multi-Scalar Processes, Networks, and Relationships." *Anthropological Theory* 16, no. 1: 98–130.

Mumford, Lewis. 1961. *The City in History: Its Origins, Its Transformations, and Its Prospects*. New York: Harcourt, Brace, and World.

Narotzky, Susana. 2016. "On Waging the Ideological War: Against the Hegemony of Form." *Anthropological Theory* 16, nos. 2–3: 263–84.

Nashashibi, Rami. 2013. "Ghetto Cosmopolitanism: Making Theory at the Margins." In *Deciphering the Global: Its Scales, Spaces and Subjects*, edited by S. Sassen, 243–64. New York: Routledge.

National Day of Prayer Task Force. 2015. "The Power of Prayer, Oct 29, 2015." Accessed October 10, 2016, at: http://www.nationaldayofprayer.org/the_power_of_prayer.

National League of Cities. 2011. *Congress of Cities and Exposition.* Accessed July 20, 2012, at: http://citysummit.nlc.org.

Neal, Zachary P. 2013. *The Connected City: How Networks Are Shaping the Modern Metropolis.* London: Routledge.

Neveu, Catherine. 2005. "Discussion: Anthropology and Citizenship." *Social Anthropology* 13: 199–202.

New Hampshire Center for Public Policy Studies. 2015. *Policy Notes: An Overview of New Hampshire's Foreign-Born Population: May 2015.* Accessed February 21, 2016, at: http://www.nhpolicy.org/UploadedFiles/Reports/ForeignBornMay2015.pdf.

New Hampshire Employment Security. 2017. "Hillsborough." Accessed March 24, 2017, at: https://www.nhes.nh.gov/elmi/products/cp/documents/hillsborough-cp.pdf.

Nijman, Jan. 2007. "Introduction: Comparative Urbanism." *Urban Geography* 28, no. 1: 1–6.

Nijman, Jan. 2012. ed. *Special Issue: Comparative Urbanism, Urban Geography* 33: 6.

Nonini, Donald M. 2012. "Toward a (Proper) Postwar History of Southeast Asian Petty Capitalism: Predation, the State, and Chinese Small Business Capital in Malaysia." In *Petty Capitalists and Globalization Flexibility, Entrepreneurship, and Economic Development,* edited by A. Smart and J. Smart, 167–200. Albany: State University of New York Press.

Nonini, Donald M. 2015. *"Getting By": A Historical Ethnography of Class and State Formation in Malaysia.* Ithaca, NY: Cornell University Press.

Novy, Johannes. 2011. *Marketing Marginalized Neighborhoods: Tourism and Leisure in the 21st Century Inner City.* PhD diss., Columbia University. http://academiccommons.columbia.edu/catalog/ac:148817.

Nowicka, Magdalena, and Anna Cieslik. 2013. "Beyond Methodological Nationalism in Insider Research with Migrants." *Migration Studies* 2, no. 1: 1–15.

Nowicka, Magdalena, and Steven Vertovec. 2014. "Introduction: Comparing Convivialities; Dreams and Realities of Living-with-Difference." *European Journal of Cultural Studies* 17, no. 4: 341–50.

NTV. 2010. *Mardin Çehre Değiştiriyor.* January 13, 2010. Accessed October 31, 2016, at: http://www.ntv.com.tr/ekonomi/mardin-cehre-degistiriyor,xfICNsTa-EOCprZi84QLgw.

Nuijten, Monique. 2013. "The Perversity of the 'Citizenship Game': Slum-Upgrading in the Urban Periphery of Recife, Brazil." *Critique of Anthropology* 33: 8–25.

Offe, Claus. 1999. "How Can We Trust Our Fellow Citizens?" In *Democracy and Trust,* edited by M. E. Warren, 42–87. Cambridge: Cambridge University Press.

Office of the Independent City Auditor. 2013. "MEDO Performance Audit: March 2013." City of Manchester. Accessed July 8, 2015, at: http://www.girardatlarge.com/wp-content/uploads/2013/08/MEDO_audit.pdf.

Oktik, Nurgun, and Fethi Nas. 2005. "Ulus-Devlet ve Topluluklar: Midyat Örneği." *Muğla Üniversitesi, Sosyal Bilimler Enstitüsü Dergisi* 15: 122–42.

Olwig, Karen Fog. 2007. *Caribbean Journeys: An Ethnography of Migration and Home in Three Family Networks.* Durham, NC: Duke University Press.

ORIS. 2017. "History and Mission." Accessed March 28, 2017, at: http://refugeesuccess.org/history-mission.

Orozco, Manuel. 2000a. "Latino Hometown Associations as Agents of Development in Latin America." Inter-American Dialogue and the Tomas Rivera Policy Institute. Los Angeles: University of Southern California.

Orozco, Manuel. 2000b. "Remittances and Markets: New Players and Practices." Working paper, Inter-American Dialogue and the Tomas Rivera Policy Institute. Los Angeles: University of Southern California.

Orozco, Manuel. 2013. *Migrant Remittances and Development in the Global Economy.* Boulder: Lynne Rienner.

Orozco, Manuel, and Eugenia Garcia-Zanello. 2009. "Hometown Associations: Transnationalism, Philanthropy, and Development." *Brown Journal of World Affairs* 15: 1–17.

Ortiz, Isabel, and Matthew Cummins. 2013. *The Age of Austerity: A Review of Public Expenditures and Adjustment Measures in 181 Countries.* New York: IPD and South Centre. Accessed February 15, 2016, at: http://policydialogue.org/files/publications/Age_of_Austerity_Ortiz_and_Cummins.pdf.

Ortner, Sherry B. 1984. "Theory in Anthropology Since the Sixties." *Comparative Studies in Society and History* 26, no. 1: 126–66.

Østergaard-Nielsen, Eva. 2010. "Codevelopment and Citizenship: The Nexus between Policies on Local Migrant Incorporation and Migrant Transnational Practices in Spain." *Ethnic and Racial Studies* 34: 20–39.

Oxfam. 2015. *Wealth: Having It All and Wanting More.* Oxfam Issue Briefing, Oxfam International. http://policy-practice.oxfam.org.uk/publications/wealth-having-it-all-and-wanting-more-338125.

Özceylan, Dilek, and Erman Coşkun. 2012. "Türkiye'deki illerin sosyo-ekonomik gelişmişlik düzeyleri ve afetlerden sosyal ve ekonomik zarar görebilirlikleri arasındaki ilişki." *İstanbul Üniversitesi İşletme Fakültesi Dergisi* 1: 31–46.

Özcoşar, İbrahim. 2006. "19. Yüzyılda Mardin Nüfusu." In *I. Uluslararası Mardin Sempozyumu Bildirileri.* İstanbul: n.p.

Özcoşar, İbrahim. 2009. *Merkezileşme Sürecinde Bir Taşra Kenti: Mardin (1800–1900).* Mardin: Mardin Artuklu Üniversitesi Yayınları.

Özok-Gündoğan, Nilay. 2005. "Social Development as a Governmental Strategy in the Southeastern Anatolia Project." *New Perspectives on Turkey* 32: 930–113.

Özmen, Abdurrahim. 2013. "Hafıza ve Hayat: Tur Abdin Süryanileri Sözlü Tarihinden Örnekler." In *Mardin Tebliğleri.* İstanbul: Hrant Dink Vakfı.

Pamuk, Şevket. 1987. *The Ottoman Empire and European Capitalism, 1820–1913: Trade, Investment, and Production.* Cambridge: Cambridge University Press.

Peck, Jamie. 2005. "Struggling with the Creative Class." *International Journal of Urban and Regional Research* 29, no 4: 740–70.

Peck, Jamie, and Nik Theodore. 2015. *Fast Policy: Experimental Statecraft at the Thresholds of Neoliberalism.* Minneapolis: University of Minnesota Press.

Pecoud, Antoine. 2000. "Thinking and Rethinking Ethnic Economies." *Diaspora* 9, no. 3: 439–62.

Pecoud, Antoine. 2004a. "Do Immigrants Have a Business Culture? The Political Epistemology of Fieldwork in Berlin's Turkish Economy." *Journal of the Society for the Anthropology of Europe* 4, no. 2: 19–25.

Pecoud, Antoine. 2004b. "Entrepreneurship and Identity: Cosmopolitanism and Cultural Competencies among German-Turkish Businesspeople in Berlin." *Journal of Ethnic and Migration Studies* 30, no.1: 3–20.

Pethe, Heike, Sabine Hafner, and Philip Lawton. 2010. "Transnational Migrants in the Creative Knowledge Industries: Amsterdam, Barcelona, Dublin and Munich." In *Making Competitive Cities*, edited by S. Musterd and A. Murie, 163–91. Hoboken, NJ: Wiley Blackwell.

Pierre, Jon. 2005. "Comparative Urban Governance: Uncovering Complex Causalities." In *Urban Affairs Review*, 40, no. 4: 71–92.

Pieterse, Jan Nederveen. 2003. "Social Capital and Migration: Beyond Ethnic Economies." *Ethnicities* 3, no. 1: 29–58.

Piketty, Thomas. 2014. *Capital in the Twenty-First Century*. Translated by A. Goldhammer. Cambridge, MA: Harvard University Press.

Piketty, Thomas. 2015. *The Economics of Inequality*. Translated by A. Goldhammer. Cambridge, MA: Harvard University Press.

Pink, Sarah. 2012. *Situating Everyday Life: Practices and Place*. London: Sage.

Pohlgeers. 2015. "Ebay Enterprise eröffnet Logistikzentrum in Halle." In *OnlinehaendlerNews*, November 17, 2015. Accessed August 5, 2016, at: https://www.onlinehaendler-news.de/handel/allgemein/20879-ebay-enterprise-eroeffnet-logistikzentrum-halle.html.

Polatel, Mehmet. 2010. "Ittihat Terakki den Kemalist Döneme Ermeni Mallari." *Toplum ve Kuram* 3: 113–53.

Ponzini, Davide. 2010. "Bilbao Effects and Narrative Defects: A Critical Reappraisal of an Urban Rhetoric." Cahiers de Recherche du Programme Villes & Territoires. Paris: Sciences Po. Accessed March 30, 2017, at: http://blogs.sciences-po.fr/recherche-villes/files/2010/08/Ponzini-Bilbao-Effects-and-Narrative-Defects.pdf.

Portes, Alejandro, and Alex Stepick. 1993. *City on the Edge: The Transformation of Miami*. Berkeley: University of California Press.

Portes, Alejandro, Cristina Escobar, and Alexandria W. Radford. 2007. "Immigrant Transnational Organizations and Development: A Comparative Study." *International Migration Review* 41: 242–81.

Portes, Alejandro, and Patricia Fernández-Kelly. 2015. *The State and the Grassroots: Immigrant Transnational Organizations in Four Continents*. New York: Berghahn.

Postkult. 2015. "Projektbericht Freiraumgalerie 2012–2014." Accessed June 14, 2016, at: http://www.freiraumgalerie.com/images/Freiraumgalerie_Evaluation%202012-2014_web.pdf.

PR Newswire. 2001. "Harvard University Names State Representative Carlos Gonzalez of Concord, New Hampshire, as a Fannie Mae Foundation Fellow." June 12, 2001. http://www.prnewswire.com/news-releases/harvard-university-names-state-representative-carlos-gonzalez-of-concord-new-hampshire-as-a-fannie-mae-foundation-fellow-72136487.html.

Prasse, Jan-Ole. 2013. "Abderhalden-Straße in Halle Wiegand legt sich auf Amo fest." *Mitteldeutsche Zeitung*, December 15–20, 2013. Accessed June 10, 2016, at: http://www.mz-web.de/halle-saale/abderhalden-strasse-in-halle-wiegand-legt-sich-auf-amo-fest-3474486.

Preston, Julia. 2013. "Ailing Midwestern Cities Extend a Welcoming Hand to Immigrants." *New York Times*, October 7, 2013. Accessed November 4, 2013, at: http://

www.nytimes.com/2013/10/07/us/ailing-cities-extend-hand-to-immigrants.html?
pagewanted=2&emc=eta1.

Price, Marie, and Lisa Benton-Short. 2008. *Migrants to the Metropolis: The Rise of Immigrant Gateway Cities.* Syracuse, NY: Syracuse University Press.

Pries, Ludger. 2007. *Rethinking Transnationalism: The Meso-Link of Organisations.* Abington, UK: Routledge.

Pries, Ludger, and Zeynep Sezgin, eds. 2012. *Cross-Border Migrant Organisations in Comparative Perspective.* London: Palgrave Macmillan.

Putnam, Robert D. 2007. "*E Pluribus Unum*: Diversity and Community in the Twenty-First Century." *Scandinavian Politica Studies in Scandinavian Politica Studies* 30, no. 2: 137–74.

Putgül, U. 2014. *Pegasus (Airlines) Magazine.* 96–108.

Quijano, Anibal. 2000. "Coloniality of Power and Eurocentrism in Latin America." *International Sociology* 15, no. 2: 215–32.

Rajaram, Prem Kumar, and Zsuzsanna Arandes. 2013. "Exceeding Categories: Law, Bureaucracy and Acts of Citizenship by Asylum Seekers in Hungary." In *Enacting European Citizenship*, edited by E. Isin and M. Seward, 195–219. Cambridge UK: Cambridge University Press.

Ranciere, Jacques. 2004. "Who Is the Subject of Human Rights?" *South Atlantic Quarterly* 103, no. 2/3: 297–310.

Ratcliffe, Peter. 2011. "From Community to Social Cohesion: Interrogating a Policy Paradigm." In *Promoting Social Cohesion: Implications for Policy and Evaluation*, edited by P. Ratcliffe and I. Newman, 1–40. Bristol, UK: Policy Press.

Rath, Jan. 2002. *Unraveling the Rag Trade: Immigrant Entrepreneurship in Seven World Cities.* New York: Oxford University Press.

Rath, Jan. 2006. *Entrepreneurship among Migrants and Returnees: Creating New Opportunities.* Accessed June 28, 2012, at: http://citeseerx.ist.psu.edu.

Rath, Jan. 2011. *Promoting Ethnic Entrepreneurship in European Cities.* Luxembourg: Eurofound Publications Office of the European Union.

Rath, Jan, and Robert Kloosterman. 2000. "Outsiders' Business: A Critical Review of Research on Immigrant Entrepreneurship." *International Migration Review* 34, no. 3: 657–81.

Rath, Jan, Robert Kloosterman, and Eran Razin. 2002. "The Economic Context, Embeddedness and Immigrant Entrepreneurs." Special issue, *International Journal of Entrepreneurial Behaviour & Research* 8: 1–2.

Rath, Jan, and Anna Swagerman. 2011. *Promoting Ethnic Entrepreneurship in European Cities.* Luxembourg: Publications Office of the European Union. Accessed February 5, 2016, at: http://www.coe.int/t/democracy/migration/Source/migration/congress_public_3.pdf.

Razin, Eran, and Andre Langlois. 1996. "Metropolitan Characteristics and Entrepreneurship among Immigrants and Ethnic Groups in Canada." *International Migration Review* 30, no. 3: 703–27.

Redfield, Robert. 1940. "The Folk Society and Culture." *American Journal of Sociology*: 731–42.

Resmi Gazete. 2006. "Kalkinma ajanslari bütçe ve muhasebe yönetmeliği." September 28, 2006. Accessed May 5, 2013, at: http://www.resmigazete.gov.tr.

Resurrection Crusade. 2004. "Calling America to Pray for America's 2004 Elections." November 2004, flyer in files of N. Glick Schiller.

Richardson, Harry W., and Chang Woon Nam, eds. 2014. "Shrinking Cities: A Global Perspective." *Population and Development Review* 40, no. 4: 751–52.

Rizga, Kristina. 2017. "Betsy DeVos Wants to Use America's Schools to Build 'God's Kingdom': Trump's Education Secretary Pick Has Spent a Lifetime Working to End Public Education as We Know It." *Mother Jones*, March/April 2017. Accessed March 14, 2017, at: http://www.motherjones.com/politics/2017/01/betsy-devos-christian-schools-vouchers-charter-education-secretary.

Robbins, Joel. 2004. "The Globalization of Pentecostal and Charismatic Christianity." *Annual Review of Anthropology* 33: 117–43.

Robidoux, Carol. 2015. "16 Manchester-Area Nonprofits Share in $262K from NH Charitable Foundation." ManchesterInkLink.com. Accessed April 5, 2016, at: https://manchesterinklink.com/16-manchester-region-nonprofits-receive-262k-in-nh-charitable-foundation-grants/.

Robinson, Jennifer. 2004. "In the Tracks of Comparative Urbanism: Difference, Urban Modernity and the Primitive." *Urban Geography* 25: 707–23.

Robinson, Jennifer. 2006. *Ordinary Cities: Between Modernity and Development.* London: Routledge.

Robinson, Jennifer. 2011. "Cities in a World of Cities: The Comparative Gesture." *International Journal of Urban and Regional Research* 35, no. 1: 1–23.

Rogaly, Ben, and Kaveri Qureshi. 2013. "Diversity, Urban Space and the Right to the Provincial City." *Identities: Global Studies in Culture and Power* 20, no. 4: 423–37.

Rogers, Shannon H., and Kevin H. Garner. 2015. "Measuring Social Capital at a Neighborhood Scale through a Community Based Framework." In *Social Capital at the Community Level: An Applied Interdisciplinary Perspective,* edited by J. M. Halstead, and S. C. Deller, 103–13. New York: Routledge.

Rorick, Beverly. 2004. "Attorneys Strive to Help Unite Congolese Family." *Bar News,* November 5, 2004. Accessed March 2016 at: https://www.nhbar.org/publications/archives/display-news-issue.asp?id=1959.

Rosaldo, Renato, and William Vincent Flores. 1997. "Identity, Conflict, and Evolving Latino Communities: Cultural Citizenship in San Jose, California." In *Latino Cultural Citizenship: Claiming Identity, Space, and Rights,* edited by W. Flores and R. Benmajor, 57–96. Boston: Beacon.

Rose, Damaris, Pia Carrasco, and Johanne Charbonneau. 1998. "The Role of 'Weak Ties' in the Settlement Experiences of Immigrant Women with Young Children: The Case of Central Americans in Montréal." Joint Centre of Excellence for Research on Immigration and Settlement. Accessed August 15, 2014, at: https://www.researchgate.net/publication/268415484_The_Role_of_Weak_Ties_in_the_Settlement_Experiences_of_Immigrant_Women_with_Young_Children_The_Case_of_Central_Americans_in_Montreal.

Rose, Nikolas, and Thomas Osborne. 2000. "Governing Cities, Governing Citizens." In *Democracy, Citizenship and the City: Rights to the Global City,* edited by E. Isin, 95–109. London: Routledge.

Rothstein, Frances Abrahamer, and Michael L. Blim. 1992. *Anthropology and the Global*

Factory: Studies of the New Industrialization in the Late Twentieth Century. New York: Bergin & Garvey.

Russell, Francis. 2014. "Turkey's Culture Club." *Guardian,* April 10, 2010. Accessed July 4, 2014, at: http://www.theguardian.com/travel/2010/apr/10/turkey-culture-archaeology-sites-history.

Safa, Hele Icken. 1974. *The Urban Poor of Puerto Rico: A Study in Development and Inequality.* New York: Holt, Rinehart, and Winston.

Şahin, Mediha, Peter Nijkamp, and Marius Rietdjik. 2009. "Cultural Diversity and Urban Innovativeness: Personal and Business Characteristics of Urban Migrant Entrepreneurs." *Innovation: The European Journal of Social Science Research* 22, no. 3: 251–81.

Salzbrunn, Monika. 2011. "Rescaling Processes in Two 'Global' Cities: Festive Events as Pathways of Migrant Incorporation." In *Locating Migration,* edited by N. Glick Schiller and A. Çağlar, 166–89. Ithaca, NY: Cornell University Press.

Sandbrook, Richard, Marc Edelman, Patrick Heller, and Judith Teichman. 2007. *Social Democracy in the Global Periphery: Origins, Challenges, Prospects.* Cambridge: Cambridge University Press.

Sassen, Saskia. 1998. *Globalization and Its Discontents: Essays on the New Mobility of People and Money.* New York: New Press.

Sassen, Saskia. 2001. *The Global City; New York, London, Tokyo.* Princeton, NJ: Princeton University Press.

Sassen, Saskia. 2002a. "Locating Cities on Global Circuits." *Environment and Urbanization* 14, no. 1: 13–30.

Sassen, Saskia. 2002b. "Towards Post-National and Denationalized Citizenship." In *Handbook of Citizenship Studies,* edited by E. F. Isin and B. S. Turner, 277–92. Thousand Oaks, CA: Sage.

Sassen, Saskia. 2008. *Territory, Authority, Rights: From Medieval to Global Assemblages.* Princeton, NJ: Princeton University Press.

Sassen, Saskia, ed. 2013. *Deciphering the Global: Its Scales, Spaces, and Subjects.* New York: Routledge.

Sassen, Saskia. 2014. *Expulsions: Brutality and Complexity in the Global Economy.* Cambridge, MA: Harvard University Press.

Schneider, Jane, and Ida Susser eds. 2009. *Wounded Cities: Destruction and Reconstruction in a Globalized World.* New York: Berg.

Scott, Eugene. 2015. "Mayors Strike Back against Governors in Refugee Fight." *cnn,* November 18, 2015. Accessed in August 2016 at: http://www.cnn.com/2015/11/18/politics/mayors-cities-governors-refugees/.

Seppelt, Enrico. 2011. "Wünsch dir was: Halles 300 Millionen Euro-Baupläne." *Hallelife.de,* September 7, 2011. Accessed July 9, 2015, at: https://hallelife.de/nachrichten/aktuelles/details/Wuensch-dir-was-Halles-300-Millionen-Euro-Bauplaene.html.

Seppelt, Enrico. 2014. "'Synagoge & Tempel': Ausstellungseröffnung zum Auftakt der Jüdischen Kulturtage." Accessed July 5, 2014, at: http://hallespektrum.de/nachrichten/kultur/synagoge2-tempel-ausstellungseroeffnung-zum-auftakt-der-juedischen-kulturtage/120167/.

Sezgin, Zeynep. 2011. "Turkish Migrants' Organizations in Germany and Their Role in the Flow of Remittances to Turkey." *International Migration and Integration* 12: 231–51.

Shafir, Gershon, ed. 1998. *The Citizenship Debates: A Reader*. Minneapolis: University of Minnesota Press.

Shore, Cris, and Susan Wright, eds. 1997. *Anthropology of Public Policy: Critical Perspectives on Governance and Power*. London: Routledge.

Shore, Cris, and Susan Wright. 2011. "Conceptualising Policy: Technologies of Governance and the Politics of Visibility." In *Policy Worlds: Anthropology and the Analysis of Contemporary Power*, edited by C. Shore, S. Wright, and D. Però, 1–27. New York: Berghahn.

Shore, Cris, Susan Wright, and Davide Però, eds. 2011. *Policy Worlds: Anthropology and the Analysis of Contemporary Power*. New York: Berghahn.

Siefer, Ted. 2014. "Manchester Mayor Gatsas Protests to Refugee Resettlement Group: What about Our Own Kids?" *New Hampshire Union Leader*, August 5, 2014. Accessed July 4, 2015, at: http://www.unionleader.com/apps/pbcs.dll/article?AID= /20140806/NEWS0606/140809428/1006.

Simmel, Georg (1910) 1949. "Sociology of Sociability." *American Journal of Sociology* 54, no. 3: 254–61.

Simmel, Georg (1903) 2002. "The Metropolis and Mental Life." In *The Blackwell City Reader*, edited by G. Bridge and S. Watson, 11–19. Oxford, UK: Blackwell.

Siu, Lok C. D. 2007. *Memories of a Future Home: Diasporic Citizenship of Chinese in Panama*. Stanford, CA: Stanford University Press.

Smith, Alice. 1999. *Dispelling the Darkness: How to Deal with Demonic Rulers*. Houston, TX: US Prayer Center.

Smith, Michael P. 2001. *Transnational Urbanism: Locating Globalization*. Malden, MA: Blackwell.

Smith, Michael P., and Louis Eduardo Guernizo, eds. 1998. *Transnationalism from Below*. New Brunswick, NJ: Rutgers University Press.

Smith, Michael P., and L. Owen Kirkpatrick, eds. 2015. *Reinventing Detroit: Urban Decline and the Politics of Possibility*. New Brunswick, NJ: Transaction Publishers.

Smith, Neil. 1995. "Remaking Scale: Competition and Cooperation in Pre-National and Postnational Europe." In *Competitive European Peripheries*, edited by H. Eskelinen and F. Snickars, 59–74. Berlin, Germany: Springer Verlag.

Smith, Neil. 1996. *The New Urban Frontier: Gentrification and the Revanchist City*. New York: Routledge.

Smith, Neil. 2002. "New Globalism, New Urbanism: Gentrification as Global Urban Strategy." *Antipode* 34: 427–50.

Sökefeld, Martin. 2006. "Mobilizing in Transnational Space: A Social Movement Approach to the Formation of Diaspora." *Global Networks* 6, no. 3: 265–84.

Sollors, Warner. 1989. *The Invention of Ethnicity*. Oxford: Oxford University Press.

Solomon, Dave. 2012. "'Silicon Millyard' Is Emerging Along the Merrimack." *New Hampshire Union Leader*, October 16, 2012. Accessed July 15, 2015, at: http://www .unionleader.com/apps/pbcs.dll/article?AID=/20121017/NEWS02/710179949.

Sørensen, Ninna Nyberg. 2008. "Migrant Transfers as a Development Tool." DIIS Working Paper 16. Accessed March 2008 at: http://www.diis.dk.

Sørensen, Ninna Nyberg. 2013. *The Migration Industry and the Commercialization of International Migration*. London: Routledge.

Southern New Hampshire Services. 2016. "History." Accessed October 26, 2016, at: http://www.snhs.org.

Soysal, Yasemin. 1994. *Limits of Citizenship: Migrants and Postnational Membership in Europe*. Chicago: University of Chicago Press.

Soysal, Yasemin. 2000. "Citizenship and Identity: Living in Diasporas in Post-War Europe?" *Ethnic and Racial Studies* 23, no. 1: 1–15.

Stack, Carol B. 1974. *All Our Kin: Strategies for Survival in a Black Community*. New York: Harper & Row.

Standing, Guy. 2011. *The Precariat: The New Dangerous Class*. London: Bloomsbury.

Star Gazete. 2011. "Mardin'in tarihi geleceğe dönüşüyor." August 9, 2011. Accessed July 16, 2014, at: http://www.restorasyonforum.com/index.php?topic=4658.0.

Strathern, Marilyn. 1996. "The Concept of Society Is Theoretically Obsolete: For the Motion." In *Key Debates in Anthropology*, edited by T. Ingold, 60–66. London: Routledge.

Studio Hillier. n.d. "J. Robert Hillier, FAIA." Accessed April 12, 2018, at: http://www.studiohillier.com/bob-hillier/.

Sum, Ngai-Ling, and Bob Jessop. 2013. *Towards a Cultural Political Economy: Putting Culture in Its Place in Political Economy*. Cheltenham, UK: Edward Elgar.

Susser, Ida. 2002. "Manuel Castells: Conceptualizing the City in the Information Age." In *The Castells Reader on Cities and Social Theory*, edited by I. Susser 1–12. Malden, MA: Blackwell.

Susser, Ida. 2012a. "Displacement for the Global Spectacle: Reshaping the 'Wounded City.'" Paper delivered at the Inequality and Displacement Conference, São Paulo, Brazil.

Susser, Ida. 2012b. *Norman Street: Poverty and Politics in an Urban Neighborhood*, updated ed. New York: Oxford University Press.

Susser, Ida, and Stephane Tonnelat. 2013. "Transformative Cities: The Three Urban Commons." *Focaal* 6 (Summer): 105–21.

Swyngedouw, Erik. 1997. "Neither Global Nor Local: 'Glocalization' and the Politics of Scale." In *Spaces of Globalization, Reasserting the Power of the Local*, edited by K. Cox, 137–66. New York: Guilford.

Swyngedouw, Erik. 2004. "Globalisation or 'Glocalisation'? Networks, Territories and Rescaling." *Cambridge Review of International Affairs* 17, no 1: 25–48.

Swyngedouw, Erik. 2011. "Interrogating Post-Democratization: Reclaiming Egalitarian Political Spaces." *Political Geography* 30: 370–80.

Syrett, Stephen, and Leandro Sepulveda. 2012. "Urban Governance and Economic Development in the Diverse City." *European Urban and Regional Studies* 19, no 3: 238–53.

Tempel, Michael. 2014. "Bauvorhaben in Halle 2014: Hier klotzen, dort kleckern." *Mitteldeutsche Zeitung*. Accessed April 18, 2015, at: https://www.mz-web.de/halle-saale/bauvorhaben-in-halle-2014-hier-klotzen--dort-kleckern-3465836.

Tepav. 2011. *trc 3 Bölgesi Dış Ekonomi Çevre Analizi*. Ankara: Tepav.

Tepav. 2012. *Istihdam İzleme Bülteni*. Accessed July 17, 2014, at: http://www.tepav.org.tr/upload/files/1477983324-1.Istihdam_Izleme_Bulteni_Subat_2012.pdf.

Theodore, Nik, and Nina Martin. 2007. "Migrant Civil Society: New Voices in the Struggle over Community Development." *Urban Affairs* 29, no. 3: 229–337.

Therborn, Göran. 2003. "Entangled Modernities." *European Journal of Social Theory* 6, no. 3: 293–305.

Tilly, Charles. 1984. *Big Structures, Large Processes, Huge Comparisons*. New York: Russell Sage Foundation.

Tilly, Charles. 1990. *Coercion, Capital, and European States, AD 990–1992*. Oxford: Basil Blackwell.

Today's Zaman. 2013. "Hewlett Packard Invests in Printing Facility in Mardin." September 23, 2013. Accessed June 10, 2014, at: http://turkey-re.com/hewlett-packard-invests-in-printing-facility-in-mardin/#sthash.Ettwachh.dpuf.

Tönnies, Ferdinand (1877) 1957. *Community and Society*. Mineola, NY: Dover.

Toprak, Duygu. 2008. "TOKİ'den Süryanilere geri dönüş konutu." *Sabah*. Accessed July 5, 2014, at: http://arsiv.sabah.com.tr/2008/06/29/haber,147A8756682C4A9 DAFAE015F4D6D0CB8.html.

Transatlantic Trends. 2014. "Transatlantic Trends 2014: Mobility, Migration and Integration Key Findings from 2014 and Selected Highlights from Transatlantic Trends and Transatlantic Trends: Immigration 2008–13." The German Marshall Fund of the United States. Accessed June 15, 2015, at: http://trends.gmfus.org/immigration-2014/.

Trauthig, Michael. 2003. "Jakob and Israel kehren Heim in die Turkei." *Stuttgarter Zeitung*, October 29, 2003.

TUİK. 2011. "Gayri Safi Katma Değer: Bölgesel Sonuçlar 2004–2011." Ankara: Türkiye İstatistik Kurumu Ulusal Hesaplar Daire Başkanlığı Yıllık Hesaplar Grubu.

TUİK. 2013. *Seçilmiş Göstergelerle Mardin 2013*. Ankara: Türkiye İstatistik Kurumu. Accessed July 13, 2014, at: http://www.TUİK.gov.tr/ilGostergeleri/iller/MARDIN .pdf.

Tuohy, D. 2011. "Manchester Embraces Its Diversity on City Website." *New Hampshire Union Leader*, June 20, 2011. Accessed August 10, 2011, at: http://www.unionleader .com/apps/pbcs.dll/article?AID=/20110621/NEWS06/706219969#sthash.zdPMuOXV .dpuf.

TURKSTAT. 2016. *Address Based Population Registration System Results*. Ankara.

Ujima Collective. 2016. "About Ujima Collective." Accessed March 24, 2017, at: http:// www.ujimacollective.mysite.com/index.html.

Ülker, Baris. 2016. *Enterprising Migrants in Berlin*. Bielefeld: transcript Verlag.

Union Leader. 2015. "Two Queen City Traditions Make for We Are One Festival." Accessed at April 15, 2016, at: http://www.unionleader.com/apps/pbcs.dll/article?AID =/20150813/NEWHAMPSHIRE02/150819729/1023/NEWS01&template=printart# sthash.DRIM39IL.dpuf.

Urak. 2011. *Türkiye İllerarası Rekabetçilik Endeksi 2009–2010*. İstanbul.

Uslu, Melih. 2013. "Bir Doğu Masalı: Mardin." Istanbul: Iletisim Yayincilik A. S. Accessed July 4, 2014, at: http://www.anadolujet.com/aj-tr/anadolujet-magazin/2013/ nisan/makaleler/bir-dogu-masali-mardin.aspx.

US Bureau of Labor Statistics. 2012. "Employment Tenure." Accessed August 28, 2014, at: https://www.bls.gov/opub/ted/2012/ted_20120920.htm.

US Bureau of Labor Statistics. 2016. "Employment Situation Summary." Accessed February 14, 2017, at: https://www.bls.gov/news.release/empsit.nro.htm.

US Census. 2000a. "New Americans." Accessed August 4, 2005, at: http://:www.census.data-Manch/2000.census.data.htm.

US Census. 2000b. "Ranking Tables for Population of Metropolitan Statistical Areas." Accessed March 20, 2017, at: https://www.census.gov/population/www/cen2000/briefs/phc-t29/tables.

US Census. 2014. "Selected Economic Characteristics: 2010–2014 American Community Survey; 5-Year Estimates." Accessed March 28, 2017, at: https://www.census.gov/quickfacts/table/POP645215/3345140.

US Census. 2017a. "Quick Facts, Manchester New Hampshire." Accessed March 28, 2017, at: https://www.census.gov/quickfacts/table/PST045215/3345140,2507000,00.

US Census. 2017b. "Quick Facts, Manchester New Hampshire." Accessed March 24, 2017, at: https://www.census.gov/quickfacts/table/POP645215/3345140.

US Conference of Mayors. 2015. "Mayors Register Their Support of the U.S. Refugee Resettlement Program." Press Release, November 20, 2015. Accessed August 28, 2016, at: https://www.usmayors.org/pressreleases/uploads/2015/1120-release-refugeeletter.pdf.

US Department of Housing and Urban Development, Archives. 2011. "Manchester Downtown Development with HUD Assistance." Accessed July 10, 2015, at: https://archives.hud.gov/local/nh/goodstories/manchesterdevelopment.cfm.

US Department of Labor, Bureau of Labor Statistics. 2012. Accessed March 12, 2013, at: http://data.bls.gov/timeseries/LAUMT33749503?data_tool=XGtable.

US Department of State. 2016. "The Diversity Visa Process." Bureau of Consular Affairs. Accessed August 28, 2016, at: https://travel.state.gov/content/visas/en/immigrate/diversity-visa/entry.html.

US Prayer Center. 2004. *Disciplining the Nations.* Accessed March 15, 2004, at: http://www.usprayercenter.org.

Vaiou, Dina, and Rouli Lykogianni. 2006. "Women, Neighbourhoods and Everyday Life." *Urban Studies* 43, no. 4: 731–43.

van der Zanden, Christine. 2014. "The United States Holocaust Memorial Museum Encyclopedia of Camps and Ghettos, 1933–1945." Center for Advanced Holocaust Studies, United States Holocaust Memorial Museum. Accessed July 9, 2015, at: http://www.ushmm.org/wlc/en/article.php?ModuleId=10007067.

van Dijk, Rijk. 2011. "Cities and the Social Construction of Hot Spots: Rescaling, Ghanaian Migrants, and the Fragmentation of Urban Spaces." In *Locating Migration: Rescaling Cities and Migrants,* edited by N. Glick Schiller and A. Çağlar, 104–22. Ithaca, NY: Cornell University Press.

van Winden, Willem. 2010. "Towards a Creative Cluster in Halle (Saale): Results of the REDIS Implementation Lab, Halle." Accessed July 11, 2015, at: https://www.yumpu.com/en/document/view/8154667/towards-a-creative-cluster-in-halle-saale-germany-urbact.

Varsanyi, Monica W. 2006. "Interrogating 'Urban Citizenship' vis-à-vis Undocumented Migration." *Citizenship Studies* 10, no. 2: 229–49.

Venice Biennale. 2006. "10th International Architecture Exhibition: Official Awards."

Accessed June 13, 2014, at: http://www.gat.st/news/10th-international-architecture-exhibition-official-awards.

Vertovec, Steven. 2007. "Super-Diversity and Its Implications." *Ethnic and Racial Studies* 30, no. 6: 1024–54.

Vertovec, Steven. 2015. "Introduction: Migration, Cities, and Diversities 'Old' and 'New'." In *Diversities Old and New: Migration and Socio-Spatial Patterns in New York, Singapore and Johannesburg*, edited by S. Vertovec, 1–20. Basingstoke, UK: Palgrave MacMillan.

Vertovec, Steven, and Susanne Wessendorf, eds. 2010. *The Multiculturalism Backlash: European Discourses, Policies and Practices*. Milton Park, UK: Routledge.

von Vasquez, Manuel, and Marie Friedmann Marquardt. 2003. *Globalizing the Sacred: Religion Across the Americas*. New Brunswick, NJ: Rutgers University Press.

Waldinger, Roger. 1986. "Immigrant Enterprise: A Critique and Reformulation." *Theory and Society* 15, no. 1: 249–85.

Waldinger, Roger. 2015. *The Cross-Border Connection: Immigrants, Emigrants, and Their Homeland*. Cambridge, MA: Harvard University Press.

Waldinger, Roger, Howard Aldrich, and Robin Ward. 1990. "Opportunities, Group Characteristics, and Strategies." In *Ethnic Entrepreneurs: Immigrant Businesses in Industrial Societies*, edited by R. Waldinger, H. Aldrich, and R. Ward, 13–48. London: Sage.

Wallerstein, Immanuel. 2011. *The Modern World System 1: Capitalist Agriculture and the Origins of the European World-Economy in the Sixteenth Century*. Berkeley: University of California Press.

Ward, Kevin. 2008. "Toward a Comparative (re)Turn in Urban Studies? Some Reflections." *Urban Geography* 29, no. 5: 405–10.

Ward, Kevin. 2010. "Towards a Relational Comparative Approach to the Study of Cities." *Progress in Human Geography* 34: 471–87.

Ward, Kevin, and Eugene McCann. 2011. "Conclusion: Cities Assembled; Space, Neoliberalization, (re)Territorialization, and Comparison." In *Mobile Urbanism: Cities and Policymaking in the Global Age*, edited by E. McCann and E. Ward, 167–84. Minneapolis: University of Minnesota Press.

Warner, Stephen R. 1998. "Immigration and Religious Communities in the United States." In *Gatherings in Diaspora: Religious Communities and the New Immigration*, edited by R. S. Warner and J. Wittner, 3–34. Philadelphia: Temple University Press.

Watson, Sophie. 2009. "The Magic of the Marketplace: Sociality in a Neglected Public Space." *Urban Studies* 46, no. 8: 1577–91.

Weber, Max. 1958 [1921]. *The City*. New York: Free Press.

Werkfeuerwehrverbandes Saxony-Anhalt e.V. 2015. "InfraLeuna GmbH." Accessed March 22, 2017, at: http://www.wfv-sachsen-anhalt.de/?page_id=64.

Wessendorf, Susanne. 2013. "Commonplace Diversity and the 'Ethos of Mixing': Perceptions of Difference in a London Neighborhood." *Identities* 20, no. 4: 407–22.

Whyte, William Foote. 1943. *Street Corner Society: The Social Structure of an Italian Slum*. Chicago: University of Chicago Press.

WikiLeaks 2005. 05ANKARA3191. "Turkey's Syriacs Skeptical about Prospects for

Greater Freedom." Released August 30, 2011. Accessed June 11, 2014, at: http://www
.atour.com/government/wikileaks/20111027p.html.

WikiLeaks 2006. 06ANKARA2387. "Turkey: Diyarbakir Syriacs Threatened, Local
Imams Encourage Anti-Christian Sentiment." Released August 30, 2011. Accessed
June 11, 2014, at: http://www.atour.com/government/wikileaks/20120219h.html.

WikiLeaks. 06ANKARA4835_a. 2006. "Ankara Media Reaction Report." Released
August 30, 2011. Accessed June 11, 2014, at: https://wikileaks.org/plusd/cables/
06ANKARA4835_a.html.

Wilson, Kenneth L., and Alejandro Portes. 1980. "Immigrant Enclaves: An Analysis of
the Labor Market Experiences of Cubans in Miami." *American Journal of Sociology*
86, no. 2: 295–319.

Wimmer, Andreas, and Nina Glick Schiller. 2002. "Methodological Nationalism and
Beyond: Nation-State Building, Migration and the Social Sciences." *Global Networks* 2, no. 4: 301–34.

Wimmer, Andreas, and Nina Glick Schiller. 2003. "Methodological Nationalism and
the Study of Migration: Beyond Nation-State Building." *International Migration Review* 37, no. 3: 576–610.

Wirth, Louis. 1938. "Urbanism as a Way of Life." *American Journal of Sociology*: 1–24.

Wirtschaftsstandort Dortmund. 2014. "Standortentwicklung/Zukunftsstandorte."
Accessed August 20, 2014, at: www.wirtschaftsfoerderung-dortmund.de/tiny/4f/.

Wise, Amanda, and Selvaraj Velayutham. 2014. "Conviviality in Everyday Multiculturalism: Some Brief Comparisons between Singapore and Sydney." *European Journal
of Cultural Studies* 17, no. 4: 406–30.

WMUR. 2016. "Black Lives Matter Protesters March in Manchester: Armed Civilians
Stand on Guard." July 23, 2016. Accessed October 10, 2016, at: http://www.wmur
.com/article/black-lives-matter-protesters-march-in-manchester/5213302.

WNYC and the Nation. 2016. *The United States of Anxiety*. Accessed on October 21,
2016, at: http://www.wnyc.org/shows/anxiety.

Wolf, Eric. 1982. *Europe and the People without History*. Berkeley: University of California Press.

Woodlief, Anthony. 1988. "The Path Dependent City." *Urban Affairs Review* 33, no. 83:
405–37.

World Bank. 2006. *Global Economic Prospects: Economic Implications of Remittances
and Migration*. Washington, DC: World Bank. Accessed July 2009 at: http://
www-wds.worldbank.org/servlet/WDSContentServer/WDSP/IB/2005/11/14/
000112742_20051114174928/Rendered/PDF/343200GEP02006.pdf.

World Bank. 2016. *Global Economic Prospects: Divergences and Risk*. Accessed July 15,
2016, at: http://www.worldbank.org/en/publication/global-economic-prospects.

World Bulletin. 2013. *Mardin's Tourism Increases with Settlement Process*. Accessed
March 18, 2015, at: http://www.worldbulletin.net/news/114717/mardins-tourism-
increases-with-settlement-process.

Wright, Susan. 2011. "Studying Policy: Methods, Paradigms, Perspectives, Introduction." In *Policy Worlds: Anthropology and the Analysis of Contemporary Power*, edited by C. Shore, S. Wright, and D. Però, 27–31. New York: Berghahn.

Xiang, Biao. 2016. "Theory as Vision." *Anthropological Theory* 16: 213–20.

Yavuz, Cihan. 2012. *Mardin'i Dinlerken: Müzeyle Başlayan Değişim*. Istanbul: Sabanci Vakfi.

Yeung, Henry Wai-chung, and Kris Olds. 2000. *Globalization of Chinese Business Firms*. London: Macmillan.

Yeoh, Brenda S. A. 2005. "The Global Cultural City? Spatial Imagineering and Politics in the (Multi)cultural Marketplaces of South-east Asia." *Urban Studies* 42, no. 5/6: 945–58.

Young, Justin R. 2015. *Social Capital in a Diversifying City: A Multi-Neighborhood Ethnographic Case Study*. Unpublished PhD manuscript, submitted to University of New Hampshire.

Young, Michael, and Peter Willmott. 1957. *Family and Kinship in East London*. Penguin: Harmondsworth.

Yüksel, Ayşe Seda. 2014. *Report on Political Economy, History, and Structural Parameters of Mardin*. Unpublished report.

Yuval-Davis, Nira. 1997. *Gender and Nation*. Thousand Oaks, CA: Sage.

Zhou, Min. 2004. "Revisiting Ethnic Entrepreneurship: Convergencies, Controversies, and Conceptual Advancements." *International Migration Review* 38: 1040–74.

Zizek, Slavoj. 2005. "Against Human Rights." *New Left Review* 34: 115–31.

Zukin, Sharon. 1995. *The Cultures of Cities*. Oxford: Blackwell.

INDEX

abandonment, 35, 39, 57, 91, 203, 217; abandoned property (Enval-i-Metruke), 75, 185–86, 187, 188. *See also* dispossession
accumulation by dispossession, 16, 17–18, 19, 20, 86–87, 120, 121, 153, 175, 207, 220
actor-network theory, 24–25
affect, 23, 124, 125, 128, 129, 131, 225
African Week. *See* cultural festivals
agency, 3, 12–13, 31, 93, 153, 210
Alternative for Germany (AfD), 220
American Muslim Alliance (AMA), 52
Amo, Anton Wilhelm, 63
Amoskeag Company, 36
anti-capitalist, 225. *See also* social movements
anti-globalization, 226. *See also* social movements
anti-immigrant, 12, 31, 45, 47, 72, 124, 212, 220, 221. *See also* social movements
anti-Islamic, 145. *See also* social movements
anti-racism, 52, 53, 68, 71, 72, 173, 176, 221. *See also* social movements
Armenians, 73, 184, 203, 231n28
aspirations, 4, 93, 123, 124, 129, 146, 173, 176, 199, 207, 225
assimilation, 21, 47, 150, 215
asylum seeker(s), 56, 63, 64, 65, 66, 68, 69, 70, 157, 159, 164, 223

belonging, 22, 27, 30, 70, 130, 149, 150, 151–52, 153, 154, 160, 218, 223

binary of difference. *See* difference: binaries of
Black Lives Matter movement, 222. *See also* social movement
borders, 3, 51, 73, 78, 88, 154, 179, 182; transborder, 50, 154, 155
bridging, 125, 126, 128
built environment, 84, 191, 195, 206
Bush, George W., 174, 175
Business and Science Support Center of Halle (Dienstleistungszentrum Wirtschaft und Wissenschaft), 59

call centers, 60, 61
capital accumulation, 1, 9, 17, 19, 22, 23, 30, 35, 62, 82, 90, 92, 124, 152, 173, 175, 211, 212, 213, 215, 219, 223, 225
capital restructuring, 12, 181
Cerullo, Morris, 167–68, 172
Christian, born-again, 30, 49, 70, 148, 154, 157, 161, 169, 170, 174, 175, 176, 214; born-again organizations, 155, 163, 164, 166–67, 171, 173; healing, 155, 156, 162–63, 167; marriage, 169–70; minority, 88, 190, 199, 200, 206, 219; missionaries, 174; networks, 154, 158, 171, 172, 173, 175, 204–5, 219; organizations, 49, 159, 168, 173, 176, 217; reverse missionaries, 149, 175
Christianity, 148, 163, 170, 171, 175; Eastern, 87–88, 179, 204, 207; Pentecostal, 148–49, 157, 160, 164, 167, 168, 173; universalism, 163

100, 119, 213; identity, 4; neighborhoods, 101; networks, 110, 118; niche, 115
ethnic Germans, 56, 230n11
ethnic lens, 3, 4–5, 11, 100, 110, 119, 120, 126, 147, 212
ethnicity, 100
ethnography, 26; bounded, 10, 218; multi-sighted, 10; multisited, 10
ethnoreligious, 4, 126, 127, 147, 150
euro, 61, 108, 112
European Commission, 64
European Union, 83, 84, 179, 197–99, 207, 214; funding, 59, 79; Turkey accession, 83, 89, 183, 190, 199, 219
evangelization, 162
everyday life, 10, 11–13, 154, 195
exclusion, 150, 153
expropriation, 187, 188. *See also* accumulation by dispossession
expulsions, 209

Family Research Council, 174
Federal Housing Authority, 133
Florida, Richard, 6
Focus on the Family, 168–69, 174
Fordism, 38
foreigner, 12, 34, 63, 72, 104–5. *See also* public foreigner
friendship, 129, 139, 233n4

genocide: Armenian and Syriac, 73, 75, 184–85, 203, 205
gentrification, 58, 67, 69, 112, 131
German federal state, 103, 160
global economy, 2, 209
global positioning, 35, 40–45, 56–62, 76–83, 109
globalization, 7, 10, 11, 16, 22, 23, 25, 97, 102, 223

Halle/Saale, 1, 2, 27, 28–29, 33–34, 35, 53–74, 95–96, 103–108, 109–18, 119–20, 157, 162, 163, 165–66, 217; city decline, 53–56; history, 54, 59, 63; Lord Mayor, 34, 63, 104, 105
Halle-Neustadt, 54, 55, 57, 64
Hanseatic League, 54
Harvey, David, 17, 224–25

heritage, 207; multifaith and multilingual, 84, 190, 191, 196, 197; site, 69; tourism industry, 189–90, 202, 203
Hometown Associations (HTA), 179, 180–81, 188, 189, 206; Kafro, 177, 179
housing, 41, 44, 50, 57, 58, 86, 131, 133; federal, 47, 49, 133
housing agencies: Department of Housing and Urban Development (HUD), 42, 44; Housing Development Administration (TOKI), 78, 193; Manchester Housing and Redevelopment Authority (MHRA), 44
human rights, 134, 198–200, 206
humanity, 210, 214

immigrants, 15, 46, 47, 53, 97, 175, 215, 221
Immigrants Rights Task Force, 53
impoverishment, 30, 44, 49, 58, 61, 82–83. *See also* poverty
industry: construction, 62, 80, 172, 193; culture, 197; defense, 50, 141, 229n4; food, 75, 80, 81, 108; logistics, 43, 60–61, 80–81; manufacturing, 39, 75, 80, 136; textiles, 40, 75. *See also* Iraq war; Syrian Civil War
infrastructure, 14, 59, 76, 81, 85, 95, 171, 203
Instrument for Pre-Accession (IPA), 190
integration, 3–4, 5, 16, 21, 64–66, 115, 126, 142, 215. *See also* assimilation
interconnectivity, 24–25
Intercultural Week. *See* cultural festivals
internally displaced people (IDP), 76, 82
international development, 180
International Monetary Fund (IMF), 181, 209
international student, 27, 54, 67, 104
investment: foreign, 39, 201; private, 29, 40–45, 56–62, 63, 76–83, 91; public, 40, 42, 49, 57, 59, 138. *See also* disinvestment
investment agencies: Invest in Mardin, 87; Manchester Economic Development Office (MEDO), 43
Iraq: Gulf War, 182; trade with, 80, 88; US invasion of, 182–83; War, 78, 175–76
Islamic Society of Greater Manchester, 49–50
Islamophobia, 145, 226

opportunity structures, 49, 96, 100, 101, 102, 103, 107, 119, 219
Organization of Free Churches (Bund freikirchlicher Pfingstgemeinden), 163, 236n4
otherizing, 20, 226
out-migration, 55, 96, 182, 184. *See also* depopulation

participant observation. *See* ethnography
path dependency, 14
Patriot Act, 45, 230n6
place-making, 21, 25
polarization, 12, 48, 64, 73, 91
positioning, 14, 15, 16, 24, 25, 35, 36–40, 53–56, 73–76, 92, 97, 104, 118, 127, 211. *See also* repositioning
poverty, 19, 44, 47, 131. *See also* urban poor
power, 11, 164; cultural, 2, 8, 13, 15, 20, 78, 93, 120, 183; economic, 62, 210; geometry, 153, 211, 212, 214, 217, 219; institutional-ized, 9, 11, 29, 180, 206; political, 1, 102, 62, 210
precarity, 19–20, 50, 119, 132, 138, 165, 225
privatization, 17, 19, 55, 220
proximal relation, 134, 135
public: debt, 35, 92, 131, 217, 222; funding, 11, 64, 86, 112; services, 91, 132, 215, 217, 225; subsidies, 81. *See also* city: funding
public enactment: human rights, 84, 200; religious diversity, 200; safety and toler-ance, 200
public foreigner, 71
public-private partnerships, 47, 81, 91
Putnam, Robert, 12, 126, 233n3

racialization, 6, 126, 211, 213, 226
racism, 56, 145, 212, 226
real estate, 81, 83, 136
refugee resettlement, 46, 51, 53, 65, 221
refugees, 5, 44, 47
relationality, 128, 213–14, 218
religious diversity, 150, 159, 160, 197, 198
religious freedom, 198, 202, 205, 206
remittance, 180, 181, 206
rents, 44, 57, 106, 112–14, 131, 132, 145. *See also* housing

repositioning, 12, 35, 41, 59, 77, 84, 93, 104, 120, 197, 211. *See also* positioning
Republican Party, 51, 124, 221
Return to Villages and the Rehabilitation Project (RVRP), 184
rights: property, 187–88, 201; religious, 187
rights to the city, 30, 209, 210, 223, 224
rule of law, 198, 200
rural-urban continuum, 125
rural-urban dichotomy, 125

sanctuary movement, 72, 220, 233n2, 234n10. *See also* social movements
Sassen, Saskia, 152–53
Saxony-Anhalt, 1, 55, 58, 60, 70, 72, 103, 104, 112, 115, 117, 124, 159, 220, 232n2, 235n3
scales (scalar), 8. *See also* multiscalar
sending-state policies, 180
shrinking cities, 56. *See also* depopulation; out-migration
Simmel, Georg, 29, 125, 128
simultaneity, 218–19
sociabilities, 12, 20, 21, 29–30, 123, 127, 128–30, 131, 145, 146, 148, 217, 218, 225; emplacement of, 124, 130, 143, 144, 145, 170, 213, 214, 221; institutional, 141–44; proximal, 131–36; workplace, 136–41
social capital, 20, 99, 126, 173
social cohesion, 127, 145. *See also* integration
Social Democratic Party (SPD), 71
social field(s), 8–9
social inequality, 127, 209
social justice, 210, 211
social justice movement, 93, 128
social media: Facebook, 216
social mobility, 19, 55, 209, 215, 220
social movements, 13, 19, 25, 70, 72, 101, 127, 146, 210, 218, 223, 225, 226
sociality, 128
solidarities, 99–100, 125–26, 128, 135, 144, 149, 222, 225, 226
strangers, 12, 125, 133, 146, 164
structural adjustment, 209, 222
superdiversity, 126–28, 213
supranational, 9, 12, 13, 21, 31, 183, 188, 206, 207, 216, 218

surveillance, 45, 52, 141, 145, 199, 226, 230n6

Swedish Assyrian Federation, 203

Syria, 2, 220, 226

Syriac: Christian(s), 30, 33, 83, 85, 86–89, 177–79, 181, 183, 184–89, 189–97; Christian persecution, 83, 88; Christian returnees, 85–87, 177, 189, 200, 201–2, 203, 206, 207; emigrants, 85–87, 179, 187–88

Syrian Civil War, 88, 90, 197, 214

Tahir, Saghir "Saggy," 51, 52, 144, 211

tax policy, 44, 136

temporality, 206, 212–14

Tigris Development Agency (DİKA), 82, 87

tolerance, 33, 93, 198, 200, 213, 225

tourism, 78, 81, 82, 84, 188, 193, 210

trade: cross-border, 182

transnational: city-making, 50; ethnic community, 180, 213; migration, 10, 23, 206

Trump, Donald J., 221, 233n2, 234n6, 236n8

Tur Abdin, 178, 185, 200, 205, 232n34, 232n2, 232n6, 237n15; Christian Orient–Friends of, 205

Turkey, 73–76, 89, 182–83; democratization, 77, 83, 198; US relations, 183, 200, 206. *See also* European Union: Turkey accession

Turkish state, 79, 90, 181, 197, 199, 208, 214, 224

typological time, 22

undocumented, 5

UNDP (United Nations Development Programme), 191

unemployment; 55, 61, 82, 157

UNESCO, 179

UNESCO World Heritage, 196, 197

unification of Germany *Wende*, 3, 55, 63, 68, 70, 103, 106, 108, 109, 112, 119, 165, 235n3

university, 67, 194; Artuklu University, 84, 89, 194, 208; Martin-Luther-Wittenberg University, 54, 230n10; University of New Hampshire, 122, 228n10, 235

urban: growth, 6, 57, 98; policy, 93; poor, 18, 47, 83, 113; renewal, 14, 38, 42, 158; restructuring, 15, 27, 101, 197, 209–11, 212, 214

Urban Redevelopment East (Stadtumbau Ost), 57, 58, 112

urban regeneration, 1–2, 7, 12, 14–15, 29–30, 33, 35, 55–56, 79, 86, 96, 103, 111, 112, 144, 189, 190–91, 217; Halle, 103–5, 106, 116–17, 158, 220; Manchester, 124, 130, 131–32, 158; Mardin, 189–96, 219; migrant business and, 100, 101, 106, 119; migrants or minorities, 35, 45–48, 62–64, 83–85

urban regeneration project, 79, 81, 93, 190, 217

US State Department, 179, 182, 205

valorization, 90, 126, 179, 181, 189–99, 206–8

value creation, 181

value-creation process, 127, 189

violence, 19, 90, 186, 190, 200, 205, 207, 208, 220, 231n28

war: global warring, 30, 90, 174. *See also* Iraq: War; Syrian Civil War

We Are One. *See* cultural festivals

Wikileaks, 178, 205, 238n23

World Bank, 191